INTERIOR DESIGN
ILLUSTRATED

☐ INTERIOR DESIGN
ILLUSTRATED

FRANCIS D.K. CHING

A VNR Book

JOHN WILEY & SONS, INC.

New York   Chichester   Weinheim   Brisbane   Singapore   Toronto

Designed by Francis D.K. Ching

This book is printed on acid-free paper. ⊖

Library of Congress Cataloging-in-Publication Data:

Ching, Francis D.K., 1943-
    Interior design illustrated.
    Includes index.
    1. Interior architecture.   2. Space (Architecture)
  3. Interior decoration—History—20th century. I. Title.
    NA2850.C45   1987   729   87-10512
ISBN 0-471-28868-3

Printed in the United States of America

20 19 18 17

CONTENTS

INTRODUCTION.............................6

1 INTERIOR
SPACE.............................9

2 INTERIOR
DESIGN.............................45

3 A DESIGN
VOCABULARY.............................87

4 INTERIOR DESIGN
ELEMENTS.............................159

5 INTERIOR ENVIRONMENTAL
SYSTEMS.............................277

BIBLIOGRAPHY.............................315

INDEX.............................315

INTRODUCTION

We spend the majority of our lives indoors, in the interior spaces created by the structures and shells of buildings. These spaces provide the physical context for much of what we do, and give substance and life to the architecture which houses them. This introductory text is a visual study of the nature and design of these interior settings.

The purpose of this primer is to introduce to students of interior design those fundamental elements which make up our interior environments. It outlines the characteristics of each element and presents the choices we have in selecting and arranging them into design patterns. In making these choices, emphasis is placed on basic design principles and how design relationships determine the functional, structural, and aesthetic qualities of interior spaces.

This exploration of the ways and means of developing interior spaces begins with space itself, for it is the prime material with which the interior designer must work.

- The first chapter – Interior SPACE – proceeds from a general discussion of architectural space to the particular characteristics of interior space in three dimensions.

- The second chapter – Interior DESIGN – outlines a method for translating programmatic needs and requirements into three-dimensional design decisions.

- The third chapter – A Design VOCABULARY – explores the fundamental elements and principles of visual design and applies each of them to the unique field of interior design.

- The fourth chapter – Interior Design ELEMENTS – describes the major categories of interior elements and discusses how each affects the functional and aesthetic development of interior spaces.

- The fifth chapter – Interior Environmental SYSTEMS – provides an outline of the environmental control systems which must be integrated into a building's interior.

Since interior design is to a great extent a visual art, drawings are used extensively to convey information, express ideas, and outline possibilities. Some of the illustrations are quite abstract; others are more specific and particular. All of them, however, should be viewed essentially as diagrams which serve to demonstrate design principles or to clarify the relationships existing between the elements of a design.

The limits of interior design are difficult to define precisely since it lies in the continuum between architecture and product design. It encompasses both visual and functional design as well as aspects of materials, construction, and technology. This introduction to interior design is therefore broad in scope. The intent, nevertheless, is to treat the subject with clarity, make it as accessible as possible, and stimulate further in-depth study and research.

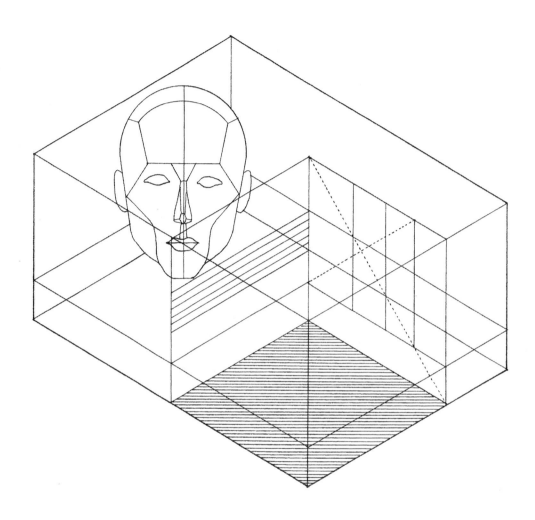

1

INTERIOR
SPACE

SPACE

Space is the prime material in the designer's palette and the essential element in interior design. Through the volume of space we not only move...we see forms, hear sounds, feel gentle breezes and the warmth of the sun, smell the fragrances of flowers in bloom. Space inherits the sensual and aesthetic characteristics of those elements in its field.

Space is a material substance like stone and wood. Yet it is inherently formless and diffuse. Universal space has no definition. Once an element is placed in its field, however, a visual relationship is established. As other elements are introduced into the field, multiple relationships are established between the space and the elements as well as among the elements themselves. Space is thus formed by these relationships and we who perceive them.

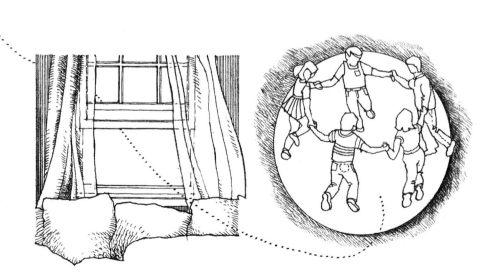

The geometric elements of point, line, plane, and volume can be arranged to articulate and define space. At the scale of architecture, these fundamental elements become linear columns and beams, and planar walls, floors, and roofs.

In architectural design, these elements are organized to give a building form, differentiate between inside and outside, and define the boundaries of interior space.

- A column marks a point in space and makes it visible.

- Two columns define a spatial membrane through which we can pass.

- Supporting a beam, the columns delineate the edges of a transparent plane.

- A wall, an opaque plane, marks off a portion of amorphous space and separates here from there.

- A floor defines a field of space with territorial boundaries.

- A roof provides shelter for the volume of space beneath it.

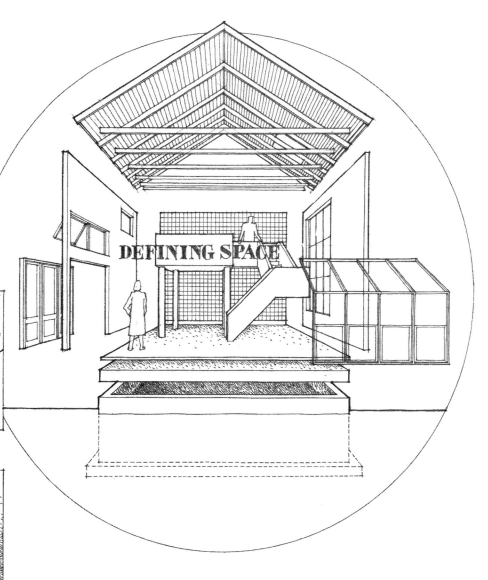

DEFINING SPACE

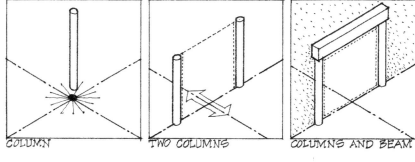

COLUMN   TWO COLUMNS   COLUMNS AND BEAM

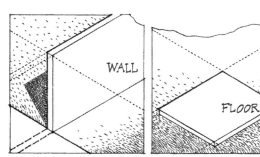

WALL

FLOOR

ROOF

EXTERIOR SPACE

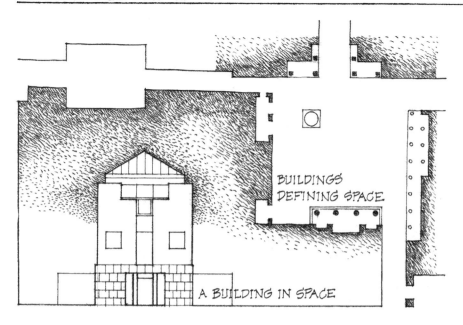

BUILDINGS DEFINING SPACE

A BUILDING IN SPACE

A building's form, scale, and spatial organization are the designer's response to a number of conditions – functional planning requirements, technological aspects of structure and construction, economic realities of cost, expressive qualities of image and style. In addition, the architecture of a building must address the physical context of its site and the issue of exterior space.

A building can be related to its site in several ways. It can merge with its setting or attempt to dominate it. It can surround and capture a portion of exterior space. One of its faces can be made special to address a feature of its site or define an edge of exterior space. In each case, due consideration should be given to the potential relationship, as defined by a building's exterior walls, between interior and exterior space.

DOMINATING

MERGING

SURROUNDING

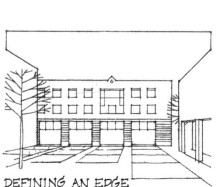

FRONTING

DEFINING AN EDGE

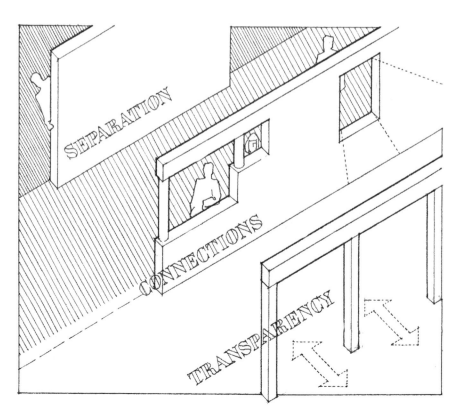

SEPARATION

CONNECTIONS

TRANSPARENCY

A building's exterior walls constitute the interface between our interior and exterior environments. In defining both interior and exterior space, they determine the character of each. They may be thick and heavy, and express a clear distinction between a controlled interior environment and the exterior space from which it is isolated. They may be thin, or even transparent, and attempt to merge inside and outside.

Windows and doorways, the openings which penetrate a building's exterior walls, are the spatial transitions between exterior and interior space. Their scale, character, and composition often tell us something about the nature of the interior spaces which lie behind them.

Special transitional spaces, belonging to both the outside world and the inside, can be used to mediate between the two environments. A familiar example in residential architecture is the porch. Cultural and climatic variations of this theme include the verandah, lanai, and arcaded gallery.

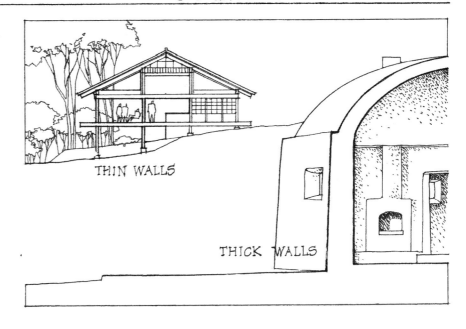

THIN WALLS

THICK WALLS

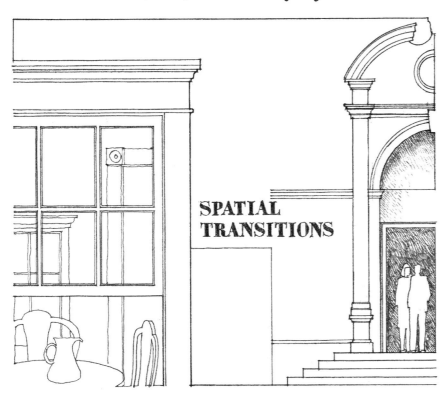

SPATIAL TRANSITIONS

INTERIOR SPACE

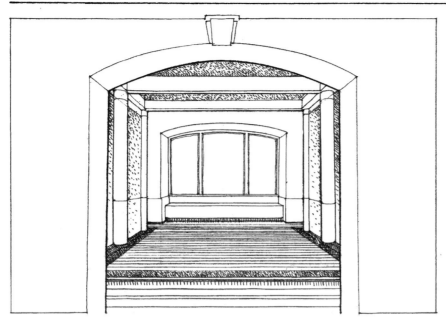

Upon entering a building, we sense shelter and enclosure. This perception is due to the surrounding floor, wall, and ceiling planes of interior space. These are the architectural elements that define the physical limits of rooms. They enclose space, articulate its boundaries, and separate it from surrounding interior spaces and the outside.

Floors, walls, and ceilings do more than mark off a simple quantity of space. Their form, configuration, and pattern of window and door openings also imbue the defined space with certain spatial or architectural qualities. We use terms such as grand hall, loft space, sun room, and alcove to describe not simply how large or small a space is, but also to characterize its scale and proportion, its quality of light, the nature of its enclosing surfaces, and how it relates to adjacent spaces.

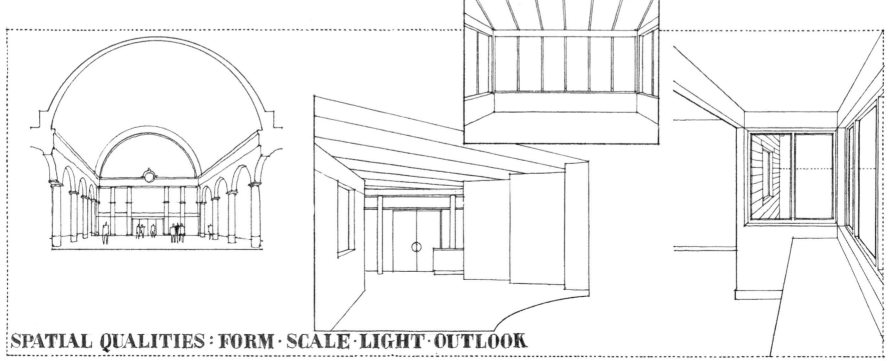

SPATIAL QUALITIES : FORM · SCALE · LIGHT · OUTLOOK

Interior design necessarily goes beyond the architectural definition of space. In planning the layout, furnishing, and enrichment of a space, the interior designer should be acutely aware of its architectural character as well as its potential for modification and enhancement. The design of interior spaces requires, therefore, an understanding of how they are formed by the building systems of structure and enclosure. With this understanding, the interior designer can effectively elect to work with, continue, or even offer a counterpoint to the essential qualities of an architectural space.

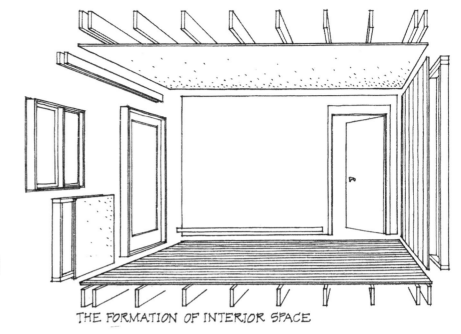

THE FORMATION OF INTERIOR SPACE

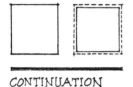  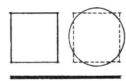

CONTINUATION   COUNTERPOINT   CONTRAST

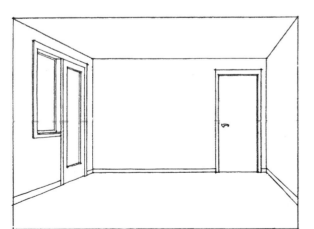

THE BASIC SHELL

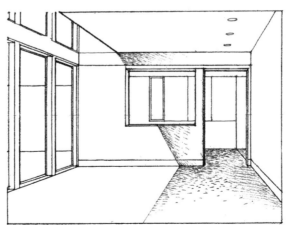

MODIFIED ARCHITECTURALLY

OR THROUGH INTERIOR DESIGN

STRUCTURING SPACE

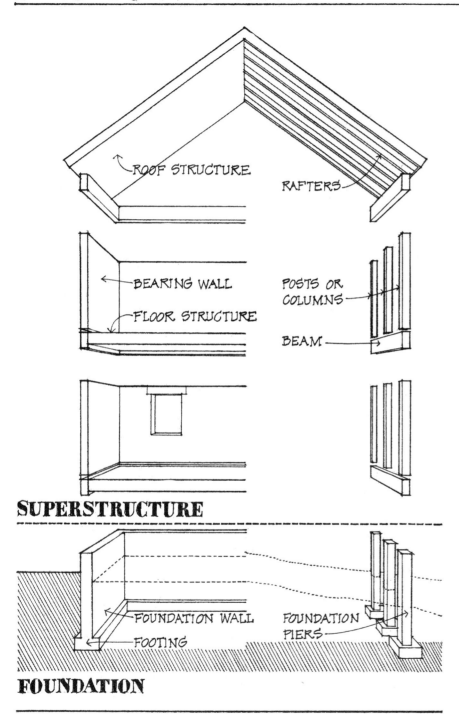

SUPERSTRUCTURE

FOUNDATION

Most buildings consist of the following constituent elements and systems.

The foundation system forms the base of a building, anchors it firmly to the ground, and supports the building elements and spaces above.

The building superstructure consists of structural floor, wall, column, and roof systems. These systems must work together to support the following types of loads.

- Dead Loads: How a building is constructed determines its dead load, which is the weight of its structural and nonstructural components, including any fixed equipment.

- Live Loads: How a building is used determines its live load, which is the weight of its occupants and any movable equipment and furnishings. In cold climates, snow imposes an additional live load on a building.

- Dynamic Loads: Where a building is located determines its potential load from the dynamic forces of wind and earthquakes.

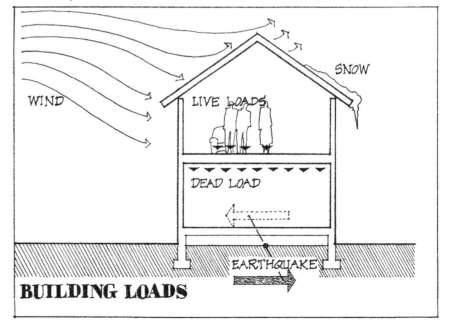

BUILDING LOADS

The building envelope consists of exterior walls, windows, doors, and roof, which protect and shelter interior spaces from the exterior environment.

Nonstructural walls, partitions, and ceilings subdivide and define interior space. They generally carry no loads other than their own weight.

Mechanical and electrical systems provide the necessary environmental conditioning of interior spaces and help make them habitable. They provide heat, ventilation, air conditioning, fresh water supply, sanitary waste facilities, electrical power, and lighting.

While the nature of a building's structural system can manifest itself in its interior spaces, the often complex networks of its mechanical and electrical systems are normally hidden from view. Interior designers, however, should be aware of those items which are visible and which directly affect the interior environment - light fixtures, electrical outlets, air supply registers and return grills, and plumbing fixtures. Also of interest are the space requirements for horizontal and vertical runs of electrical and plumbing lines, and air ducts.

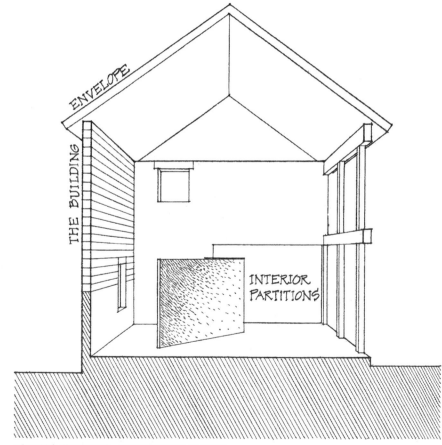

BUILDING ENVELOPE

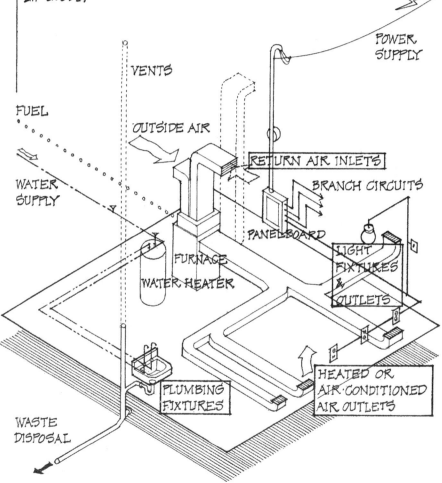

ELECTRICAL · MECHANICAL SYSTEMS

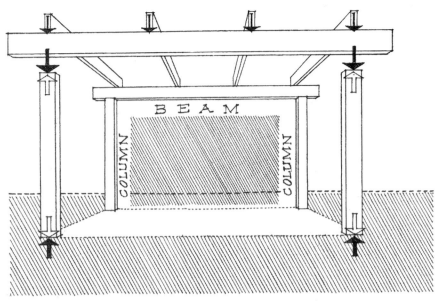

LINEAR STRUCTURAL SYSTEMS

A building's structural system is formed according to the geometry of its materials and how they react to the forces applied to them. This structural form and geometry, in turn, influence the dimensions, proportion, and arrangement of the interior spaces within the building volume.

The two basic linear structural elements are the column and the beam. A column is a vertical support which transmits compressive forces downward along its shaft. The thicker a column is in relation to its height, the greater its load-bearing capacity and its ability to resist buckling due to off-center loading or lateral forces.

A beam is a horizontal member which transmits forces perpendicular to itself along its length to its supports. It is subject to bending which results in a combination of compressive and tensile stresses. These stresses are proportionally greater at the upper and lower edges of a beam. Increasing depth and placing material where stresses are greatest optimizes a beam's performance.

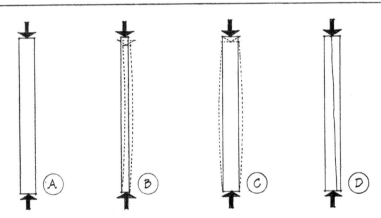

A. COLUMNS ARE SUBJECT TO COMPRESSION
B. SLENDER COLUMNS ARE SUSCEPTIBLE TO BUCKLING
C. THICK COLUMNS MAY COMPRESS, OR
D. IN THE CASE OF TIMBER OR CONCRETE, SPLIT OR FRACTURE

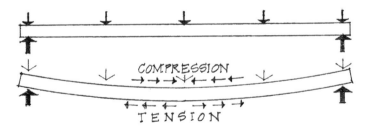

■ BEAMS ARE SUBJECT TO BENDING

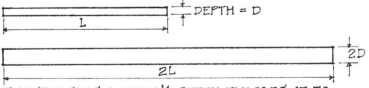

■ INCREASING A BEAM'S DEPTH ENABLES IT TO SPAN FARTHER

Columns mark points in space and provide a measure for its horizontal divisions. Beams make structural and visual connections across space, between their supports. Together, columns and beams form a skeletal framework around interconnected volumes of space.

While a linear structural system may suggest a grid layout of repetitive spaces, floor, wall, and ceiling planes are necessary for the support and enclosure of interior space. Girders, beams, and joists support floor and ceiling planes, which define the vertical limits of space. Wall planes need not be load bearing and do not have to be aligned with the columns of a structural frame. They are free to define the horizontal dimensions of space according to need, desire, or circumstance.

Linear structural systems are cumulative by nature and eminently flexible. They allow for growth, change, and the adaptation of individual spaces to their specific uses.

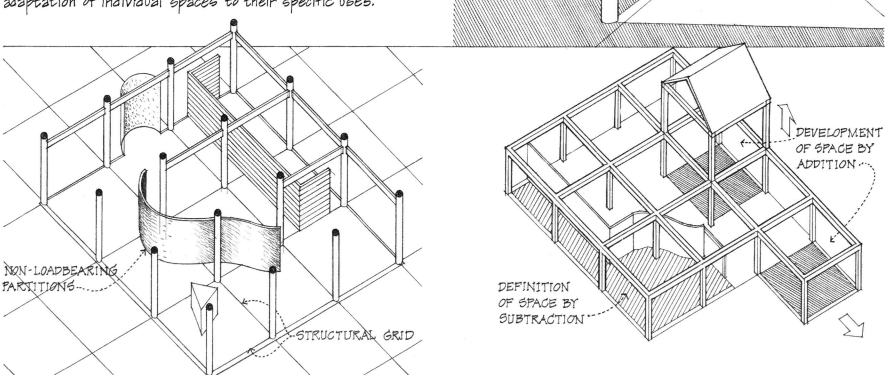

NON-LOADBEARING PARTITIONS

STRUCTURAL GRID

DEVELOPMENT OF SPACE BY ADDITION

DEFINITION OF SPACE BY SUBTRACTION

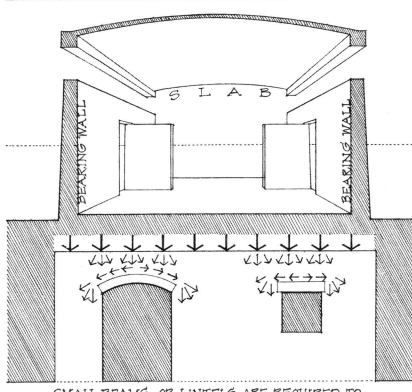

The two principal types of planar structural elements are the load-bearing wall and the horizontal slab. A bearing wall transmits compressive forces, applied along its top edge, to the ground. An exterior wall must also be able to resist lateral forces, such as wind above ground and water and earth pressures below.

A common pattern for bearing walls is a parallel layout spanned by floor joists and roof rafters, or by horizontal slabs. For lateral stability, cross walls are often used to help brace bearing walls.

Window and door openings within a bearing wall tend to weaken its structural integrity. Any opening must be spanned by a short beam called a lintel to support the wall load above.

While linear structural elements outline the edges of spatial volumes, planar elements such as the bearing wall define the physical limits of space. They provide a real sense of enclosure and privacy as well as serve as barriers against the elements.

SMALL BEAMS OR LINTELS ARE REQUIRED TO SPAN OPENINGS IN BEARING WALLS

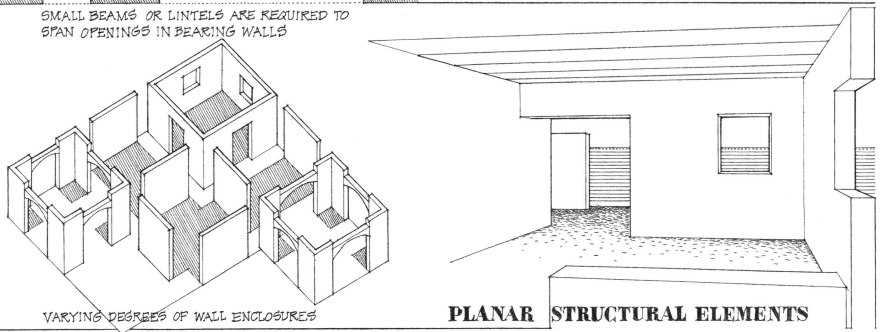

VARYING DEGREES OF WALL ENCLOSURES

PLANAR STRUCTURAL ELEMENTS

A slab is a horizontal structural plane of reinforced concrete. It is able to support both concentrated and distributed loads well since the resulting stresses can fan out across the plane of the slab and take various paths to the slab supports.

When supported along two edges, a slab can be considered to be a wide, shallow beam extending in one direction. Supported along four sides, a slab becomes a two-way structural element. For greater efficiency and reduced weight, a slab can be modified in section to incorporate ribs.

When integrally connected with reinforced concrete columns, flat slabs can be supported without beams. They form horizontal layers of space punctuated only by the shafts of the supporting columns.

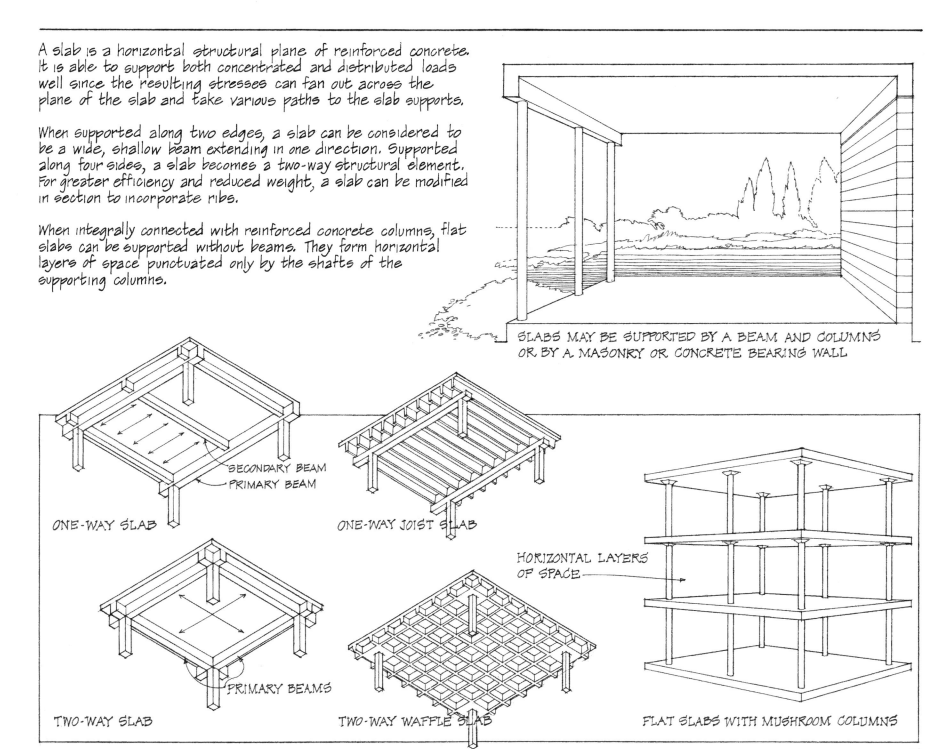

SLABS MAY BE SUPPORTED BY A BEAM AND COLUMNS OR BY A MASONRY OR CONCRETE BEARING WALL

SECONDARY BEAM
PRIMARY BEAM

ONE-WAY SLAB

ONE-WAY JOIST SLAB

PRIMARY BEAMS

TWO-WAY SLAB

TWO-WAY WAFFLE SLAB

HORIZONTAL LAYERS OF SPACE

FLAT SLABS WITH MUSHROOM COLUMNS

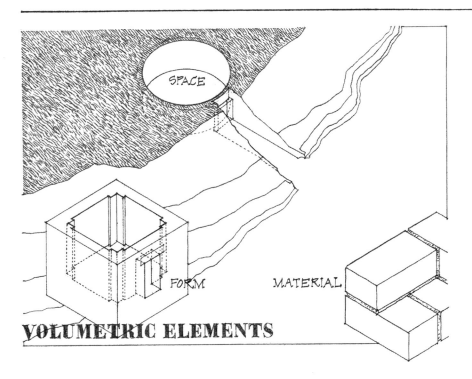

SPACE

FORM

MATERIAL

VOLUMETRIC ELEMENTS

A volumetric structural system consists of three-dimensional mass. The mass of the material used fills the void of space. Out of the mass is carved the volume of interior space.

Because of the efficiency of engineering methods and the strength of modern building materials, pure volumetric systems are quite rare today. At a small scale, however, stone and clay masonry units can be seen to be volumetric structural elements. At a larger scale, any building that encloses interior space can be viewed as a three-dimensional structure which must have strength in width, length, and depth.

Most structural systems are in fact composites of linear, planar, and volumetric elements. No one system is superior to all others in all situations. For the structural designer, each presents advantages and disadvantages, depending on the size, location, and intended use of a building. In interior design, we should be aware of the character of the interior spaces each system defines.

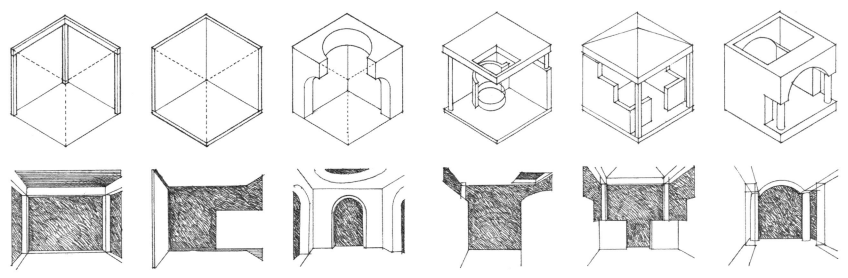

COMPOSITE SYSTEMS   COMBINING LINEAR, PLANAR, AND VOLUMETRIC ELEMENTS INTO COMPOSITIONS OF FORMS AND SPACE

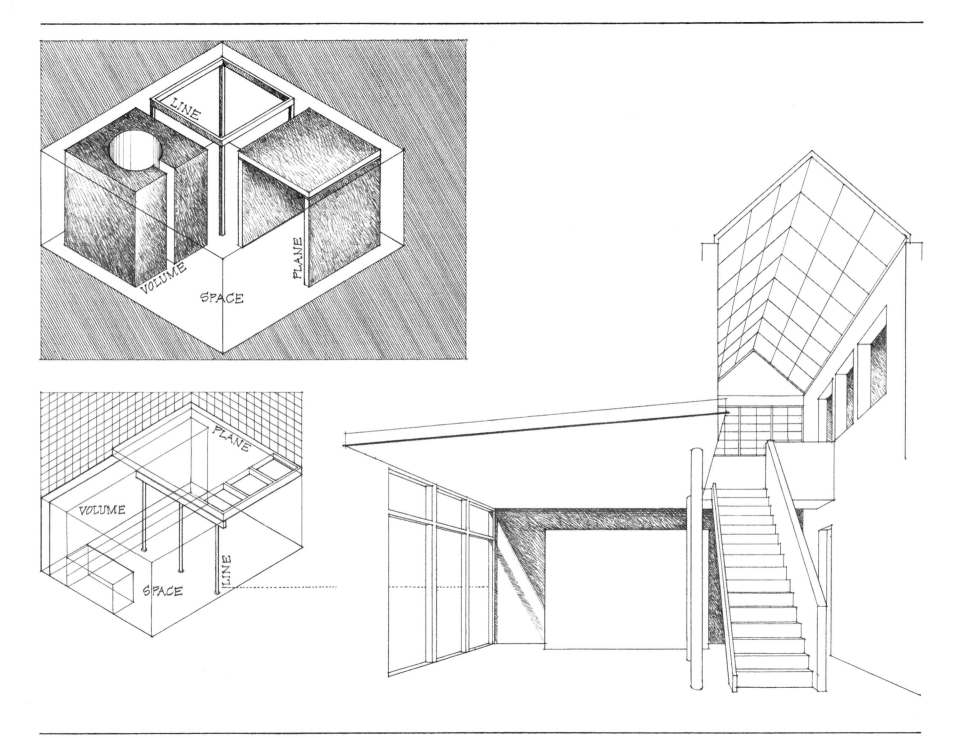

LINE

VOLUME

SPACE

PLANE

PLANE

VOLUME

SPACE

LINE

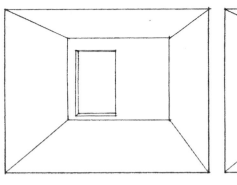

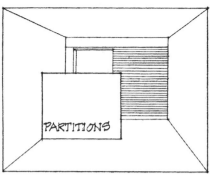

PARTITIONS

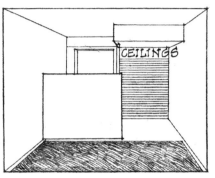

CEILINGS

FURNITURE

A building's structural system sets up the basic form and pattern of its interior spaces. These spaces, however, are ultimately structured by the elements of interior design. The term structure is not used here in the sense of physical support. It refers to the selection and arrangement of interior elements such that their visual relationships define and organize the interior space of a room.

Non-loadbearing walls and suspended ceilings are often used to define or modify space within the structural framework or shell of a building.

Within a large space, the form and arrangement of furnishings can also function as walls, provide a sense of enclosure, and define spatial patterns. Even a single element, by its form, scale, or style, can dominate a room and organize a field of space about itself.

Light, and the patterns of light and dark it creates, can call our attention to one area of a room, de-emphasize others, and thereby create divisions of space.

STRUCTURING SPACE

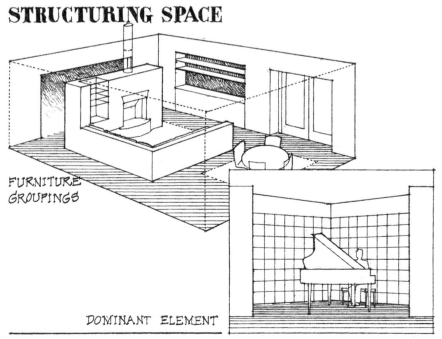

FURNITURE GROUPINGS

DOMINANT ELEMENT

WITH

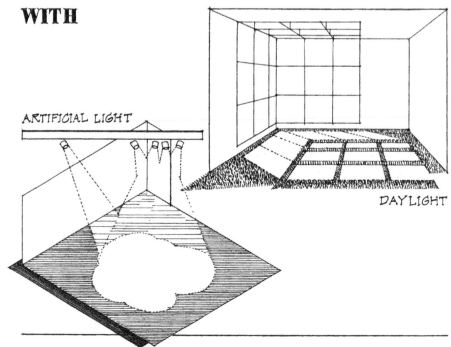

ARTIFICIAL LIGHT

DAYLIGHT

The surface treatment of wall, floor, and ceiling planes can articulate the spatial boundaries of a room. Their color, texture, and pattern affect our perception of their relative positions in space and, therefore, our awareness of the room's dimensions, scale, and proportion.

Even the acoustic nature of a room's surfaces can affect the apparent boundaries of the space. Soft, absorbent surfaces muffle sounds and can expand the acoustical boundaries of a room. Hard surfaces that reflect sounds within a room can emphasize the physical boundaries of the space.

Finally, space is structured by how we use it. The nature of our activities and the rituals we develop in performing them influence how we plan, arrange, and organize interior space.

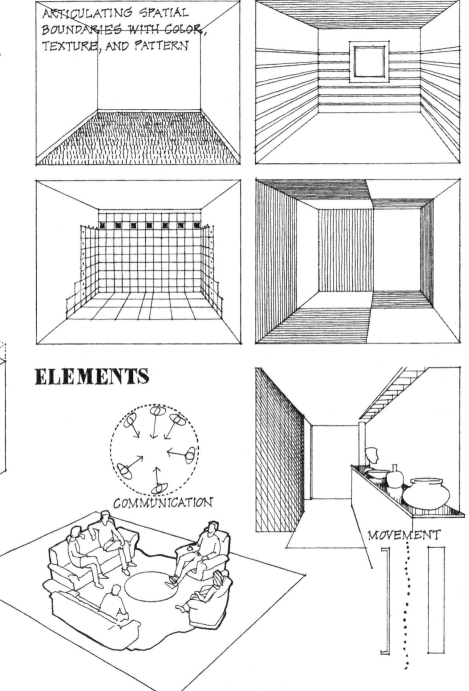

ARTICULATING SPATIAL BOUNDARIES WITH COLOR, TEXTURE, AND PATTERN

INTERIOR DESIGN ELEMENTS

INDIVIDUAL OR GROUP ACTIVITIES

COMMUNICATION

MOVEMENT

SPATIAL FORM

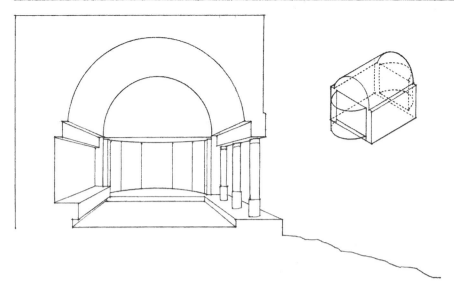

Interior spaces are formed first by a building's structural system, further defined by wall and ceiling planes, and related to other spaces by windows and doorways. Every building has a recognizable pattern of these elements and systems. Each pattern has an inherent geometry which molds or carves out a volume of space into its likeness.

It is useful to be able to read this figure-ground relationship between the form of space-defining elements and that of the space defined. Either the structure or the space can dominate this relationship. Whichever appears to dominate, we should be able to perceive the other as an equal partner in the relationship.

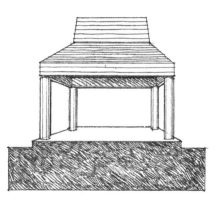

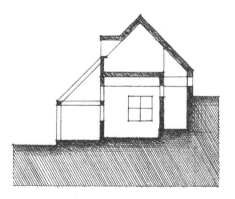

It is equally useful to see this alternating figure-ground relationship occurring as interior design elements, such as tables and chairs, are introduced and arranged within an interior space.

When a chair is placed in a room, it not only occupies space. It also creates a spatial relationship between itself and the surrounding enclosure. We should see more than the form of the chair. We should also recognize the form of the space surrounding the chair after it has filled some of the void.

As more elements are introduced into the pattern, the spatial relationships multiply. The elements begin to organize into sets or groups, each of which not only occupies space but also defines and articulates the spatial form.

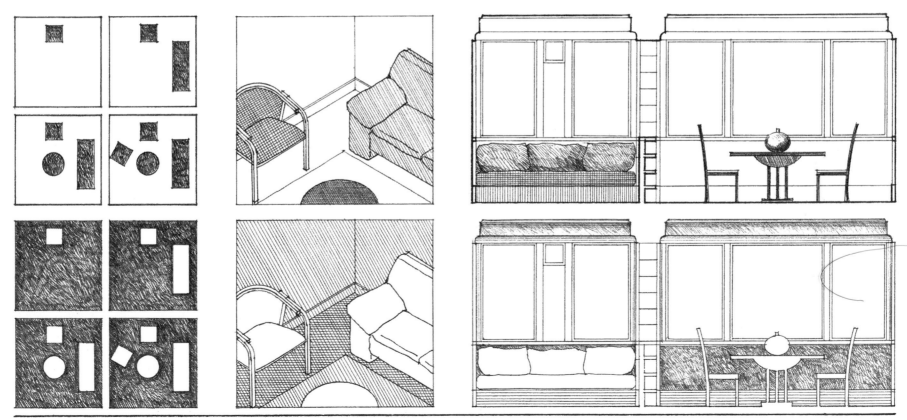

SPATIAL DIMENSIONS

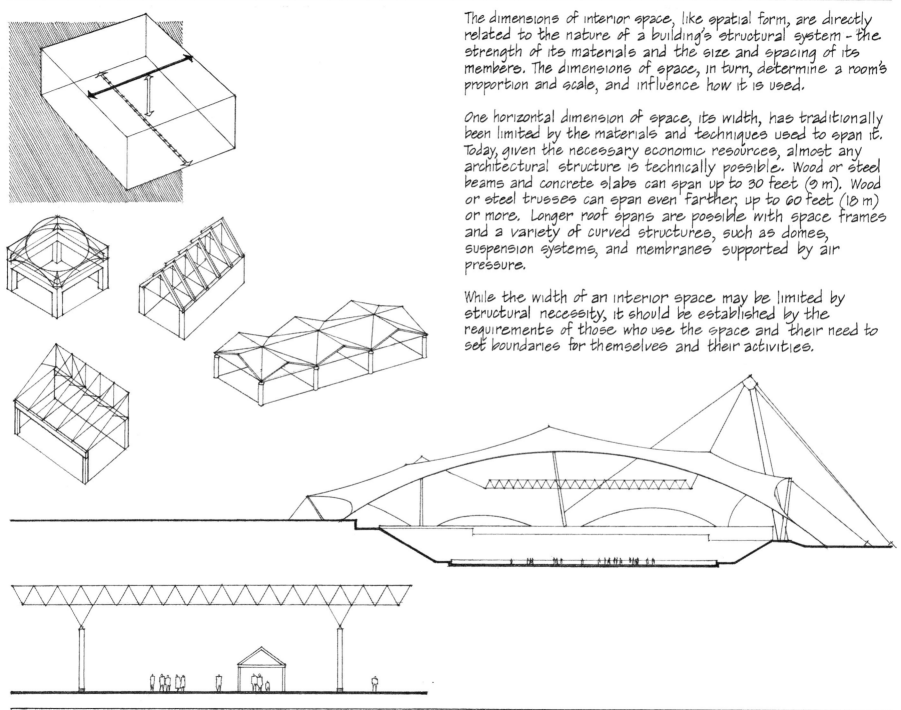

The dimensions of interior space, like spatial form, are directly related to the nature of a building's structural system - the strength of its materials and the size and spacing of its members. The dimensions of space, in turn, determine a room's proportion and scale, and influence how it is used.

One horizontal dimension of space, its width, has traditionally been limited by the materials and techniques used to span it. Today, given the necessary economic resources, almost any architectural structure is technically possible. Wood or steel beams and concrete slabs can span up to 30 feet (9 m). Wood or steel trusses can span even farther, up to 60 feet (18 m) or more. Longer roof spans are possible with space frames and a variety of curved structures, such as domes, suspension systems, and membranes supported by air pressure.

While the width of an interior space may be limited by structural necessity, it should be established by the requirements of those who use the space and their need to set boundaries for themselves and their activities.

The other horizontal dimension of space, its length, is limited by desire and circumstance. Together with width, the length of a space determines the proportion of a room's plan shape.

A square room, where the length of the space equals its width, is static in quality and often formal in character. The equality of the four sides focuses in on the room's center. This centrality can be enhanced or emphasized by covering the space with a pyramidal or dome structure.

To de-emphasize the centrality of a square room, the form of the ceiling can be made asymmetrical, or one or more of the wall planes can be treated differently from the others.

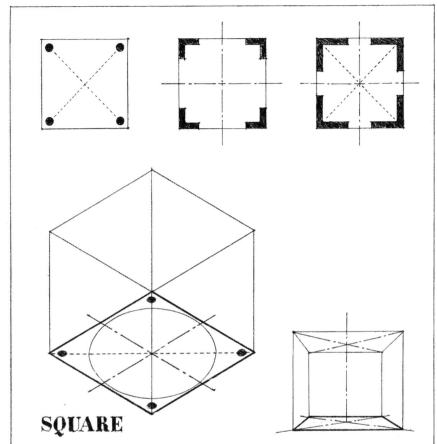

SQUARE

ROOF FORMS EMPHASIZING THE CENTRALITY OF SQUARE ROOMS

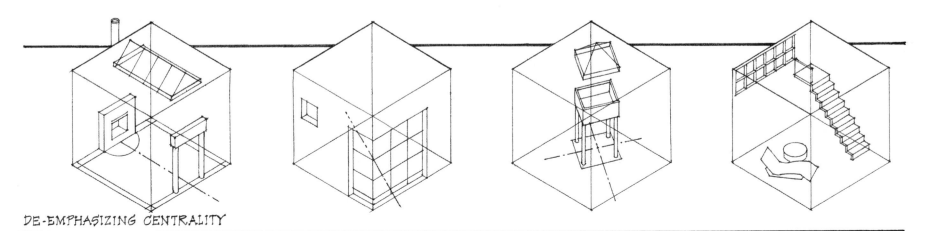

DE-EMPHASIZING CENTRALITY

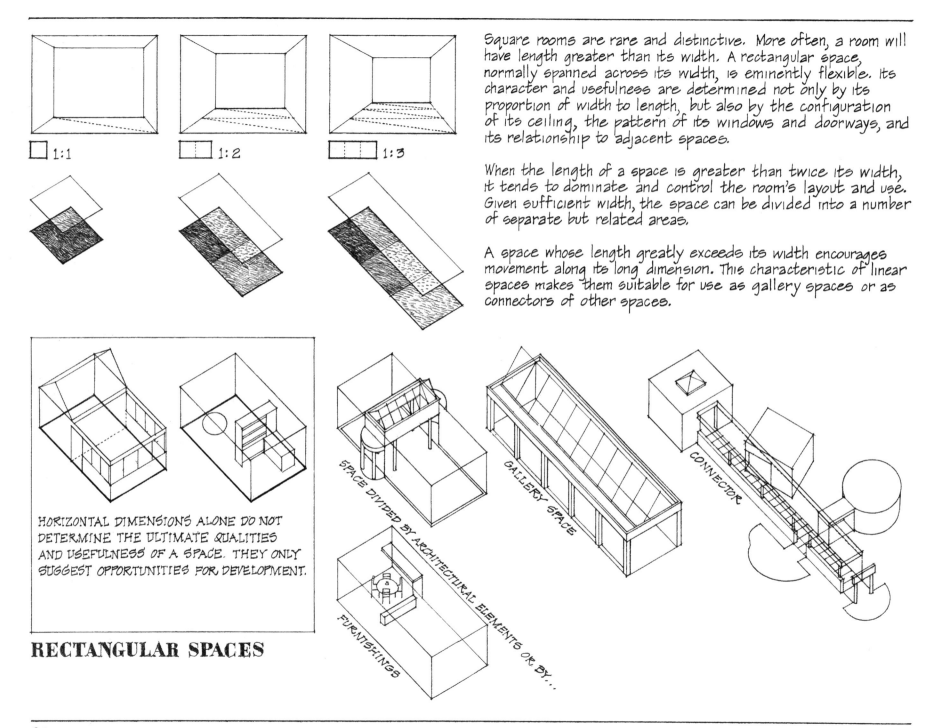

Square rooms are rare and distinctive. More often, a room will have length greater than its width. A rectangular space, normally spanned across its width, is eminently flexible. Its character and usefulness are determined not only by its proportion of width to length, but also by the configuration of its ceiling, the pattern of its windows and doorways, and its relationship to adjacent spaces.

When the length of a space is greater than twice its width, it tends to dominate and control the room's layout and use. Given sufficient width, the space can be divided into a number of separate but related areas.

A space whose length greatly exceeds its width encourages movement along its long dimension. This characteristic of linear spaces makes them suitable for use as gallery spaces or as connectors of other spaces.

1:1 1:2 1:3

HORIZONTAL DIMENSIONS ALONE DO NOT DETERMINE THE ULTIMATE QUALITIES AND USEFULNESS OF A SPACE. THEY ONLY SUGGEST OPPORTUNITIES FOR DEVELOPMENT.

RECTANGULAR SPACES

SPACE DIVIDED BY ARCHITECTURAL ELEMENTS OR BY...

FURNISHINGS

GALLERY SPACE

CONNECTOR

Both square and rectangular spaces can be altered by addition or subtraction, or by merging with adjacent spaces. These modifications can be used to create an alcove space or to reflect an adjoining circumstance or site feature.

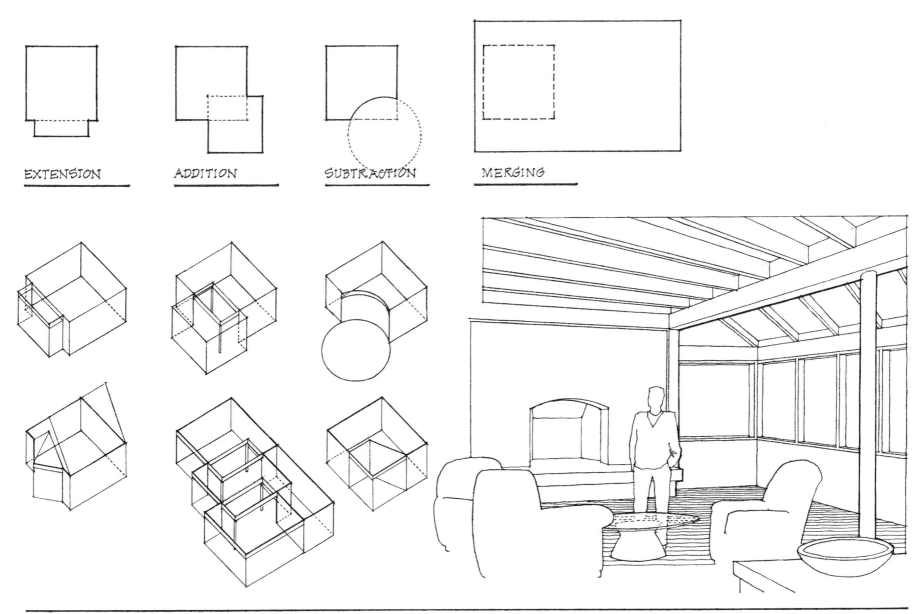

EXTENSION
ADDITION
SUBTRACTION
MERGING

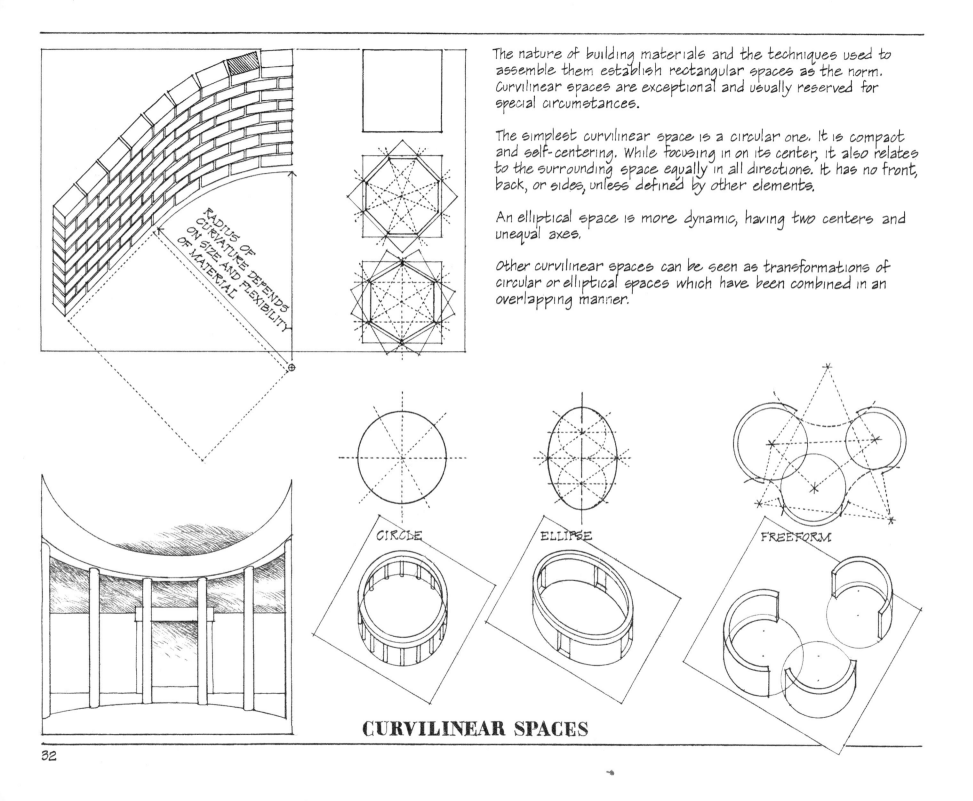

The nature of building materials and the techniques used to assemble them establish rectangular spaces as the norm. Curvilinear spaces are exceptional and usually reserved for special circumstances.

The simplest curvilinear space is a circular one. It is compact and self-centering. While focusing in on its center, it also relates to the surrounding space equally in all directions. It has no front, back, or sides, unless defined by other elements.

An elliptical space is more dynamic, having two centers and unequal axes.

Other curvilinear spaces can be seen as transformations of circular or elliptical spaces which have been combined in an overlapping manner.

RADIUS OF CURVATURE DEPENDS ON SIZE AND FLEXIBILITY OF MATERIAL

CIRCLE

ELLIPSE

FREEFORM

CURVILINEAR SPACES

Within a rectilinear context, a curvilinear space is highly visible. Its contrasting geometry can be used to express the importance or uniqueness of its function. It can define a freestanding volume within a larger space. It can serve as a central space about which other rooms are gathered. It can articulate the edge of a space and reflect an exterior condition of the building site.

Curved walls are dynamic and visually active, leading our eyes along their curvature. The concave aspect of a curved wall encloses and focuses inward on space, while its convex aspect pushes space outward.

An important consideration when dealing with a curvilinear space is the integration of furniture and other interior elements into its volume. One way of resolving conflicting geometries is to arrange interior forms as freestanding objects within the curvilinear space. Another is to integrate the form of built-in furniture and fixtures with the curved boundaries of the space.

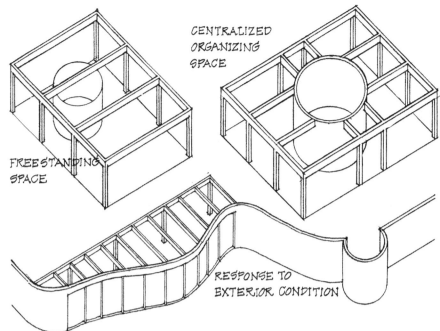

CENTRALIZED ORGANIZING SPACE

FREESTANDING SPACE

RESPONSE TO EXTERIOR CONDITION

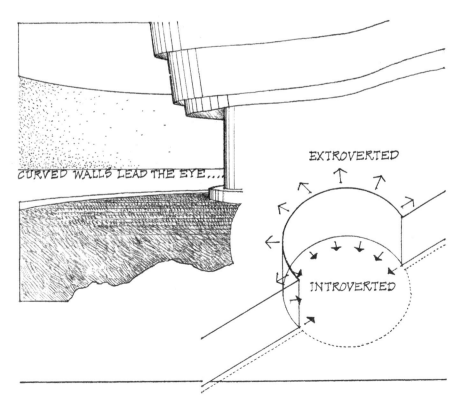

CURVED WALLS LEAD THE EYE....

EXTROVERTED

INTROVERTED

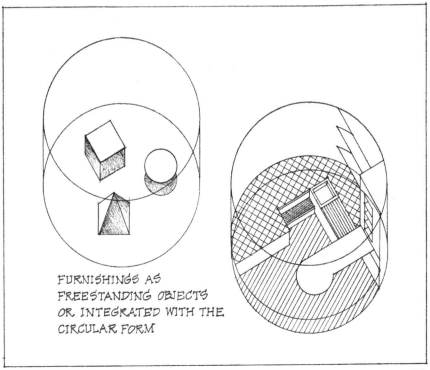

FURNISHINGS AS FREESTANDING OBJECTS OR INTEGRATED WITH THE CIRCULAR FORM

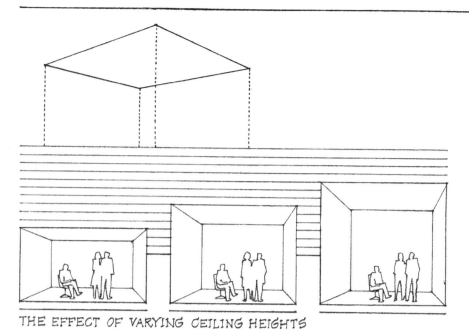

THE EFFECT OF VARYING CEILING HEIGHTS

The third dimension of interior space, its height, is established by the ceiling plane. This vertical dimension is as influential as the horizontal dimensions of space in forming the spatial quality of a room.

While our perception of a room's horizontal dimensions is often distorted by the foreshortening of perspective, we can more accurately sense the relationship between the height of a space and our own body height. A measurable change in the height of a ceiling seems to have a greater effect on our impression of a space than a similar change in its width or length.

High ceilings are often associated with feelings of loftiness or grandeur. Low ceilings often have connotations of cave-like coziness and intimacy. Our perception of the scale of a space, however, is affected not by the height of the ceiling alone, but by its relationship to the width and length of the space.

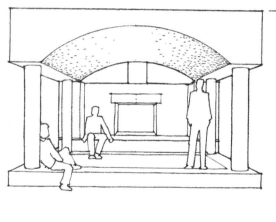

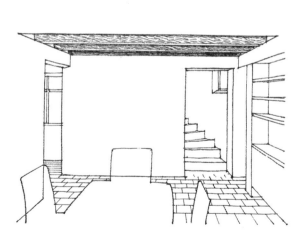

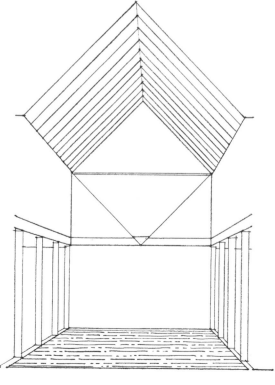

THE HEIGHT OF A SPACE

A ceiling defined by a floor plane above is typically flat. A ceiling created by a roof structure can reflect its form and the manner in which it spans the space. Shed, gable, and vaulted ceiling forms give direction to space, while domed and pyramidal ceilings emphasize the center of a space.

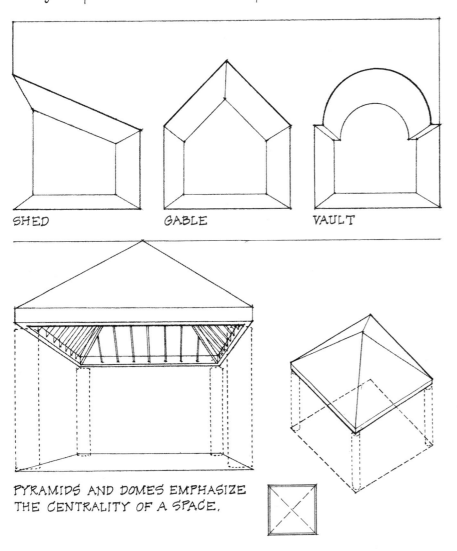

SHED   GABLE   VAULT

PYRAMIDS AND DOMES EMPHASIZE THE CENTRALITY OF A SPACE.

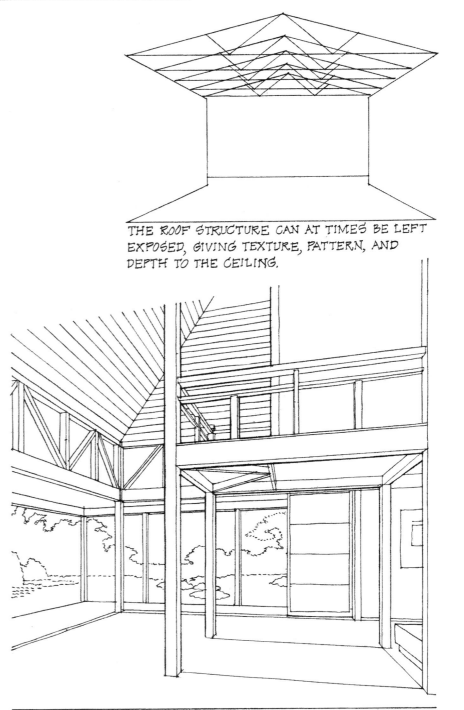

THE ROOF STRUCTURE CAN AT TIMES BE LEFT EXPOSED, GIVING TEXTURE, PATTERN, AND DEPTH TO THE CEILING.

SPATIAL TRANSITIONS

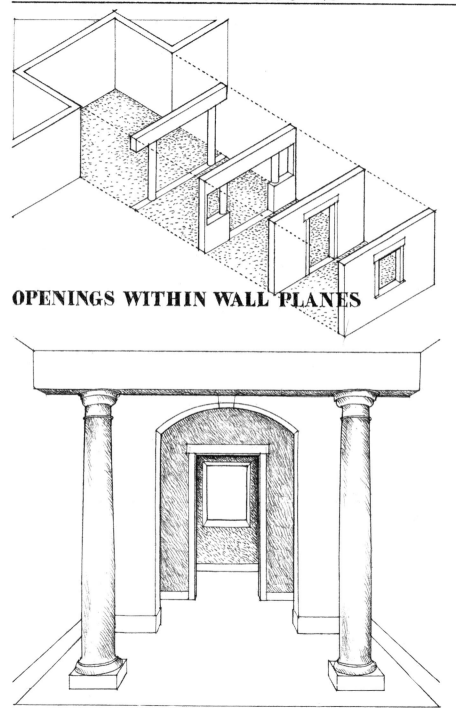

OPENINGS WITHIN WALL PLANES

Although individual spaces may be designed and formed for a certain purpose or to house certain activities, they are gathered together within a building's enclosure because they are functionally related to one another, they are used by a common group of people, or they share a common purpose. How interior spaces are related to one another is determined not only by their relative position in a building's spatial pattern, but also by the nature of the spaces which connect them and the boundaries which they have in common.

Floor, wall, and ceiling planes serve to define and isolate a portion of space. Of these, the wall plane, being perpendicular to our normal line of sight, has the greatest effect as a spatial boundary. It limits our visual field and serves as a barrier to our movement. Openings within the wall plane, windows and doorways, re-establish contact with the surrounding spaces from which the room was originally cut off.

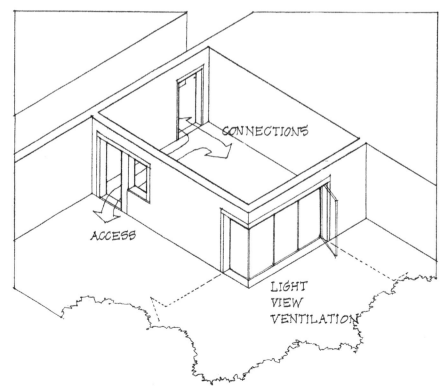

CONNECTIONS

ACCESS

LIGHT
VIEW
VENTILATION

Doorways provide physical access from one space to another. When closed, they shut a room off from adjacent spaces. When open, they establish visual, spatial, and acoustical links between spaces. Large open doorways erode the integrity of a room's enclosure and strengthen its connection with adjacent spaces or the outdoors.

The thickness of the wall separating two spaces is exposed at a doorway. This depth determines the degree of separation we sense as we pass through the doorway from one space to another. The scale and treatment of the doorway itself can also provide a visual clue to the nature of the space being entered.

The number and location of doorways along a room's perimeter affects our pattern of movement within the space, and how we may arrange its furnishings and organize our activities.

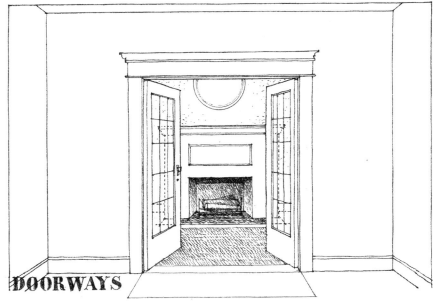

DOORWAYS

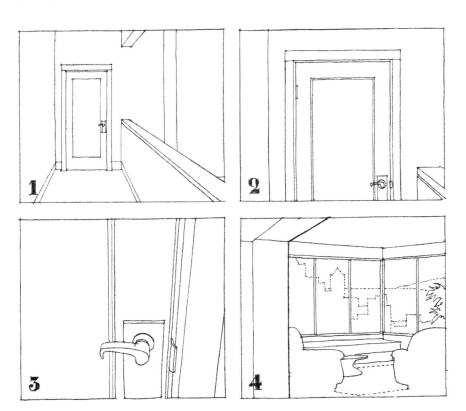

1

2

3

4

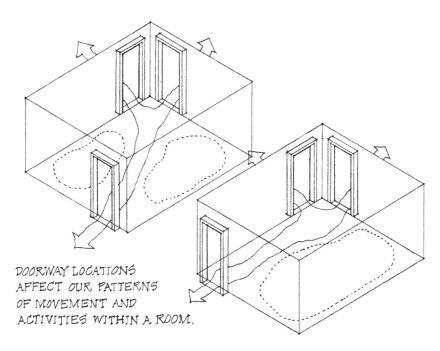

DOORWAY LOCATIONS AFFECT OUR PATTERNS OF MOVEMENT AND ACTIVITIES WITHIN A ROOM.

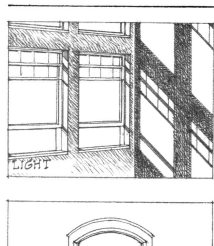

LIGHT

VIEW

DEGREE OF ENCLOSURE

OR TRANSPARENCY

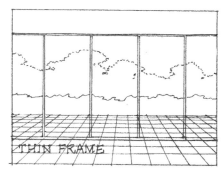

THIN FRAME

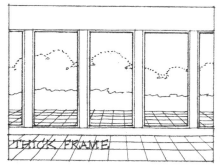

THICK FRAME

INTERIOR WINDOWS

Windows let light and air into the interior spaces of buildings and provide views of the outdoors or from one space to another. Their size and placement, relative to the wall plane in which they occur, also affect the degree of separation between an interior space and the exterior environment.

Windows framed within a wall plane attract our attention with their brightness and outlook, but maintain the enclosure provided by the wall. Large windows and glass walls attempt, at least visually, to merge indoor and outdoor space. The visual treatment of the window frames in each case can either emphasize or minimize the perceived limits of interior space.

Interior windows can, in a similar manner, visually expand a room beyond its physical boundaries and allow it to become an integral part of the surrounding interior space.

WINDOWS

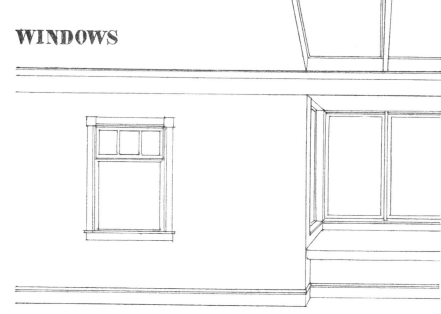

Stairways are also important forms of spatial transitions between rooms. An exterior set of steps leading to a building's entrance can serve to separate private domain from public passage and enhance the act of entry into a transitional space, like a porch or terrace.

Interior stairways connect the various levels of a building. The manner in which they perform this function shapes our movement in space - how we approach a stairway, the pace and style of our ascent and descent, and what we have an opportunity to do along the way. Wide, shallow steps can serve as an invitation, while a narrow, steep stairway can lead to more private places. Landings which interrupt a flight of steps can allow a stairway to change direction and give us room for pause, rest, and outlook.

The space a stairway occupies can be great, but its form can be fit into an interior in several ways. It can fill and provide a focus for a space, run along one of its edges, or wrap around a room. It can be woven into the boundaries of a space, or be extended into a series of terraces.

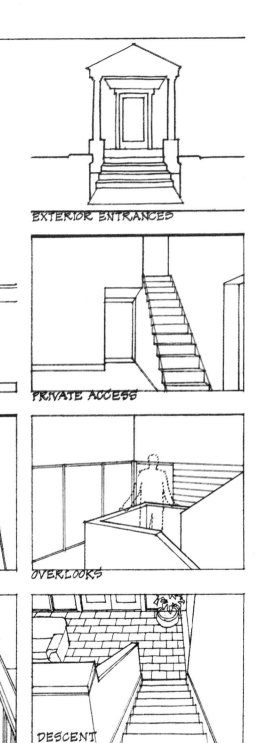

EXTERIOR ENTRANCES

PUBLIC APPROACH

PRIVATE ACCESS

VISIBLE LANDINGS INVITE

OVERLOOKS

ASCENT

DESCENT

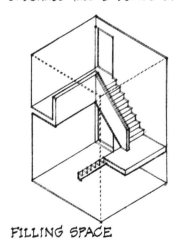

FILLING SPACE

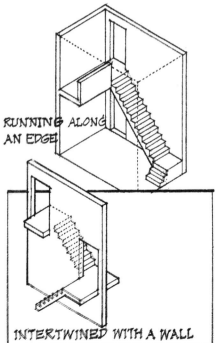

RUNNING ALONG AN EDGE

INTERTWINED WITH A WALL

STAIRWAYS

MODIFYING SPACE

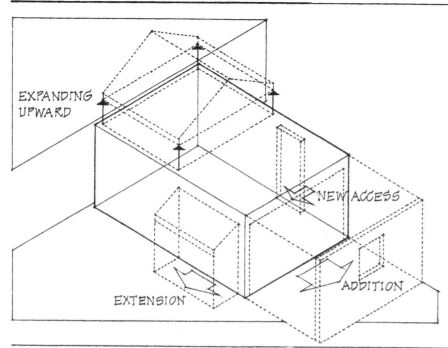

EXPANDING UPWARD

NEW ACCESS

EXTENSION

ADDITION

The architectural planning and design for a new building takes into account the nature of the activities to be housed, the spatial requirements for form, scale, and light, and the desired relationships among the various interior spaces. When an existing building is to be used for activities other than those for which it was originally intended, however, activity requirements must be matched with the existing conditions. Where a misfit occurs, a modification of the existing spaces may be required.

Two major types of alteration can be considered. The first involves structural changes in the boundaries of interior space and is of a more permanent nature than the second, which involves nonstructural modifications and enhancement accomplished through interior design.

A structural change usually involves removing or adding walls in order to alter the shape and rearrange the pattern of existing spaces, or add on new space.

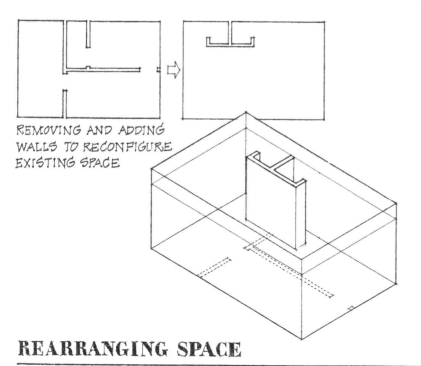

REMOVING AND ADDING WALLS TO RECONFIGURE EXISTING SPACE

REARRANGING SPACE

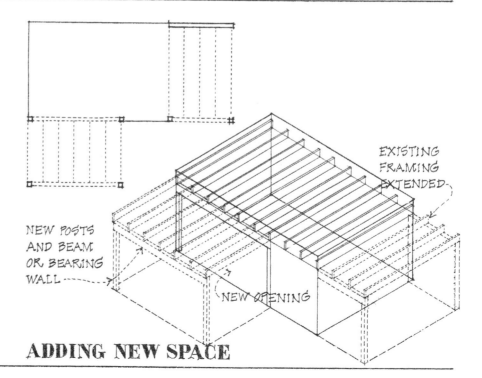

EXISTING FRAMING EXTENDED

NEW POSTS AND BEAM OR BEARING WALL

NEW OPENING

ADDING NEW SPACE

Within the boundaries of space, the existing pattern of openings can also be altered. Windows may be enlarged or added for better daylighting or to take advantage of a view. A doorway may be moved or added for better access to a space or to improve the paths of movement within the room. A large doorway may be created to merge two adjacent spaces.

Any changes in the physical boundaries of a space must be carefully planned so that the structural integrity of a building is not adversely disturbed. A portion of a load-bearing wall can be removed if a post-and-beam system is substituted, and the support system below is able to bear the concentrated loads of the new posts. Similarly, new openings in a bearing wall can be created if adequate lintels are installed to carry the wall loads above the openings.

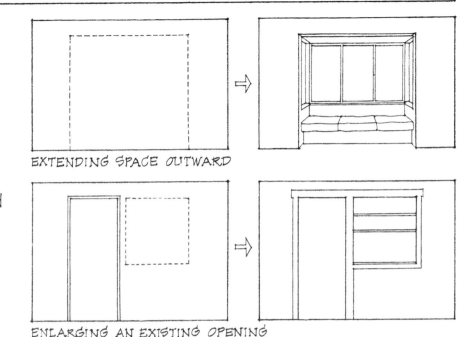

EXTENDING SPACE OUTWARD

ENLARGING AN EXISTING OPENING

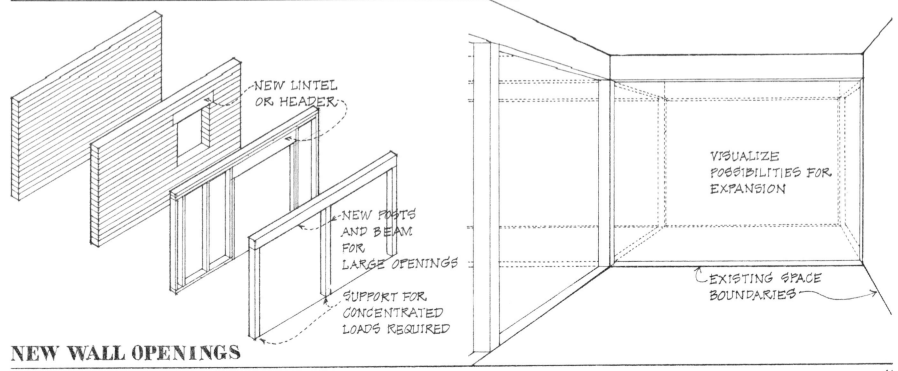

NEW LINTEL OR HEADER

NEW POSTS AND BEAM FOR LARGE OPENINGS

SUPPORT FOR CONCENTRATED LOADS REQUIRED

VISUALIZE POSSIBILITIES FOR EXPANSION

EXISTING SPACE BOUNDARIES

NEW WALL OPENINGS

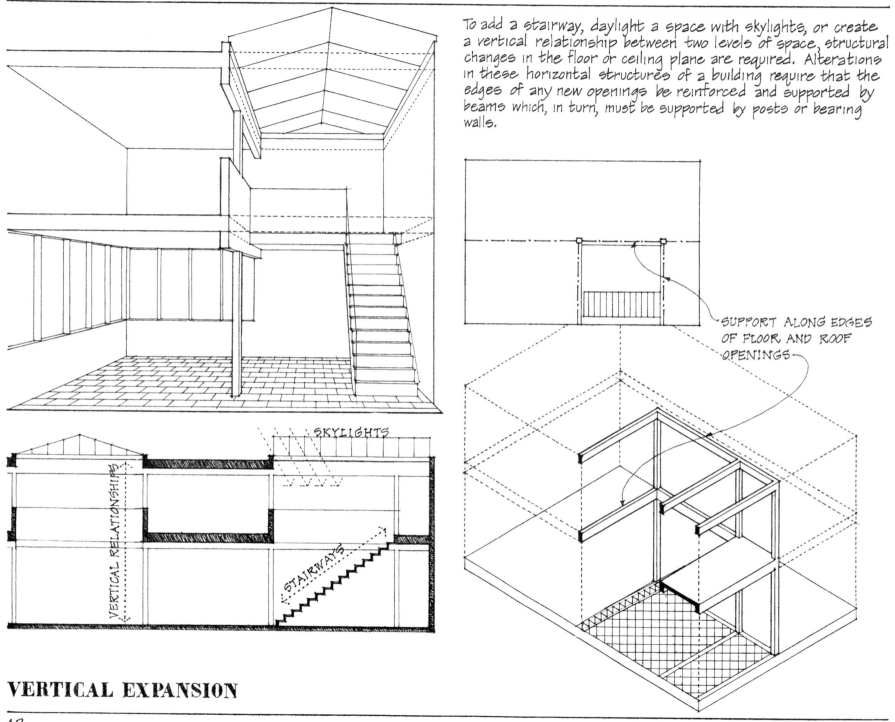

To add a stairway, daylight a space with skylights, or create a vertical relationship between two levels of space, structural changes in the floor or ceiling plane are required. Alterations in these horizontal structures of a building require that the edges of any new openings be reinforced and supported by beams which, in turn, must be supported by posts or bearing walls.

SUPPORT ALONG EDGES OF FLOOR AND ROOF OPENINGS

SKYLIGHTS

VERTICAL RELATIONSHIPS

STAIRWAYS

VERTICAL EXPANSION

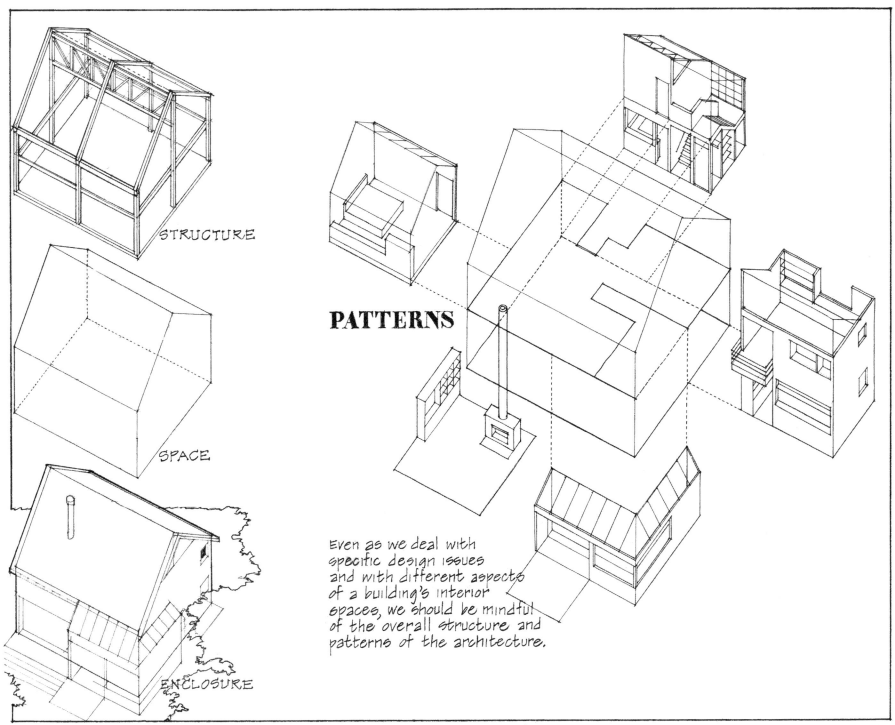

STRUCTURE

SPACE

ENCLOSURE

PATTERNS

Even as we deal with
specific design issues
and with different aspects
of a building's interior
spaces, we should be mindful
of the overall structure and
patterns of the architecture.

Major structural changes in a space require the assistance of a professional engineer, architect, or builder. Interior spaces can, however, also be modified and enhanced with nonstructural alterations. While structural changes alter the physical boundaries of space, nonstructural alterations are based on how we perceive, use, and inhabit space. This is the point where we enter the realm of interior design.

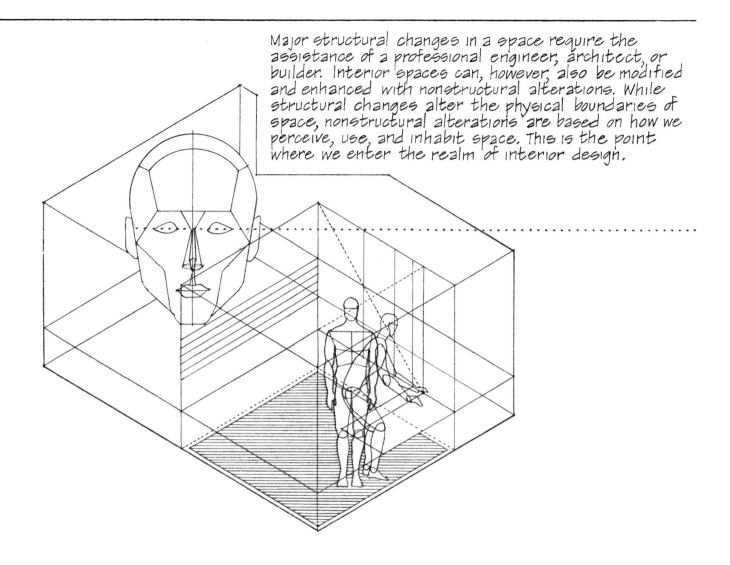

2

INTERIOR
DESIGN

INTERIOR DESIGN

Interior design is the planning, layout, and design of the interior spaces within buildings. These physical settings satisfy our basic need for shelter and protection; they set the stage for and influence the shape of our activities; they nurture our aspirations and express the ideas which accompany our actions; they affect our outlook, mood, and personality. The purpose of interior design, therefore, is the functional improvement, aesthetic enrichment, and psychological enhancement of interior space.

The purpose of any design is to organize its parts into a coherent whole in order to achieve certain goals. In interior design, selected elements are arranged into three-dimensional patterns according to functional, aesthetic, and behavioral guidelines. The relationships among the elements established by these patterns ultimately determine the visual qualities and functional fitness of an interior space, and influence how we perceive and use it.

PLANNING LAYOUT DESIGN OF THE PARTS

THE ARCHITECTURAL CONTEXT

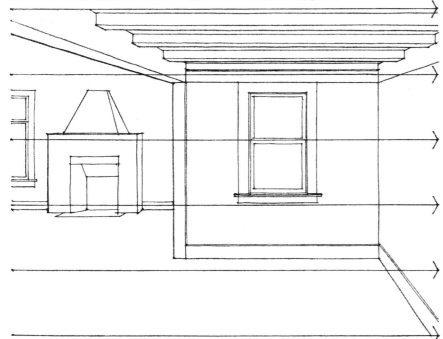

INTERIOR ELEMENTS

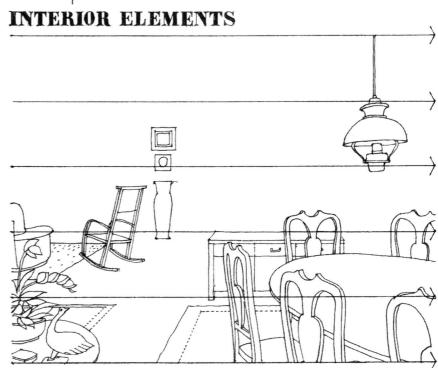

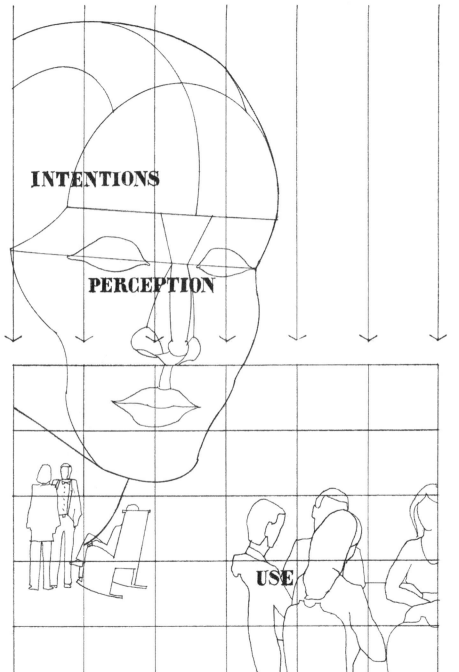

INTENTIONS

PERCEPTION

USE

INTO A WHOLE

THE INTERIOR ENVIRONMENT

DESIGN PROCESS

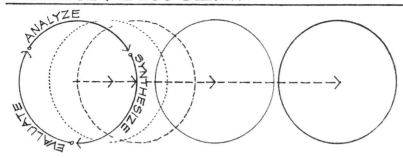

We determine which elements to use and how to arrange them into patterns through the process of design. Although presented as a linear series of steps, the design process is more often a cyclical one in which a sequence of careful analysis, synthesis, and evaluation of available information, insights, and possible solutions is repeated until a successful fit between what exists and what is desired is achieved.

ANALYSIS:

THE ABILITY TO DEFINE AND UNDERSTAND THE NATURE OF THE DESIGN PROBLEM ADEQUATELY IS AN ESSENTIAL PART OF THE SOLUTION.

WHAT EXISTS ?

☐ DOCUMENT PHYSICAL/CULTURAL CONTEXT
☐ DESCRIBE EXISTING ELEMENTS
☐ WHAT CAN CHANGE...WHAT CANNOT ?

WHAT'S DESIRED ?

☐ IDENTIFY USER NEEDS AND PREFERENCES
☐ SET GOALS:
  o FUNCTIONAL REQUIREMENTS
  o AESTHETIC IMAGE AND STYLE
  o PSYCHOLOGICAL STIMULUS AND MEANING

WHAT'S POSSIBLE ?

☐ WHAT CAN BE ALTERED...WHAT CANNOT ?
☐ WHAT CAN BE CONTROLLED...WHAT CANNOT ?
☐ WHAT IS ALLOWED...WHAT IS PROHIBITED ?
☐ DEFINE LIMITS: TIME, ECONOMIC, LEGAL, TECHNICAL

The design problem is first defined. This definition should include a specification of how the design solution should perform. Goals and objectives should be set.

An analysis of the problem requires that it be broken down into parts, issues clarified, and values assigned to the various aspects of the problem. Analysis also involves gathering relevant information that would help us understand the nature of the problem and develop appropriate responses. From the outset, it is worthwhile knowing what limitations will help shape the design solution. Any givens - what can change and what cannot be altered - should be determined. Any constraints - financial, legal, or technical - which will impinge on the design solution should be noted.

As we cycle through the design process, a clearer understanding of the problem should emerge. New information may be uncovered or be required which could alter our perception of the problem and its solution. The analysis of a problem, therefore, often continues throughout the design process.

DEVELOP HYPOTHESES ......>

MAKE PROJECTIONS ......>

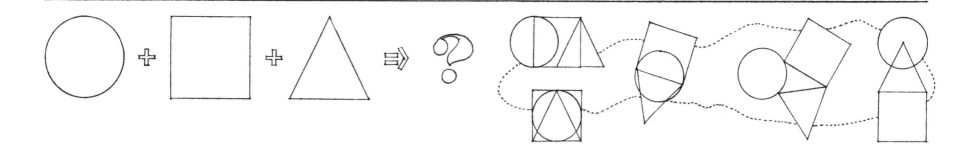

From the analysis of the problem and its parts, we can begin to formulate possible solutions. This requires synthesizing - bringing together and integrating - responses to the various issues and aspects of the problem into coherent solutions.

There are several approaches one can take to generate ideas and synthesize possible solutions to a problem:

- Isolate one or two key issues which have value or importance assigned to them, and develop solutions around them.

- Study analogous situations and use them as models for developing possible solutions to the problem at hand.

- Develop ideal solutions for parts of the problem which can then be integrated into whole solutions and be tempered by the reality of what exists.

It is difficult to develop a good idea without having many to begin with.

SYNTHESIS:

DESIGN REQUIRES RATIONAL THOUGHT BASED ON KNOWLEDGE AND UNDERSTANDING GAINED THROUGH EXPERIENCE AND RESEARCH. ALSO PLAYING EQUAL ROLES ARE INTUITION AND IMAGINATION, WHICH ADD THE CREATIVE DIMENSION TO THE RATIONAL DESIGN PROCESS.

SELECT THE PARTS

☐ SELECT AND ASSIGN VALUES TO KEY ISSUES OR ELEMENTS
☐ STUDY THE NATURE OF THE PARTS
☐ VISUALIZE THE WAYS THE PARTS CAN FIT TOGETHER

GENERATE IDEAS

☐ LOOK AT THE SITUATION FROM DIFFERENT POINTS OF VIEW
☐ MANIPULATE THE PARTS TO SEE HOW A CHANGE MIGHT AFFECT THE WHOLE
☐ SEARCH FOR WAYS TO COMBINE SEVERAL GOOD IDEAS INTO A BETTER ONE

INTEGRATE INTO A WHOLE

☐

SIMULATE POSSIBILITIES

TEST & REFINE IDEAS

EVALUATION:

DESIGN REQUIRES A CRITICAL REVIEW OF ALTERNATIVES AND CAREFUL WEIGHING OF THE STRENGTHS AND WEAKNESSES OF EACH PROPOSAL UNTIL THE BEST POSSIBLE FIT BETWEEN PROBLEM AND SOLUTION IS ACHIEVED.

COMPARE ALTERNATIVES

☐ COMPARE EACH ALTERNATIVE WITH DESIGN GOALS AND CRITERIA.
☐ WEIGH THE BENEFITS AND STRENGTHS AGAINST THE COSTS AND LIABILITIES OF EACH ALTERNATIVE.
☐ RANK ALTERNATIVES IN TERMS OF SUITABILITY AND EFFECTIVENESS

MAKE DESIGN DECISIONS
☐

DEVELOP & REFINE DESIGN
☐

IMPLEMENT DESIGN
☐

Given a range of possible solutions, each must be evaluated according to the criteria set forth in the problem statement and further clarified in the problem analysis.

Successive explorations of the problem and the evaluation of alternative solutions should help narrow down the choices for design development. While the initial stages of the design process encourage divergent thinking about the problem, this latter phase requires a convergent focus on a specific design solution.

Once a final decision has been made, the design proposal is developed, refined, and prepared for implementation. This includes the production of working drawings and specifications, and other services related to purchasing, construction, and supervision.

No design process is complete until a design solution which has been implemented is evaluated for its effectiveness in solving a given problem. This critical appraisal of a completed design can build up our knowledge base, sharpen our intuition, and provide valuable lessons that may be applied in future work.

RE·EVALUATE COMPLETED DESIGN ⟩

One of the idiosyncrasies of the design process is that it does not always lead simply and inevitably to a single, obvious, correct answer. In fact, there is often more than one valid solution to a design problem. How then can we judge whether a design is good or bad?

A design may be good, in the judgment of the designer, the client, or the people who experience and use the design, for any of several reasons:

- A design may be good because it functions well - it works.

- A design may be good because it is affordable - it is economical, efficient, and durable.

- A design may be good because it looks good - it is aesthetically pleasing.

- A design may be good because it recreates a feeling remembered from another time and place - it carries meaning.

- At times, we may judge a design to be good because we feel it follows current design trends - it is in fashion - or because of the impression it will make on others - it enhances our status.

As the foregoing suggests, there are several kinds of meaning which can be conveyed by a design. Some operate at a level generally understood and accepted by the general public. Others are more readily discerned by specific groups of people. Successful designs usually operate at more than one level of meaning and thus appeal to a wide range of people.

A good design, therefore, should be understandable. Knowing why something was done helps to make a design comprehensible. If a design does not express an idea, communicate a meaning, or elicit a response, either it will be ignored or it will appear to be a bad design.

DESIGN CRITERIA

In defining and analyzing a design problem, one also develops goals and criteria by which the effectiveness of a solution can be measured. Regardless of the nature of the interior design problem being addressed, there are several criteria with which we should be concerned.

• FUNCTION & PURPOSE

First, the intended function of the design must be satisfied and its purpose fulfilled.

• UTILITY & ECONOMY

Second, a design should exhibit utility, honesty, and economy in its selection and use of materials.

• FORM & STYLE

Third, the design should be aesthetically pleasing to the eye and our other body senses.

• IMAGE & MEANING

Fourth, the design should project an image and promote associations which carry meaning for the people who use and experience it.

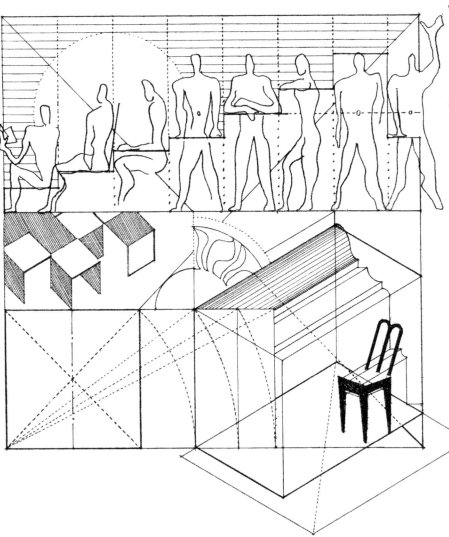

A prime criterion for judging the success of an interior design is whether it is functional. Function is the most fundamental level of design. We design to improve the functioning of interior spaces and make our tasks and activities within them more convenient, comfortable, and pleasurable. The proper functioning of a design is, of course, directly related to the purposes of those who inhabit and use it.

To help understand, and ultimately to fulfill, the function and purpose of an interior space, it is necessary to carefully analyze the users' and activity requirements for that space. The following outline can help the designer program these requirements, translate these needs into forms and patterns, and integrate them into the spatial context.

OUTLINE

• ANALYSIS
• SYNTHESIS
• EVALUATION

1. USER REQUIREMENTS

IDENTIFY USERS

☐ Individual or group
☐ If group, how many?
☐ Specific or anonymous
☐ Age group
☐
☐

IDENTIFY NEEDS

☐ Group needs
☐ Specific individual needs

TERRITORIAL REQUIREMENTS:
☐ Personal space
☐ Privacy
☐ Interaction
☐ Access

☐ Favored objects
☐ Favorite colors
☐ Special places
☐ Special interests
☐
☐

2. ACTIVITY REQUIREMENTS

IDENTIFY PRIMARY & SECONDARY ACTIVITIES

☐ Name and function of primary activity
☐ Names and functions of secondary or related activities

....
....
....

ANALYZE NATURE OF THE ACTIVITIES

☐ Active or passive
☐ Noisy or quiet
☐ Public, small group, or private

☐ If space is to be used for more than one activity, how compatible are the activities?

☐ How often is the space to be used?
☐ What times of day or night?

REQUIREMENTS FOR:
☐ Privacy and enclosure
☐ Access
☐ Flexibility
☐ Light
☐ Acoustic quality
☐ ....
☐ ....

3. FURNISHING REQUIREMENTS

DETERMINE FURNISHING & EQUIPMENT REQUIREMENTS FOR EACH ACTIVITY

☐ Number, type, and style of:
☐ Seating
☐ Tables
☐ Work surfaces
☐ Storage and display units
☐ Accessories

☐ Other special equipment required:
☐ Lighting
☐ Electrical
☐ Mechanical

DETERMINE DESIRED QUALITIES OF PIECES

☐ Requirements for:
☐ Comfort
☐ Safety
☐ Variety
☐ Flexibility
☐ Style
☐ Durability
☐ Maintenance

DETERMINE POSSIBLE ARRANGEMENTS

☐ Functional groupings
☐ Tailored arrangements
☐ Flexible arrangements

4. SPACE ANALYSIS

DOCUMENT EXISTING OR PROPOSED SPACE

☐ Measure and draw plan, sections, and interior elevations

ANALYZE SPACE

☐ Form, scale, and proportion of the space
☐ Doorway locations, points of access, and the circulation paths they suggest
☐ Windows, and the light, views, and ventilation they afford
☐ Wall, floor, and ceiling materials
☐ Significant architectural details

☐ Location of electrical and mechanical fixtures and outlets

☐ What modifications would be feasible, if necessary?

☐ . . . .
☐ . . . .

5. DIMENSIONAL REQUIREMENTS

DETERMINE REQUIRED DIMENSIONS FOR SPACE AND FURNITURE GROUPINGS

☐ Area required for each functional grouping of furniture

☐ Space required for:
☐ Access to and movement within and between activity areas
☐ Number of people served
☐ Appropriate social distances and interaction

DETERMINE FIT BETWEEN ACTIVITY & DIMENSIONS OF SPACE

☐ Study ways activity groupings can be accommodated within the shape and proportion of the floor area and the vertical dimension of the space.

6. DESIRED QUALITIES

DETERMINE QUALITIES APPROPRIATE TO SPATIAL CONTEXT AND COMPATIBLE WITH CLIENT'S OR USERS' NEEDS OR WISHES

☐ Feeling, mood, or atmosphere
☐ Image and style

☐ Degree of spatial enclosure
☐ Comfort and security

☐ Quality of light
☐ Focus and orientation of space
☐ Color and tone

☐ Acoustical environment
☐ Thermal environment

☐ Flexibility

7. DESIRED RELATIONSHIPS

DESIRED RELATIONSHIPS BETWEEN:

☐ Related activity areas
☐ Activity areas and space for movement
☐ Room and adjacent spaces
☐ Room and the outside

DESIRED ZONING OF ACTIVITIES

☐ Organization of activities into groups or sets according to compatibility and use

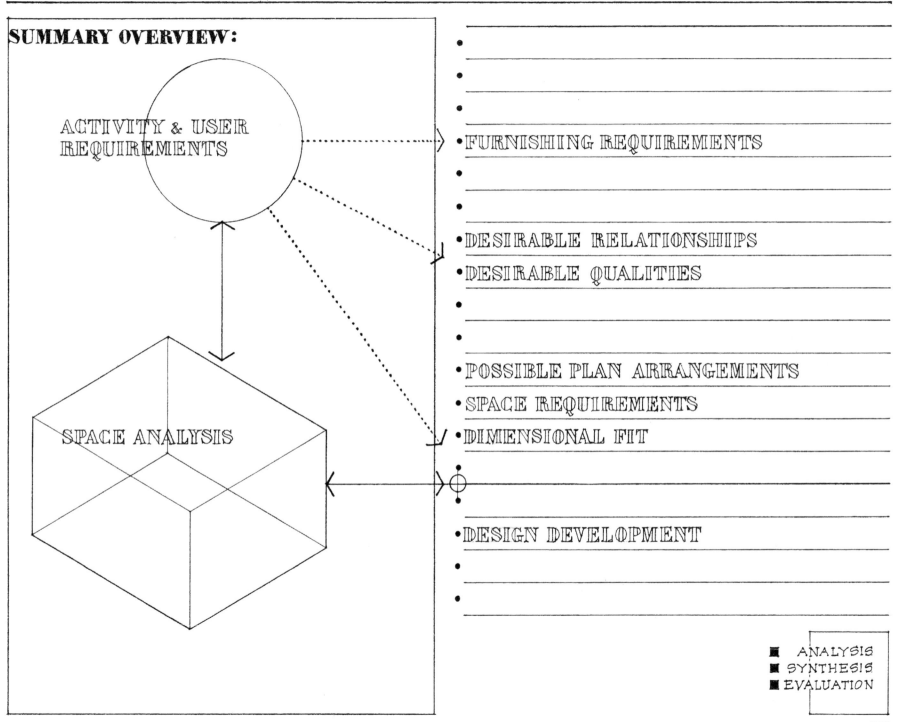

SUMMARY OVERVIEW:

ACTIVITY & USER
REQUIREMENTS

SPACE ANALYSIS

- FURNISHING REQUIREMENTS

- DESIRABLE RELATIONSHIPS
- DESIRABLE QUALITIES

- POSSIBLE PLAN ARRANGEMENTS
- SPACE REQUIREMENTS
- DIMENSIONAL FIT

- DESIGN DEVELOPMENT

■ ANALYSIS
■ SYNTHESIS
■ EVALUATION

HUMAN FACTORS

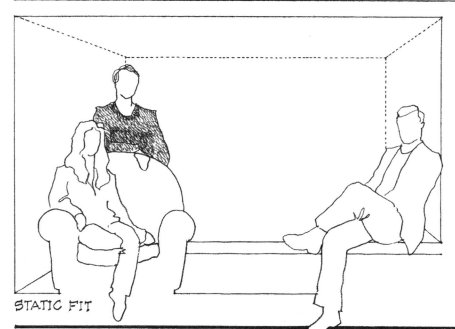

STATIC FIT

The interior spaces of buildings are designed as places for human movement, activity, and repose. There should be, therefore, a fit between the form and dimensions of interior space and our own body dimensions. This fit can be a static one as when we sit in a chair, lean against a railing, or nestle within an alcove space.

There can also be a dynamic fit as when we enter a building's foyer, walk up a stairway, or move through the rooms and halls of a building.

A third type of fit is how a space accommodates our need to maintain appropriate social distances and to have control over our personal space.

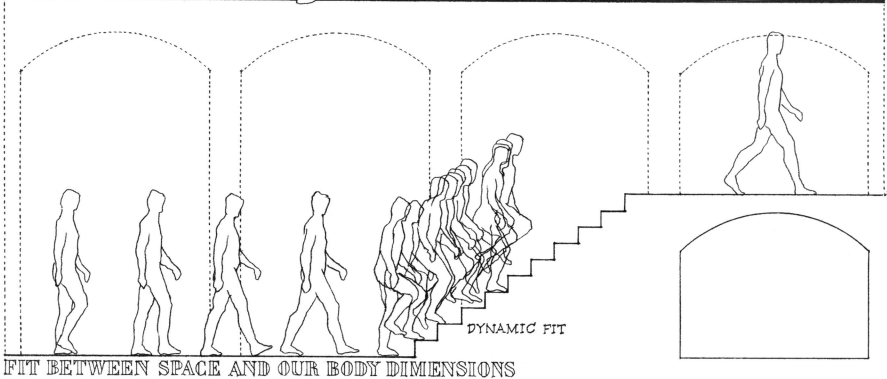

DYNAMIC FIT

FIT BETWEEN SPACE AND OUR BODY DIMENSIONS

In addition to these physical and psychological dimensions, space also has tactile, auditory, olfactory, and thermal characteristics that influence how we feel and what we do within it.

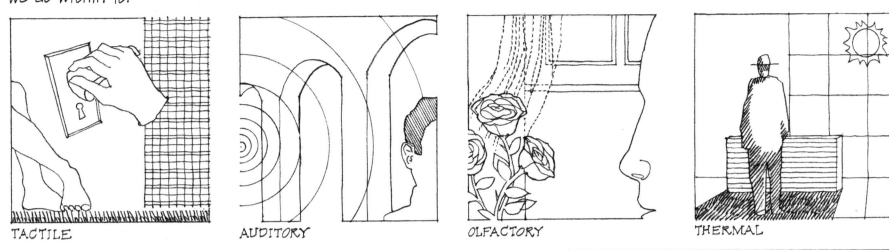

TACTILE

AUDITORY

OLFACTORY

THERMAL

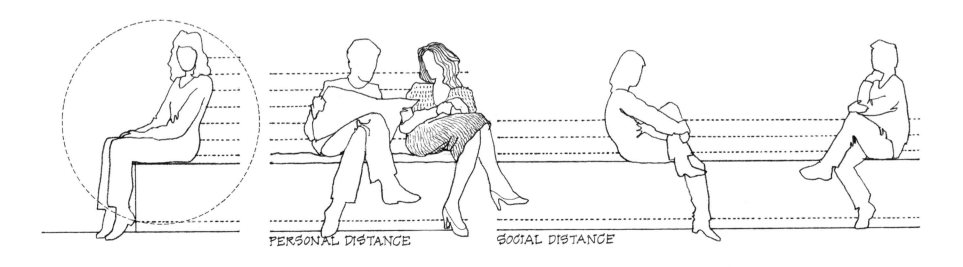

PERSONAL DISTANCE

SOCIAL DISTANCE

PERSONAL SPACE

HUMAN DIMENSIONS

Our body dimensions, and the way we move through and perceive space, are prime determinants of architectural and interior design. In the following section, basic human dimensions are illustrated for standing, walking, sitting, ascending or descending stairs, lying down, reaching, and viewing. Dimensional guidelines are also given for group activities, such as dining or conversing.

It should be noted there is a difference between the structural dimensions of our bodies and those dimensional requirements which result from how we reach for something on a shelf, sit down at a table, walk down a set of stairs, or interact with other people. These are functional dimensions and will vary according to the nature of the activity engaged in and the social situation.

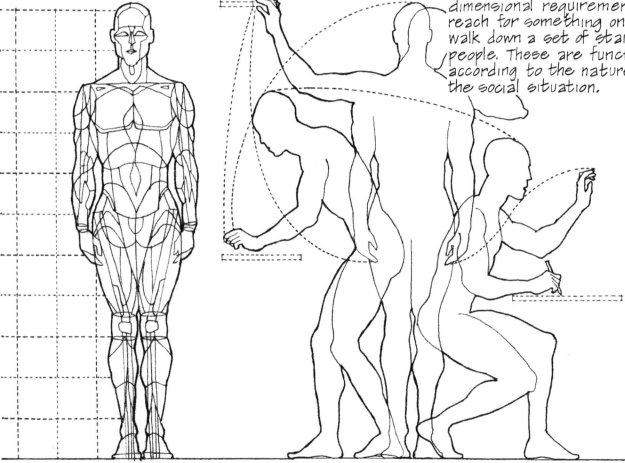

STRUCTURAL   VS.   FUNCTIONAL DIMENSIONS

Caution should always be exercised whenever you use any set of dimensional tables or illustrations such as these. These are based on typical or average measurements which may have to be modified to satisfy specific user needs. Variations from the norm will always exist due to the differences between men and women, among various age and racial groups, even from one individual to the next.

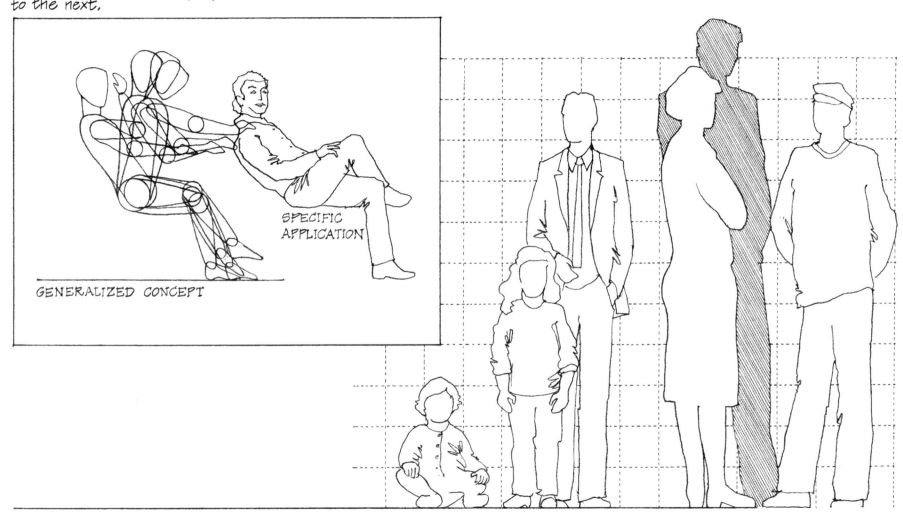

SPECIFIC APPLICATION

GENERALIZED CONCEPT

SIGNIFICANCE OF INDIVIDUAL VARIATIONS

BASIC HUMAN DIMENSIONS

NOTE ON DIMENSIONS:
Unless otherwise specified, dimensions are in inches, with their metric equivalents in millimeters (shown in parentheses).

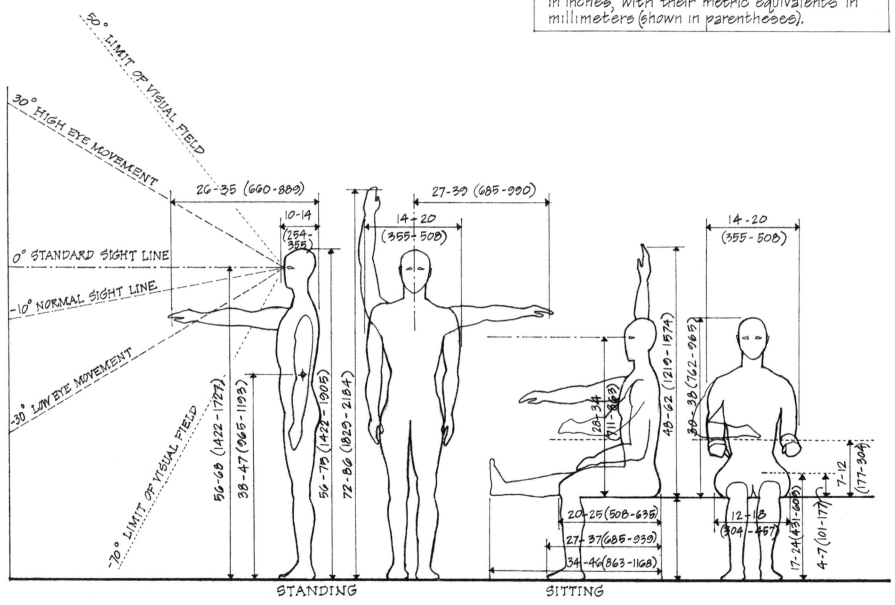

STANDING

SITTING

DISTANCE ZONES

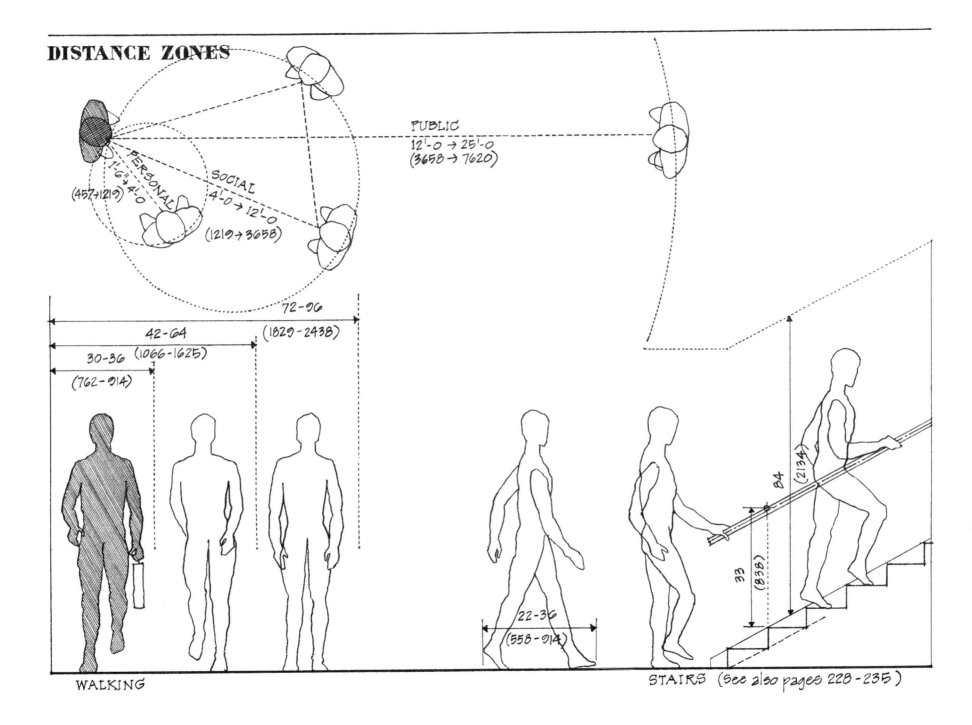

PUBLIC
12'-0 → 25'-0
(3658 → 7620)

PERSONAL
1'-6" → 4'-0
(457 → 1219)

SOCIAL
4'-0 → 12'-0
(1219 → 3658)

72-96
(1829 - 2438)

42-64 (1066-1625)

30-36
(762 - 914)

22-36
(558 - 914)

84
(2134)

33
(838)

WALKING

STAIRS (see also pages 228 - 235)

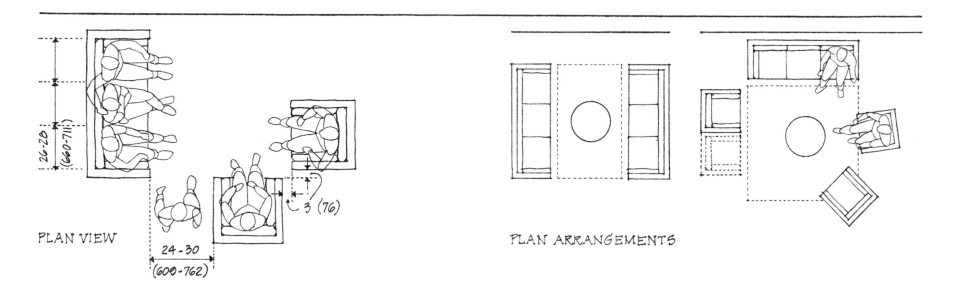

PLAN VIEW

26-28 (660-711)

3 (76)

24-30 (609-762)

PLAN ARRANGEMENTS

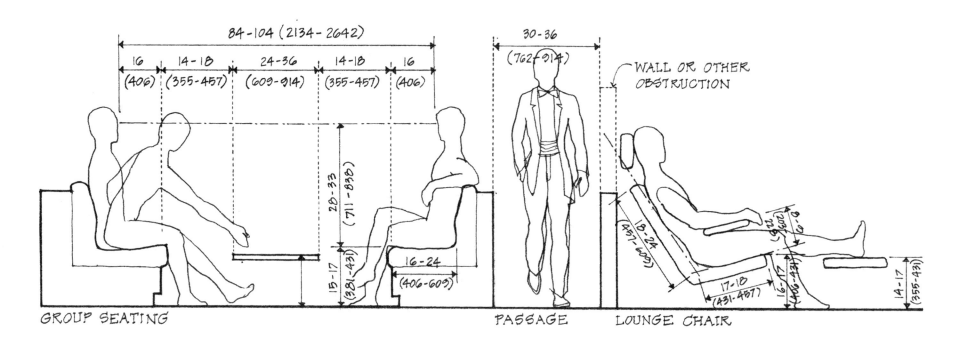

84-104 (2134-2642)

16 (406)   14-18 (355-457)   24-36 (609-914)   14-18 (355-457)   16 (406)

28-33 (711-838)

15-17 (381-431)

16-24 (406-609)

GROUP SEATING

30-36 (762-914)

WALL OR OTHER OBSTRUCTION

PASSAGE

18-24 (457-609)

17-18 (431-457)

16-17 (406-431)

14-17 (355-431)

LOUNGE CHAIR

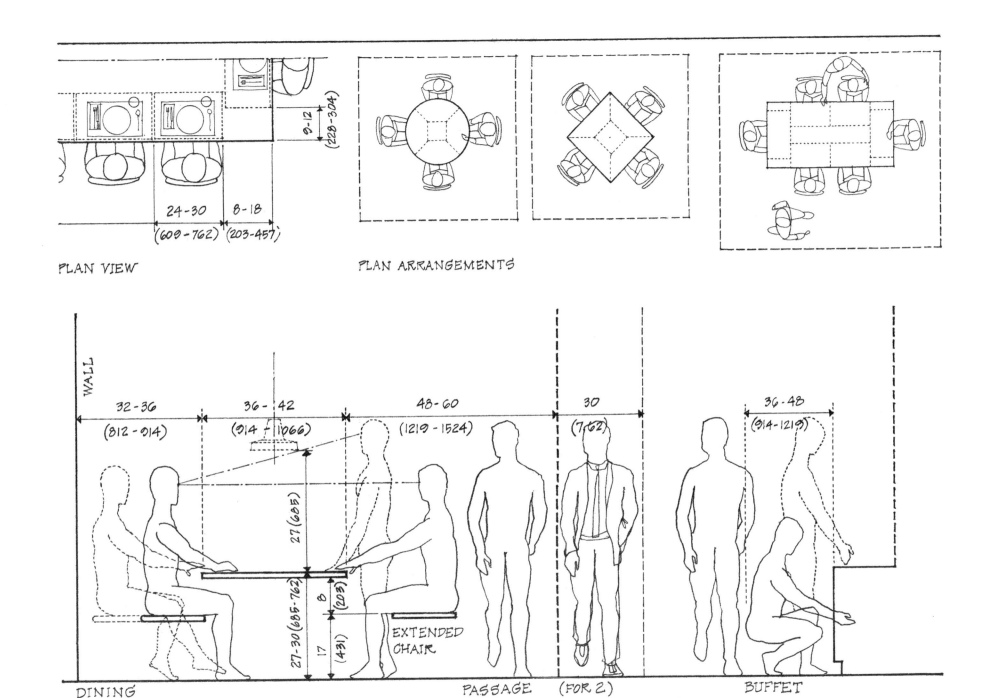

PLAN VIEW

PLAN ARRANGEMENTS

24-30
(609-762)

8-18
(203-457)

9-12
(228-304)

32-36
(812-914)

36-42
(914-1066)

48-60
(1219-1524)

30
(762)

36-48
(914-1219)

WALL

27(685)

8
(203)

27-30(685-762)

17
(431)

EXTENDED
CHAIR

DINING

PASSAGE   (FOR 2)

BUFFET

65

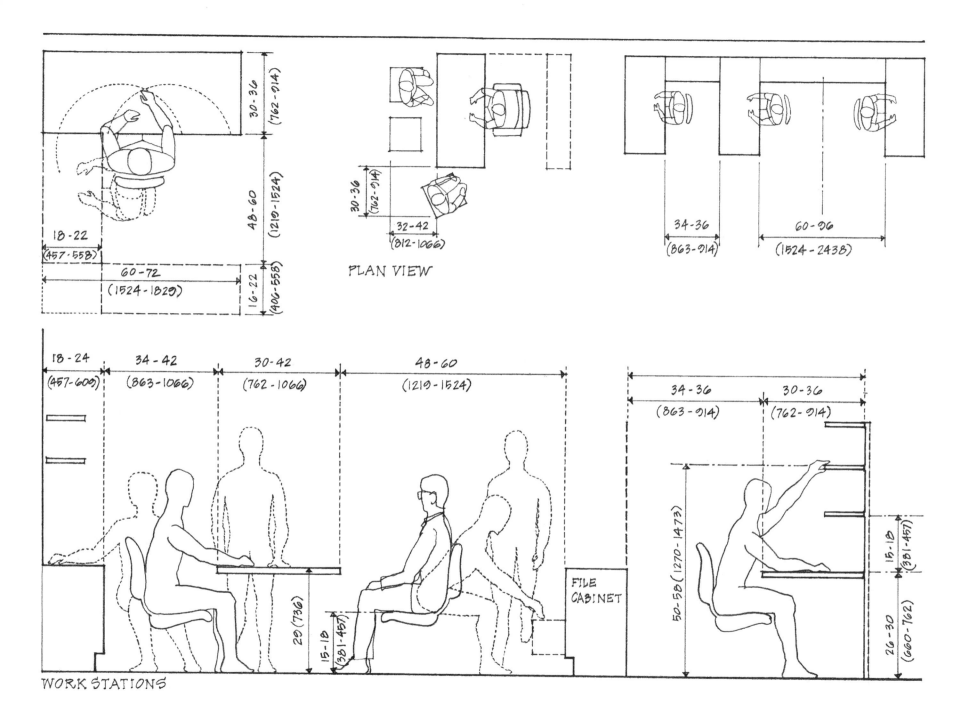

30-36
(762-914)

48-60
(1219-1524)

18-22
(457-558)

60-72
(1524-1829)

16-22
(406-558)

PLAN VIEW

30-36
(762-914)

32-42
(812-1066)

34-36
(863-914)

60-96
(1524-2438)

18-24
(457-600)

34-42
(863-1066)

30-42
(762-1066)

48-60
(1219-1524)

34-36
(863-914)

30-36
(762-914)

50-58 (1270-1473)

15-18
(381-457)

26-30
(660-762)

29 (736)

15-18
(381-457)

FILE
CABINET

WORK STATIONS

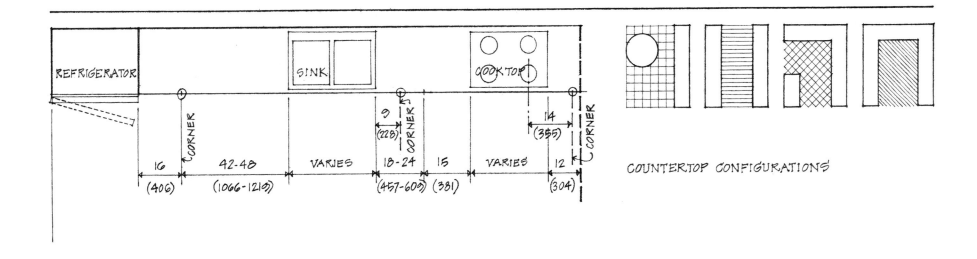

REFRIGERATOR

SINK

COOKTOP

CORNER

CORNER

CORNER

16
(406)

42-48
(1066-1219)

VARIES

9
(228)

18-24
(457-609)

15
(381)

VARIES

12
(304)

14
(355)

COUNTERTOP CONFIGURATIONS

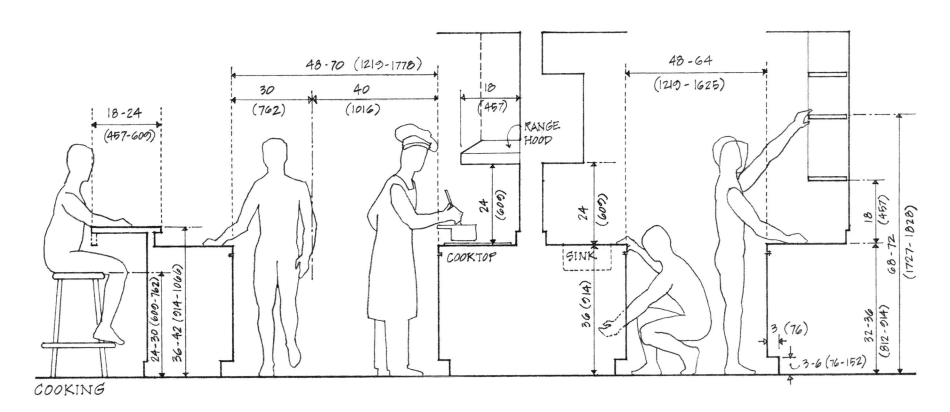

18-24
(457-609)

48-70 (1219-1778)

30
(762)

40
(1016)

18
(457)

RANGE HOOD

24
(609)

COOKTOP

SINK

24
(609)

36 (914)

48-64
(1219-1625)

18
(457)

3 (76)

3-6 (76-152)

68-72
(1727-1828)

32-36
(812-914)

24-30 (609-762)

36-42 (914-1066)

COOKING

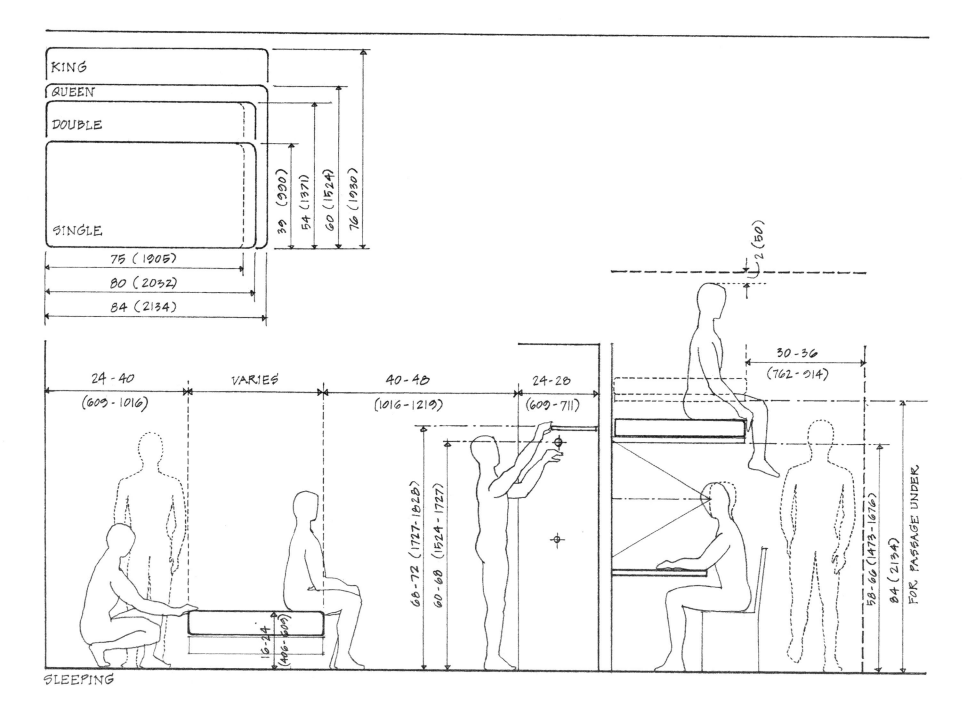

KING

QUEEN

DOUBLE

SINGLE

39 (990)
54 (1371)
60 (1524)
76 (1930)

75 (1905)
80 (2032)
84 (2134)

2 (50)

30 - 36
(762 - 914)

24 - 40
(609 - 1016)

VARIES

40 - 48
(1016 - 1219)

24 - 28
(609 - 711)

68 - 72 (1727 - 1828)
60 - 68 (1524 - 1727)

16 - 24
(609 - 406)

58 - 66 (1473 - 1676)

84 (2134)

FOR PASSAGE UNDER

SLEEPING

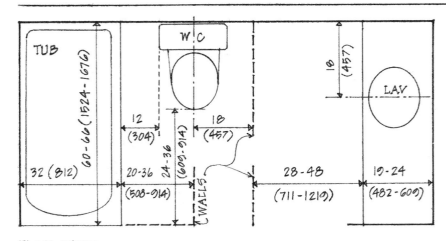

PLAN VIEW

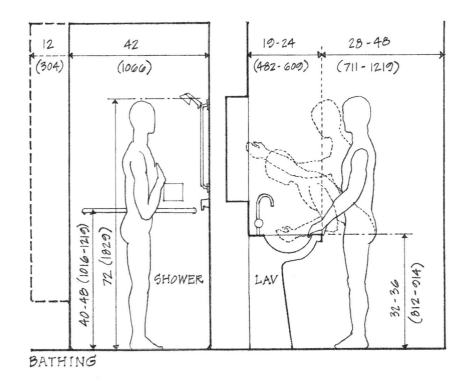

BATHING

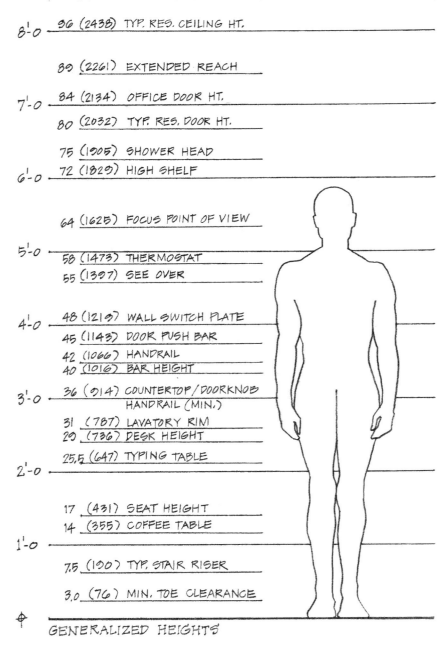

GENERALIZED HEIGHTS

8'-0	96 (2438)	TYP. RES. CEILING HT.
	89 (2261)	EXTENDED REACH
7'-0	84 (2134)	OFFICE DOOR HT.
	80 (2032)	TYP. RES. DOOR HT.
	75 (1905)	SHOWER HEAD
6'-0	72 (1829)	HIGH SHELF
	64 (1625)	FOCUS POINT OF VIEW
5'-0	58 (1473)	THERMOSTAT
	55 (1397)	SEE OVER
4'-0	48 (1219)	WALL SWITCH PLATE
	45 (1143)	DOOR PUSH BAR
	42 (1066)	HANDRAIL
	40 (1016)	BAR HEIGHT
3'-0	36 (914)	COUNTERTOP/DOORKNOB HANDRAIL (MIN.)
	31 (787)	LAVATORY RIM
	29 (736)	DESK HEIGHT
	25.5 (647)	TYPING TABLE
2'-0		
	17 (431)	SEAT HEIGHT
	14 (355)	COFFEE TABLE
1'-0		
	7.5 (190)	TYP. STAIR RISER
	3.0 (76)	MIN. TOE CLEARANCE

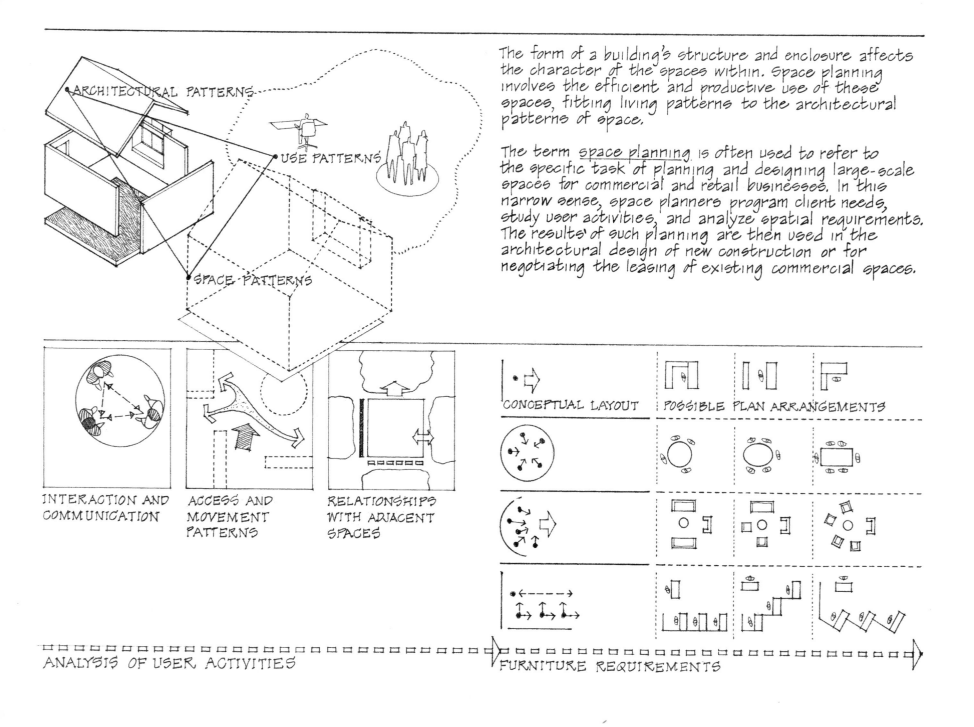

The form of a building's structure and enclosure affects the character of the spaces within. Space planning involves the efficient and productive use of these spaces, fitting living patterns to the architectural patterns of space.

The term space planning is often used to refer to the specific task of planning and designing large-scale spaces for commercial and retail businesses. In this narrow sense, space planners program client needs, study user activities, and analyze spatial requirements. The results of such planning are then used in the architectural design of new construction or for negotiating the leasing of existing commercial spaces.

ARCHITECTURAL PATTERNS

USE PATTERNS

SPACE PATTERNS

INTERACTION AND COMMUNICATION

ACCESS AND MOVEMENT PATTERNS

RELATIONSHIPS WITH ADJACENT SPACES

CONCEPTUAL LAYOUT   POSSIBLE PLAN ARRANGEMENTS

ANALYSIS OF USER ACTIVITIES

FURNITURE REQUIREMENTS

In a broader sense, all interior designers are involved in the planning and layout of interior spaces, whether small or large, residential or commercial. Once a design program has been outlined and developed from an analysis of the client's or users' needs, the design task is to properly allocate the available or desired interior spaces for the various required activities.

Area requirements can be estimated from an analysis of the number of people served, the furnishings and equipment they require, and the nature of the activity that will go on in each space. These area requirements can then be translated into rough blocks of space, and related to each other and to the architectural context in a functional and aesthetic manner.

SITE CONTEXT   DAYLIGHT   ARCHITECTURE

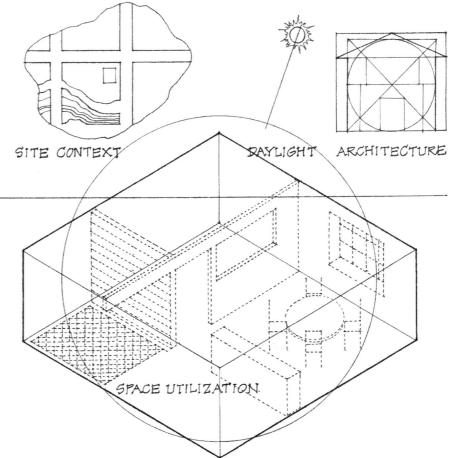

PROPORTION AND SCALE

DIMENSIONS

SHAPE AND SIGNIFICANT
FEATURES

SPACE UTILIZATION

ANALYSIS OF EXISTING OR PROPOSED SPACE   INTEGRATION

ACTIVITY RELATIONSHIPS

Whether collaborating on the design of a new building or planning the remodeling of an existing structure, the interior designer strives for a proper fit between the demands of activities and the architectural nature of the spaces that house them.

Certain activities may need to be closely related or adjacent to each other, while others may be more distant or isolated for privacy. Some activities may require easy accessibility, while others may need controlled entries and exits. Some activities may require daylighting or natural ventilation, while others may not need to be located near exterior windows. Some activities may have specific spatial requirements, while others may be more flexible or be able to share a common space.

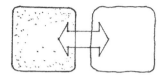

WHICH ACTIVITIES SHOULD BE CLOSELY RELATED?

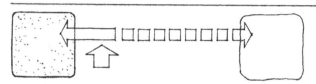

WHICH ACTIVITIES CAN BE ISOLATED BY ENCLOSURE OR DISTANCE?

WHAT DEGREE OF ACCESSIBILITY IS REQUIRED?

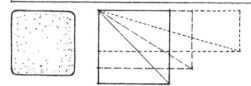

ARE THERE SPECIFIC PROPORTIONAL REQUIREMENTS?

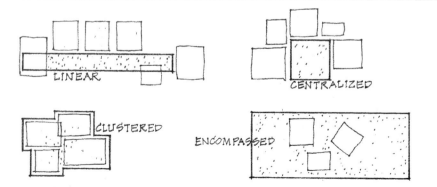

LINEAR

CENTRALIZED

CLUSTERED

ENCOMPASSED

DO ACTIVITY RELATIONSHIPS SUGGEST A SPATIAL PATTERN?

CAN ANY ACTIVITIES SHARE THE SAME SPACE?

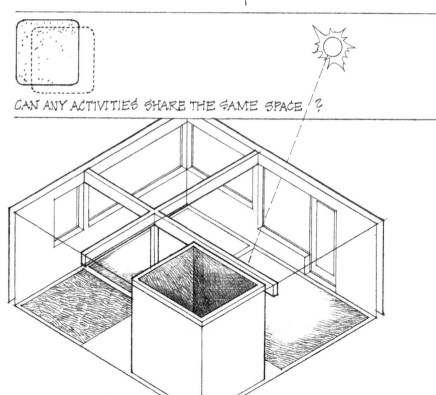

WHICH ACTIVITIES REQUIRE DAYLIGHT AND VENTILATION?

As interior areas are organized on the basis of these considerations, along with considerations of the building site and adjacent structures, the shape and form of a new building will begin to develop.

When dealing with an existing structure, the available spaces usually provide clues as to how they can best be utilized. The entries into a space may define a pattern of movement that divides the area into certain zones. Some zones may be more readily accessible than others. Some may be clearly large enough to accommodate group activities, while others are not. Some may have access to exterior windows or skylights for daylighting or ventilation; others may be internalized. Some may include a natural center of interest, such as a view window or a fireplace.

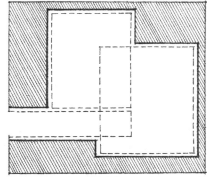

DIVISION SUGGESTED BY ROOM SHAPE OR BY ARCHITECTURE?

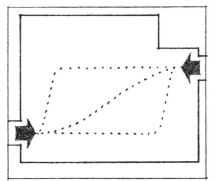

POSSIBLE PATHS OF MOVEMENT?

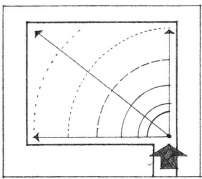

ACCESSIBILITY OF ZONES?

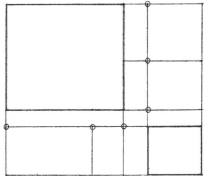

SIZE AND PROPORTION OF ZONES?

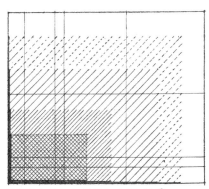

DAYLIGHT AVAILABLE?

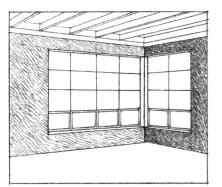

IS THERE AN EXTERNAL OUTLOOK?

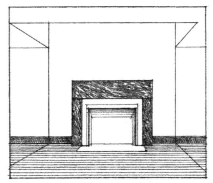

AN INTERNAL FOCUS?

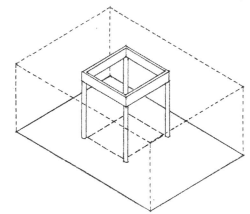

PLAN ARRANGEMENTS

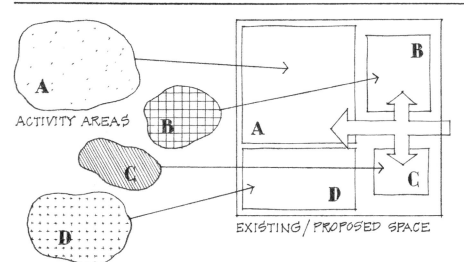

ACTIVITY AREAS

EXISTING / PROPOSED SPACE

From the preceding activity and space analyses, one can begin to match the space requirements of each activity to the characteristics of the available spaces. The design task then shifts to selecting and arranging furnishings, finishes, and lighting into three-dimensional patterns within the given spatial boundaries. These arrangements of shapes and forms in space should respond both to functional and aesthetic criteria.

FUNCTION

- FUNCTIONAL GROUPING OF FURNITURE
- APPROPRIATE DIMENSIONS AND CLEARANCES
- APPROPRIATE SOCIAL DISTANCES
- SUITABLE VISUAL AND ACOUSTICAL PRIVACY
- ADEQUATE FLEXIBILITY OR ADAPTABILITY
- APPROPRIATE LIGHTING AND OTHER ELECTRICAL OR MECHANICAL SERVICES

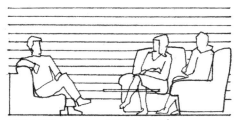

FUNCTIONAL GROUPINGS

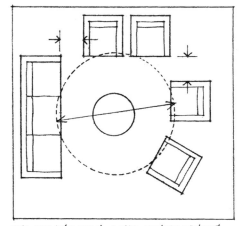

DIMENSIONS AND DISTANCES

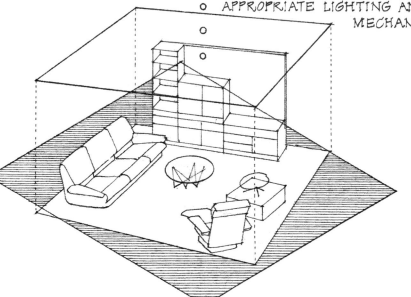

DEFINITION AND PRIVACY

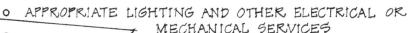

FLEXIBILITY

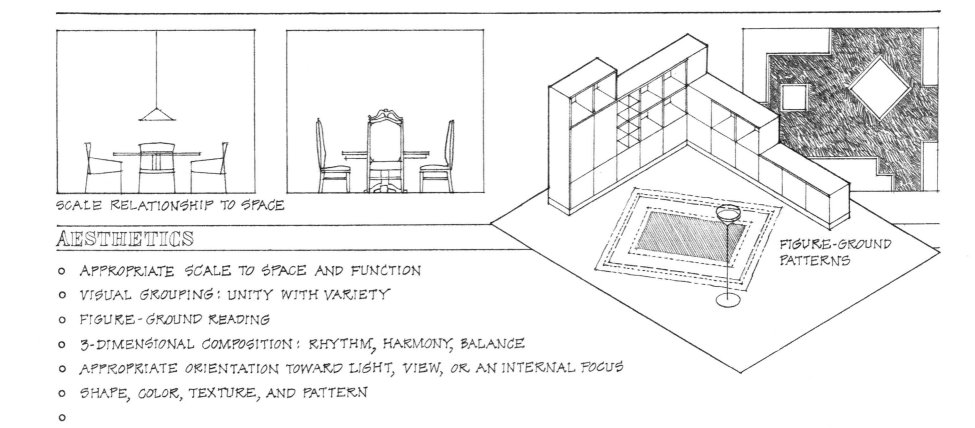

SCALE RELATIONSHIP TO SPACE

FIGURE-GROUND PATTERNS

AESTHETICS

- APPROPRIATE SCALE TO SPACE AND FUNCTION
- VISUAL GROUPING: UNITY WITH VARIETY
- FIGURE-GROUND READING
- 3-DIMENSIONAL COMPOSITION: RHYTHM, HARMONY, BALANCE
- APPROPRIATE ORIENTATION TOWARD LIGHT, VIEW, OR AN INTERNAL FOCUS
- SHAPE, COLOR, TEXTURE, AND PATTERN
-
-

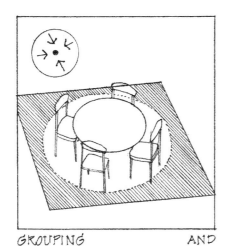
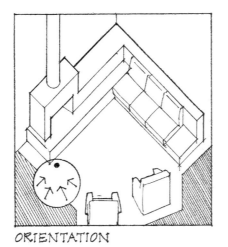

GROUPING   AND   ORIENTATION   OBJECTS IN SPACE   OR   MERGING WITH SPACE

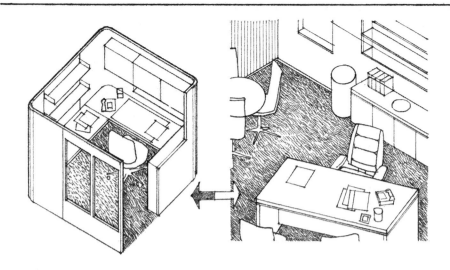

Plan arrangements can be generally classified into two broad categories, according to how each uses the available space. The first exhibits a tight fit between the nature of the activity and the arrangement of furniture and equipment. This may be particularly appropriate when space is at a premium, or when functional efficiency is important. Because a tight fit arrangement may not be readily adaptable to other uses, it is important that it be laid out with great care for its intended use.

TIGHT FIT

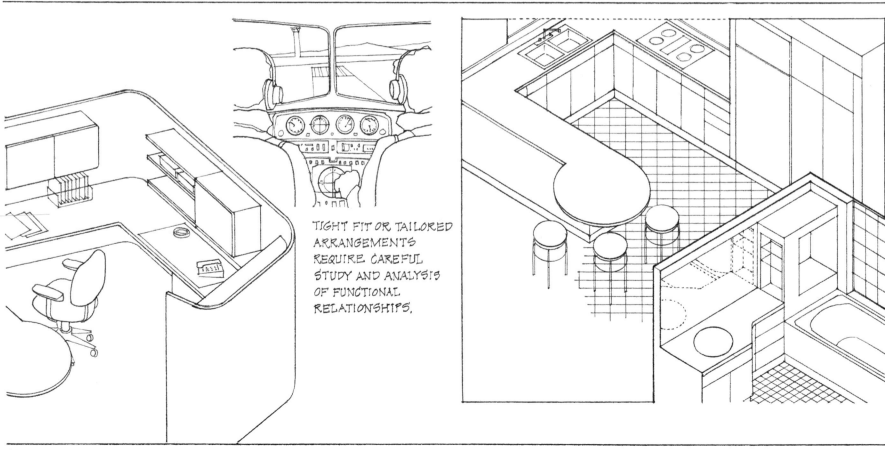

TIGHT FIT OR TAILORED ARRANGEMENTS REQUIRE CAREFUL STUDY AND ANALYSIS OF FUNCTIONAL RELATIONSHIPS.

A tight fit arrangement usually employs modular or unit furniture components which can be combined in a number of ways to form integrated, often multifunctional, structures. Such structures utilize space efficiently and leave a maximum amount of floor area around them. A tailored arrangement of modular furniture can also be used to define a space within a larger volume for greater privacy or intimacy.

Carried to an extreme, a tight fit arrangement can be built in place and become a permanent extension of a room's architecture. Like modular and unit arrangements, built-in furniture utilizes space efficiently, conveys an orderly, unified appearance, and can help mitigate visual clutter in a space.

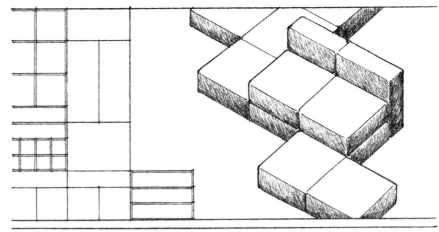

MODULAR FURNISHINGS ARE FLEXIBLE AND SPACE-EFFICIENT

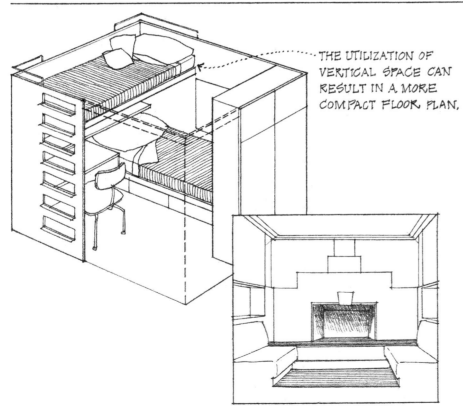

THE UTILIZATION OF VERTICAL SPACE CAN RESULT IN A MORE COMPACT FLOOR PLAN.

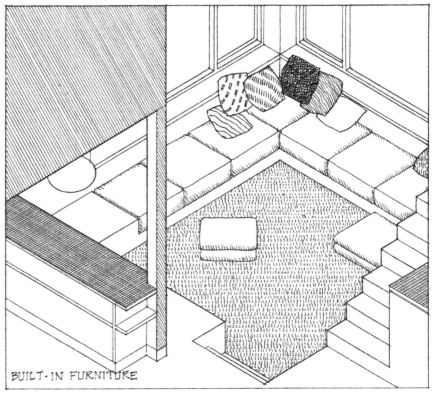

BUILT-IN FURNITURE

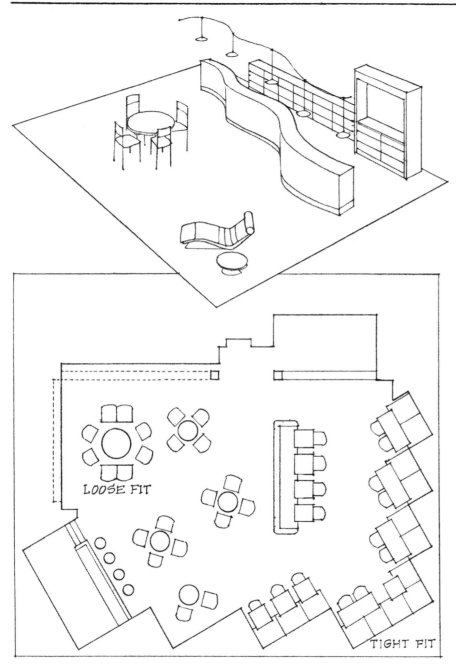

LOOSE FIT

TIGHT FIT

A second, more common type of plan arrangement exhibits a looser fit between function and space. Loose fit arrangements are desirable for the flexibility and diversity they afford.

Most rooms with a loose fit arrangement can accommodate a variety of uses, especially if the furniture used can be easily moved and rearranged. This inherent flexibility in adapting to changes in use or circumstance makes a loose fit arrangement the more common method for laying out furniture in a space. It also offers the opportunity for a greater mix of furniture types, sizes, and styles to be selected over time to suit almost any design situation.

LOOSE FIT

LOOSE FIT ARRANGEMENTS REQUIRE THOUGHTFUL COMPOSITION OF THREE-DIMENSIONAL FORMS IN SPACE.

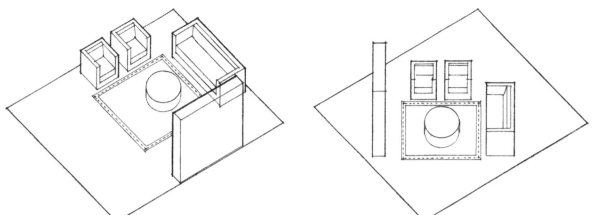

LOOSE FIT ARRANGEMENTS CAN REFLECT CHANGES IN USE OR CIRCUMSTANCE

GRAPHIC REPRESENTATION

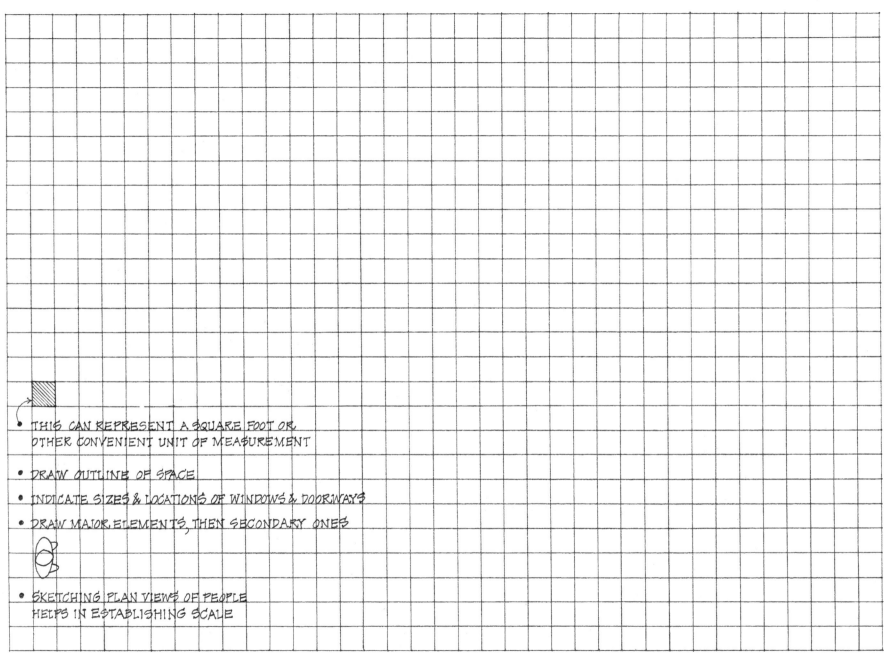

- THIS CAN REPRESENT A SQUARE FOOT OR OTHER CONVENIENT UNIT OF MEASUREMENT

- DRAW OUTLINE OF SPACE

- INDICATE SIZES & LOCATIONS OF WINDOWS & DOORWAYS

- DRAW MAJOR ELEMENTS, THEN SECONDARY ONES

- SKETCHING PLAN VIEWS OF PEOPLE HELPS IN ESTABLISHING SCALE

PLAN DRAWINGS ARE VIEWS LOOKING DOWN INTO AN INTERIOR SPACE AFTER A HORIZONTAL CUT IS MADE.

Drawings are valuable aids in visualizing design ideas, exploring possibilities, and communicating proposals to others. These grids represent the major types of drawings used by designers. They can be used as base drawings by laying tracing paper over them and sketching the possibilities you envision. Analyze your ideas, synthesize the good ones, and evaluate the results.

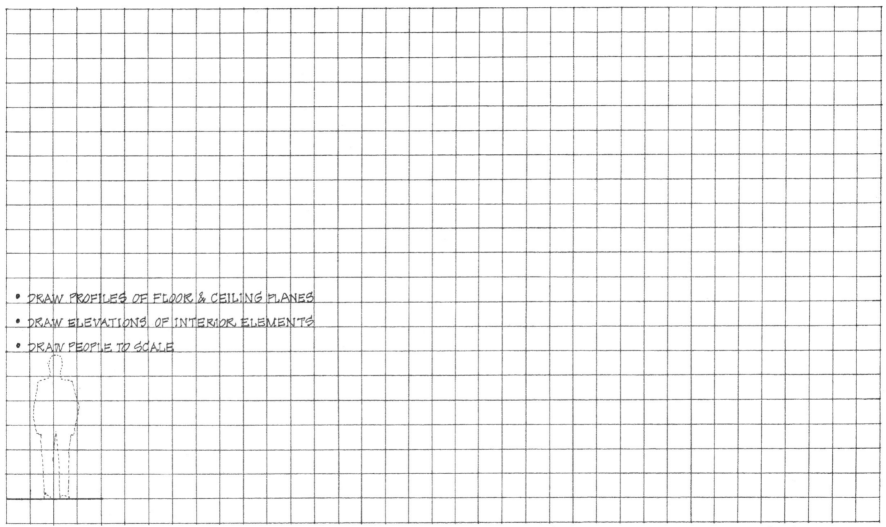

- DRAW PROFILES OF FLOOR & CEILING PLANES
- DRAW ELEVATIONS OF INTERIOR ELEMENTS
- DRAW PEOPLE TO SCALE

SECTION DRAWINGS REPRESENT WHAT IS SEEN AFTER A VERTICAL CUT IS MADE THROUGH AN INTERIOR SPACE.

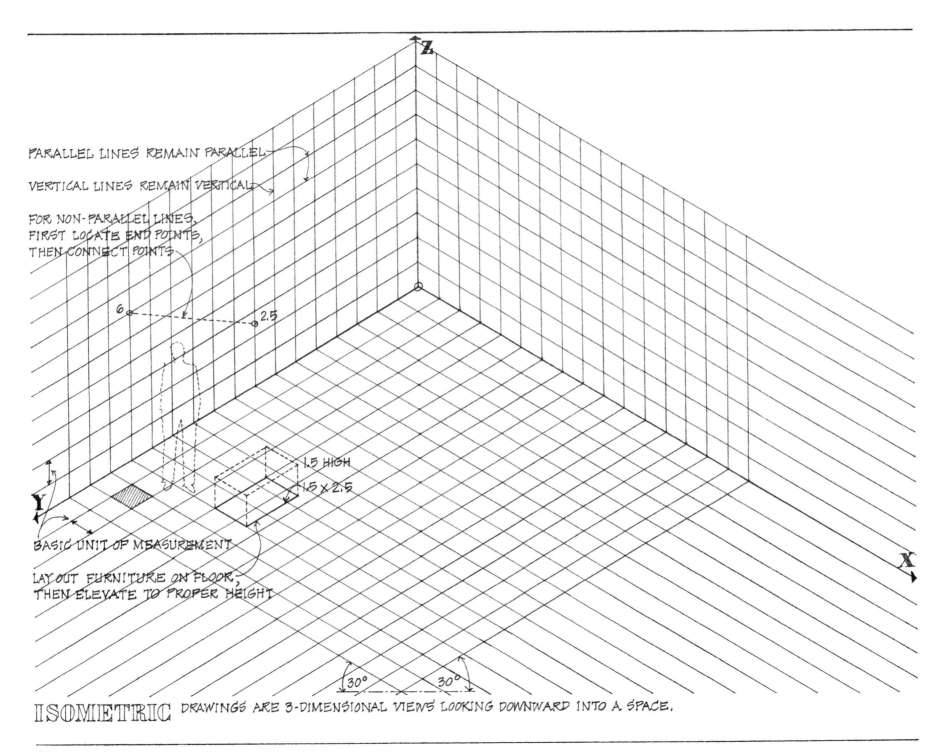

PARALLEL LINES REMAIN PARALLEL

VERTICAL LINES REMAIN VERTICAL

FOR NON-PARALLEL LINES,
FIRST LOCATE END POINTS,
THEN CONNECT POINTS

6

2.5

1.5 HIGH

1.5 X 2.5

Y

BASIC UNIT OF MEASUREMENT

LAY OUT FURNITURE ON FLOOR,
THEN ELEVATE TO PROPER HEIGHT

X

30°   30°

ISOMETRIC DRAWINGS ARE 3-DIMENSIONAL VIEWS LOOKING DOWNWARD INTO A SPACE.

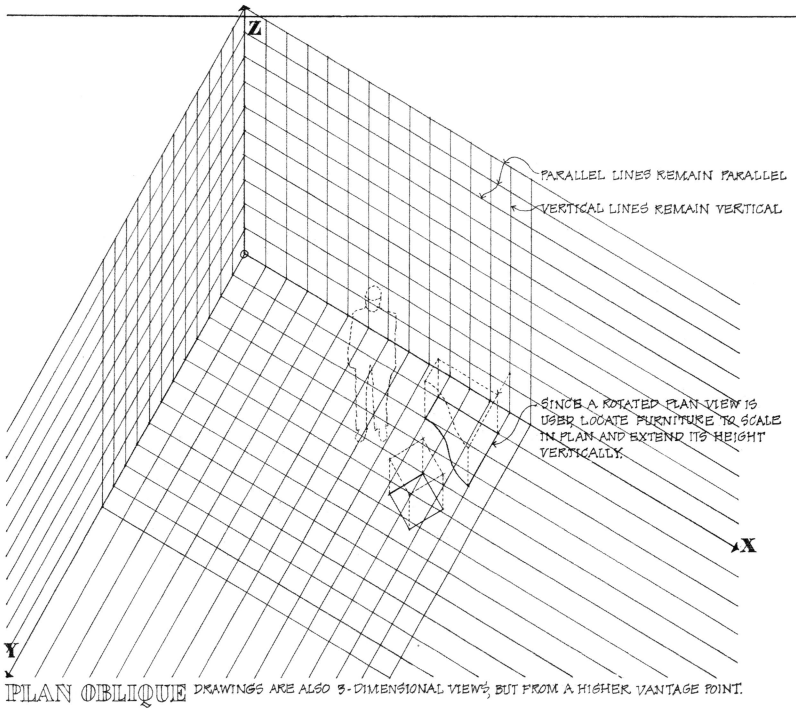

Z

PARALLEL LINES REMAIN PARALLEL

VERTICAL LINES REMAIN VERTICAL

SINCE A ROTATED PLAN VIEW IS
USED, LOCATE FURNITURE TO SCALE
IN PLAN AND EXTEND ITS HEIGHT
VERTICALLY.

X

Y

PLAN OBLIQUE DRAWINGS ARE ALSO 3-DIMENSIONAL VIEWS, BUT FROM A HIGHER VANTAGE POINT.

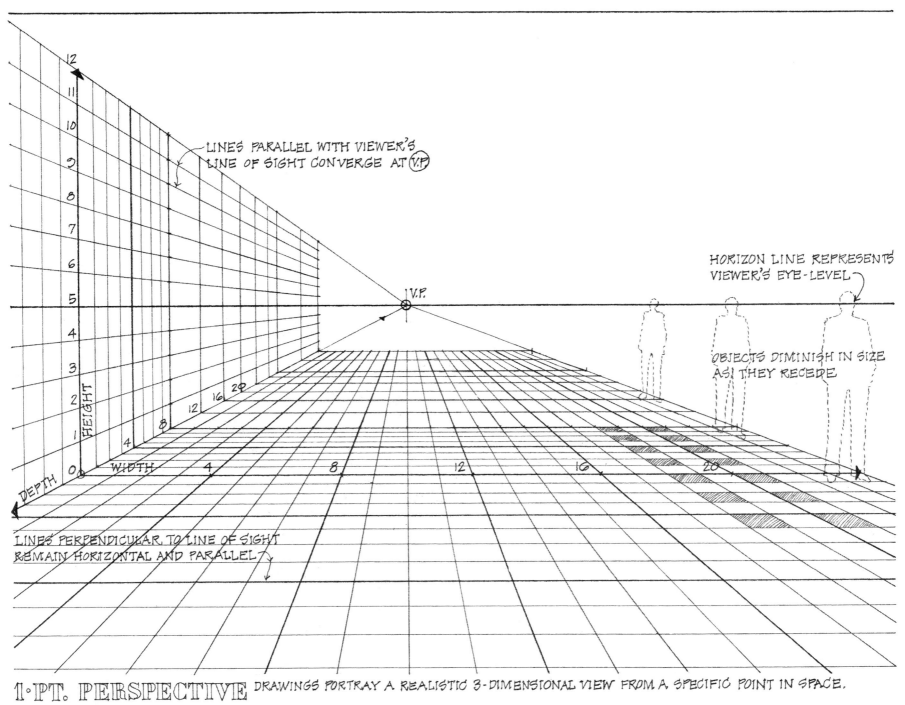

LINES PARALLEL WITH VIEWER'S LINE OF SIGHT CONVERGE AT (V.P.)

HORIZON LINE REPRESENTS VIEWER'S EYE-LEVEL

V.P.

OBJECTS DIMINISH IN SIZE AS THEY RECEDE

HEIGHT

DEPTH

WIDTH

LINES PERPENDICULAR TO LINE OF SIGHT REMAIN HORIZONTAL AND PARALLEL

1·PT. PERSPECTIVE DRAWINGS PORTRAY A REALISTIC 3-DIMENSIONAL VIEW FROM A SPECIFIC POINT IN SPACE.

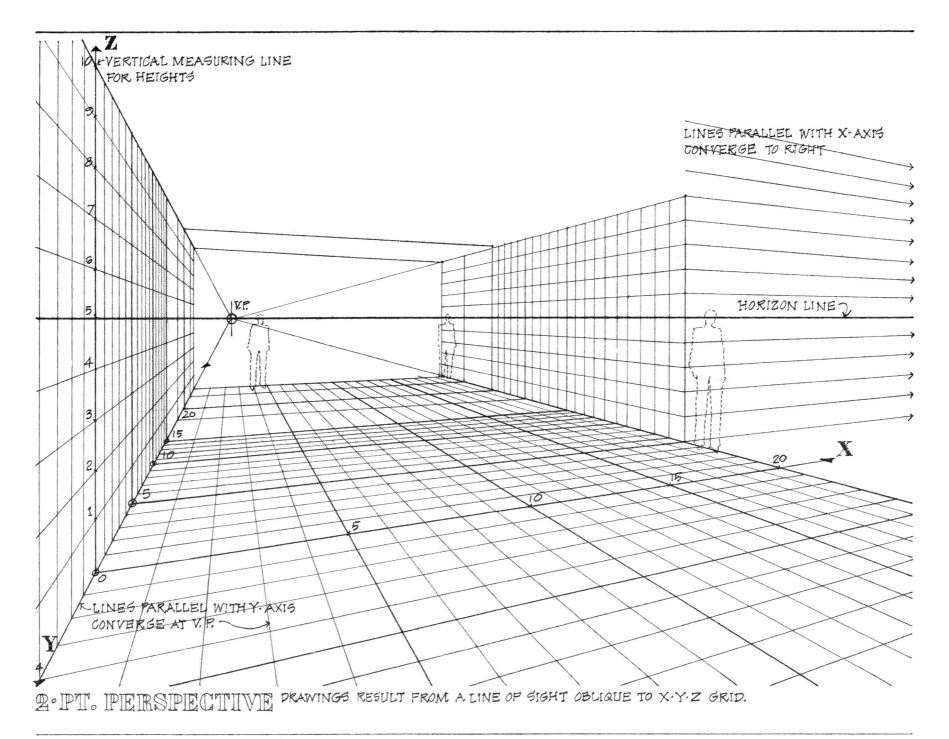

Z — VERTICAL MEASURING LINE FOR HEIGHTS

LINES PARALLEL WITH X-AXIS CONVERGE TO RIGHT

HORIZON LINE

V.P.

LINES PARALLEL WITH Y-AXIS CONVERGE AT V.P.

X

Y

2·PT. PERSPECTIVE DRAWINGS RESULT FROM A LINE OF SIGHT OBLIQUE TO X·Y·Z GRID.

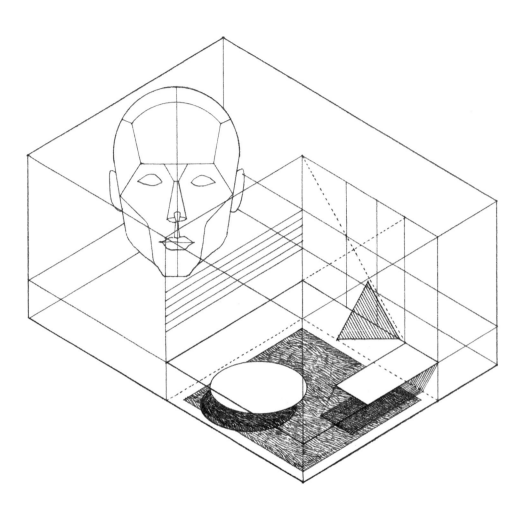

86

A DESIGN
VOCABULARY

VISUAL PERCEPTION

Our perception of the visual shape, size, color, and texture of things is affected by the optical environment in which we see them and the relationships we can discern between them and their visual setting. If our visual field were undifferentiated we would see nothingness. As a perceptible change in tonal value, color, and texture occurred, however, we would begin to discern an object or figure as differentiated from its background. In order to read the lines, shapes, and forms of objects in our field of vision, therefore, we must first perceive contrast between them and their background.

Those elements which appear to stand out from or in front of their background are called figures. In addition to tonal value contrast, what distinguish a figure from its background are its shape and size relative to that of its field. While a figure shares a common border with its background, it has a more distinct and recognizable shape which makes it appear as an object. Figures are sometimes referred to as positive elements - having a positive shape - while backgrounds are described as negative or neutral elements - lacking a clear or discernible shape.

VISUAL CONTRAST

FIGURE - GROUND RELATIONSHIPS

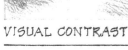

Figures are most discernible when surrounded by a generous amount of space or background. When the size of a figure is such that it crowds its background, the background can develop its own distinct shape and interact with the shape of the figure. At times, an ambiguous figure-ground relationship can occur wherein elements in a composition can be seen alternately, but not simultaneously, as both figure and ground.

Our visual world is, in reality, a composite image constructed from a continuous array of figure-ground relationships. In interior design, these relationships can be seen to exist at several scales, depending on one's point of view.

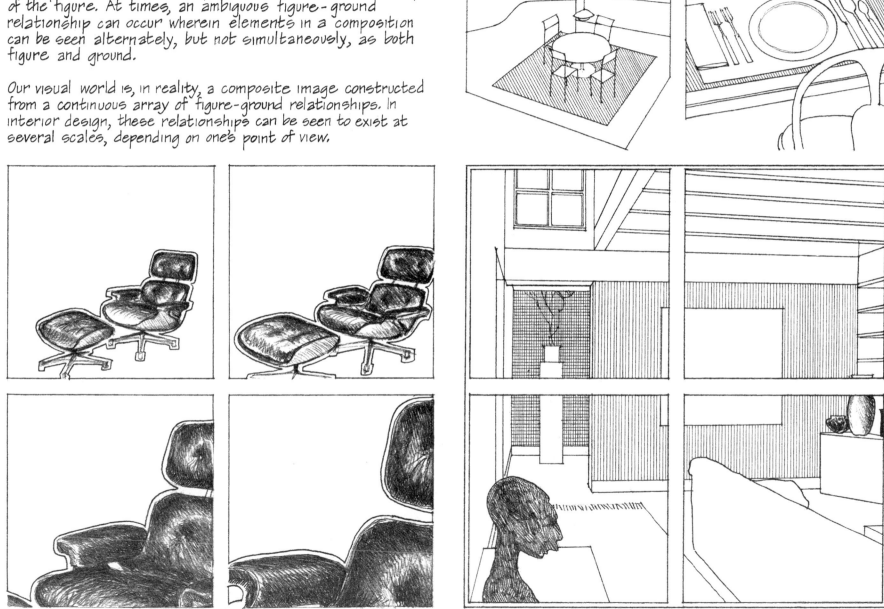

INTERIORS: COMPOSITE LAYERS OF FIGURE-GROUND PATTERNS AND RELATIONSHIPS AT VARIOUS SCALES.

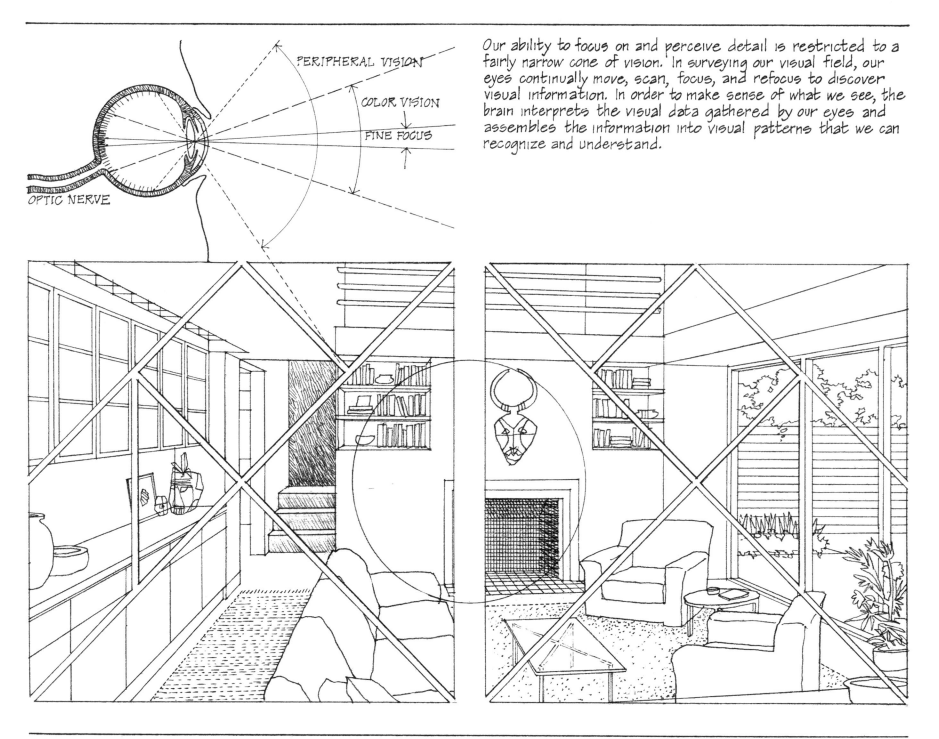

PERIPHERAL VISION

COLOR VISION

FINE FOCUS

OPTIC NERVE

Our ability to focus on and perceive detail is restricted to a fairly narrow cone of vision. In surveying our visual field, our eyes continually move, scan, focus, and refocus to discover visual information. In order to make sense of what we see, the brain interprets the visual data gathered by our eyes and assembles the information into visual patterns that we can recognize and understand.

The normal process of perception is utilitarian and geared toward recognition. When we see a chair, we recognize it to be a chair if its form and configuration fit a pattern established by chairs we have seen and used in the past. If we look carefully, however, we would also be able to perceive the chair's specific shape, size, proportion, color, texture, and material. This ability to see beyond recognition and utility is extremely important to designers. We must continually strive to see and be conscious of the specific visual characteristics of things and how they relate and interact to form the aesthetic quality of our visual environments.

VISUAL CHARACTERISTICS:

☐ A DESIGN VOCABULARY

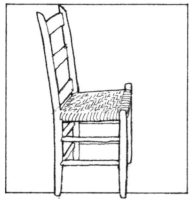

FORM
SHAPE
COLOR
TEXTURE
LIGHT
PROPORTION
SCALE

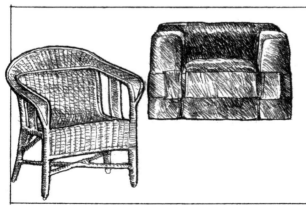  

BALANCE
HARMONY
UNITY & VARIETY
RHYTHM
EMPHASIS

FORM

P
O
I
N
T ....LINE

PLANE

VOLUME

The point is the generator of all form. As a point moves, it leaves a trace of a line - the first dimension. As the line shifts in a direction other than its own, it defines a plane - a two-dimensional element. The plane, extended in a direction oblique or perpendicular to its surface, forms a three-dimensional volume.

Point, line, plane, and volume. These are the primary elements of form. All visible forms are, in reality, three-dimensional. In describing form, these primary elements differ according to their relative dimensions of length, width, and depth - a matter of proportion and scale.

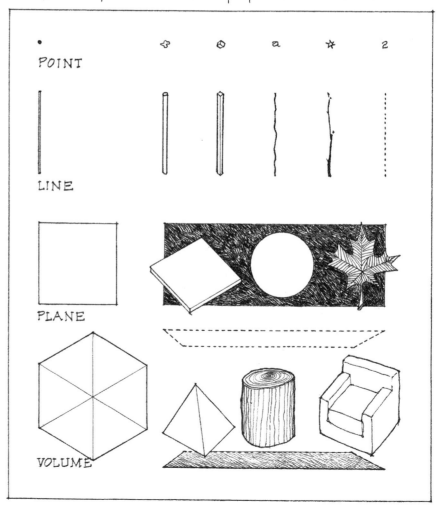

POINT

LINE

PLANE

VOLUME

A point marks a location in space. Conceptually, it has no length, width, or depth. It is, therefore, static and directionless. As the prime generator of form, a point can mark the ends of a line, the intersection of two lines, or the corner where the lines of a plane or volume meet.

As a visible form, a point is most commonly manifested as a dot, a circular shape that is small relative to its field. Other shapes can also be seen as point-forms if sufficiently small, compact, and nondirectional.

When at the center of a field or space, a point is stable and at rest, and capable of organizing other elements about itself. When moved off-center, it retains its self-centering quality but becomes more dynamic. Visual tension is created between the point and its field. Point-generated forms, such as the circle and the sphere, share this self-centering quality of the point.

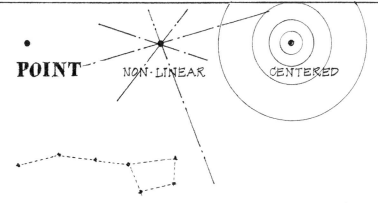

POINT　　NON-LINEAR　　　CENTERED

MULTIPLE POINTS DEFINING LINES AND PATTERNS

▲　★　a　♥　◆　✗

RELATIVELY SMALL SHAPES READ AS POINTS

POINT-GENERATED FORMS — THE CIRCLE AND THE SPHERE — ARE SELF-CENTERING.

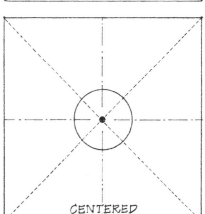

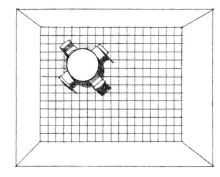

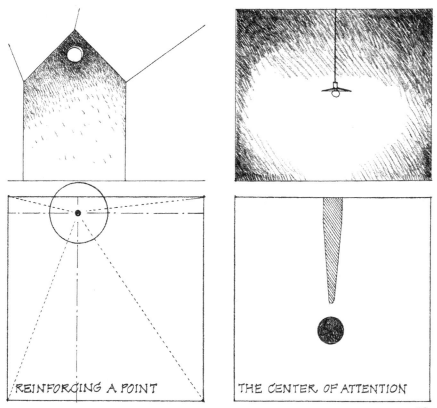

CENTERED

OFF-CENTER

REINFORCING A POINT

THE CENTER OF ATTENTION

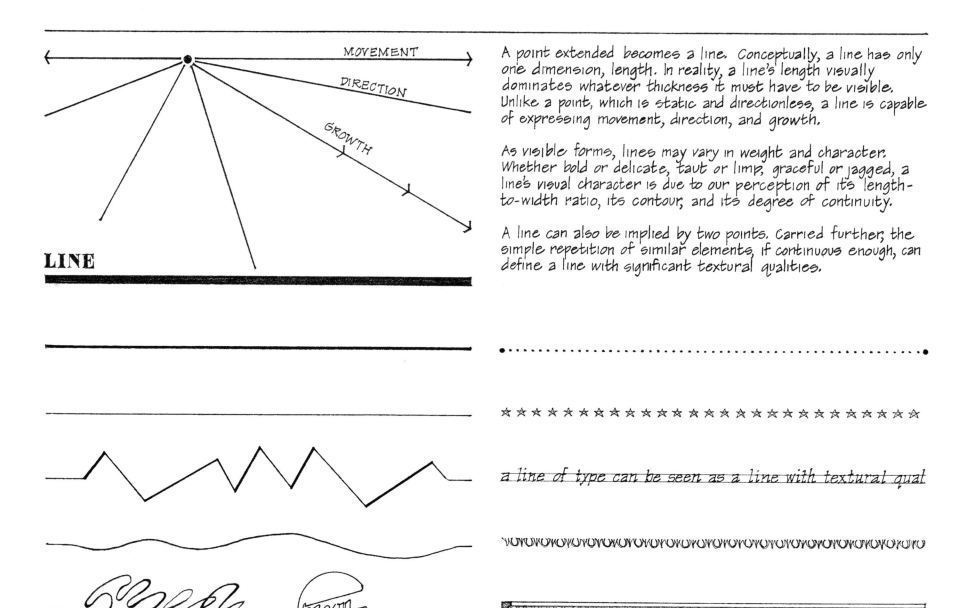

LINE

A point extended becomes a line. Conceptually, a line has only one dimension, length. In reality, a line's length visually dominates whatever thickness it must have to be visible. Unlike a point, which is static and directionless, a line is capable of expressing movement, direction, and growth.

As visible forms, lines may vary in weight and character. Whether bold or delicate, taut or limp, graceful or jagged, a line's visual character is due to our perception of its length-to-width ratio, its contour, and its degree of continuity.

A line can also be implied by two points. Carried further, the simple repetition of similar elements, if continuous enough, can define a line with significant textural qualities.

LINES VARYING IN WEIGHT, CONTOUR, AND TEXTURE

A straight line represents the tension that exists between two points. An important characteristic of a straight line is its direction. A horizontal line can represent stability, repose, or the plane upon which we stand or move. In contrast to this, a vertical line can express a state of equilibrium with the force of gravity.

Diagonal lines, deviations from the horizontal and the vertical, can be seen as rising or falling. In either case, they imply movement and are visually active and dynamic.

A curved line represents movement deflected by lateral forces. Curved lines tend to express gentle movement. Depending on their orientation, they can be uplifting or represent solidity and attachment to the earth. Small curves can express playfulness, energy, or the patterns of biological growth.

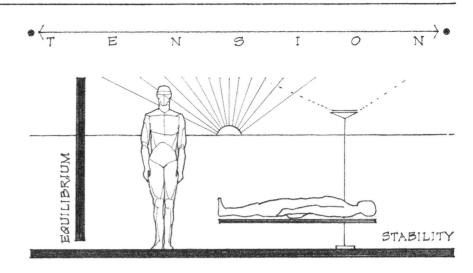

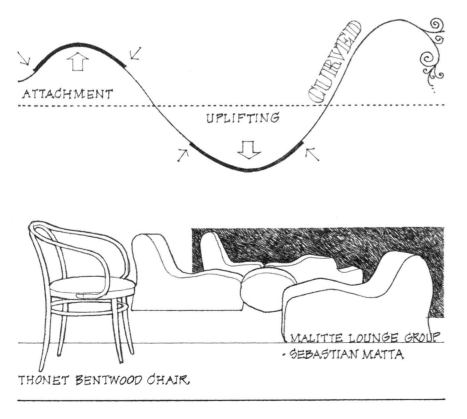

THONET BENTWOOD CHAIR

MALITTE LOUNGE GROUP
· SEBASTIAN MATTA

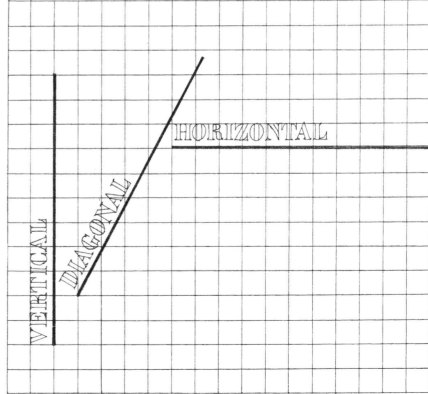

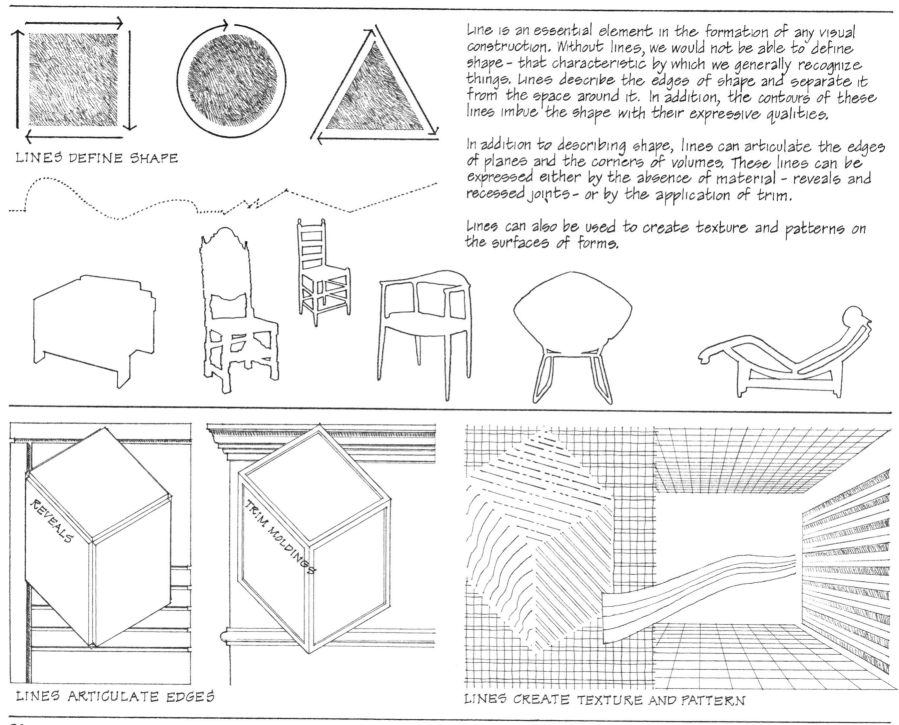

LINES DEFINE SHAPE

Line is an essential element in the formation of any visual construction. Without lines, we would not be able to define shape - that characteristic by which we generally recognize things. Lines describe the edges of shape and separate it from the space around it. In addition, the contours of these lines imbue the shape with their expressive qualities.

In addition to describing shape, lines can articulate the edges of planes and the corners of volumes. These lines can be expressed either by the absence of material - reveals and recessed joints - or by the application of trim.

Lines can also be used to create texture and patterns on the surfaces of forms.

REVEALS

TRIM MOLDINGS

LINES ARTICULATE EDGES

LINES CREATE TEXTURE AND PATTERN

Linear forms have traditionally been used to provide vertical support, span and express movement across space, and define the edges of spatial volumes. This structural role of linear elements can be seen at the scale of both architecture and interior space and furnishings.

Within the design process itself, lines are used simply as regulating devices to express relationships and establish patterns among design elements.

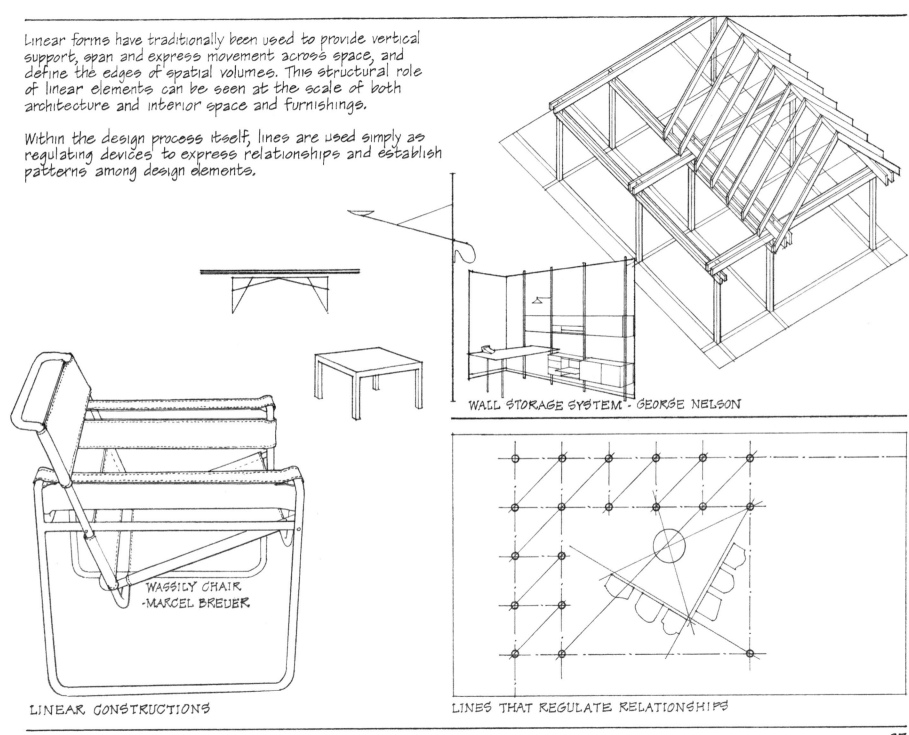

WALL STORAGE SYSTEM - GEORGE NELSON

WASSILY CHAIR -MARCEL BREUER

LINEAR CONSTRUCTIONS

LINES THAT REGULATE RELATIONSHIPS

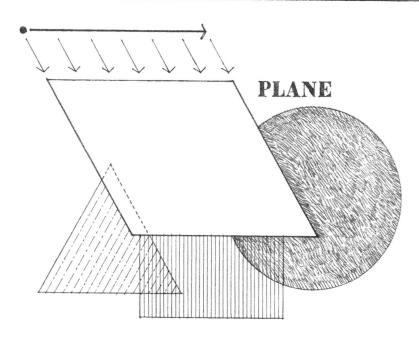

PLANE

A line shifted in a direction other than its intrinsic direction defines a plane. Conceptually, a plane has two dimensions, width and length, but no depth. In reality, a plane's width and length dominate whatever thickness it must have to be visible.

Shape is the primary characteristic of a plane. It is described by the contour of the lines defining the edges of the plane. Since our perception of a plane's shape can be distorted by perspective, we see the true shape of a plane only when we view it frontally.

In addition to shape, planar forms have significant surface qualities of material, color, texture, and pattern. These visual characteristics affect a plane's:

- Visual weight and stability
- Perceived size, proportion, and position in space
- Light reflectivity
- Tactile qualities
- Acoustic properties

SHAPE IS A PLANE'S DOMINANT CHARACTERISTIC.

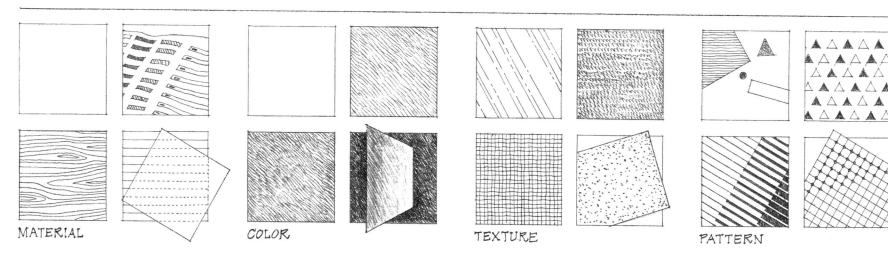

MATERIAL   COLOR   TEXTURE   PATTERN

SURFACE CHARACTERISTICS OF PLANAR ELEMENTS

Planar forms are fundamental elements of architectural and interior design. Floor, wall, and ceiling or roof planes serve to enclose and define three-dimensional volumes of space. Their specific visual characteristics and their relationships in space determine the form and character of the spaces they define. Within these spaces, furnishings and other interior design elements can also be seen to consist of planar forms.

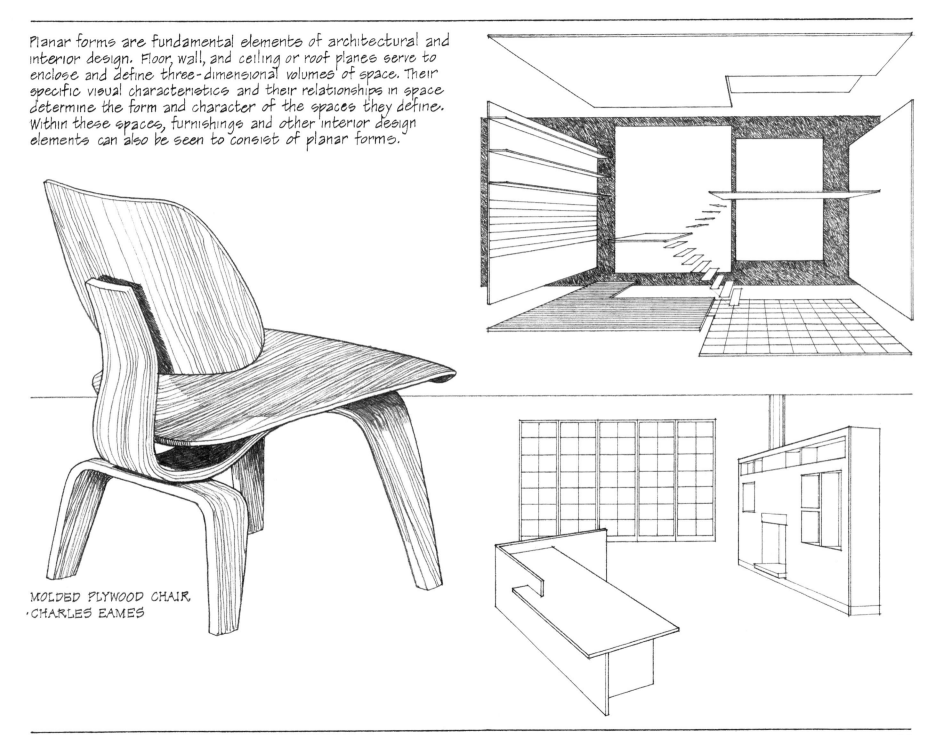

MOLDED PLYWOOD CHAIR
·CHARLES EAMES

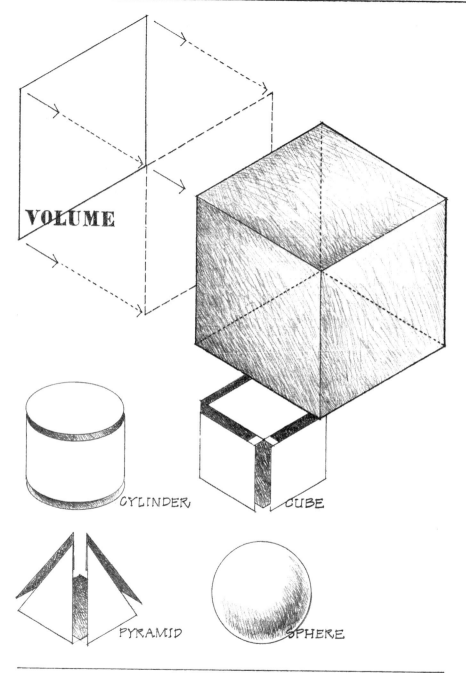

VOLUME

CYLINDER

CUBE

PYRAMID

SPHERE

A plane extended in a direction other than along its surface forms a volume. Conceptually and in reality a volume exists in three dimensions.

Form is the term we use to describe the contour and overall structure of a volume. The specific form of a volume is determined by the shapes and interrelationships of the lines and planes that describe the boundaries of the volume.

As the three-dimensional element of architectural and interior design, a volume can be either solid (space displaced by mass) or a void (space enclosed by planar forms).

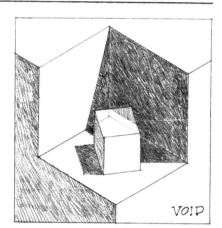

SOLID

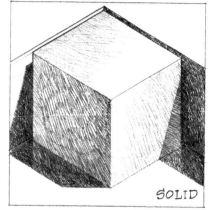

VOID

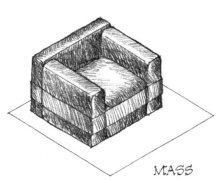

MASS

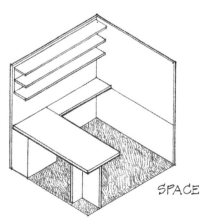

SPACE

Solid forms and spatial voids. . .This duality represents the essential unity of opposites which shapes the reality of architecture and interior design. Visible forms give space dimension, scale, color, and texture, while space reveals the forms. This symbiotic relationship between form and space can be seen at several scales in interior design.

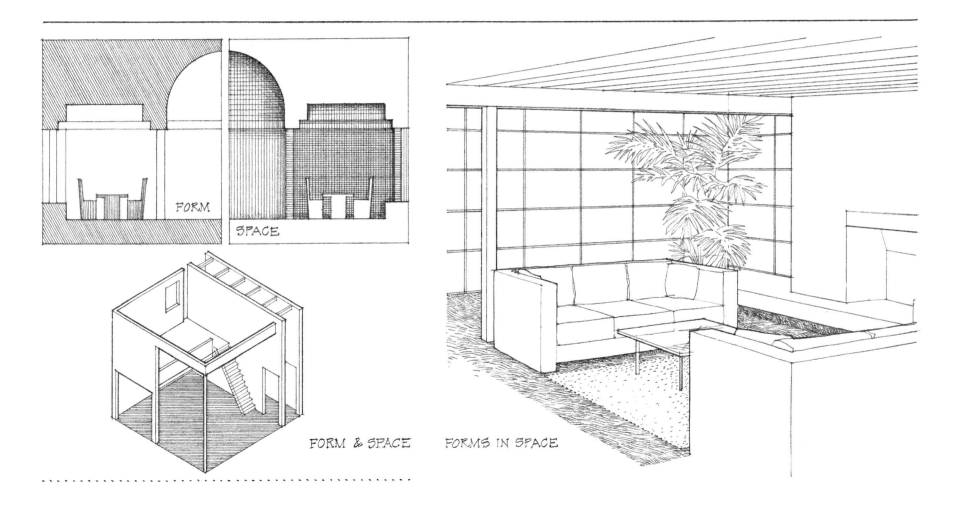

FORM

SPACE

FORM & SPACE   FORMS IN SPACE

SHAPE

NATURAL SHAPES

NON-OBJECTIVE SHAPES

GEOMETRIC SHAPES

Shape is the primary means by which we distinguish one form from another. It may refer to the contour of a line, the outline of a plane, or the boundary of a three-dimensional mass. In each case, shape is defined by the specific configuration of the lines or planes which separate a form from its background or surrounding space.

There are several broad categories of shapes. Natural shapes represent the images and forms of our natural world. These shapes may be abstracted, usually through a process of simplification, and still retain the essential characteristics of their natural sources.

Non-objective shapes make no obvious reference to a specific object or to a particular subject matter. Some non-objective shapes may result from a process, such as calligraphy, and carry meaning as symbols. Others may be geometric and elicit responses based on their purely visual qualities.

Geometric shapes dominate the built environment of both architecture and interior design. There are two separate and distinct types of geometric shapes – rectilinear and curvilinear. In their most regular form, curvilinear shapes are circular while rectilinear shapes include the series of polygons which can be inscribed within a circle. Of these, the most significant geometric shapes are the circle, the triangle, and the square. Extended into the third dimension, these primary shapes generate the sphere, the cylinder, the cone, the pyramid, and the cube.

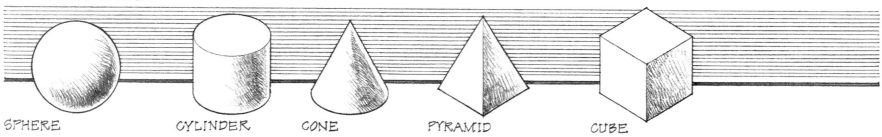

SPHERE   CYLINDER   CONE   PYRAMID   CUBE

The circle is a compact, introverted shape which has as its natural focus its centerpoint. It represents unity, continuity, and economy of form.

A circular shape is normally stable and self-centering in its environment. When associated with other lines and shapes, however, a circle can appear to have apparent motion.

Other curvilinear lines and shapes can be seen to be fragments or combinations of circular shapes. Whether regular or irregular, curvilinear shapes are capable of expressing softness of form, fluidity of movement, or the nature of biological growth.

CIRCLE

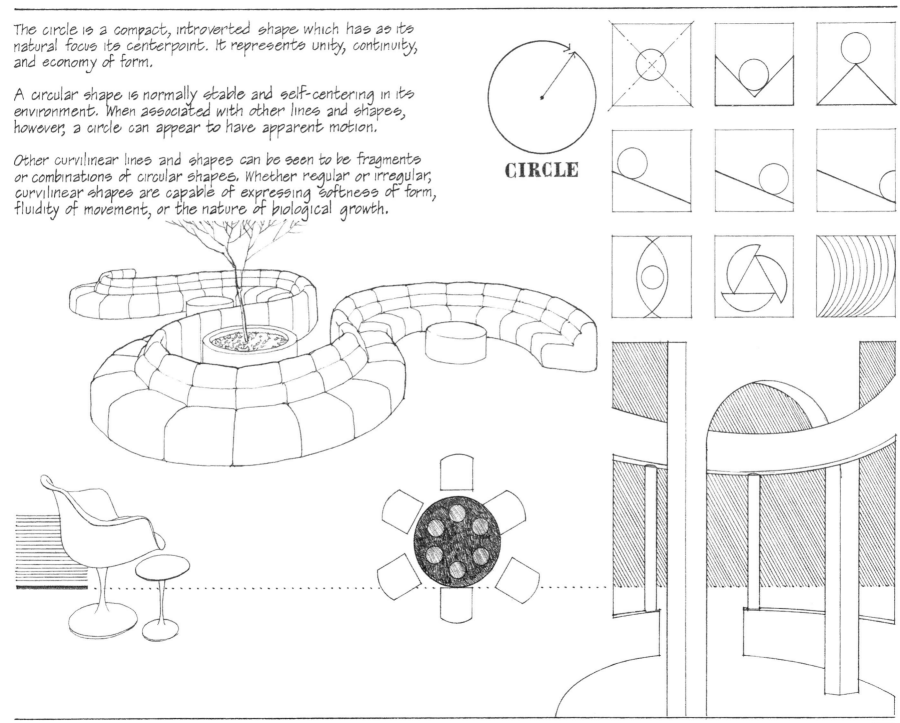

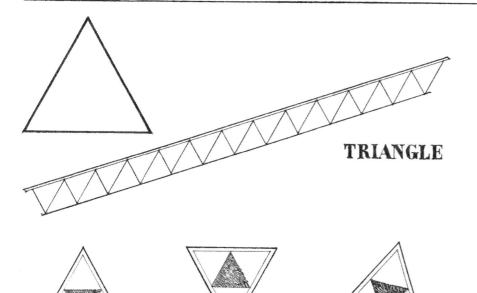

TRIANGLE

The triangle represents stability. Triangular shapes and patterns are often used in structural systems since their configuration cannot be altered without bending or breaking one of their sides.

From a purely visual point of view, a triangular shape is also stable when resting on one of its sides. When tipped to stand on one of its points, however, the triangular shape becomes dynamic. It can exist in a precarious state of balance or imply motion as it tends to fall over onto one of its sides.

The dynamic quality of a triangular shape is also due to the angular relationships of its three sides. Because these angles can vary, triangles are more flexible than squares and rectangles. In addition, triangles can be conveniently combined to form any number of square, rectangular, and other polygonal shapes.

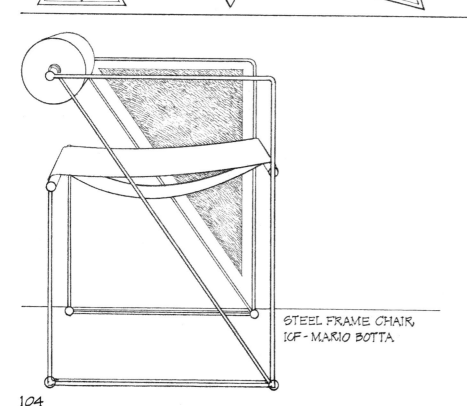

STEEL FRAME CHAIR,
ICF - MARIO BOTTA

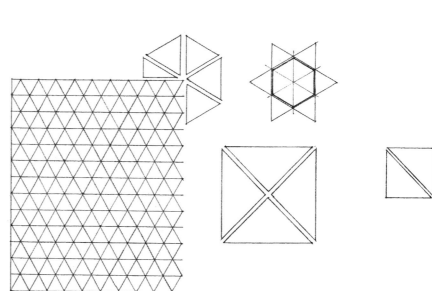

The square represents the pure and the rational. The equality of its four sides and its four right angles contributes to its regularity and visual clarity.

A square shape has no preferred or dominant direction. Like the triangle, the square is a stable, tranquil figure when resting on one of its sides, but becomes dynamic when standing on one of its corners.

All other rectangles can be considered to be variations of the square with the addition of width or length. While the clarity and stability of rectangular shapes can lead to visual monotony, variety can be introduced by varying their size, proportion, color, texture, placement, or orientation.

Rectangular shapes are clearly the norm in architectural and interior design. They are easily measured, drawn, and manufactured, and they fit together readily and snugly in construction.

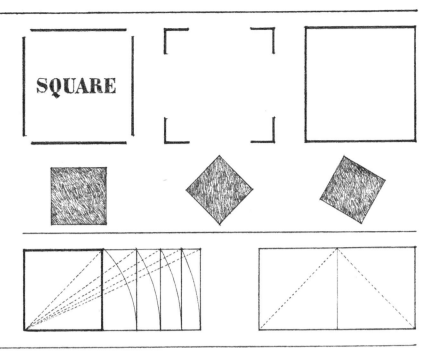

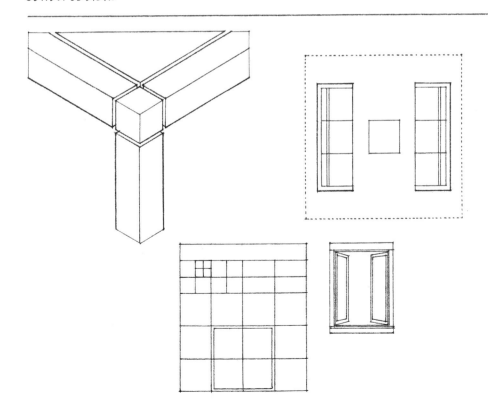

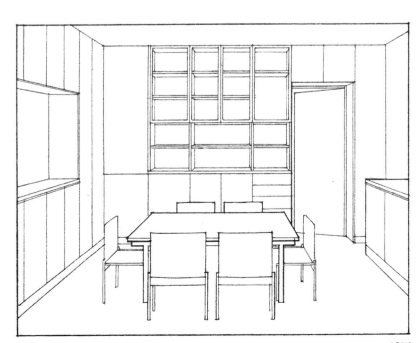

COLOR

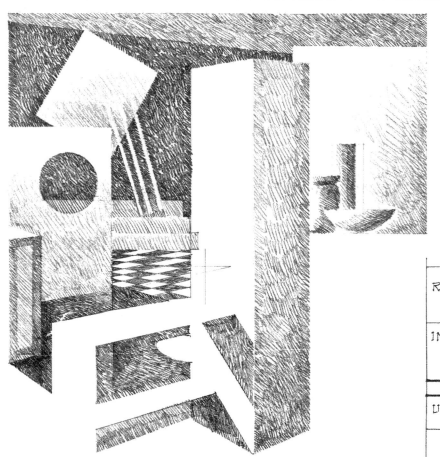

Color is, like shape and texture, an inherent visual property of all form. We are surrounded by color in our environmental settings. The colors we attribute to objects, however, find their source in the light that illuminates and reveals form and space. Without light, color does not exist.

The science of physics deals with color as a property of light. Within the visible spectrum of light, color is determined by wavelength; starting at the longest wavelength with red, we proceed through the spectrum of orange, yellow, green, blue, and violet to arrive at the shortest visible wavelengths. When these colored lights are present in a light source in approximately equal quantities, they combine to produce white light—light that is apparently colorless.

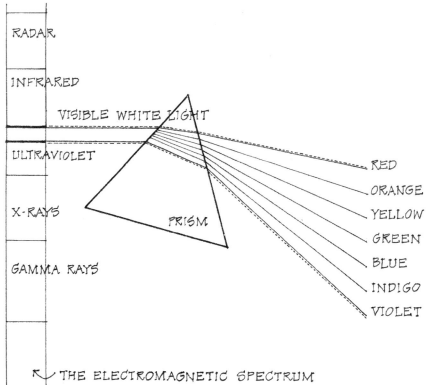

RADAR

INFRARED

VISIBLE WHITE LIGHT

ULTRAVIOLET

X-RAYS

PRISM

GAMMA RAYS

RED
ORANGE
YELLOW
GREEN
BLUE
INDIGO
VIOLET

THE ELECTROMAGNETIC SPECTRUM

When white light falls on an opaque object, selective absorption occurs. The surface of the object absorbs certain wavelengths of light and reflects others. Our eyes apprehend the color of the reflected light as the color of the object.

White light, such as noon sunlight, is composed of the entire spectrum of colored lights. Some light sources, such as fluorescent lamps or light reflected off of a colored wall, may not be well balanced and lack part of the spectrum. This lack of certain colors would make a surface illuminated by such light appear to also lack those colors.

Which wavelengths or bands of light are absorbed and which are reflected as object color is determined by the pigmentation of a surface. A red surface appears red because it absorbs most of the blue and green light falling on it and reflects the red part of the spectrum; a blue surface absorbs the reds. Similarly, a black surface absorbs the entire spectrum; a white surface reflects all of it.

A surface has the natural pigmentation of its material. This coloration can be altered with the application of paints, stains, or dyes which contain color pigments. While colored light is additive in nature, color pigments are subtractive. Each pigment absorbs certain proportions of white light. When pigments are mixed, their absorptions combine to subtract various colors of the spectrum. The colors that remain determine the hue, value, and intensity of the mixed pigment.

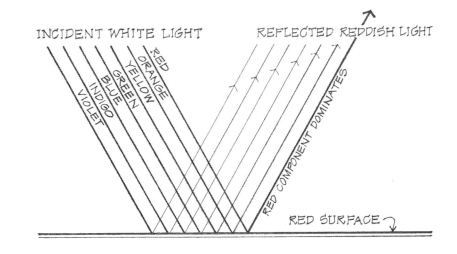

INCIDENT WHITE LIGHT   REFLECTED REDDISH LIGHT

RED
ORANGE
YELLOW
GREEN
BLUE
INDIGO
VIOLET

RED COMPONENT DOMINATES

RED SURFACE

LIGHT: ADDITIVE COLOR MIXTURE

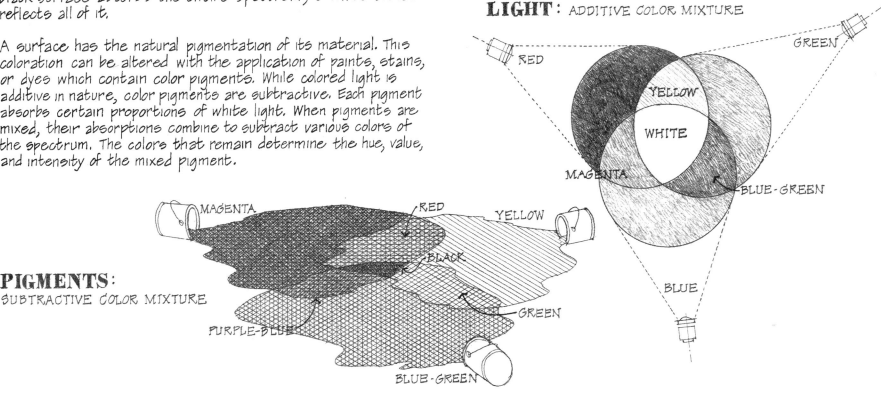

RED

GREEN

YELLOW

WHITE

MAGENTA

BLUE-GREEN

BLUE

PIGMENTS:
SUBTRACTIVE COLOR MIXTURE

MAGENTA

RED

YELLOW

BLACK

GREEN

PURPLE-BLUE

BLUE-GREEN

Color has three dimensions:

1. HUE — The attribute by which we recognize and describe a color, such as red or yellow.

2. VALUE — The degree of lightness or darkness of a color in relation to white and black.

3. INTENSITY — The degree of purity or saturation of a color when compared to a gray of the same value.

All of these attributes of color are necessarily interrelated. Each principal hue has a normal value. Pure yellow, for example, is lighter in value than pure blue. If white, black, or a complementary hue is added to a color to lighten or darken its value, its intensity will also be diminished. It is difficult to adjust one attribute of a color without simultaneously altering the other two.

A number of color systems attempt to organize colors and their attributes into a visible order. The simplest type, such as the Brewster or Prang color wheel, organizes color pigments into primary, secondary, and tertiary hues.

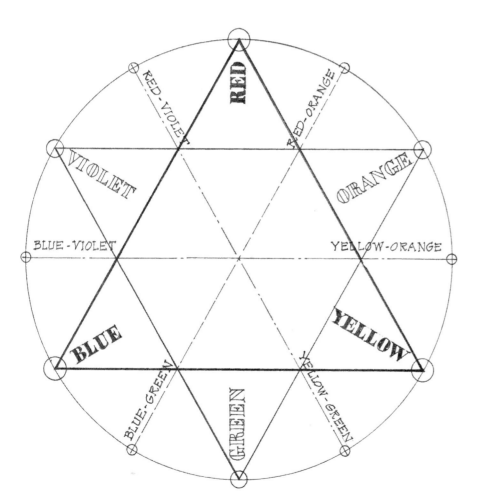

A more comprehensive system for the accurate specification and description of color is the Munsell system, developed by Albert H. Munsell. The system arranges colors into three orderly scales of uniform visual steps according to their attributes of hue, value, and chroma (intensity).

The Munsell system is based on five principal hues and five intermediate hues. These ten major hues are positioned ten hue steps apart and arranged horizontally in a circle.

Extending vertically through the center of the hue circle is a scale of neutral gray values, graded in ten equal visual steps from black to white.

Radiating out from the vertical scale of values are equal steps of chroma or intensity. The number of steps will vary according to the attainable saturation of each color's hue and value.

With this system, a specific color can be identified with the following notation: Hue Value/Chroma, or H V/c. For example, 5R 5/14 would indicate a pure red at middle value and maximum chroma.

While the ability to accurately communicate the hue, value, and intensity of a specific color without an actual sample is important in science, commerce, and industry, color names and notations cannot adequately describe the visual sensation of color. Actual color samples, seen in the color of light, is essential in the design of color schemes.

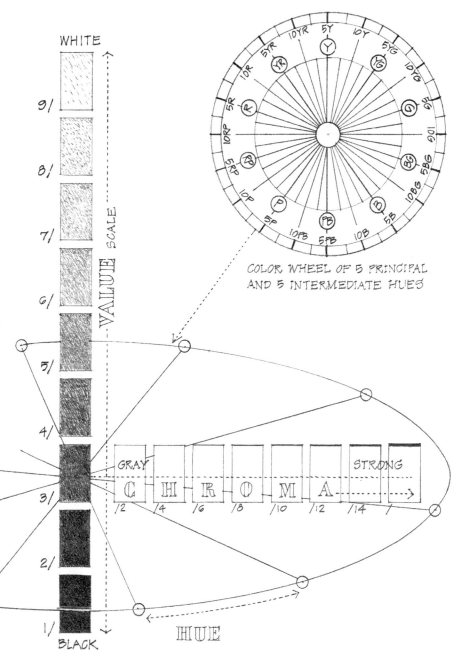

COLOR WHEEL OF 5 PRINCIPAL AND 5 INTERMEDIATE HUES

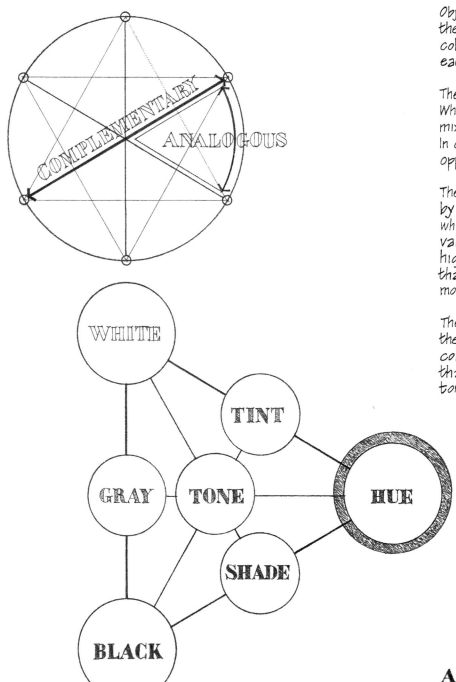

Object colorants, such as paints and dyes, are means to modify the color of the illuminating light, which we interpret to be the color of the object. In mixing the pigments of paints and dyes, each of the attributes of color can be altered.

The hue of a color can be changed by mixing it with other hues. When neighboring or analogous hues on the color wheel are mixed, harmonious and closely related hues are created. In contrast to this, mixing complementary hues, hues directly opposite of each other on the color wheel, produces neutral hues.

The value of a color can be raised by adding white and lowered by adding black. Lightening a hue's normal value by adding white creates a tint of that hue; darkening the hue's normal value with black creates a shade of the hue. A normally high-value color, such as yellow, is capable of more shades than tints, while a low-value color, such as red, is able to have more tints than shades.

The intensity of a color can be strengthened by adding more of the dominant hue. It can be lowered by mixing gray with the color or by adding to the color its complementary hue. Hues that are grayed or neutralized in this manner are often called tones.

ALTERING COLORS: WITH PIGMENTS....

Apparent changes in an object's color can also result from the effects of light and from the juxtaposition of surrounding or background colors. These factors are especially important to the interior designer, who must carefully consider how the colors of elements in an interior space interact and how they are rendered by the light illuminating them.

Light of a particular hue, other than white, is rarely used for general illumination. Not all sources of white light, however, are spectrally well balanced. Incandescent bulbs cast a warm glow, while many fluorescents cast a cool light. Daylight, too, can be warm or cool, depending on the time of day and the direction from which it comes. Even the color of a large reflecting surface can tint the light within an interior space.

Warm light tends to accentuate warm colors and neutralize cool hues, while cool light intensifies cool colors and weakens warm hues. If light is tinted with a particular hue, it will raise the intensity of colors of that hue, and neutralize colors of a complementary hue.

The apparent value of a color can also be altered by the amount of light used to illuminate it. Lowering the amount of illumination will darken a color's value and neutralize its hue. Raising the lighting level will lighten the color's value and enhance its intensity. High levels of illumination, however, can also tend to make colors appear less saturated or washed out.

Since the natural fluctuations of light in an interior setting alter colors in often subtle ways, it is always best to test colors in the environment in which they are to be viewed, under both daylight and nighttime conditions.

...OR WITH LIGHT

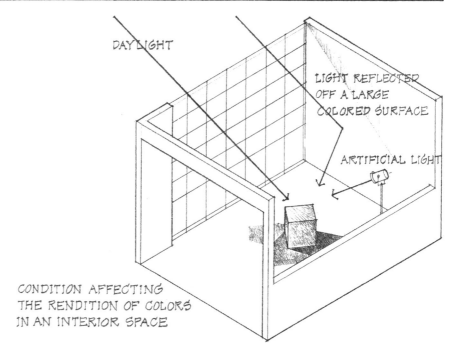

DAYLIGHT

LIGHT REFLECTED OFF A LARGE COLORED SURFACE

ARTIFICIAL LIGHT

CONDITION AFFECTING THE RENDITION OF COLORS IN AN INTERIOR SPACE

HIGH LIGHT LEVEL | MEDIUM LEVEL | LOW LEVEL

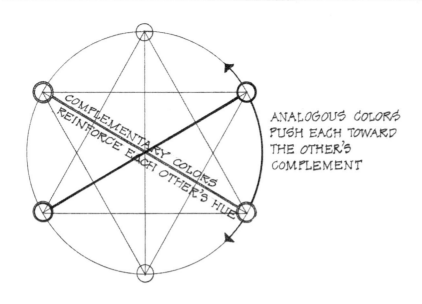

ANALOGOUS COLORS PUSH EACH TOWARD THE OTHER'S COMPLEMENT

While mixing two complementary color pigments results in a neutralized or grayed hue, placing them next to each other can produce the opposite effect. In the phenomenon known as simultaneous contrast, the eye tends to generate a color's complementary hue and project it as an afterimage on adjacent colors. Thus two complementary colors placed side by side tend to heighten each other's saturation and brilliance without an apparent change in hue.

When the two colors are not complementary, each will tint the other with its own complement and shift it towards that hue. The result is that the two colors are pushed farther apart in hue.

Simultaneous contrast in hue is most easily perceived when two colors are fairly uniform in value. If one color is much lighter or darker than the other, the effects of contrasting values become more noticeable.

THE EFFECTS OF ADJACENT COLORS: SIMULTANANEOUS CONTRAST

USE THE SUPERIMPOSED SQUARES BELOW AS TEMPLATES TO STUDY THE EFFECT OF SIMULTANEOUS CONTRAST ON THE HUES OF ADJACENT COLORS.

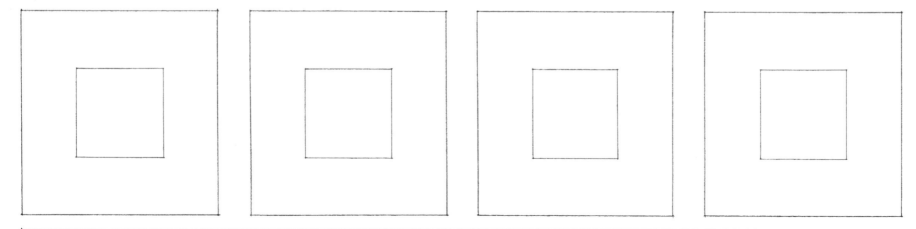

Simultaneous contrast also affects the apparent value of a color, which can be made to appear lighter or darker according to the value of its background color. A light color will tend to deepen a dark color while a dark color will tend to brighten a light color.

Both black and white have a visible effect on colors when brought into contact with them. Surrounding colors with black tends to make them richer and more vibrant, while outlining with white often has the opposite effect. A large area of white will reflect light onto adjacent colors, while thin white lines tend to spread and tint the hues they separate.

The effects of contrasting hues and values depend on areas large enough to be perceived as separate colors. If the areas are small and closely spaced, the eye does not have enough time to adjust to their differences and mixes the colors optically. The effects of optical mixing are often used in the weaving of textiles to create an impression of many hues and values with a limited number of colored yarns or threads.

USE THESE SUPERIMPOSED SQUARES AS TEMPLATES TO STUDY THE EFFECT OF SIMULTANEOUS CONTRAST ON THE VALUES OF ADJACENT COLORS.

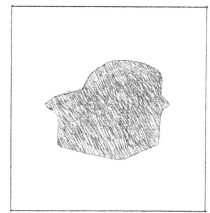

SIMULTANEOUS CONTRAST OF VALUE

SURROUNDING WITH WHITE........OR BLACK

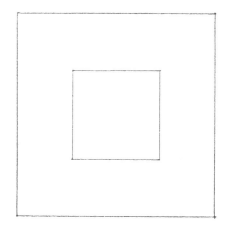
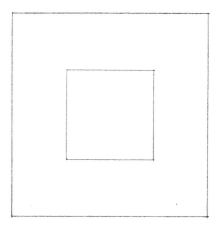

COLOR PATTERN

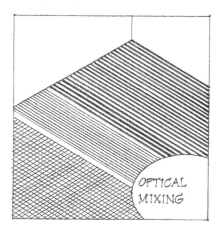

OPTICAL MIXING

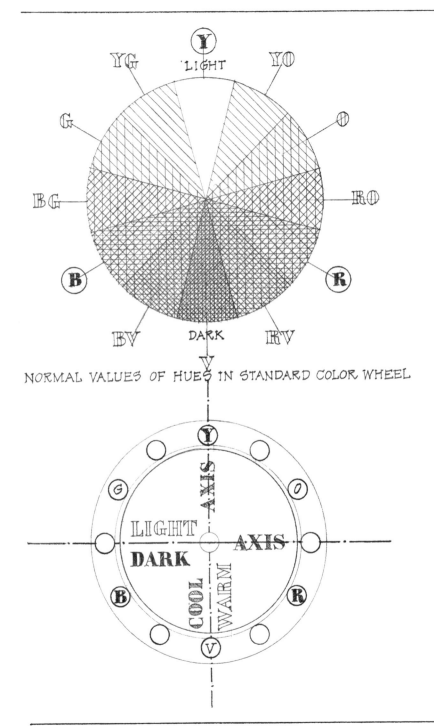

NORMAL VALUES OF HUES IN STANDARD COLOR WHEEL

In addition to how colors interact and alter one another's attributes, it is important to note how color might affect our perception of form and the dimensions and qualities of interior space.

The warmth or coolness of a color's hue, along with its relative value and degree of saturation, determines the visual force with which it attracts our attention, brings an object into focus, and creates space. The following generalizations summarize some of these effects of color.

Warm hues and high intensities are said to be visually active and stimulating, while cool hues and low intensities are more subdued and relaxing. Light values tend to be cheerful, middle values undemanding, and dark values somber.

Bright, saturated colors and any strong contrasts attract our attention; grayed hues and middle values are less forceful. Contrasting values in particular make us aware of shapes and forms. Contrasting hues and saturations can also define shape, but if they are too similar in value, the definition they afford will be less distinct.

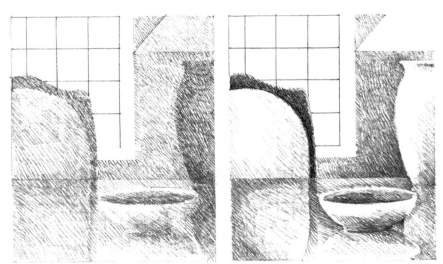

VALUE CONTRAST AIDS IN OUR PERCEPTION OF SHAPE

Deep, cool colors appear to contract. Light, warm colors tend to expand and increase the apparent size of an object, especially when seen against a dark background.

When used on an enclosing plane of a space, light values, cool hues, and grayed colors appear to recede and increase apparent distance. They can therefore be used to enhance the spaciousness of a room, and increase its apparent width, length, or ceiling height.

Warm hues appear to advance; dark values and saturated colors suggest nearness. These traits can be used to diminish the scale of a space or, in an illusionary way, shorten one of a room's dimensions.

 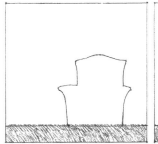 

LIGHT ON LIGHT   DARK ON LIGHT   LIGHT ON DARK

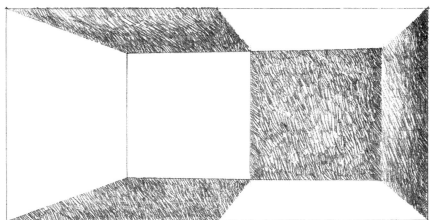

THE EFFECT OF COLOR ON SPATIAL BOUNDARIES

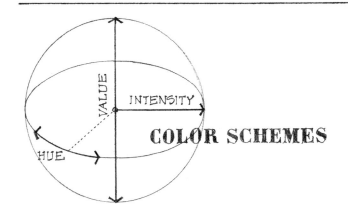

COLOR SCHEMES

Although each of us may have favorite colors and a distinct dislike of others, there is no such thing as a good or bad color. Some colors are simply in or out of fashion at a given time; others may be appropriate or inappropriate given a specific color scheme. The suitability of a color depends ultimately on how and where it is used, and how it fits into the palette of a color scheme.

If colors are like the notes of a musical scale, then color schemes are like musical chords, structuring color groups according to certain visual relationships among their attributes of hue, value, and intensity. The following color schemes are based on the hue relationships within a color group.

There are two broad categories of hue schemes, related and contrasting. Related hue schemes, based on either a single hue or a series of analogous hues, promote harmony and unity. Variety can be introduced by varying value and intensity, including small amounts of other hues as accents, or bringing shape, form, and texture into play.

Contrasting hue schemes, based on complementary or triadic color combinations, are inherently more rich and varied since they always include both warm and cool hues.

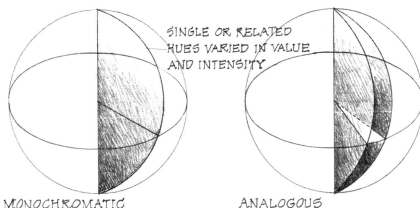

SINGLE OR RELATED HUES VARIED IN VALUE AND INTENSITY

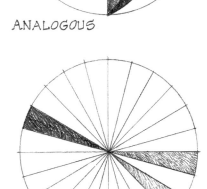

MONOCHROMATIC   ANALOGOUS

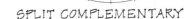

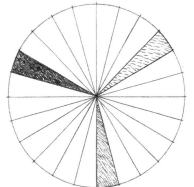

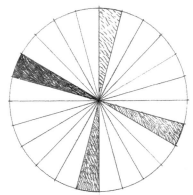

COMPLEMENTARY   SPLIT COMPLEMENTARY   TRIADIC   DOUBLE COMPLEMENTARY

Hue schemes merely outline the approaches one can take in organizing a combination of hues. In designing a color scheme, other color relationships must also be considered.

The color triangle developed by Faber Birren illustrates how modified colors - tints, tones, and shades - might be related in a harmonious sequence. The triangle is based on the three basic elements, pure color, white, and black. They combine to create the secondary forms of tint, shade, gray, and tone. Any of the straight-line paths defines a harmonious sequence since each involves a series of visually related elements.

Ultimately, whether a color scheme is lively and exuberant or restful and quiet will depend on the chromatic and tonal values of the hues chosen. Large intervals between the colors and values will create lively contrasts and dramatic effects. Small intervals will result in more subtle contrasts and patterns.

SMALL INTERVALS   LARGE INTERVALS

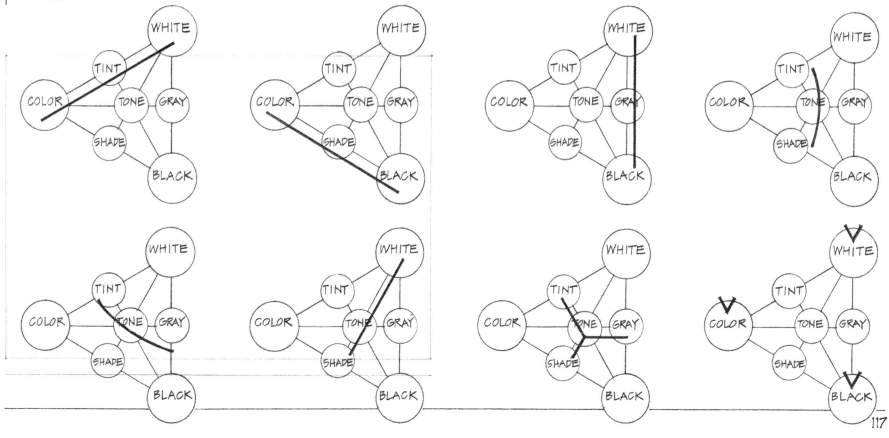

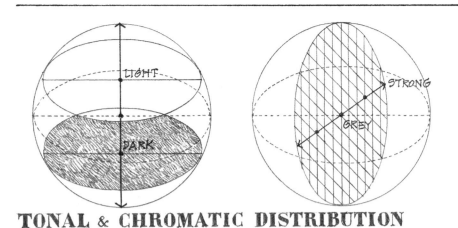

TONAL & CHROMATIC DISTRIBUTION

In developing a color scheme for an interior space, one must consider carefully the chromatic and tonal key to be established and the distribution of the colors. The scheme must not only satisfy the purpose and use of the space but also take into account its architectural character.

Decisions must be made regarding the major planes of an interior space and how color might be used to modify their apparent size, shape, scale, and distance. Which elements are to form the background, middleground, and foreground? Are there architectural or structural features which should be accentuated, or undesirable elements to be minimized?

Traditionally, the largest surfaces of a room, its floor, walls, and ceiling, have the most neutralized values. Against this background, secondary elements such as large pieces of furniture or area rugs can have greater chromatic intensity. Finally, accent pieces, accessories, and other small-scale elements can have the strongest chroma for balance and to create interest.

Neutralized color schemes are the most flexible. For a more dramatic effect, the main areas of a room can be given the more intense values while secondary elements have lesser intensity. Large areas of intense color should be used with caution, particularly in a small room. They reduce apparent distance and can be visually demanding.

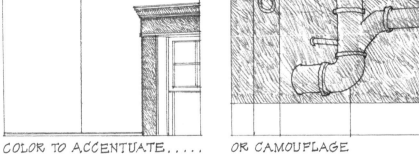
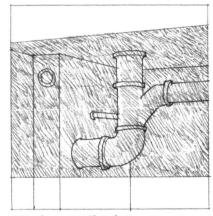

COLOR TO ACCENTUATE..... OR CAMOUFLAGE

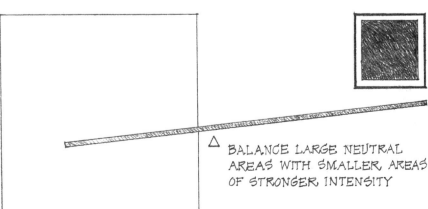

△ BALANCE LARGE NEUTRAL AREAS WITH SMALLER AREAS OF STRONGER INTENSITY

LARGE AREAS OF INTENSE COLOR CAN BE BOTH DRAMATIC AND VISUALLY DEMANDING

Of equal importance to chromatic distribution is tonal distribution, the pattern of lights and darks in a space. It is generally best to use varying amounts of light and dark values with a range of middle values to serve as transitional tones. Avoid using equal amounts of light and dark unless a fragmented effect is desired.

Typically, large areas of light value are offset by smaller areas . . . . > of medium and dark values. This use of light values is particularly appropriate when the efficient use of available light is important. Dark color schemes can absorb much of the light within a space, resulting in a significant loss of illumination.

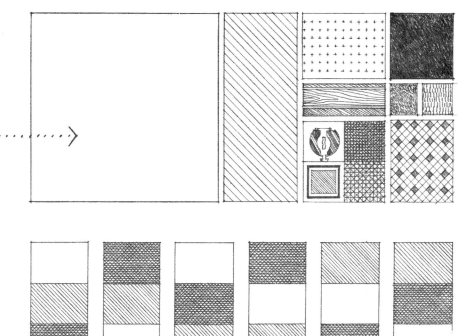

Another way of distributing values is to follow the pattern of nature. In this tonal sequence, the floor plane has the darkest value, surrounding walls are in the middle to light range, and the ceiling above is fairly light. Of course, the distribution of values and their degree of contrast will also depend on the size, shape, and scale of the space. Since light values tend to recede while dark values advance, their placement can modify our perception of these spatial dimensions.

VERTICAL DISTRIBUTION PATTERNS OF TONAL VALUES

TEXTURE

TEXTURE: THE 3-DIMENSIONAL STRUCTURE OF A SURFACE

Texture is that specific quality of a surface which results from its three-dimensional structure. Texture is most often used to describe the relative smoothness or roughness of a surface. It can also be used to describe the characteristic surface qualities of familiar materials, such as the roughness of stone, the grain of wood, and the weave of a fabric.

There are two basic types of texture. Tactile texture is real and can be felt by touch; visual texture is seen by the eye. All tactile textures provide visual texture as well. Visual texture, on the other hand, may be illusory or real.

Our senses of sight and touch are closely intertwined. As our eyes read the visual texture of a surface, we often respond to its apparent tactile quality without actually touching it. We base these physical reactions to the textural qualities of surfaces on previous associations with similar materials.

PHYSICAL TEXTURE

VISUAL TEXTURE

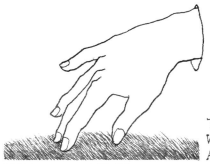

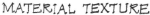

MATERIAL TEXTURE

TEXTURE IS INTERTWINED WITH OUR SENSES OF TOUCH AND SIGHT.

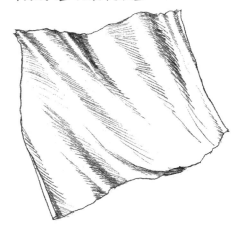

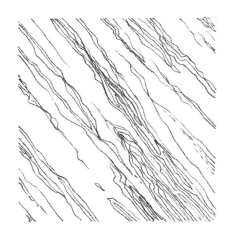

Scale, viewing distance, and light are important modifying factors in our perception of texture and the surfaces they articulate.

All materials have some degree of texture. But the finer the scale of a textural pattern, the smoother it will appear to be. Even coarse textures, when seen from a distance, can appear to be relatively smooth. Only upon closer viewing would the texture's coarseness become evident.

The relative scale of a texture can affect the apparent shape and position of a plane in space. Textures with a directional grain can accentuate a plane's length or width. Coarse textures can make a plane appear closer, reduce its scale, and increase its visual weight. In general, textures tend to visually fill the space in which they exist.

TEXTURE & SCALE: FAR   NEAR

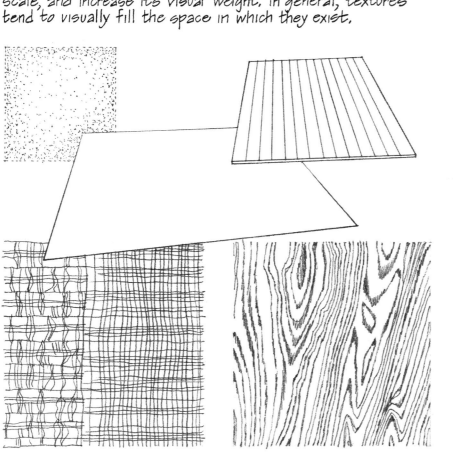

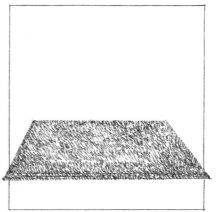

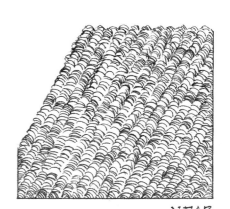

FAR   NEAR

TEXTURE & LIGHT

Light influences our perception of texture and, in turn, is affected by the texture it illuminates. Direct light falling across a surface with physical texture will enhance its visual texture. Diffused lighting de-emphasizes physical texture and can even obscure its three-dimensional structure.

Smooth, shiny surfaces reflect light brilliantly, appear sharply in focus, and attract our attention. Surfaces with a matte or medium-rough texture absorb and diffuse light unevenly and therefore appear less bright than a similarly colored but smoother surface. Very rough surfaces, when illuminated with direct lighting, cast distinct shadow patterns of light and dark.

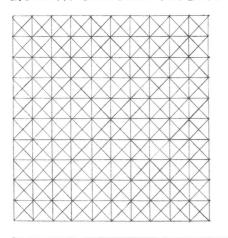

LIGHTING DIRECTION AFFECTS OUR READING OF TEXTURE

SHINY SURFACES REFLECT

MATTE SURFACES DIFFUSE

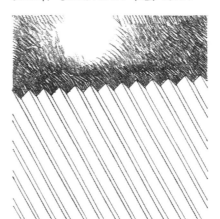

Contrast influences how strong or subtle a texture will appear to be. A texture seen against a uniformly smooth background will appear more obvious than when placed in juxtaposition with a similar texture. When seen against a coarser background, the texture will appear to be finer and reduced in scale.

Finally, texture is a factor in the maintenance of the materials and surfaces of a space. Smooth surfaces show dirt and wear but are relatively easy to clean, while rough surfaces may conceal dirt but are difficult to maintain.

CONTRAST AFFECTS THE APPARENT STRENGTH OR SUBTLETY OF ADJACENT TEXTURES.

TEXTURE CAN ALSO RESULT FROM THE MANNER IN WHICH MATERIALS ARE ASSEMBLED IN CONSTRUCTION.

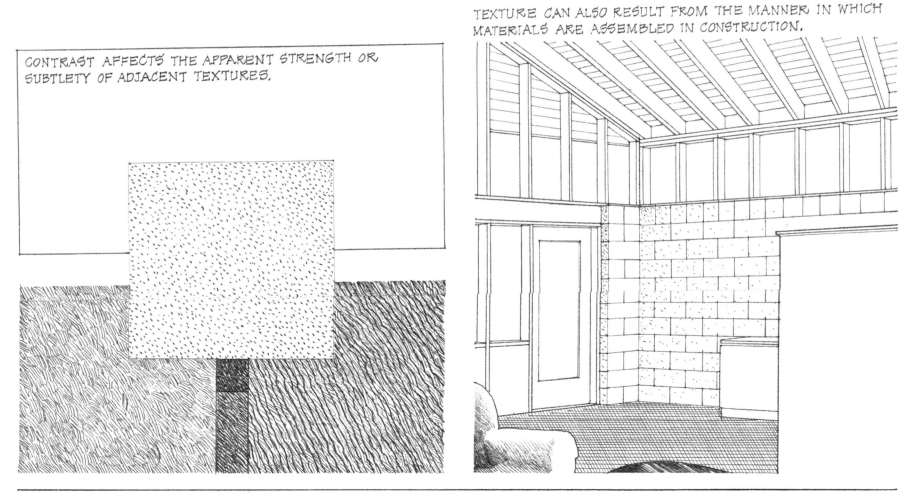

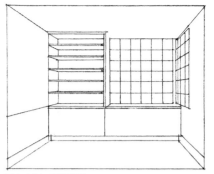

NO TEXTURE.................WITH TEXTURE

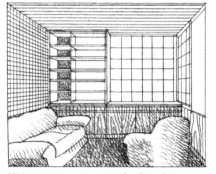
TEXTURE FILLING SPACE

COMPETING TEXTURES

Texture is an intrinsic characteristic of the materials we use to define, furnish, and embellish interior space. How we combine and compose differing textures is just as important as the composition of color and light, and should suit the desired character and use of a space.

The scale of a textural pattern should be related to the scale of a space and its major surfaces, as well as to the size of secondary elements within the space. Since texture tends to visually fill space, any textures used in a small room should be subtle or used sparingly. In a large room, texture can be used to reduce the scale of the space or to define a more intimate area within it.

A room with little textural variation can be bland. Combinations of hard and soft, even and uneven, and shiny and dull textures can be used to create variety and interest. In the selection and distribution of textures, moderation should be exercised and attention paid to their ordering and sequence. Harmony among contrasting textures can be sustained if they share a common trait, such as degree of light reflectance or visual weight.

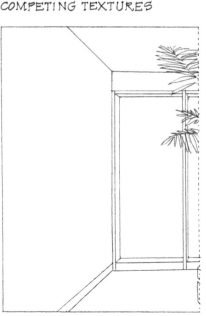

Texture and pattern are closely related design elements. Pattern is the decorative design or ornamentation of a surface which is almost always based on the repetition of a design motif. The repetitive design of a pattern often gives the ornamented surface a textural quality as well. When the elements that create a pattern become so small that they lose their individual identity and blend into a tone, they become more texture than pattern.

A pattern may be structural or applied. A structural pattern results from the intrinsic nature of a material and the way it is processed, fabricated, or assembled. An applied pattern is added to a surface after it is structurally complete.

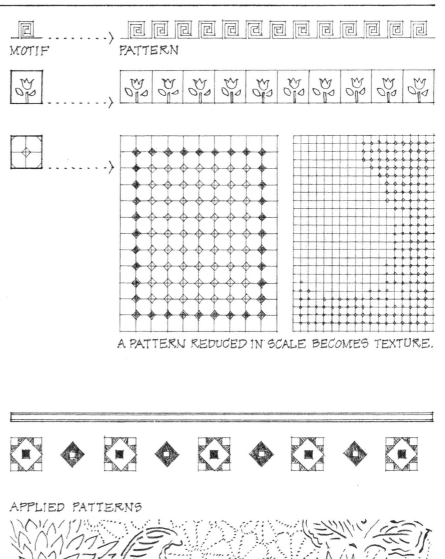

MOTIF   PATTERN

A PATTERN REDUCED IN SCALE BECOMES TEXTURE.

TEXTURE & PATTERN

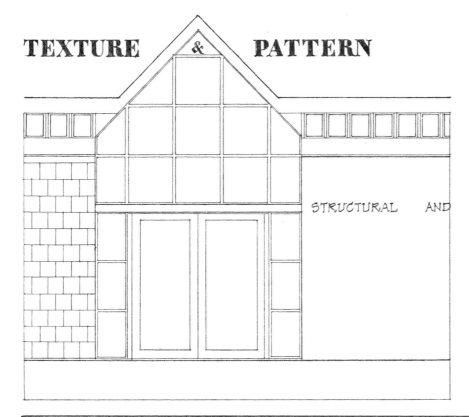

STRUCTURAL   AND

APPLIED PATTERNS

LIGHT

LIGHT ANIMATES SPACE AND REVEALS FORMS AND TEXTURES

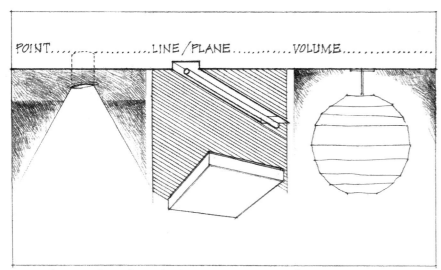

POINT.............LINE/PLANE...........VOLUME.................

FORMS OF LIGHT SOURCES AND LUMINAIRES

Light is the prime animator of interior space. Without light, there would be no visible form, color, or texture, nor any visible enclosure of interior space. The first function of lighting design, therefore, is to illuminate the forms and space of an interior environment, and allow users to undertake activities and perform tasks with appropriate speed, accuracy, and comfort.

The Zonal Cavity Method (see pages 301 - 305) for calculating the number of luminaires required to provide a specified level of illumination is a useful technique, especially when one designs general lighting for uniformly lit spaces. Note, however, that a specific level of illumination can be supplied by various combinations of luminaires. The choice of what types of luminaires are used and how they are laid out should be based not only on visibility requirements but also on the nature of the space being illuminated and the activities of its users. The lighting design should address not only the quantity of light required but also its quality.

The layout of luminaires and the pattern of light they radiate should be coordinated with the architectural features of a space and the pattern of its use. Since our eyes seek the brightest objects and the strongest tonal contrasts in their field of vision, this coordination is particularly important in the planning of localized or task lighting.

For the purpose of planning the visual composition of a lighting design, a light source can be considered to have the form of a point, a line, a plane, or a volume. If the light source is shielded from view, then the form of its light and the shape of its surface illumination should be considered. Whether the pattern of light sources is regular or varied, a lighting design should be balanced in its composition, provide an appropriate sense of rhythm, and give emphasis to what is important.

There are three methods for illuminating a space: general, local, and accent lighting. General or ambient lighting illuminates a room in a fairly uniform, generally diffuse manner. The dispersed quality of the illumination can effectively reduce the contrast between task lighting and the surrounding surfaces of a room. General lighting can also be used to soften shadows, smooth out and expand the corners of a room, and provide a comfortable level of illumination for safe movement and general maintenance.

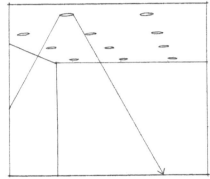

POINT SOURCES - DIRECT

Recessed downlights must have a wide beam spread to provide general lighting effectively.

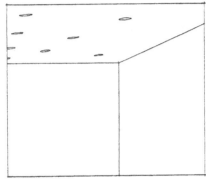

POINT SOURCES - DIRECT

Not being visually active, recessed downlights can be spaced evenly or unevenly.

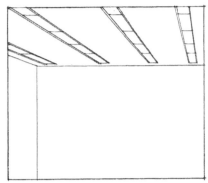

LINEAR SOURCES - DIRECT

Fluorescent luminaires parallel to our line of sight can accentuate depth.

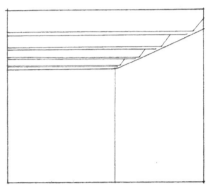

LINEAR SOURCES - DIRECT

The same fixtures perpendicular to our line of sight can increase apparent width.

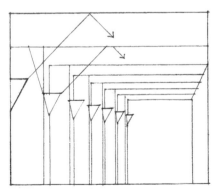

POINT SOURCES - INDIRECT

With wide-spread beams, indirect lighting fixtures can provide general lighting.

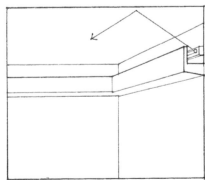

LINEAR SOURCE - INDIRECT

Cove lighting borders a room and uses the ceiling as a reflector to provide general lighting.

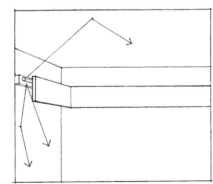

LINEAR - DIRECT/INDIRECT

Similar to cove lighting, valence lighting also illuminates the wall planes below.

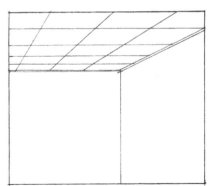

PLANAR SOURCE - DIRECT

Luminous ceilings combine high illumination and diffusion with low brightness.

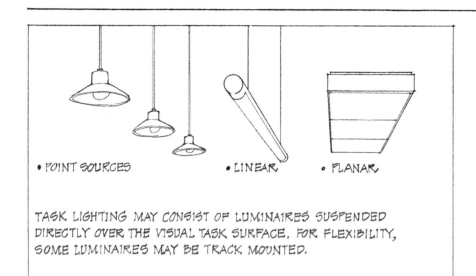

- POINT SOURCES   • LINEAR   • PLANAR

TASK LIGHTING MAY CONSIST OF LUMINAIRES SUSPENDED DIRECTLY OVER THE VISUAL TASK SURFACE. FOR FLEXIBILITY, SOME LUMINAIRES MAY BE TRACK MOUNTED.

TASK LIGHTING

Local or task lighting illuminates specific areas of a space for the performance of visual tasks or activities. The light sources are usually placed close to - either above or beside - the task surface, enabling the available wattage to be used more efficiently than with general lighting. The luminaires are normally of the direct type, and adjustability in terms of brightness (with dimmers or rheostats) and direction is always desirable.

To minimize the risk of an unacceptable brightness ratio between task and surroundings, task lighting is often combined with general lighting. Depending on the types of luminaires used, local lighting can also contribute to the general illumination of a space.

In addition to making a visual task easier to see, local lighting can also create variety and interest, partition a space into a number of areas, encompass a furniture grouping, or reinforce the social character of a room.

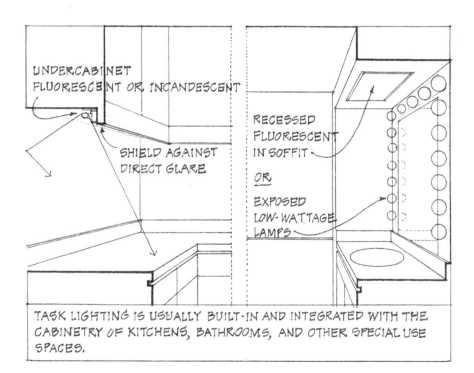

UNDERCABINET FLUORESCENT OR INCANDESCENT

SHIELD AGAINST DIRECT GLARE

RECESSED FLUORESCENT IN SOFFIT

OR

EXPOSED LOW-WATTAGE LAMPS

TASK LIGHTING IS USUALLY BUILT-IN AND INTEGRATED WITH THE CABINETRY OF KITCHENS, BATHROOMS, AND OTHER SPECIAL USE SPACES.

IN WORK SPACES, ADJUSTABLE LIGHT FIXTURES ARE OFTEN DESIRABLE TO PREVENT BOTH DIRECT AND INDIRECT GLARE.

TABLE AND FLOOR LAMPS ARE SUITABLE FOR READING IF POSITIONED CORRECTLY

Accent lighting is a form of local lighting which creates focal points or rhythmic patterns of light and dark within a space. Instead of serving simply to illuminate a task or activity, accent lighting can be used to relieve the monotony of general lighting, emphasize a room's features, or highlight art objects or prized possessions.

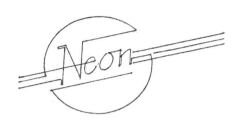

ACCENT LIGHTING

RECESSED DOWNLIGHTS CAN PROVIDE DIFFERENT TYPES OF LIGHT DEPENDING ON THE TYPE OF LAMP AND INTERNAL REFLECTOR USED.

CAST SHADOWS   FRAME ARTWORK   EMPHASIZE TEXTURE

DOWNLIGHTS WITH RELATIVELY WIDE-SPREAD BEAMS ARE USED TO WASH WALLS WITH LIGHT. THE UNIFORMITY OF THE ILLUMINATION DEPENDS ON HOW WIDELY THE LUMINAIRES ARE SPACED AND HOW FAR THEY ARE SET FROM THE WALL.

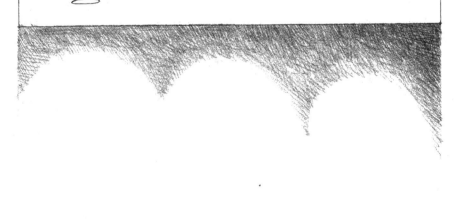

DESIGN PRINCIPLES

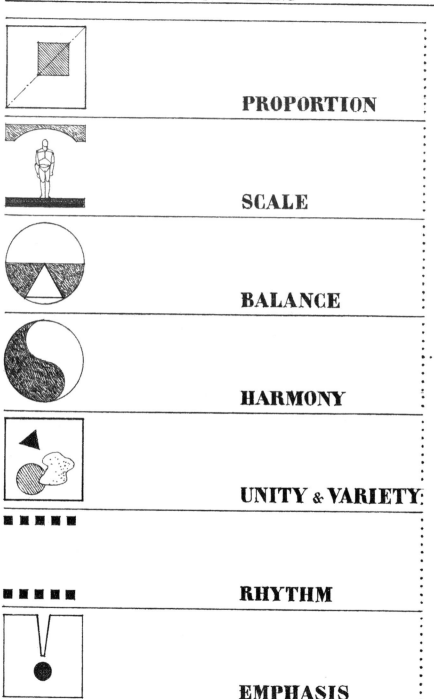

PROPORTION

SCALE

BALANCE

HARMONY

UNITY & VARIETY

RHYTHM

EMPHASIS

Interior design involves the selection of interior design elements and the arrangement of them within a spatial enclosure to satisfy certain functional and aesthetic needs and wishes. This arrangement of elements in a space includes the act of making patterns. No one single part or element in a space stands alone. In a design pattern, all of the parts, elements, or pieces depend on one another for their visual impact, function, and meaning.

We are concerned here with the visual relationships established among the interior design elements in a space. The following design principles are not intended to be 'hard and fast rules, but rather guidelines to the possible ways design elements can be arranged into recognizable patterns. Ultimately, we must learn to judge the appropriateness of a pattern, its visual role in a space, and its meaning to the users of the space. These principles, however, can help develop and maintain a sense of visual order among the design elements of a space while accommodating their intended use and function.

⟩ARRANGING DESIGN PATTERNS

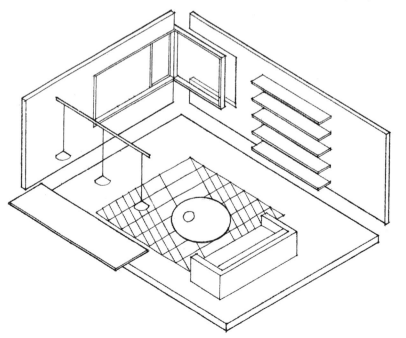

Proportion refers to the relationship of one part to another or to the whole, or between one object and another. This relationship may be one of magnitude, quantity, or degree.

MAGNITUDE

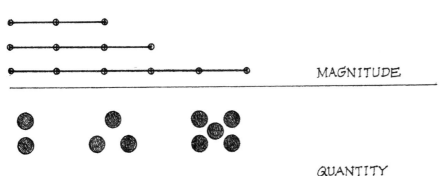

QUANTITY

DEGREE

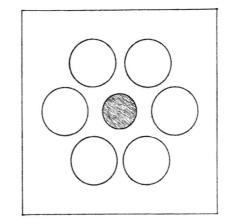 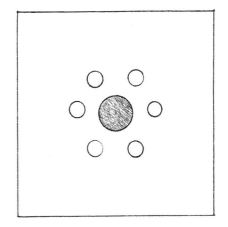

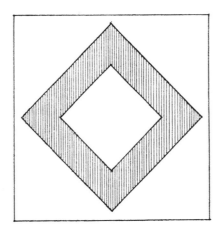 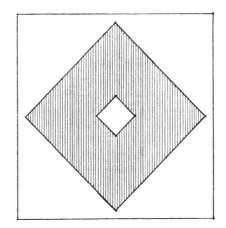

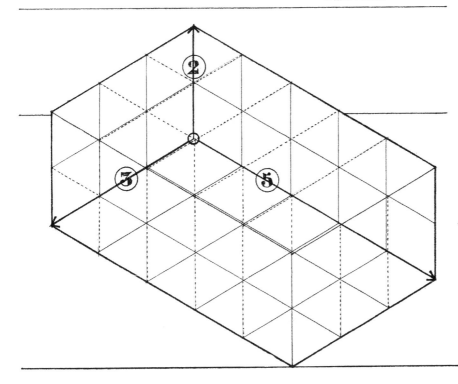

PROPORTION

THE APPARENT SIZE OF AN OBJECT IS INFLUENCED BY THE RELATIVE SIZES OF OTHER OBJECTS IN ITS ENVIRONMENT.

◁ WHEN DEALING WITH FORMS IN SPACE, ONE MUST CONSIDER PROPORTION IN THREE DIMENSIONS.

RATIO .... **A : B** $\dfrac{A}{B}$

PROPORTION... **A : B : C** $\dfrac{A}{B} = \dfrac{B}{C}$

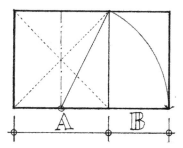

GOLDEN SECTION :
$$\dfrac{B}{A} = \dfrac{A}{A+B}$$

In the course of history, several mathematical or geometric methods have been developed to determine the ideal proportion of things. These proportioning systems go beyond functional and technical determinants in an attempt to establish a measure of beauty — an aesthetic rationale for the dimensional relationships among the parts and elements of a visual construction.

According to Euclid, the ancient Greek mathematician, a ratio refers to the quantitative comparison of two similar things, while proportion refers to the equality of ratios. Underlying any proportioning system, therefore, is a characteristic ratio, a permanent quality that is transmitted from one ratio to another.

Perhaps the most familiar proportioning system is the golden section established by the ancient Greeks. It defines the unique relationship between two unequal parts of a whole in which the ratio between the smaller and greater parts is equal to the ratio between the greater part and the whole.

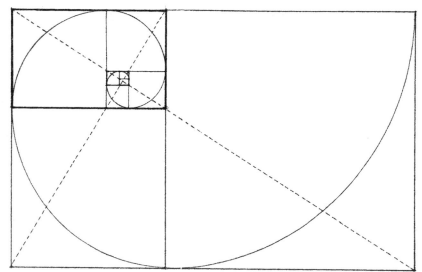

A HARMONIC COMPOSITION OF GOLDEN RECTANGLES

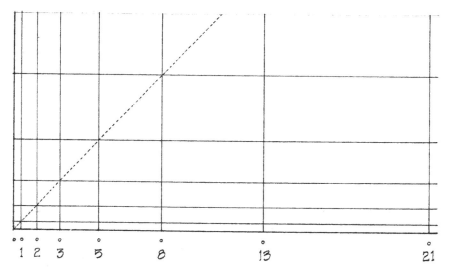

1, 1, 2, 3, 5, 8, 13, 21, 34, 55 ....

THE FIBONACCI SERIES IS A PROGRESSION OF WHOLE NUMBERS WHERE EACH TERM IS THE SUM OF THE PRECEDING TWO. THE RATIO BETWEEN TWO CONSECUTIVE TERMS APPROXIMATES THE GOLDEN SECTION.

Although often defined in mathematical terms, a proportioning system establishes a consistent set of visual relationships among the parts of a composition. It can be a useful design tool in promoting unity and harmony. Our perception of the physical dimensions of things is, however, often imprecise. The foreshortening of perspective, viewing distance, even cultural bias, can distort our perception.

The matter of proportion is still primarily one of critical visual judgment. In this respect, significant differences in the relative dimensions of things are important. Ultimately, a proportion will appear to be correct for a given situation when we sense that neither too little nor too much of an element or characteristic is present.

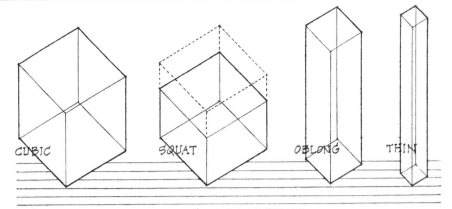

SIGNIFICANT DIFFERENCES IN PROPORTION

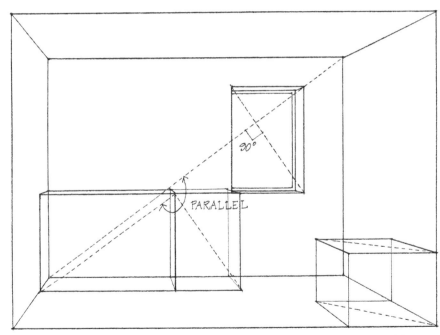

DIAGONALS WHICH ARE PARALLEL OR PERPENDICULAR TO EACH OTHER INDICATE THAT THE RECTANGLES THEY BISECT HAVE SIMILAR PROPORTIONS.

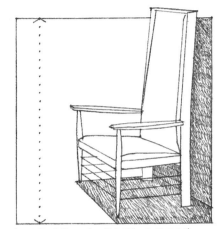
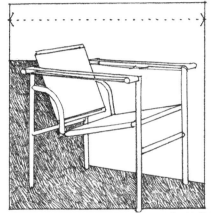

FURNITURE THAT DIFFERS SIGNIFICANTLY IN ITS PROPORTIONS

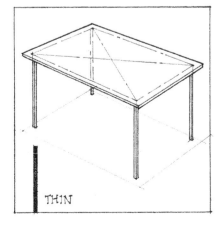
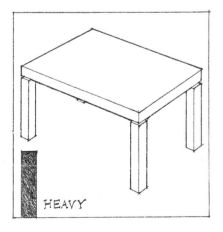

PROPORTIONAL RELATIONSHIPS

In interior design, we are concerned with the proportional relationships between the parts of a design element, between several design elements, and between the elements and the spatial form and enclosure.

PROPORTIONAL DIFFERENCES

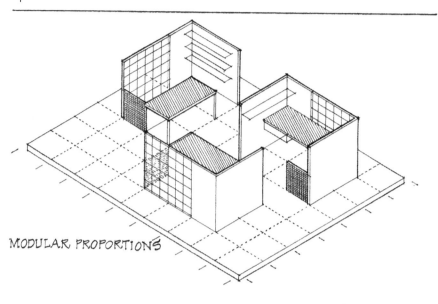

MODULAR PROPORTIONS

BETWEEN PARTS OF AN ELEMENT

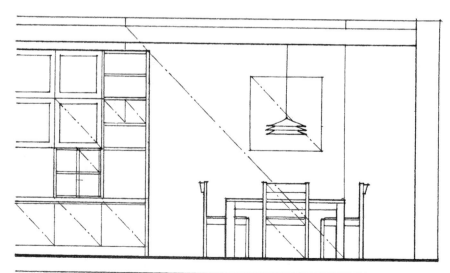

BETWEEN ELEMENTS

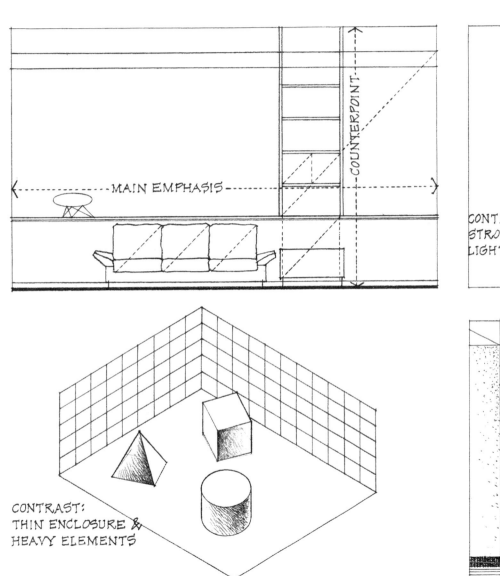

MAIN EMPHASIS

COUNTERPOINT

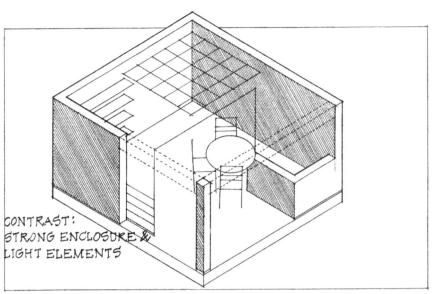

CONTRAST:
STRONG ENCLOSURE &
LIGHT ELEMENTS

CONTRAST:
THIN ENCLOSURE &
HEAVY ELEMENTS

BETWEEN ELEMENTS & SPATIAL ENCLOSURE

SCALE

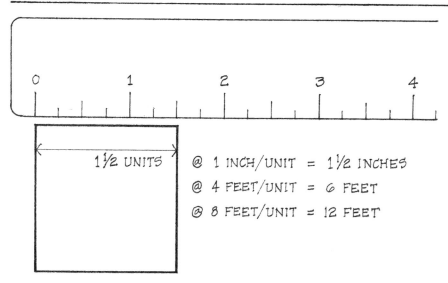

1½ UNITS

@ 1 INCH/UNIT = 1½ INCHES
@ 4 FEET/UNIT = 6 FEET
@ 8 FEET/UNIT = 12 FEET

The design principle of scale is related to proportion. Both proportion and scale deal with the relative sizes of things. If there is a difference, proportion pertains to the relationships between the parts of a composition, while scale refers specifically to the size of something, relative to some known standard or recognized constant.

Mechanical scale is the calculation of something's physical size according to a standard system of measurement. For example, we can say that a table is, according to the U.S. Customary System, 3 feet wide, 6 feet long, and 29 inches high. If we are familiar with this system and with objects of similar size, we can visualize how big the table is. Using the International Metric System, the same table would measure 914 mm wide, 1829 mm long, and 737 mm high.

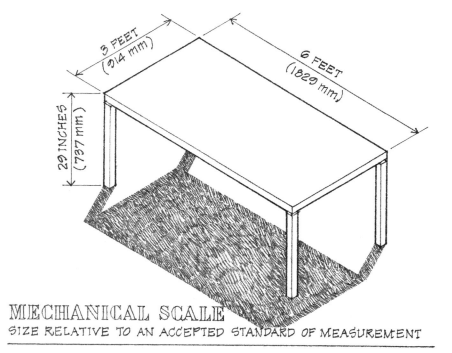

3 FEET (914 mm)

6 FEET (1829 mm)

29 INCHES (737 mm)

MECHANICAL SCALE
SIZE RELATIVE TO AN ACCEPTED STANDARD OF MEASUREMENT

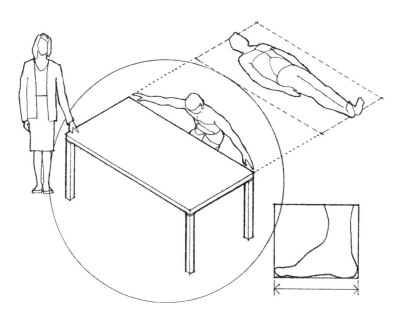

OUR BODIES CAN ALSO SERVE AS A SYSTEM OF MEASUREMENT

Visual scale refers to the bigness something appears to have when measured against other things around it. Thus, an object's scale is often a judgment we make based on the relative or known sizes of other nearby or surrounding elements. For example, the aforementioned table can appear to be in scale or out of scale with a room, depending on the relative size and proportions of the space.

We can refer to something as being small-scale if we are measuring it against other things which are generally much larger in size. Similarly, an object can be considered to be large-scale if it is grouped with relatively small items, or if it appears to be larger than what is considered normal or average in size.

SMALL-SCALE SPACE OR LARGE-SCALE FURNITURE

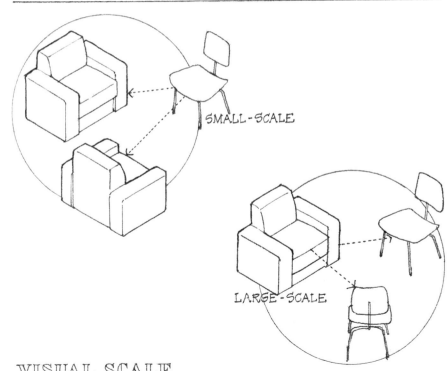

SMALL-SCALE

LARGE-SCALE

VISUAL SCALE
SIZE RELATIVE TO OTHER OBJECTS IN THE ENVIRONMENT........

OR TO THE SURROUNDING SPACE

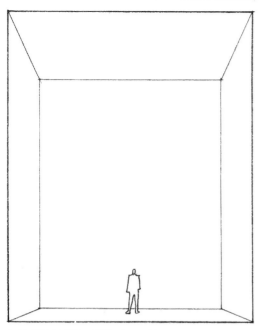

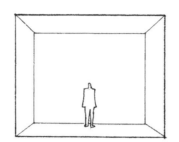

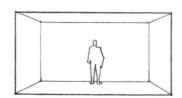

Human scale refers to the feeling of bigness something gives us. If the dimensions of an interior space or the sizes of elements within it make us feel small, we can say they lack human scale. If, on the other hand, the space does not dwarf us or if the elements offer a comfortable fit with our dimensional requirements of reach, clearance, or movement, we can say they are human in scale.

Most of the elements we use to ascertain human scale are those whose dimensions we have become accustomed to through contact and use. These include doorways, stairs, tables and counters, and various types of seating. These elements can be used to humanize a space that would otherwise lack human scale.

HUMAN SCALE

THE FEELING OF SMALLNESS OR BIGNESS A SPACE OR AN INTERIOR ELEMENT GIVES US.

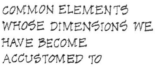

COMMON ELEMENTS WHOSE DIMENSIONS WE HAVE BECOME ACCUSTOMED TO

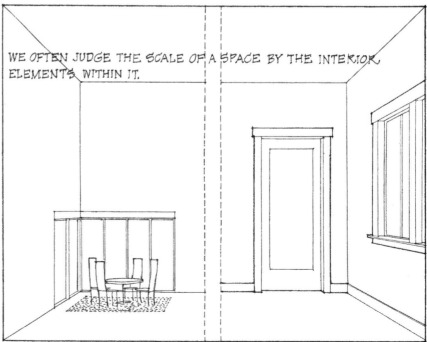

WE OFTEN JUDGE THE SCALE OF A SPACE BY THE INTERIOR ELEMENTS WITHIN IT.

The issue of scale in an interior space is not limited to one set of relationships. Interior elements can be related simultaneously to the whole space, to each other, and to those people who use the space. It is not unusual for some elements to have a normal, orderly scale relationship but have an exceptional scale when compared to other elements. Unusually scaled elements can be used to attract attention or create and emphasize a focal point.

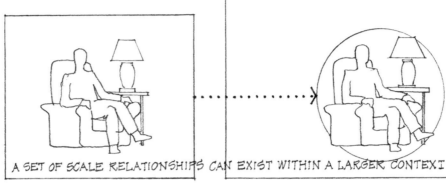

A SET OF SCALE RELATIONSHIPS CAN EXIST WITHIN A LARGER CONTEXT

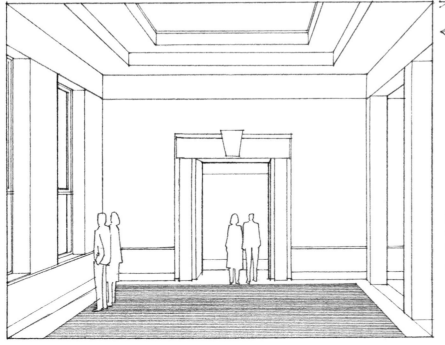

FIREPLACE MASS SCALED TO SPACE WHILE RAISED HEARTH IS AT SEAT HEIGHT.

DOORWAY AND WINDOWS ARE SCALED TO SPACE WHILE SILL HEIGHTS AND WAINSCOT RETAIN A MORE HUMAN SCALE.

BALANCE

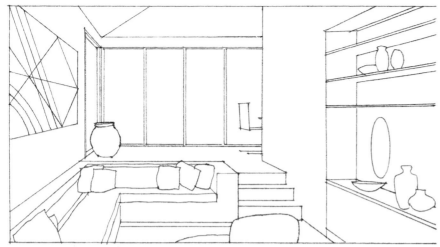

INTERIORS: A MIX OF SHAPES, COLORS, AND TEXTURES

Interior spaces – and their elements of enclosure, furnishings, lighting, and accessories – often include a mix of shapes, sizes, colors, and textures. How these elements are organized is a response to functional needs and aesthetic desires. At the same time, these elements should be arranged to achieve visual balance – a state of equilibrium among the visual forces projected by the elements.

Each element in the ensemble of interior space has specific characteristics of shape, form, size, color, and texture. These characteristics, along with the factors of location and orientation, determine the visual weight of each element and how much attention each will attract in the overall pattern of space.

Characteristics that will enhance or increase the visual weight of an element – and attract our attention – are:

- Irregular or contrasting shapes
- Bright colors and contrasting textures
- Large dimensions and unusual proportions
- Elaborate details

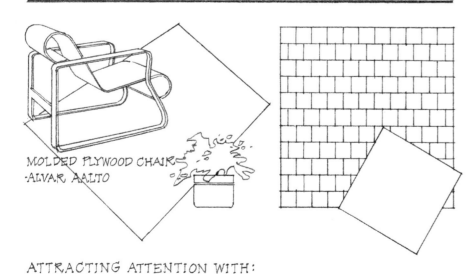

MOLDED PLYWOOD CHAIR -ALVAR AALTO

ATTRACTING ATTENTION WITH:

IRREGULAR SHAPES   CONTRASTING TEXTURES   UNUSUAL PROPORTIONS   ELABORATE DETAILS

Our perception of a room and the composition of its elements is altered as we use it and move through its space. Our perspective varies as our point of view shifts from here to there. A room also undergoes changes over time as it is illuminated by the light of day and lamps at night, occupied by people and paraphernalia, and modified by time itself. The visual balance among the elements in a space should therefore be considered in three dimensions and be strong enough to withstand the changes brought about through time and use.

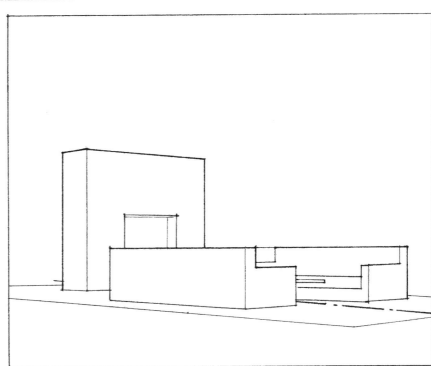

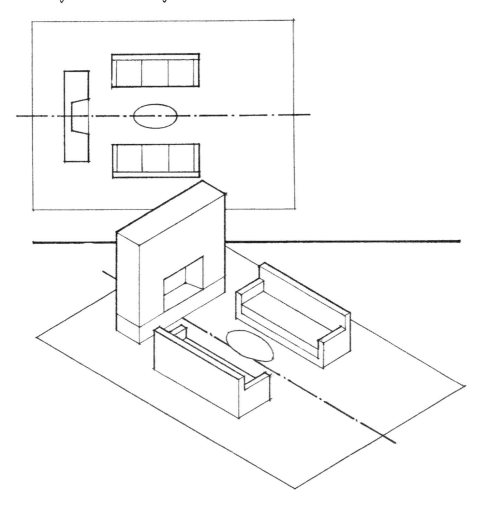

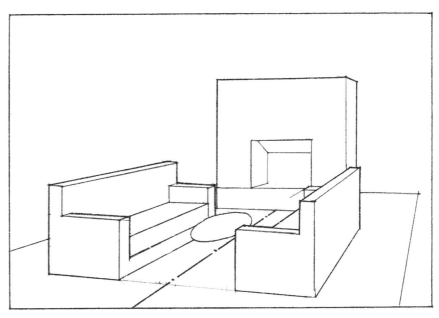

VISUAL BALANCE MUST BE CONSIDERED IN THREE DIMENSIONS.

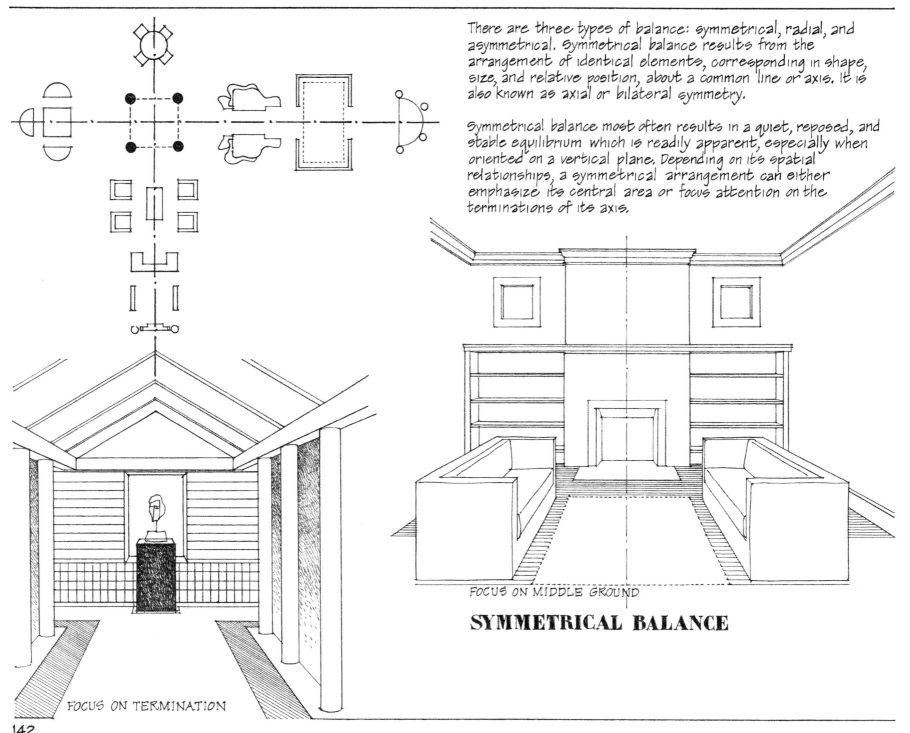

There are three types of balance: symmetrical, radial, and asymmetrical. Symmetrical balance results from the arrangement of identical elements, corresponding in shape, size, and relative position, about a common line or axis. It is also known as axial or bilateral symmetry.

Symmetrical balance most often results in a quiet, reposed, and stable equilibrium which is readily apparent, especially when oriented on a vertical plane. Depending on its spatial relationships, a symmetrical arrangement can either emphasize its central area or focus attention on the terminations of its axis.

FOCUS ON TERMINATION

FOCUS ON MIDDLE GROUND

SYMMETRICAL BALANCE

Symmetry is a simple yet powerful device to establish visual order. If carried far enough, it can impose a strict formality on an interior space. Total symmetry, however, is often undesirable or difficult to achieve, because of function or circumstance.

It is often possible or desirable to arrange one or more parts of a space in a symmetrical manner and produce local symmetry. Symmetrical groupings within a space are easily recognized and have a quality of wholeness that can serve to simplify or organize the room's composition.

The second type of balance, radial balance, results from the arrangement of elements about a center point. It produces a centralized composition which stresses the middle ground as a focal point. The elements can focus inward toward the center, face outward from the center, or simply be placed about a central element.

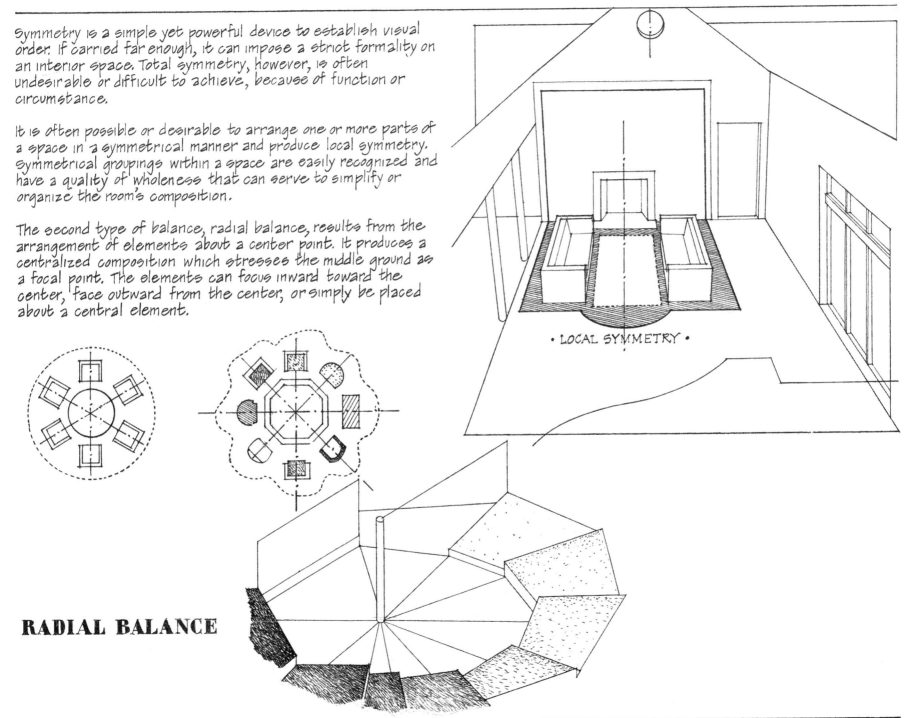

· LOCAL SYMMETRY ·

RADIAL BALANCE

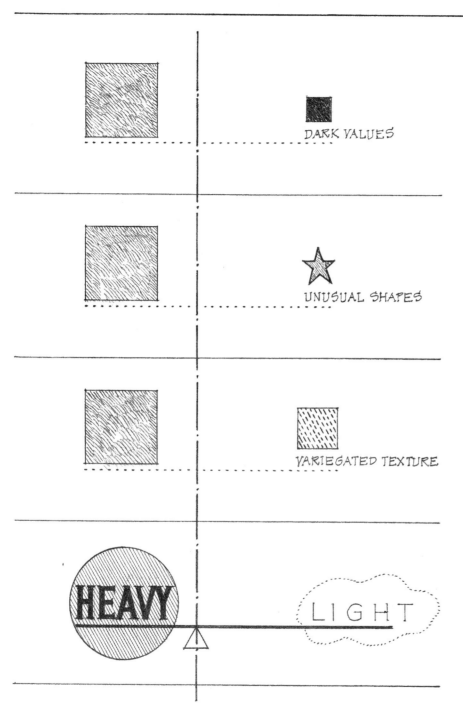

DARK VALUES

UNUSUAL SHAPES

VARIEGATED TEXTURE

HEAVY   LIGHT

Asymmetry is recognized as the lack of correspondence in size, shape, color, or relative position among the elements of a composition. While a symmetrical composition requires the use of pairs of identical elements, an asymmetrical composition incorporates dissimilar elements.

To achieve an occult or optical balance, an asymmetrical composition must take into account the visual weight or force of each of its elements and employ the principle of leverage in their arrangement. Elements which are visually forceful and attract our attention – unusual shapes, bright colors, dark values, variegated textures – must be counterbalanced by less forceful elements which are larger or placed farther away from the center of the composition.

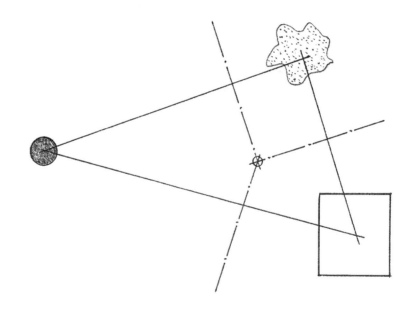

ASYMMETRICAL BALANCE

Asymmetrical balance is not as obvious as symmetry and is often more visually active and dynamic. It is capable of expressing movement, change, even exuberance. It is also more flexible than symmetry and can adapt more readily to varying conditions of function, space, and circumstance.

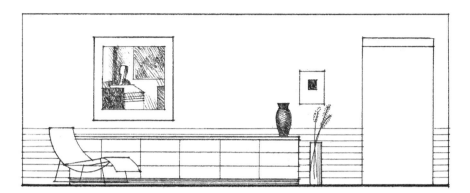

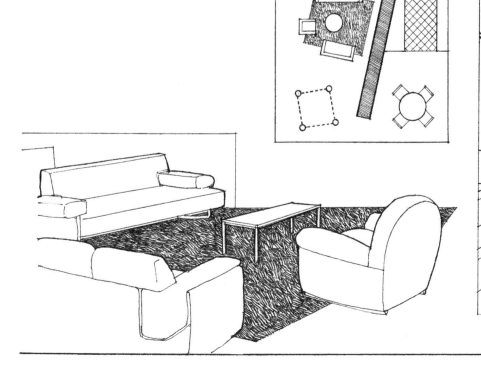

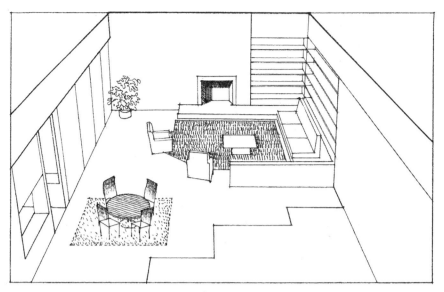

HARMONY

Harmony can be defined as consonance or the pleasing agreement of parts or combination of parts in a composition. While balance achieves unity through the careful arrangement of both similar and dissimilar elements, the principle of harmony involves the careful selection of elements that share a common trait or characteristic, such as shape, color, texture, or material. It is the repetition of a common trait that produces unity and visual harmony among the elements in an interior setting.

SHARING A COMMON TRAIT:

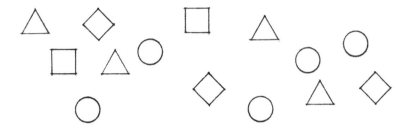

A COMMON SIZE

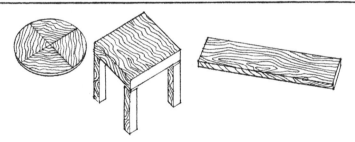

SIMILAR COLORS OR VALUES

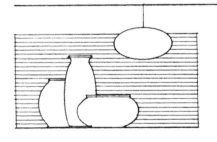
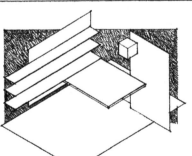

A COMMON SHAPE

SIMILAR MATERIALS

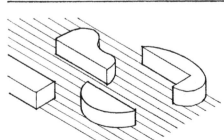
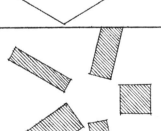

A SIMILAR ORIENTATION

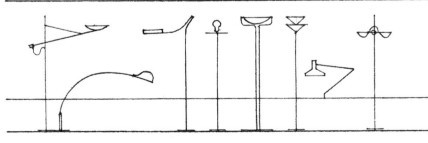

SIMILAR DETAIL CHARACTERISTICS

Harmony, when carried too far in the use of elements with similar traits, can result in a unified but uninteresting composition. Variety, on the other hand, when carried to an extreme for the sake of interest, can result in visual chaos. It is the careful and artistic tension between order and disorder – between unity and variety – that enlivens harmony and creates interest in an interior setting.

INTRODUCING VARIETY:

GIVEN A SET OF IDENTICAL SHAPES, VARIETY CAN BE INTRODUCED BY:

VARYING ORIENTATION

VARYING SIZE

VARYING DETAIL CHARACTERISTICS

VARYING TEXTURE

VARYING COLOR

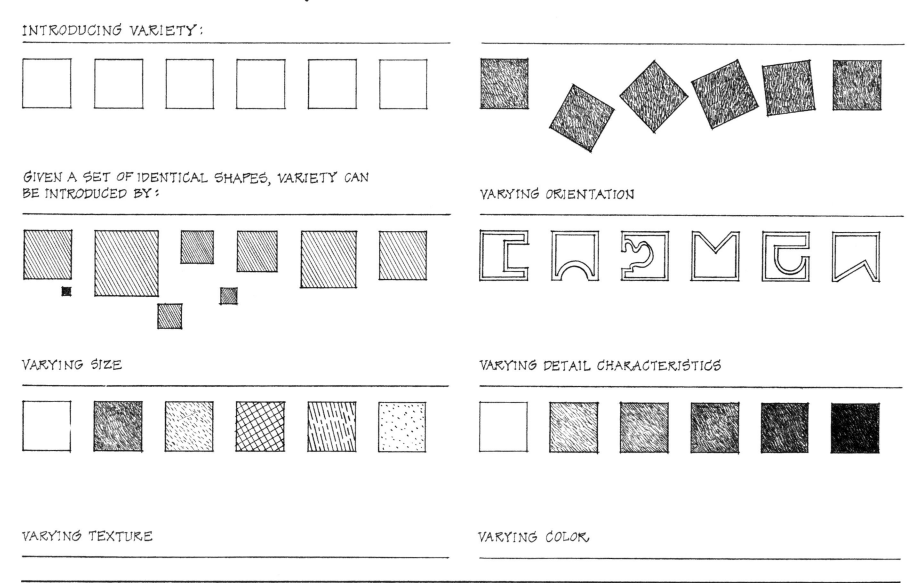

UNITY & VARIETY

It is important to note that the principles of balance and harmony, in promoting unity, do not exclude the pursuit of variety and interest. Rather, the means for achieving balance and harmony are intended to include in their patterns the presence of dissimilar elements and characteristics.

For example, asymmetrical balance produces equilibrium among elements that differ in size, shape, color, or texture. The harmony produced by elements that share a common characteristic permits the same elements to also have a variety of unique, individual traits.

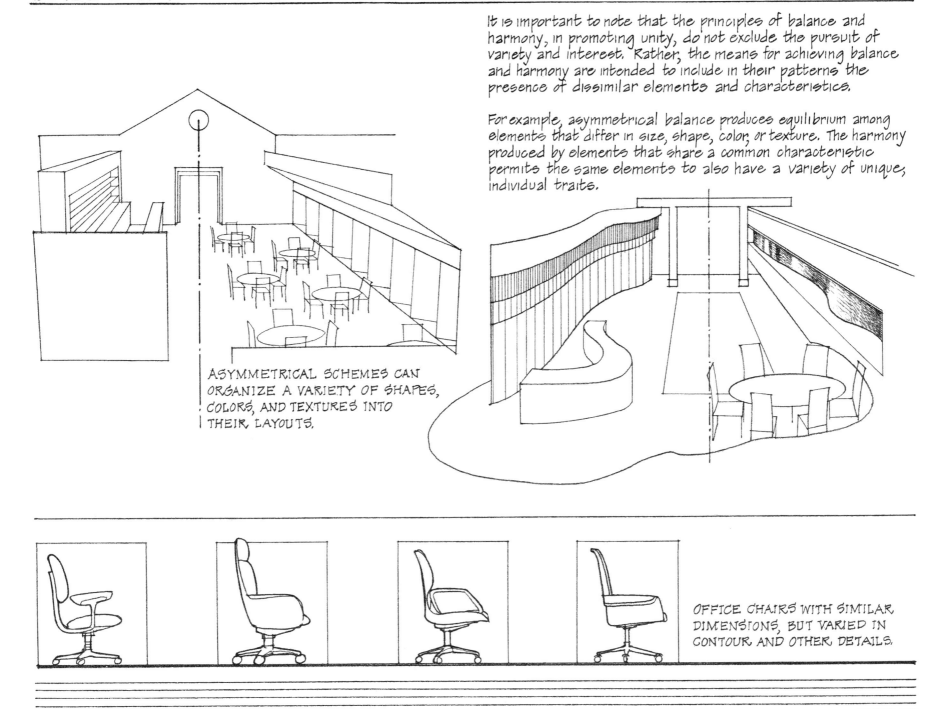

ASYMMETRICAL SCHEMES CAN ORGANIZE A VARIETY OF SHAPES, COLORS, AND TEXTURES INTO THEIR LAYOUTS.

OFFICE CHAIRS WITH SIMILAR DIMENSIONS, BUT VARIED IN CONTOUR AND OTHER DETAILS.

Another method for organizing a number of dissimilar elements is simply to arrange them in close proximity to one another. We tend to read such a grouping as an entity to the exclusion of other elements farther away. To further reinforce the visual unity of the composition, continuity of line or contour can be established among the elements' shapes.

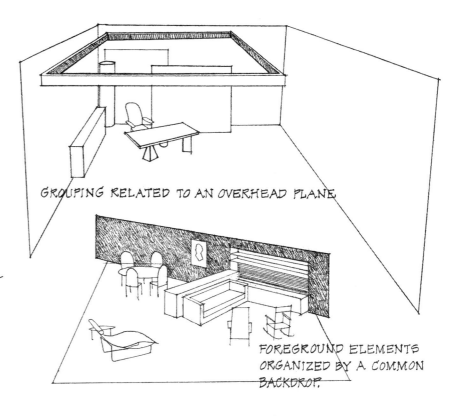

GROUPING RELATED TO AN OVERHEAD PLANE

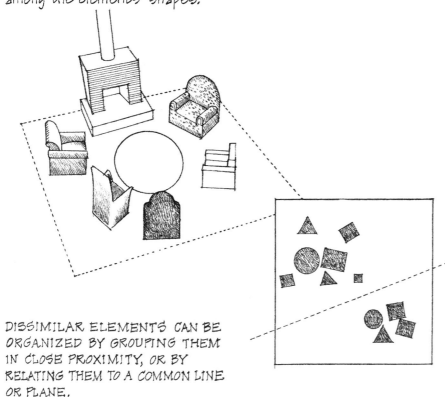

DISSIMILAR ELEMENTS CAN BE ORGANIZED BY GROUPING THEM IN CLOSE PROXIMITY, OR BY RELATING THEM TO A COMMON LINE OR PLANE.

FOREGROUND ELEMENTS ORGANIZED BY A COMMON BACKDROP.

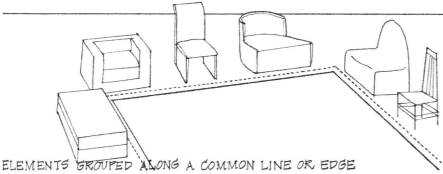

ELEMENTS GROUPED ALONG A COMMON LINE OR EDGE

RHYTHM

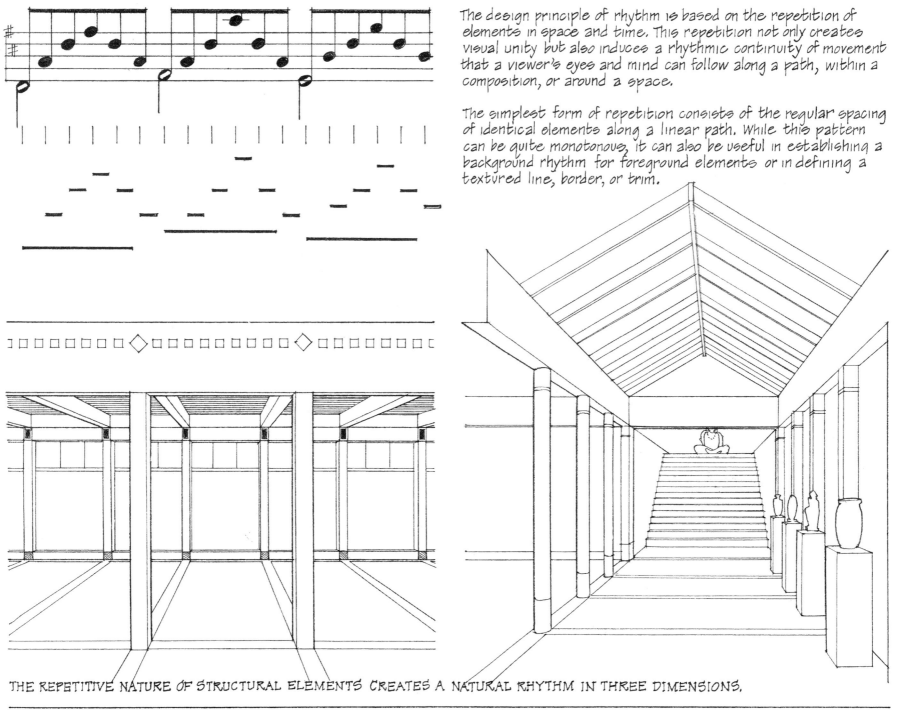

The design principle of rhythm is based on the repetition of elements in space and time. This repetition not only creates visual unity but also induces a rhythmic continuity of movement that a viewer's eyes and mind can follow along a path, within a composition, or around a space.

The simplest form of repetition consists of the regular spacing of identical elements along a linear path. While this pattern can be quite monotonous, it can also be useful in establishing a background rhythm for foreground elements or in defining a textured line, border, or trim.

THE REPETITIVE NATURE OF STRUCTURAL ELEMENTS CREATES A NATURAL RHYTHM IN THREE DIMENSIONS.

More intricate patterns of rhythm can be produced by taking into account the tendency for elements to be visually related by their proximity to one another or their sharing of a common trait.

The spacing of the recurring elements, and thus the pace of the visual rhythm, can be varied to create sets and subsets and to emphasize certain points in the pattern. The resulting rhythm may be graceful and flowing, or crisp and sharp. The contour of the rhythmic pattern and the shape of the individual elements can further reinforce the nature of the sequence.

While the recurring elements must, for continuity, share a common trait, they can also vary in shape, detail, color, or texture. These differences, whether subtle or distinct, create visual interest and can introduce other levels of complexity. An alternating rhythm can be superimposed over a more regular one, or the variations can be progressively graded in size or color value to give direction to the sequence.

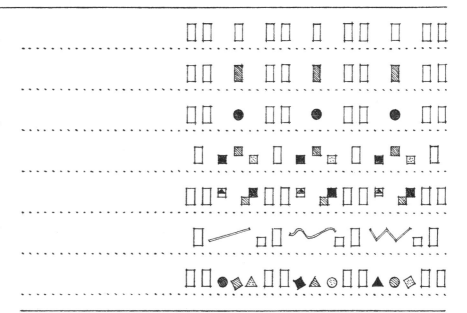

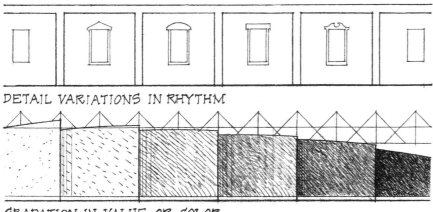

DETAIL VARIATIONS IN RHYTHM

GRADATION IN VALUE OR COLOR

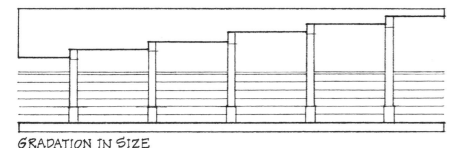

GRADATION IN SIZE

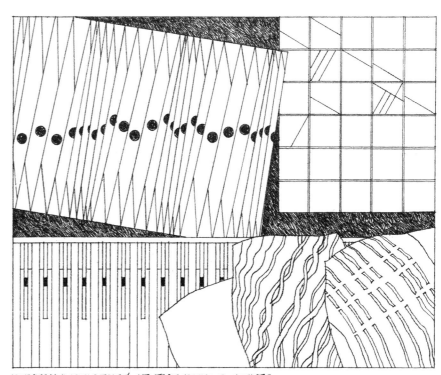

RHYTHM EXISTING AT THE DETAIL LEVEL

Visual rhythm is most easily recognized when the repetition forms a linear pattern. Within an interior space, however, nonlinear sequences of shape, color, and texture can provide more subtle rhythms which may not be immediately obvious to the eye.

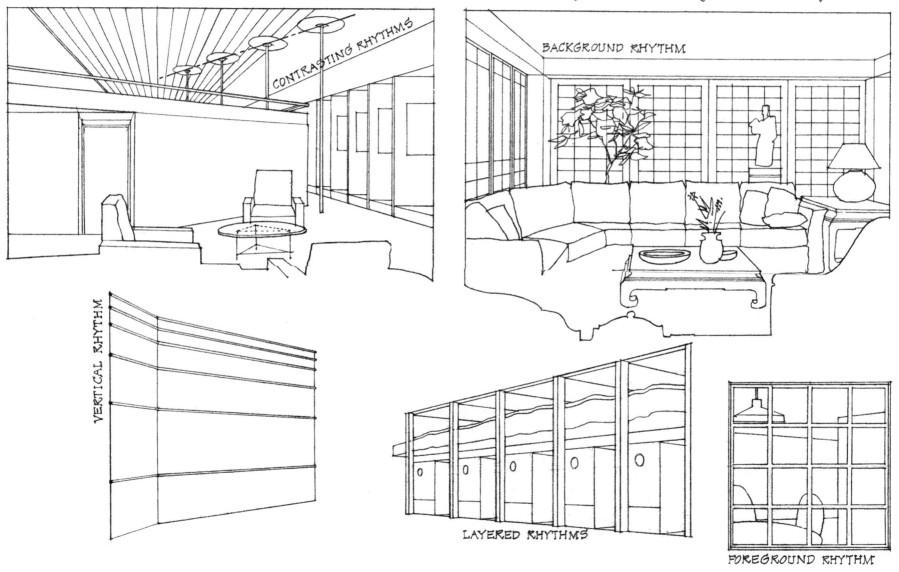

CONTRASTING RHYTHMS

BACKGROUND RHYTHM

VERTICAL RHYTHM

LAYERED RHYTHMS

FOREGROUND RHYTHM

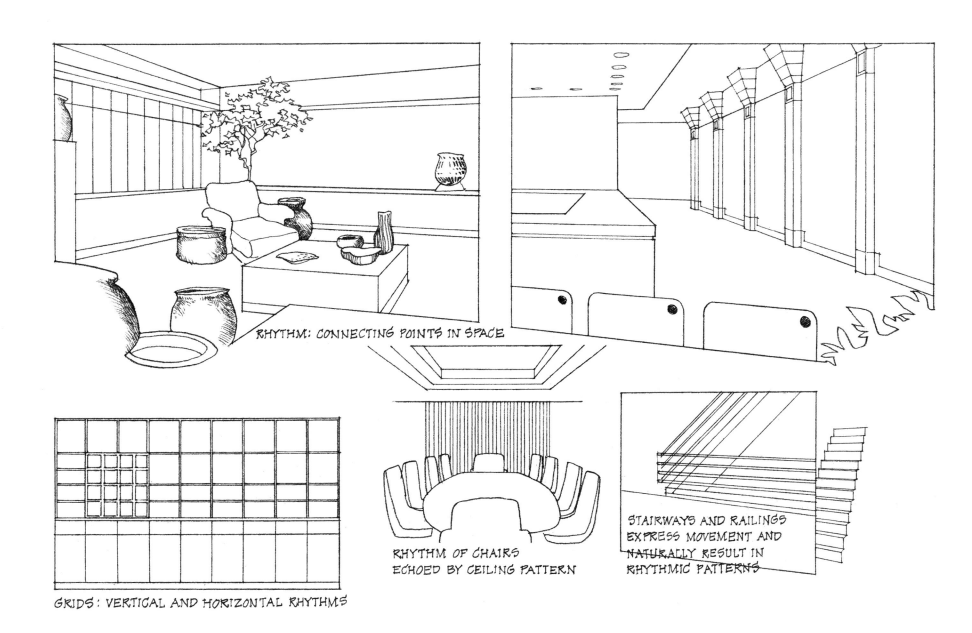

RHYTHM: CONNECTING POINTS IN SPACE

GRIDS: VERTICAL AND HORIZONTAL RHYTHMS

RHYTHM OF CHAIRS
ECHOED BY CEILING PATTERN

STAIRWAYS AND RAILINGS
EXPRESS MOVEMENT AND
NATURALLY RESULT IN
RHYTHMIC PATTERNS

EMPHASIS

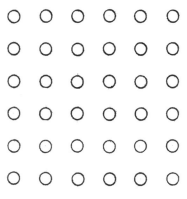

NO DOMINANT ELEMENTS -
NO EMPHASIS

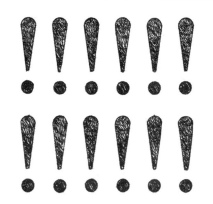

TOO MANY DOMINANT
ELEMENTS - NO EMPHASIS

The principle of emphasis assumes the coexistence of dominant and subordinate elements in the composition of an interior setting. A design without any dominant elements would be bland and monotonous. If there are too many assertive elements, the design would be cluttered and chaotic, detracting from what may truly be important. Each part of a design should be given proper significance according to its degree of importance in the overall scheme.

An important element or feature can be given visual emphasis by endowing it with significant size, a unique shape, or a contrasting color, value, or texture. In each case, a discernible contrast must be established between the dominant element or feature and the subordinate aspects of the space. Such contrast would attract our attention by interrupting the normal pattern of the composition.

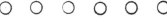

POINTS OF EMPHASIS CAN BE
CREATED BY A PERCEPTIBLE
CONTRAST IN SIZE, SHAPE,
COLOR, OR VALUE.

! EXCEPTIONAL SHAPE

! EXCEPTIONAL SIZE

An element or feature can also be visually emphasized by its strategic position and orientation in a space. It can be centered within the space or serve as the centerpiece of a symmetrical organization. In an asymmetric composition, it can be offset or isolated from the rest of the elements. It can be the termination of a linear sequence or a path of movement.

To further enhance its visual importance, an element can be oriented to contrast with the normal geometry of the space and the other elements within it. It can be lit in a special manner. The lines of secondary and subordinate elements can be arranged to focus our attention on the significant element or feature.

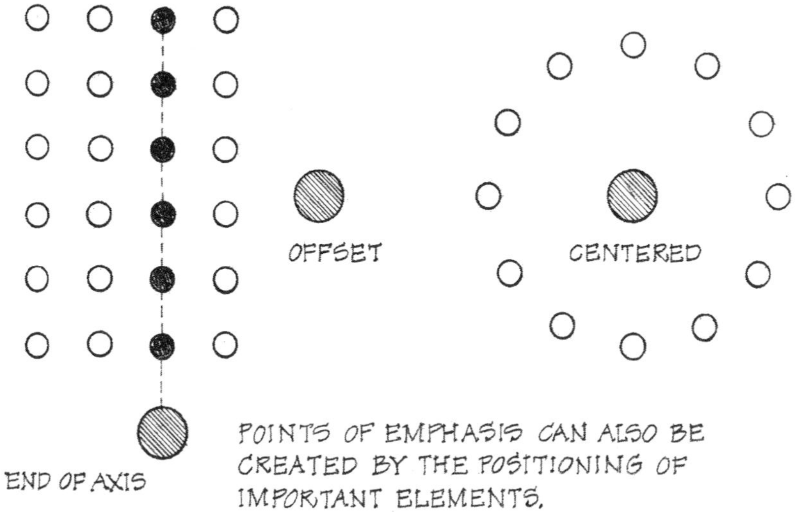

OFFSET

CENTERED

END OF AXIS

POINTS OF EMPHASIS CAN ALSO BE CREATED BY THE POSITIONING OF IMPORTANT ELEMENTS.

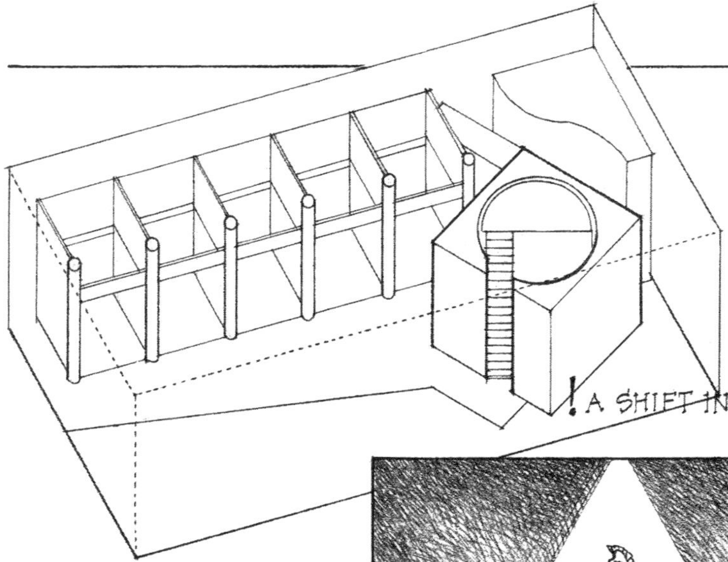

! A SHIFT IN GEOMETRY

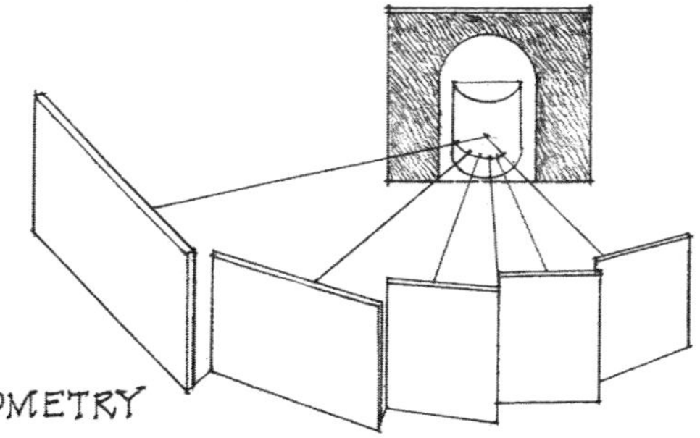

! CENTER OF FOCUS

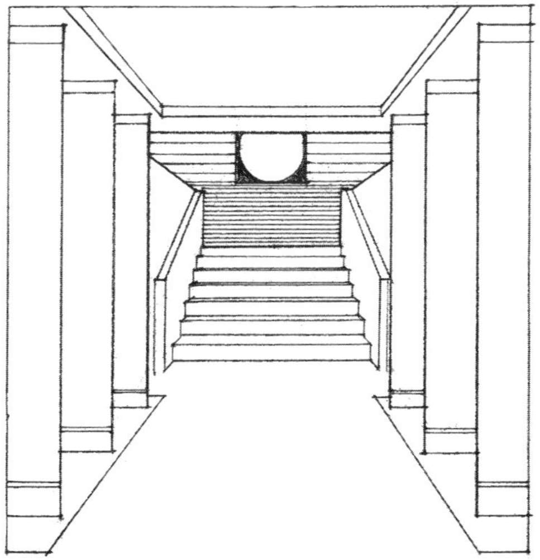

! TERMINATION OF AN AXIS

! SPOTLIGHTED

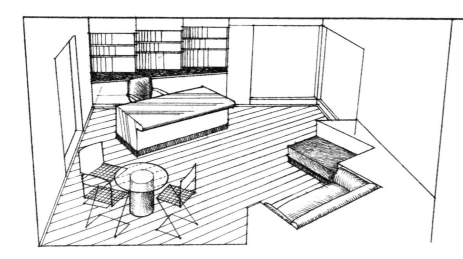

Just as there may be varying degrees of importance among the elements in an interior setting, there can also be varying degrees of emphasis given to them. Once the significant elements or features are established, then a strategy for orchestrating the subordinate elements must be devised to enhance the dominant ones.

A room's focal points should be created with some subtlety and restraint. They should not be so visually dominant that they cease to be integral parts of the overall design. Secondary points of emphasis - visual accents - can often help knit together dominant and subordinate elements. Following the principle of harmony, related shapes, colors, and values can also help retain unity of design.

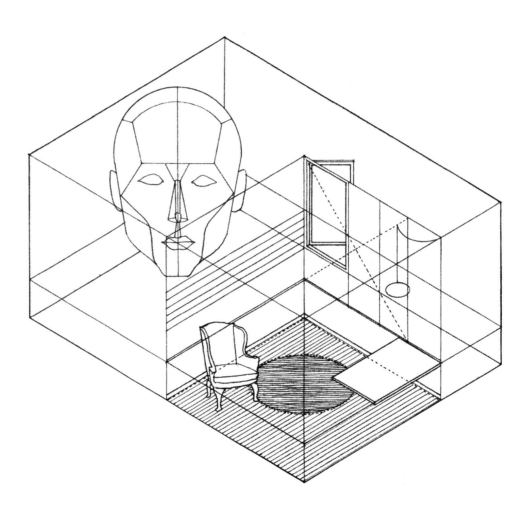

INTERIOR DESIGN
ELEMENTS

INTERIOR DESIGN ELEMENTS

Interior spaces within buildings are defined by the architectural elements of structure and enclosure - columns, walls, floors, and roofs. These elements give a building its form, demarcate a portion of infinite space, and set up a pattern of interior spaces. This chapter outlines the major elements of interior design with which we develop, modify, and enhance these interior spaces and make them habitable - functionally fit, aesthetically pleasing, and psychologically satisfying - for our activities.

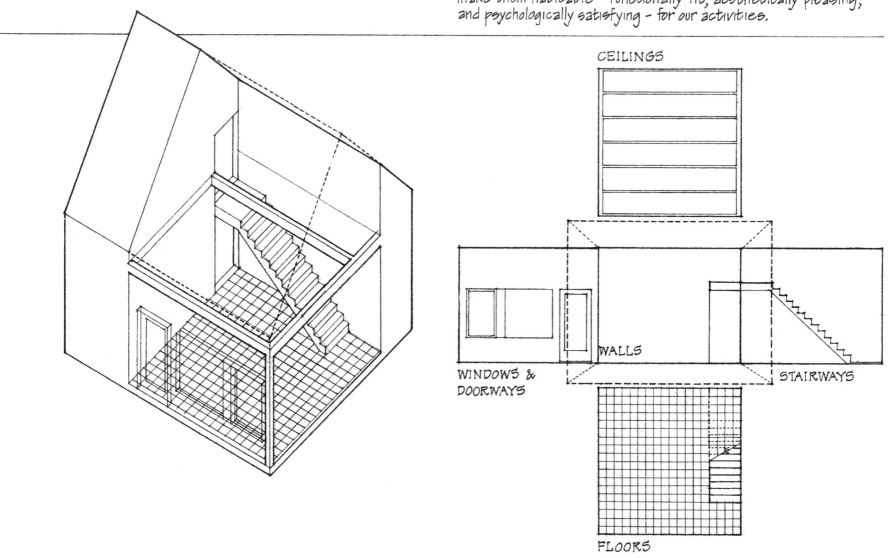

CEILINGS

WINDOWS & DOORWAYS

WALLS

STAIRWAYS

FLOORS

These design elements, and the choices they represent, are the interior designer's palette. The manner in which we select and manipulate these elements into a spatial, visual, sensory pattern will affect not only the function and use of a space but also its expressive qualities of form and style.

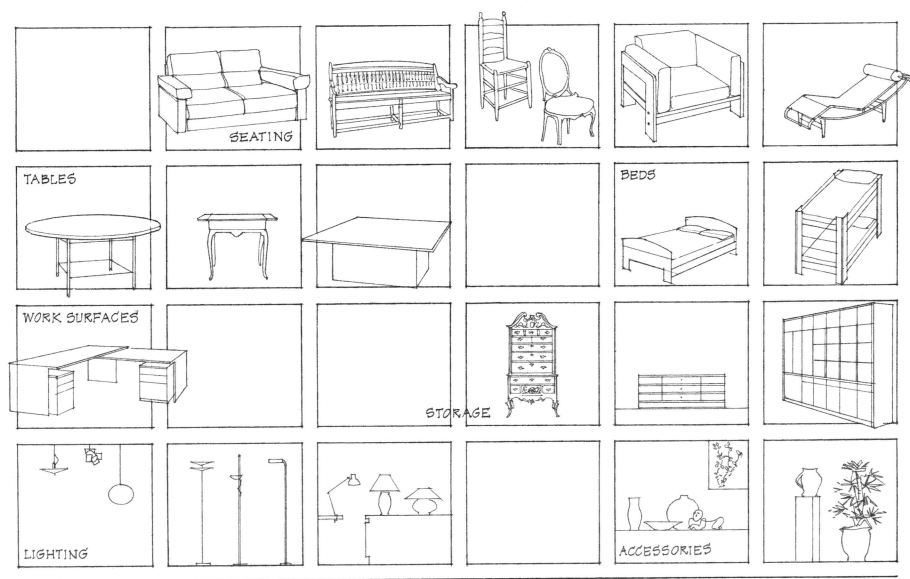

SEATING

TABLES

WORK SURFACES

STORAGE

LIGHTING

BEDS

ACCESSORIES

FLOORS

Floors are the flat, level base planes of interior space. As the platforms that support our interior activities and furnishings, they must be structured to carry these loads safely, and their surfaces must be durable enough to withstand continual use and wear.

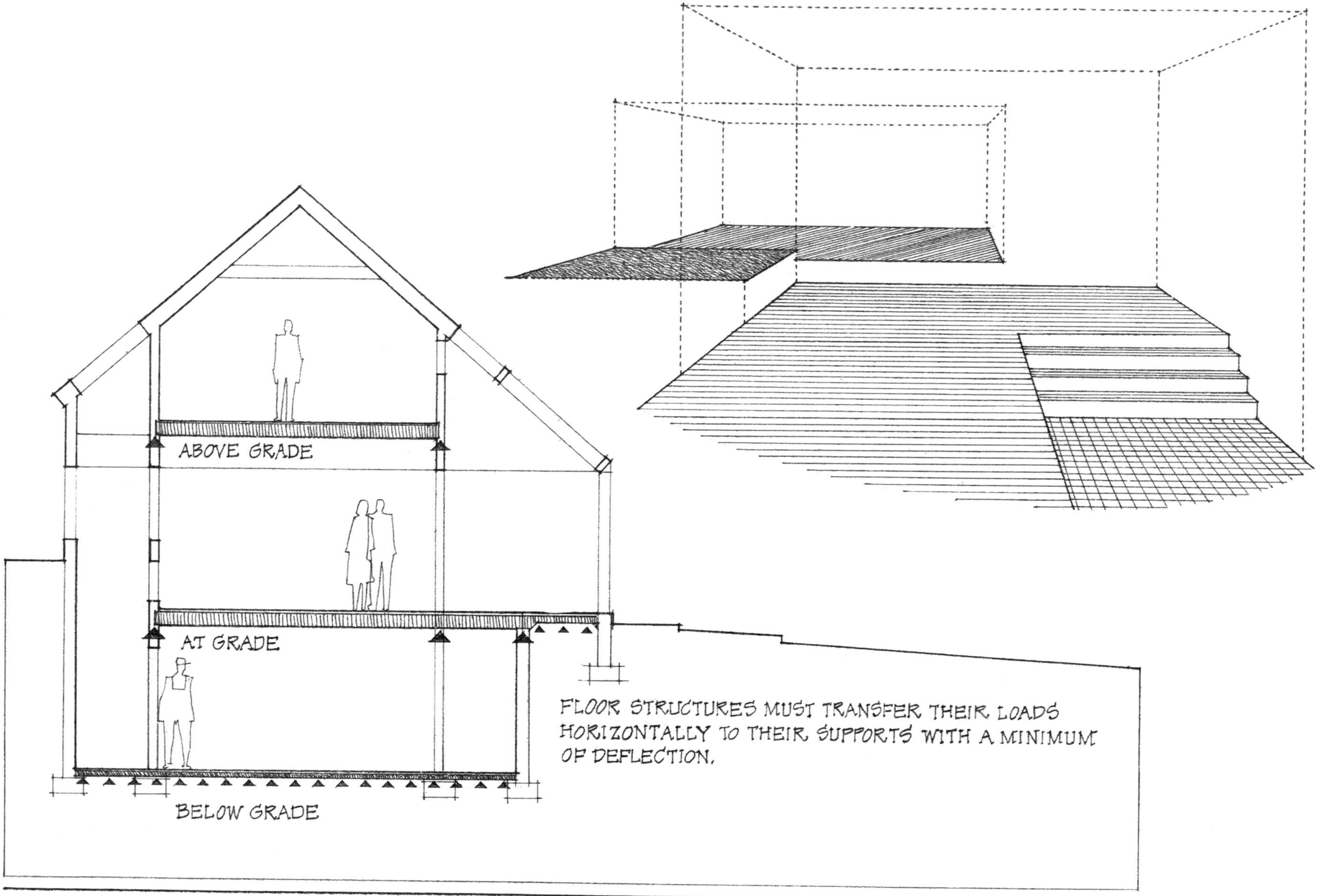

ABOVE GRADE

AT GRADE

BELOW GRADE

FLOOR STRUCTURES MUST TRANSFER THEIR LOADS HORIZONTALLY TO THEIR SUPPORTS WITH A MINIMUM OF DEFLECTION.

A typical floor consists of a series of joists spanning beams or load-bearing walls. This horizontal frame is then layered with a subfloor - a structural material such as plywood or steel decking capable of extending across the joists. The subfloor and joists are secured so that they act together as a structural unit in resisting stresses and transferring loads.

A floor may also consist of a concrete slab, reinforced with steel and capable of extending in one or two directions. The form of a slab's underside often reflects the manner in which it extends across space and transfers its loads. Instead of being cast monolithically in place, a slab can also be precast as planks.

Whether a floor is a concrete slab or framed with joists, its surface must be smooth, level, and dense enough to receive the finish flooring material. To compensate for any roughness or uneveness, a layer of underlayment or a cement topping is required for some flooring materials.

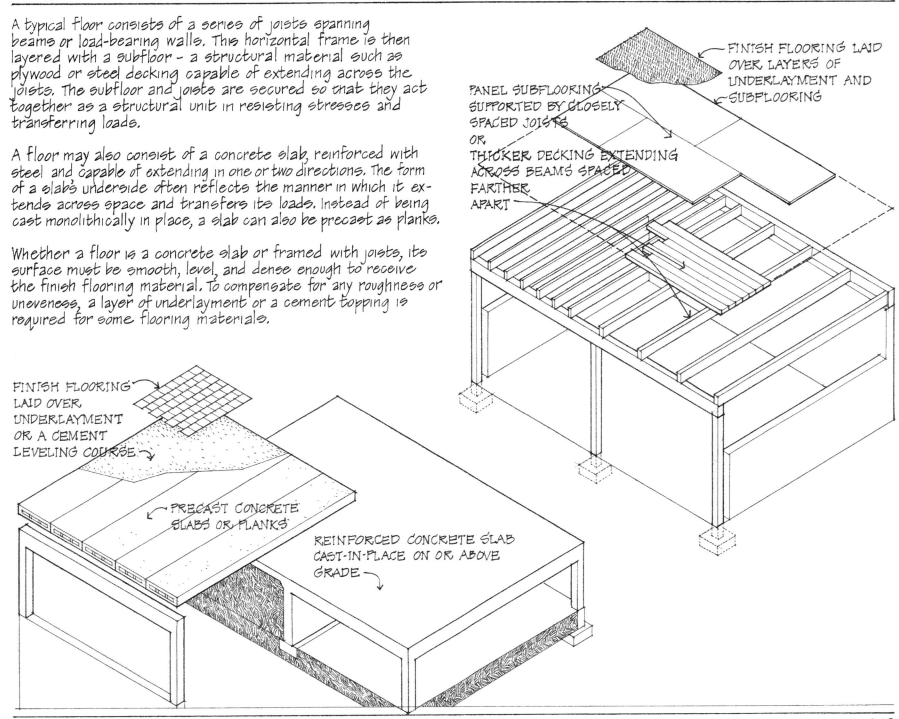

FINISH FLOORING LAID OVER LAYERS OF UNDERLAYMENT AND SUBFLOORING

PANEL SUBFLOORING SUPPORTED BY CLOSELY SPACED JOISTS
OR
THICKER DECKING EXTENDING ACROSS BEAMS SPACED FARTHER APART

FINISH FLOORING LAID OVER UNDERLAYMENT OR A CEMENT LEVELING COURSE

PRECAST CONCRETE SLABS OR PLANKS

REINFORCED CONCRETE SLAB CAST-IN-PLACE ON OR ABOVE GRADE

The finish flooring is the final layer of the floor structure. Since the flooring is subject to direct wear and represents a major portion of a room's surface area, it should be selected with both functional and aesthetic criteria in mind.

Durability is of utmost importance because of the wear and use a flooring material must withstand from our feet as well as the occasional moving of furniture and equipment. The flooring material should be resistant to physical abrasion, denting, and scuffing.

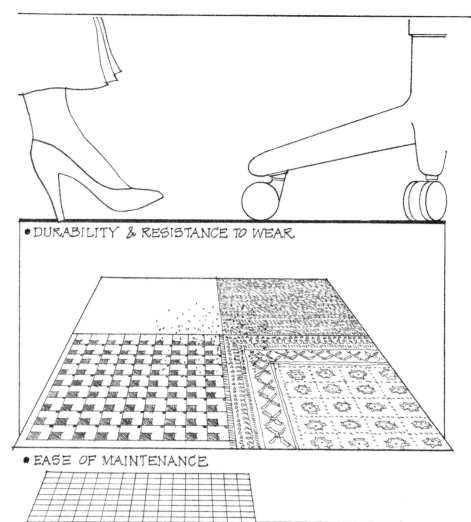

• DURABILITY & RESISTANCE TO WEAR

• EASE OF MAINTENANCE

• COMFORT UNDERFOOT

Directly related to a flooring's durability is the ease with which it can be maintained in good condition. For durability as well as ease of maintenance, a flooring material should be resistant to dirt, moisture, grease, and staining, especially in work and high-traffic areas.

There are several strategies for disguising the dirt that normally collects on a floor. One is to use neutral colors of middle value. Another is to use a pattern that camouflages any dirt and surface marks. Still another is to use a material whose natural color and texture is attractive and more noticeable than any dirt on the floor.

Foot comfort is related to the degree of resilience a flooring material has and, to a lesser degree, its warmth.

The warmth of a floor may be real or apparent. A flooring material may be warmed by radiant heat and kept warm by insulating the floor. The flooring may also appear warm if it has a soft texture, a middle to dark value, or a warm hue. Of course, in warm climates, a cool floor surface would be more comfortable than a warm one.

FINISH FLOORING: FUNCTIONAL CRITERIA

In areas susceptible to wetting, it is advisable to avoid using hard, slick flooring materials.

Hard floor surfaces reflect airborne sound originating from within a room, and amplify impact noise caused by our footwear or the moving of equipment. Resilient flooring can cushion some of this impact noise. Soft, plush, or porous flooring materials reduce impact noise as well as help muffle airborne sound reaching their surfaces.

Light-colored flooring will reflect more of the light falling on its surface and help make a room seem brighter than will dark, textured flooring.

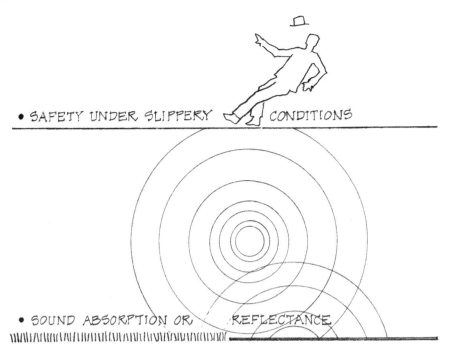

• SAFETY UNDER SLIPPERY CONDITIONS

• SOUND ABSORPTION OR REFLECTANCE

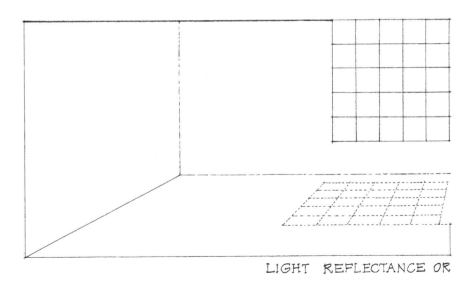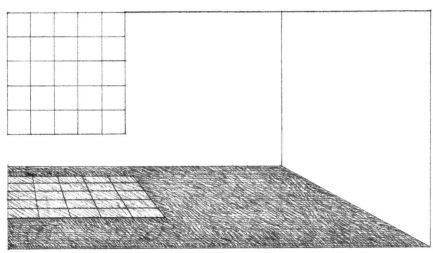

LIGHT REFLECTANCE OR ABSORPTION

Although generally considered to be a utilitarian surface and a visual background for an interior space, the floor can, through its color, pattern, and texture, play an active role in determining the character of a space.

A light-colored floor will enhance the light level within a room, while a dark floor will absorb much of the light falling on its surface. A warm, light color has an elevating effect on a floor, while a warm, dark floor conveys a sense of security. A cool, light color suggests spaciousness and emphasizes the smoothness of polished floors. A cool, dark color gives a floor plane depth and weight.

• COLOR

Unlike the wall and ceiling surfaces of a room, a floor transmits its tactile qualities - its texture and density - directly to us as we walk across its surface.

The physical texture of a flooring material and how the material is laid are directly related to the visual pattern created. It is this visual texture that communicates to us the nature of the flooring material and the character of a space.

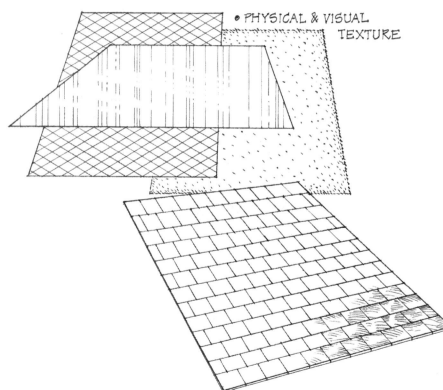

• PHYSICAL & VISUAL
   TEXTURE

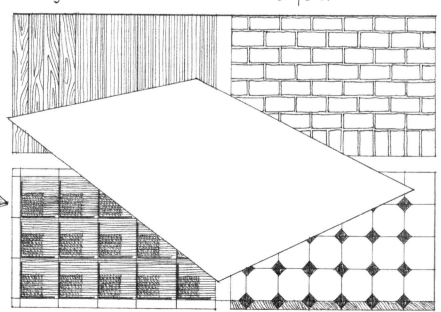

FINISH FLOORING: AESTHETIC CRITERIA

While a neutral, patternless floor can serve as a simple background for a room's occupants and furnishings, a floor can also become, through the use of pattern, a dominant element in an interior space. The pattern can be used to define areas, suggest paths of movement, or simply provide textural interest.

Our perception of a flooring pattern is affected by the laws of perspective. Thus a small-scale pattern may often be seen as a fine texture or a blended tone rather than as a composition of individual design elements.

In addition, any continuous linear elements in a flooring pattern will dominate. Directional patterns can often affect the apparent proportion of a floor, either exaggerating or foreshortening one of its dimensions.

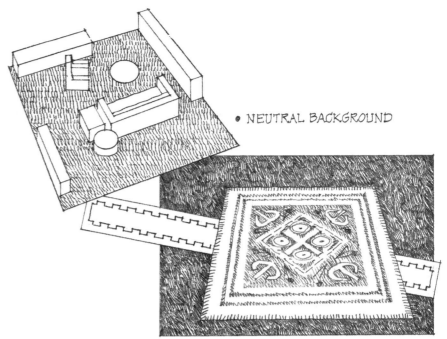

• NEUTRAL BACKGROUND

• ACTIVE DESIGN ELEMENT

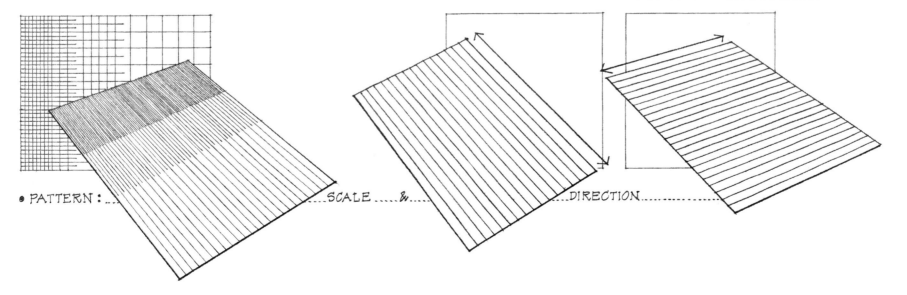

• PATTERN: SCALE & DIRECTION

WOOD FLOORING

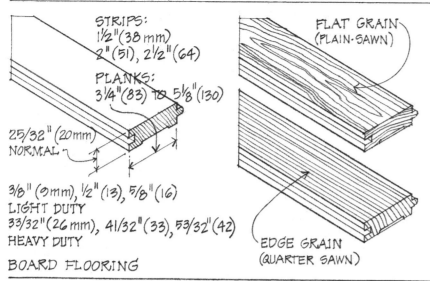

STRIPS:
1½" (38 mm)
2" (51), 2½" (64)

PLANKS:
3¼" (83) TO 5⅛" (130)

25/32" (20mm)
NORMAL

3/8" (9mm), ½" (13), 5/8" (16)
LIGHT DUTY
33/32" (26mm), 41/32" (33), 53/32" (42)
HEAVY DUTY

BOARD FLOORING

FLAT GRAIN
(PLAIN-SAWN)

EDGE GRAIN
(QUARTER SAWN)

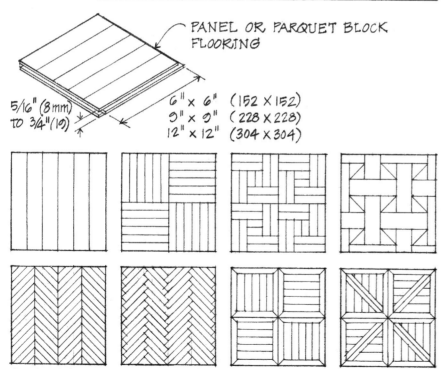

PANEL OR PARQUET BLOCK
FLOORING

5/16" (8mm)
TO 3/4" (19)

6" x 6"   (152 x 152)
9" x 9"   (228 x 228)
12" x 12" (304 x 304)

PANEL OR PARQUET PATTERNS

Wood flooring is admired for its warm, natural appearance and its attractive blend of comfort, resilience, and durability. It is also fairly easy to maintain and, if damaged, can be refinished or replaced.

Durable, close-grained species of hardwoods (white and red oak, maple, birch, beech, and pecan) and softwoods (Southern pine, Douglas fir, Western larch, hemlock, and others) are used for wood flooring. Of these, oak, Southern pine, and Douglas fir are the most common. The best grades are Clear or Select and will minimize or exclude defects, such as knots, streaks, checks, and torn grain.

Wood flooring is available in boards or manufactured blocks and panels. Board flooring is usually in the form of narrow strips, although planks up to 6" (152 mm) wide are also available in the softwoods. Parquet blocks consist of strip flooring factory-assembled into squares with various geometric patterns. Prefinished panels which have the appearance of traditional strip flooring are another type of factory-made flooring.

Wood flooring is most often finished with clear polyurethane, varnish, or a penetrating sealer; the finishes can range from high gloss to satin or a dull sheen. Ideally, the finish should enhance the durability of the wood and its resistance to water, dirt, and staining without concealing the wood's natural beauty. Stains are used to add some color to the natural color of the wood without obscuring the wood grain. Wood flooring can also be painted or even stenciled, but painted surfaces require more maintenance.

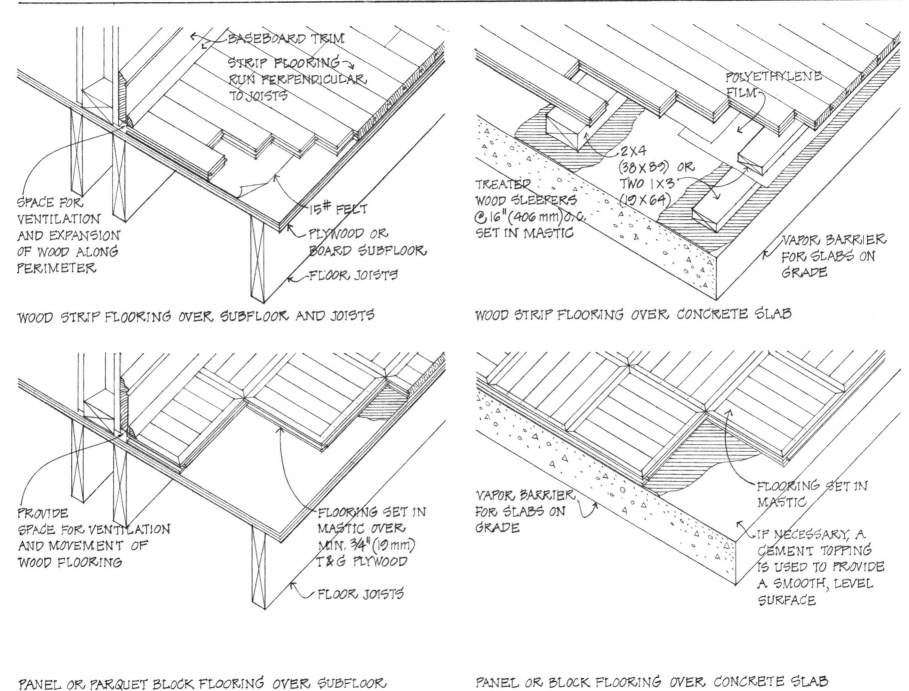

BASEBOARD TRIM

STRIP FLOORING RUN PERPENDICULAR TO JOISTS

SPACE FOR VENTILATION AND EXPANSION OF WOOD ALONG PERIMETER

15# FELT

PLYWOOD OR BOARD SUBFLOOR

FLOOR JOISTS

WOOD STRIP FLOORING OVER SUBFLOOR AND JOISTS

POLYETHYLENE FILM

2X4 (38X89) OR TWO 1X3 (19X64)

TREATED WOOD SLEEPERS @ 16" (406 mm) O.C. SET IN MASTIC

VAPOR BARRIER FOR SLABS ON GRADE

WOOD STRIP FLOORING OVER CONCRETE SLAB

PROVIDE SPACE FOR VENTILATION AND MOVEMENT OF WOOD FLOORING

FLOORING SET IN MASTIC OVER MIN. 3/4" (19 mm) T&G PLYWOOD

FLOOR JOISTS

PANEL OR PARQUET BLOCK FLOORING OVER SUBFLOOR

VAPOR BARRIER FOR SLABS ON GRADE

FLOORING SET IN MASTIC

IF NECESSARY, A CEMENT TOPPING IS USED TO PROVIDE A SMOOTH, LEVEL SURFACE

PANEL OR BLOCK FLOORING OVER CONCRETE SLAB

TILE & STONE FLOORING

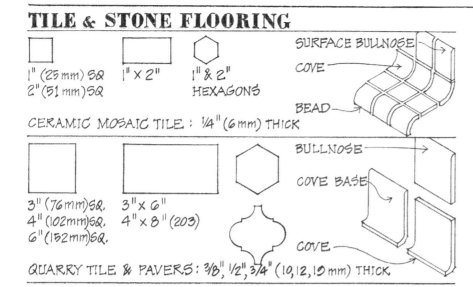

1" (25mm) SQ
2" (51mm) SQ

1" x 2"

1" & 2" HEXAGONS

SURFACE BULLNOSE

COVE

BEAD

CERAMIC MOSAIC TILE : ¼" (6mm) THICK

3" (76mm) SQ.
4" (102mm) SQ.
6" (152mm) SQ.

3" x 6"
4" x 8" (203)

BULLNOSE

COVE BASE

COVE

QUARRY TILE & PAVERS : ⅜", ½", ¾" (10,12,19 mm) THICK.

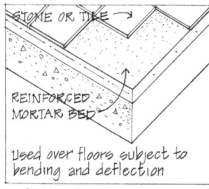

STONE OR TILE

REINFORCED MORTAR BED

Used over floors subject to bending and deflection

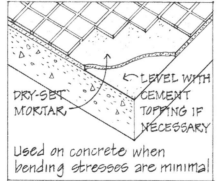

DRY-SET MORTAR

LEVEL WITH CEMENT TOPPING IF NECESSARY

Used on concrete when bending stresses are minimal

INSTALLATION OVER CONCRETE SLABS

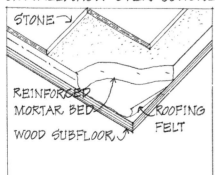

STONE

REINFORCED MORTAR BED

WOOD SUBFLOOR

ROOFING FELT

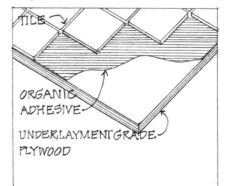

TILE

ORGANIC ADHESIVE

UNDERLAYMENT GRADE PLYWOOD

INSTALLATION OVER WOOD FLOORS

Tile and stone flooring materials are solid and durable. Depending on the shape of the individual pieces and the pattern in which they are laid, these flooring materials can have a cool, formal appearance or convey an informal feeling to a room.

Ceramic tile used for flooring are the mosaics - relatively small, modular units of natural clay or porcelain composition. The natural clay type is unglazed, with muted earth colors; the porcelains can have bright colors and are vitreous (made dense and impervious).

Quarry tiles and pavers are larger modular flooring materials. Quarry tiles are unglazed units of heat-hardened clay; pavers are similar to ceramic mosaic tile. Both are practically impervious to moisture, dirt, and stains.

Stone flooring materials provide a solid, permanent, highly durable floor surface. Colors range from the tans, beiges, and reddish browns of flagstone to the grays and blacks of slate. A random pattern of flagstone conveys an informal feeling. Slate, available in square or irregular shapes, can be formal or informal. Marble lends itself to formal elegance.

Concrete can also be used as a finish flooring surface if smooth and level enough. It should be sealed against stains and grease. It can be painted, stained, or integrally colored when cast. An exposed aggregate finish can provide textural interest. Terrazzo is a special type of exposed aggregate finish with mosaic-like patterns created by the marble chips used.

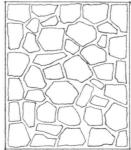

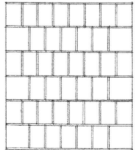

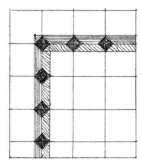

STONE FLOORING PATTERNS

Resilient flooring materials provide an economical, dense, non-absorbent flooring surface with relatively good durability and ease of maintenance. Their degree of resilience enables them to resist permanent indentation while contributing to their quietness and comfort underfoot. The degree of comfort provided will depend not only on the material's resilience, but also on the type of backing used and the hardness of the supporting substrate.

Linoleum and vinyl sheets come in rolls 6 feet (1829 mm) to 15 feet (4572 mm) wide. The other resilient flooring materials are available as tiles, typically 9 inches (228 mm) and 12 inches (304 mm) square. While sheet goods provide a seamless floor, tiles are easier to install if the floor outline is irregular. Individual tiles can also be replaced if damaged.

None of the resilient flooring types is superior in all respects. Listed below are the types which perform well in specific areas.

RESILIENCE & QUIETNESS	Cork tile, rubber tile, cork tile with vinyl coating, vinyl sheet
RESISTANCE TO: INDENTATION	Vinyl tiles and sheets, cork tile with vinyl coating, cork and rubber tiles
STAINING	Vinyl tiles and sheets, vinyl asbestos tile, linoleum
GREASE	Vinyl tiles and sheets, cork tile with vinyl coating, linoleum, vinyl asbestos tile
CIGARETTE BURNS	Cork tile, Rubber tile, cork tile with vinyl coating, vinyl tile
EASE OF MAINTENANCE	Vinyl tiles and sheets, vinyl asbestos tile, cork tile with vinyl coating.

The wood or concrete substrate for resilient flooring should be clean, dry, flat, and smooth since any irregularities in the base material would show through.

RESILIENT FLOORING

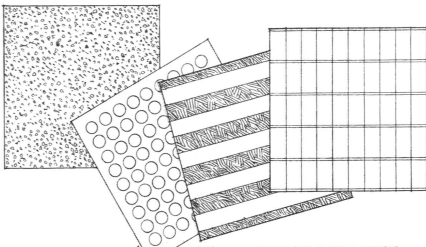

RESILIENT FLOORING PRODUCTS ARE AVAILABLE IN A WIDE RANGE OF COLORS AND PATTERNS.

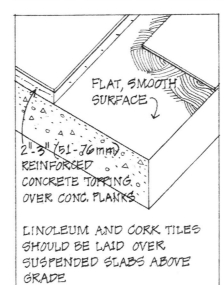

FLAT, SMOOTH SURFACE

2"-3" (51-76 mm) REINFORCED CONCRETE TOPPING OVER CONC. PLANKS

LINOLEUM AND CORK TILES SHOULD BE LAID OVER SUSPENDED SLABS ABOVE GRADE

CONCRETE FLOORS

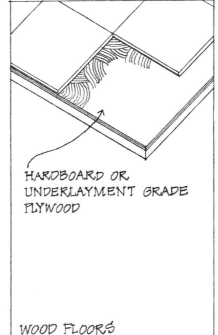

HARDBOARD OR UNDERLAYMENT GRADE PLYWOOD

WOOD FLOORS

INSTALLATION

FLOOR COVERINGS

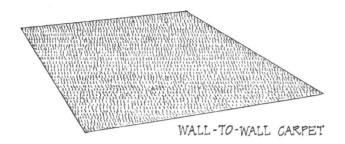

WALL-TO-WALL CARPET

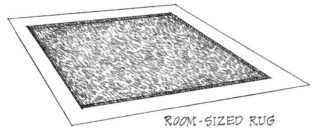

ROOM-SIZED RUG

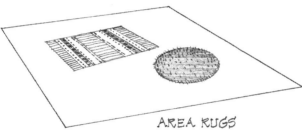

AREA RUGS

FACE YARNS

PRIMARY BACKING (some carpets also have a secondary backing)

Cushion or Pad

Floor coverings - as opposed to flooring materials - refer to carpeting and rugs. These soft coverings provide floors with both visual and textural softness, resilience, and warmth in a wide range of colors and patterns. These qualities, in turn, enable carpeting to absorb sound, reduce impact noise, and provide a comfortable and safe surface to walk on. As a group, carpeting is also fairly easy to maintain.

There are two major categories of soft floor coverings -- carpeting and rugs. Carpeting is manufactured in strips 15 inches to 27 feet wide. It is sold by the square yard, cut to fit, and normally fastened to a floor with tackless strips or adhesive.

Carpeting normally is installed wall-to-wall, covering the entire floor of a room. It can be laid directly over a subfloor and underlayment pad, obviating the need for a finish floor. It can also be laid over an existing floor.

Because carpeting is usually fastened to a floor, it must be cleaned in place and cannot be turned to equalize wear. It is also difficult to move and, if moved, only a portion can be reused.

CARPET FIBERS

WOOL	Excellent resilience and warmth: good soil, flame and solvent resistance; cleanable
ACRYLIC	Approximates wool in appearance; good crush resistance; mildew and moisture resistant
NYLON	Predominant face fiber; excellent wearability; soil and mildew resistant; anti-static properties achieved through the use of conductive filaments
POLYESTER	Combines look of wool with durability of nylon; good soil- and abrasion-resistance; low cost
OLEFIN	(Polypropylene) Good resistance to abrasion, soil, and mildew; used extensively in outdoor carpeting
COTTON	Not as durable as other face fibers, but softness and colorability used to advantage in flat-woven rugs

Each carpet manufacturer offers blends of the generic face fibers which improve on specific characteristics such as durability, soil-resistance, cleanability, color, and luster.

Carpet tiles are modular pieces of carpet which can be laid to resemble a seamless wall-to-wall installation, or can be arranged in subtle or bold patterns. They offer the following advantages:

- They can be easily cut to fit odd-shaped contours with a minimum of waste.
- Individual tiles can be replaced if worn or damaged.
- Carpet tiles can be moved easily and reused.
- In commercial installations, the tiles can be removed for access to underfloor utilities.

Residential carpet tiles are 9 or 12 inches square with a rubber backing and self-stick adhesive. Commercial-grade carpet tiles are 18 inches square with a backing strong enough to prevent shrinkage or expansion of the tile and to protect the carpet edges from unraveling. Some commercial-grade carpet tiles are intended to be glued down, while others are laid loosely with only enough adhesive to prevent the tiles from shifting along the edges of the installation and in high-traffic areas.

CARPET CONSTRUCTION

FACE YARNS
PRIMARY BACKING
LATEX
SECONDARY BACKING

TUFTED

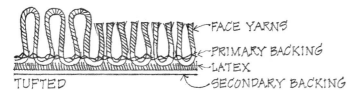

FACE YARNS
INTERWOVEN WARP AND WEFT YARNS

WOVEN

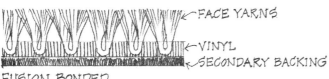

FACE YARNS
VINYL
SECONDARY BACKING

FUSION BONDED

TUFTED CARPET:
The majority of carpet produced today is tufted. Tufting involves stitching face yarns into a backing material with multi-needled machines. The fibers are secured to the pre-woven backing with a heavy latex coating. A secondary backing may be added for greater dimensional stability.

WOVEN CARPET:
Woven carpet is longer wearing and more stable than tufted carpet, but it is slower and more expensive to produce. There is no separate backing since the backing yarns are interwoven with the face yarns. There are three basic weaving techniques: Velvet, Wilton, and Axminster.

FUSION BONDED:
Fusion bonding is a method wherein face yarns are heat-fused to a vinyl backing that is supported by other materials.

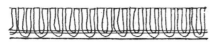

PLUSH
Smooth cut pile; cut yarn ends blend; when dense pile is cut close, called velvet plush.

TWIST OR FRIEZE
Heavier, rougher texture than plush; twist set into yarn.

SAXONY PLUSH
Texture between plush and shag; thicker yarn.

SHAG
Very textured surface created by long, twisted yarns.

LEVEL LOOP
Looped tufts are at the same height; very sturdy; little textural variation.

HI-LO LOOP
Adds another dimension to the loop texture.

RIBBED LOOP
Creates directional, ribbed or corrugated texture.

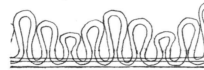

MULTILEVEL LOOP
Capable of producing sculptured patterns.

CUT AND LOOP
Cut and uncut loops alternate in a uniform fashion; adds a degree of softness and warmth to loop texture.

CUT AND LOOP
Texture is mostly loop pile with symmetrical geometric figures created by cut rows.

After color, texture is a carpet's prime visual characteristic. The various carpet textures available are a result of the pile construction, pile height, and the manner in which the carpet is cut. There are three major groups of carpet textures:

- CUT PILE, where every yarn loop is cut, can produce a range of textures from informal shags to short, dense velvets. Cut pile can be produced in tufted, woven, or bonded constructions.

- LOOP PILE is tougher and more easily maintained than cut pile, but is less versatile in color and pattern. Loop pile also lacks the softness of cut pile since light tends to be reflected off the carpet surface. Loop pile can be produced through tufted, woven, and knitted techniques.

- COMBINATION LOOP AND PILE adds a degree of warmth to all-loop pile. It can be produced in tufted and woven constructions.

SOME USEFUL TERMS

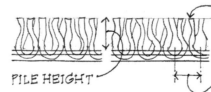

PILE HEIGHT

PITCH refers to the number of ends of yarn in 27" (685 mm) of width of woven carpet

GAUGE refers to the needle spacing across the width of a tufting machine; expressed in fractions of an inch.

FACE WEIGHT is the total weight of face yarns measured in oz./sq.yd.

DENSITY is a measure of the amount of pile fiber by weight in a given area of carpet. Increased density generally results in better performance.

$$\text{DENSITY} = \frac{\text{AVG. PILE WEIGHT } (oz/yd^2)}{\text{AVG. PILE HEIGHT (inches)}}$$

Rugs are single pieces of floor coverings manufactured or cut to standard sizes, often with a finished border. They are not intended to cover the entire floor of a room and are therefore simply laid over another finish flooring material.

Room-sized rugs cover most of a room's floor, leaving a strip of finish flooring exposed along the room's edges. They approximate the appearance of wall-to-wall carpeting but can be moved if desired, removed for cleaning when necessary, and turned for more even distribution of wear.

Area rugs cover a smaller portion of a room's floor, and can be used to define an area, unify a furniture grouping, or delineate a path. Decorative rugs, especially handmade ones, can also serve as a dominant design element and provide a focal point for a room's arrangement.

AFGHANISTAN BOKHARA

CHINESE BENGALI

INDIAN NUMDAH

NAVAJO RUG

WALLS

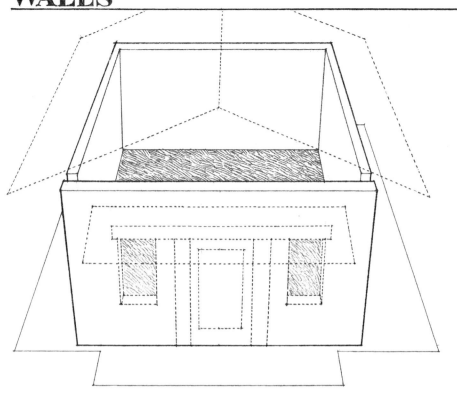

Walls are essential architectural elements of any building. They have traditionally served as structural supports for floors above grade, ceilings, and roofs. They form the facades of buildings. They provide protection and privacy for the interior spaces they create.

As structural elements, walls must be laid out in a pattern that is coordinated with the spans of the floor and roof structures they support. At the same time, this structural pattern will begin to dictate the possible sizes, shapes, and layouts of interior spaces.

When the size and shape requirements of interior spaces and the activities they house do not or would not correspond well with a firm pattern of structural walls, a post-and-beam system can be used. Nonstructural walls and partitions could then be free to define and enclose interior spaces as required. This is often done in commercial, multistory, and other buildings where flexibility in the layout of spaces is desirable.

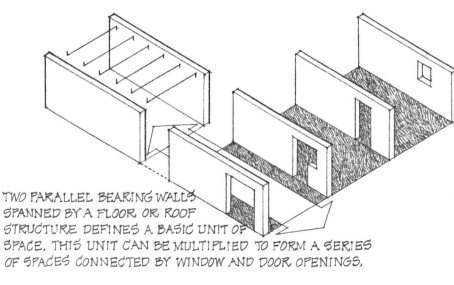

TWO PARALLEL BEARING WALLS SPANNED BY A FLOOR OR ROOF STRUCTURE DEFINES A BASIC UNIT OF SPACE. THIS UNIT CAN BE MULTIPLIED TO FORM A SERIES OF SPACES CONNECTED BY WINDOW AND DOOR OPENINGS.

ROTATING THE DIRECTION OF THE SPAN CAN LEAD TO THE CREATION OF MORE COMPLEX SPATIAL RELATIONSHIPS.

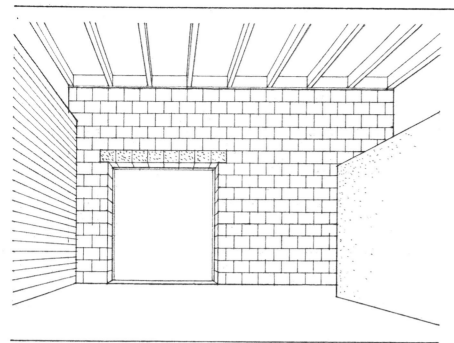

BEARING WALLS DEFINE THE BOUNDARIES OF SPACE.

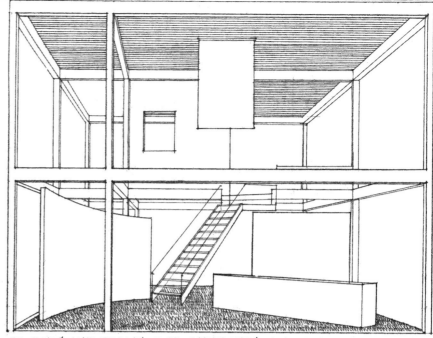

COLUMNS AND BEAMS IMPLY THE EDGES OF INTERIOR SPACE.

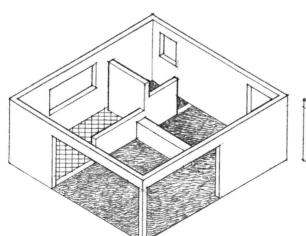

NON-BEARING PARTITIONS SERVE TO SUBDIVIDE LARGE INTERIOR SPACES.

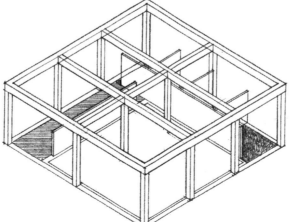

POST-AND-BEAM STRUCTURAL SYSTEMS DEFINE A GRID OF INTERCONNECTED SPACES.

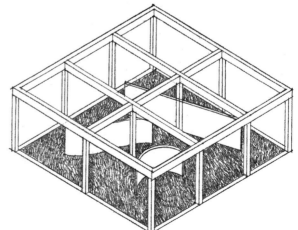

WITHIN THIS GRID, NON-BEARING PARTITIONS CAN DEFINE SPACES AS REQUIRED.

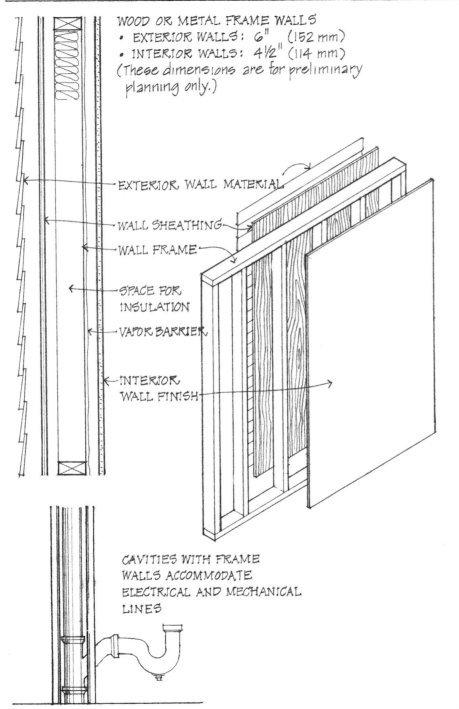

WOOD OR METAL FRAME WALLS
- EXTERIOR WALLS: 6" (152 mm)
- INTERIOR WALLS: 4½" (114 mm)

(These dimensions are for preliminary planning only.)

EXTERIOR WALL MATERIAL

WALL SHEATHING

WALL FRAME

SPACE FOR INSULATION

VAPOR BARRIER

INTERIOR WALL FINISH

CAVITIES WITH FRAME WALLS ACCOMMODATE ELECTRICAL AND MECHANICAL LINES

Most walls are made up of several layers of materials. The wall frame itself usually consists of wood or metal studs tied together by sole and top plates. Onto this frame are laid one or more layers of sheet material, such as plywood or gypsum board, which help to make the wall rigid.

The sheet material may serve as the finish surface on the exterior faces of walls, but more often, it serves as a support for a separate layer of siding, shingles, stucco, or masonry veneer. In either case, the exterior wall surface must be weather-resistant.

Interior wall surfaces do not have to withstand climatic elements and can therefore be selected from a wider range of materials.

To control the passage of heat, moisture, and sound through a wall's thickness, a wall construction can be layered or filled with an insulating material and lined with a vapor barrier.

EXTERIOR WALLS MUST CONTROL PASSAGE OF HEAT, MOISTURE, AND SOUND, AND WITHSTAND:

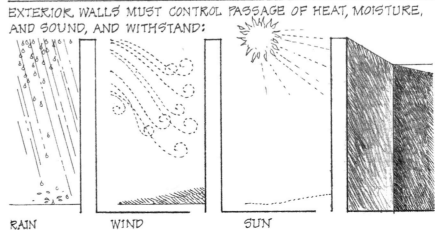

RAIN   WIND   SUN

Walls of concrete, masonry, or stone are usually employed as load-bearing walls in situations that require fire-resistant construction, or where the natural color, texture, and permanence of brick or stone are desired.

Concrete and masonry walls are usually thicker than stud frame walls since they depend on their mass for their strength and stability. While strong in compression, they require cross walls and steel reinforcement to resist bending from lateral forces.

The attractive color and texture of stone and brick are, of course, almost always left exposed as the finish wall surface. Even concrete and concrete masonry walls can now be constructed with attractive colors and textures. If desired, however, a separate finish can be applied over furring.

Concrete and masonry walls are fire-resistant but comparatively poor thermal insulators. Space for insulation and cavities for mechanical, plumbing, or electrical lines must be planned for prior to construction.

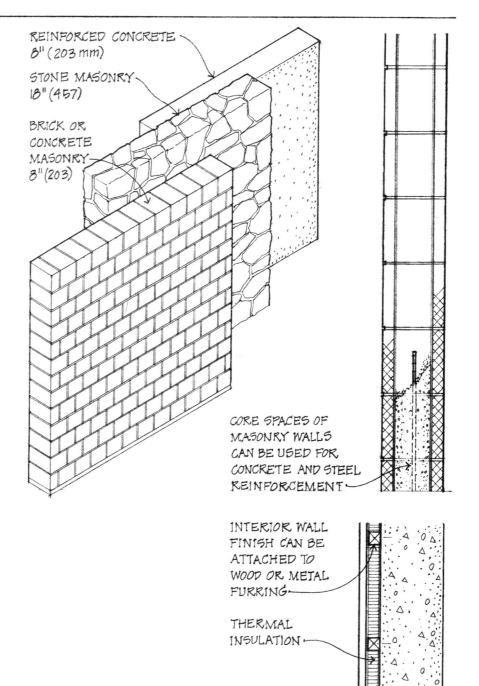

REINFORCED CONCRETE 8" (203 mm)

STONE MASONRY 18" (457)

BRICK OR CONCRETE MASONRY 8" (203)

CORE SPACES OF MASONRY WALLS CAN BE USED FOR CONCRETE AND STEEL REINFORCEMENT

INTERIOR WALL FINISH CAN BE ATTACHED TO WOOD OR METAL FURRING

THERMAL INSULATION

INTERIOR WALLS CONTROL:

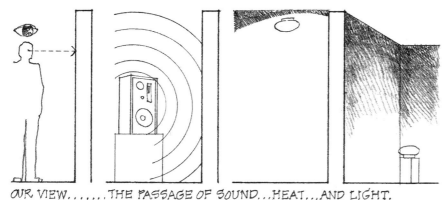

OUR VIEW.......THE PASSAGE OF SOUND...HEAT...AND LIGHT.

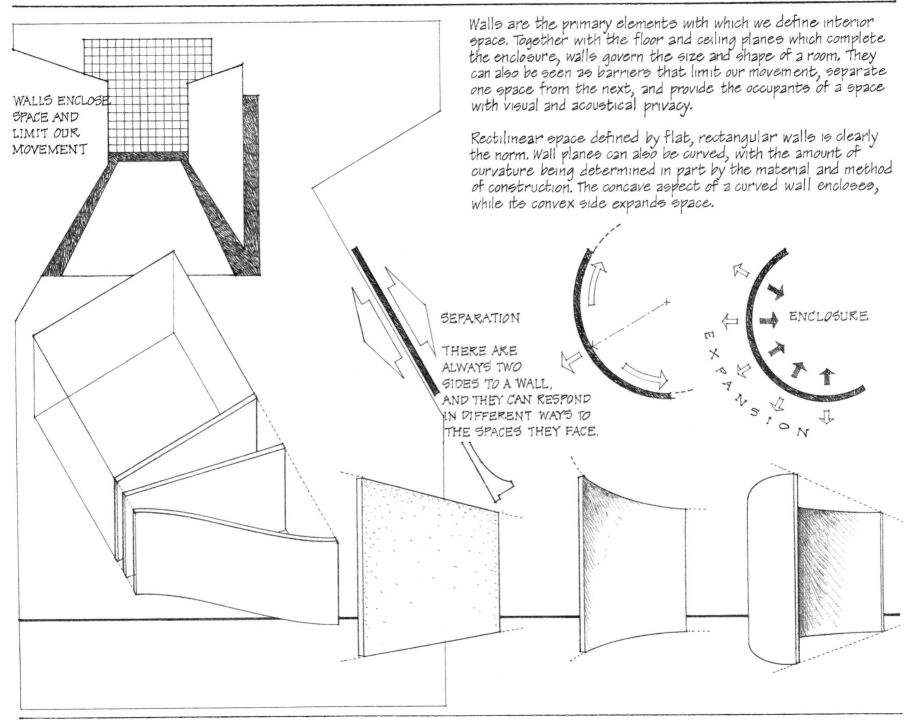

WALLS ENCLOSE
SPACE AND
LIMIT OUR
MOVEMENT

Walls are the primary elements with which we define interior space. Together with the floor and ceiling planes which complete the enclosure, walls govern the size and shape of a room. They can also be seen as barriers that limit our movement, separate one space from the next, and provide the occupants of a space with visual and acoustical privacy.

Rectilinear space defined by flat, rectangular walls is clearly the norm. Wall planes can also be curved, with the amount of curvature being determined in part by the material and method of construction. The concave aspect of a curved wall encloses, while its convex side expands space.

SEPARATION

THERE ARE ALWAYS TWO SIDES TO A WALL, AND THEY CAN RESPOND IN DIFFERENT WAYS TO THE SPACES THEY FACE.

ENCLOSURE

EXPANSION

Openings within or between wall planes allow for continuity and our physical movement between spaces, as well as the passage of light, heat, and sound. As they increase in size, the openings also begin to erode the sense of enclosure the walls provide and visually expand the space to include adjacent spaces. Views seen through the openings become part of the enclosed space. Enlarging the openings further would result ultimately in an implied separation of space defined by a framework of columns and beams.

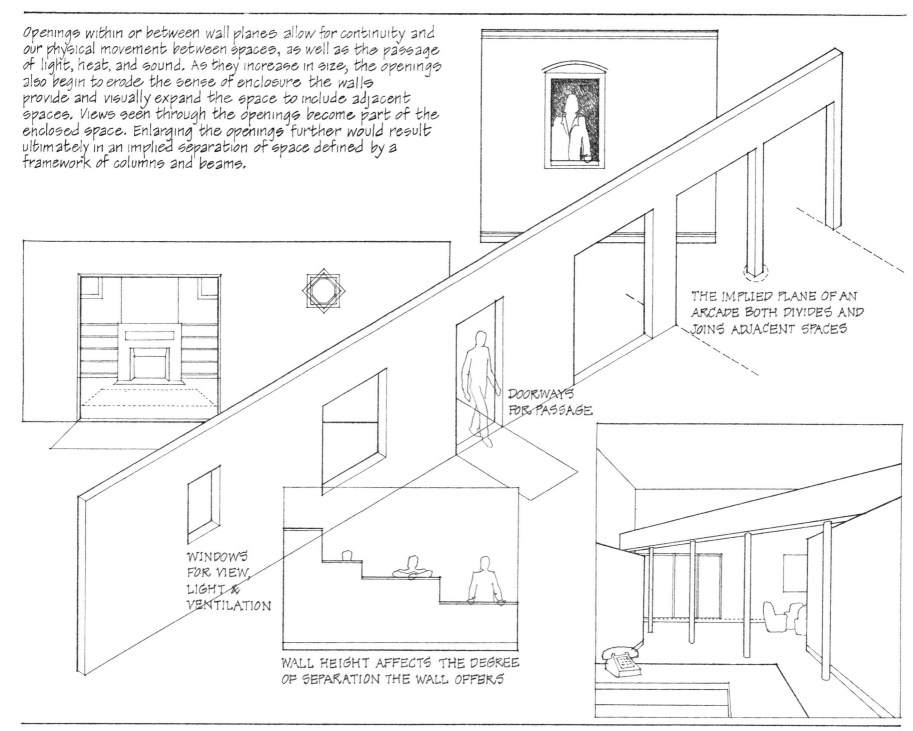

THE IMPLIED PLANE OF AN ARCADE BOTH DIVIDES AND JOINS ADJACENT SPACES

DOORWAYS FOR PASSAGE

WINDOWS FOR VIEW, LIGHT & VENTILATION

WALL HEIGHT AFFECTS THE DEGREE OF SEPARATION THE WALL OFFERS

181

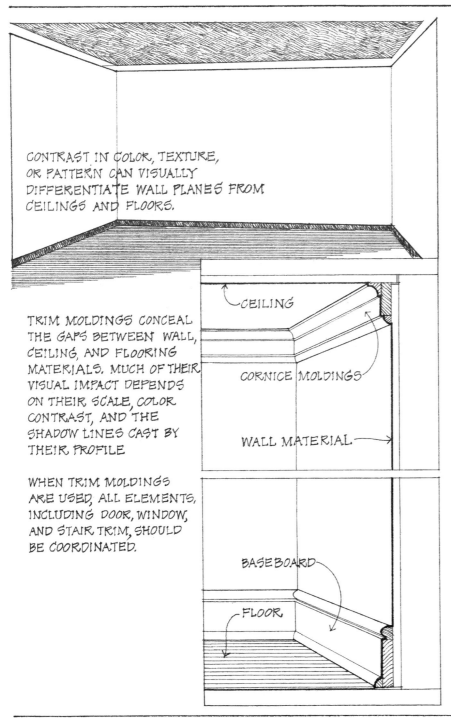

CONTRAST IN COLOR, TEXTURE, OR PATTERN CAN VISUALLY DIFFERENTIATE WALL PLANES FROM CEILINGS AND FLOORS.

TRIM MOLDINGS CONCEAL THE GAPS BETWEEN WALL, CEILING, AND FLOORING MATERIALS. MUCH OF THEIR VISUAL IMPACT DEPENDS ON THEIR SCALE, COLOR CONTRAST, AND THE SHADOW LINES CAST BY THEIR PROFILE

WHEN TRIM MOLDINGS ARE USED, ALL ELEMENTS, INCLUDING DOOR, WINDOW, AND STAIR TRIM, SHOULD BE COORDINATED.

CEILING

CORNICE MOLDINGS

WALL MATERIAL

BASEBOARD

FLOOR

A wall can be visually differentiated from either the adjoining wall or ceiling plane by a change of color, texture, or material. The distinction can be made clearer with either trimwork or a reveal.

Trimwork, such as base and crown moldings, serve to conceal the unfinished construction joints and gaps between materials and to embellish architectural surfaces. They can be simple or complex, depending on their scale, profile, and finish.

A reveal is a continuous recess that visually separates the meeting of two planes and articulates their edges. When two planes meet in this manner, their surfaces must have finished or trimmed edges when exposed to our view.

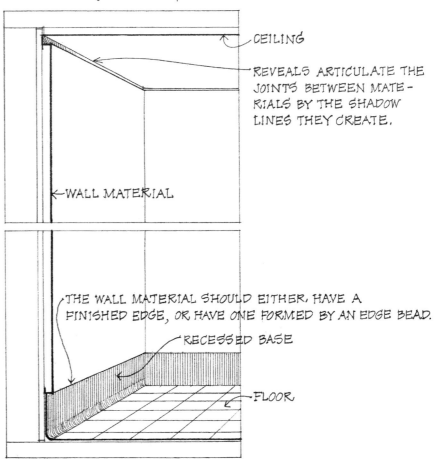

CEILING

REVEALS ARTICULATE THE JOINTS BETWEEN MATERIALS BY THE SHADOW LINES THEY CREATE.

WALL MATERIAL

THE WALL MATERIAL SHOULD EITHER HAVE A FINISHED EDGE, OR HAVE ONE FORMED BY AN EDGE BEAD.

RECESSED BASE

FLOOR

A wall surface material can be a continuation of the floor or ceiling treatment. Continuing the floor treatment up the lower portion of a wall can visually enlarge the floor area while reducing the apparent wall height. Continuing the ceiling treatment down a portion of a wall can similarly reduce the vertical scale of the wall.

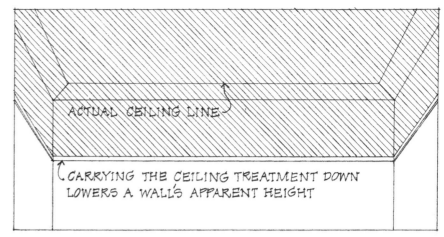

ACTUAL CEILING LINE

CARRYING THE CEILING TREATMENT DOWN LOWERS A WALL'S APPARENT HEIGHT

WALL AND CEILING SURFACES TYPICALLY ARE FINISHED IN A SIMILAR MANNER. FOR A SMOOTHER TRANSITION A COVE CAN BE USED.

DADO CAP

A DADO OR WAINSCOT REFERS TO THE LOWER PORTION OF A WALL THAT IS FINISHED DIFFERENTLY FROM THE UPPER SECTION. A DADO CAP MAY BE NECESSARY TO MAKE THE TRANSITION BETWEEN THE TWO WALL MATERIALS.

CARRYING FLOORING SUCH AS CARPET UP WALL VISUALLY ENLARGES FLOOR AREA.

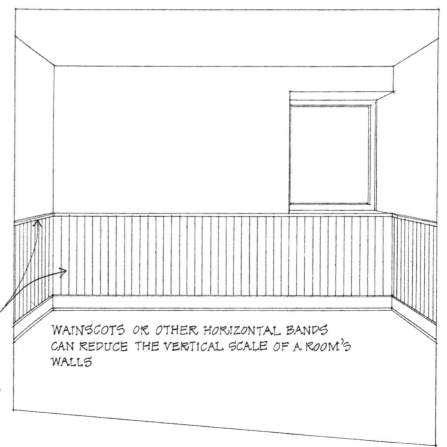

WAINSCOTS OR OTHER HORIZONTAL BANDS CAN REDUCE THE VERTICAL SCALE OF A ROOM'S WALLS

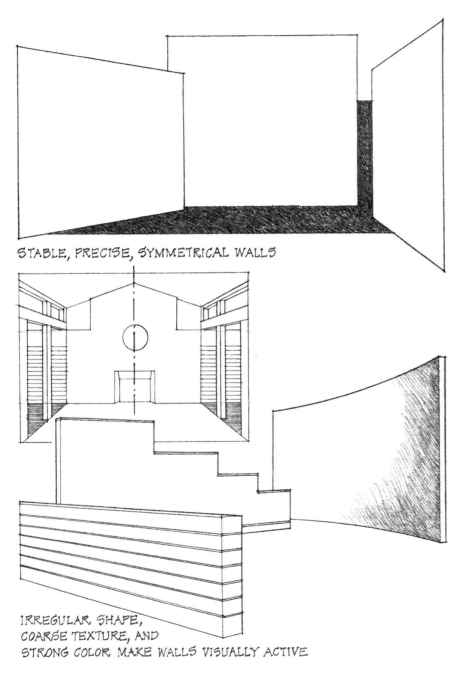

STABLE, PRECISE, SYMMETRICAL WALLS

IRREGULAR SHAPE,
COARSE TEXTURE, AND
STRONG COLOR MAKE WALLS VISUALLY ACTIVE

The vertical orientation of walls makes them visually active in our field of vision. In defining the boundaries of a room, they give form and shape to the space and play a major role in determining its character.

Stable, precise, symmetrical walls convey a feeling of formality, one which can be considerably enhanced with the use of smooth textures. Irregularly shaped walls, on the other hand, are more dynamic. When combined with a rough texture, they can impart an informal character to a space.

Walls provide a background for a room's furnishings and occupants. If smooth and neutral in color, they serve as passive backdrops for foreground elements. When irregular in shape, or given texture, pattern, or a vigorous color, the walls become more active and compete for our attention.

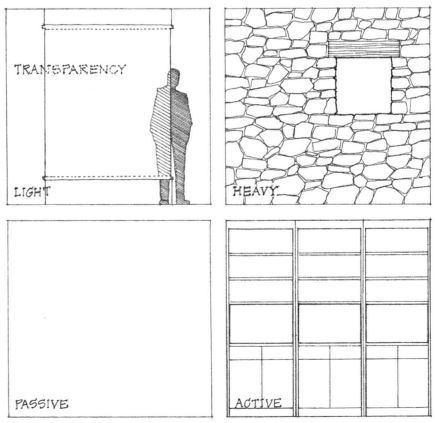

TRANSPARENCY

LIGHT

HEAVY

PASSIVE

ACTIVE

Light-colored walls reflect light effectively and serve as efficient backdrops for elements placed in front of them. Light, warm colors on a wall exude warmth, while light, cool colors increase a room's spaciousness.

Dark-colored walls absorb light, make a room more difficult to illuminate, and convey an enclosed, intimate feeling.

A wall's texture also affects how much light it will reflect or absorb. Smooth walls reflect more light than textured ones, which tend to diffuse the light striking their surfaces. In a similar manner, smooth, hard wall surfaces will reflect more sound back into a space than porous or soft-textured walls.

COLOR, PATTERN, AND TEXTURE CAN BE USED TO DIFFERENTIATE ONE WALL PLANE FROM THE NEXT AND TO ARTICULATE THE FORM OF THE SPACE.

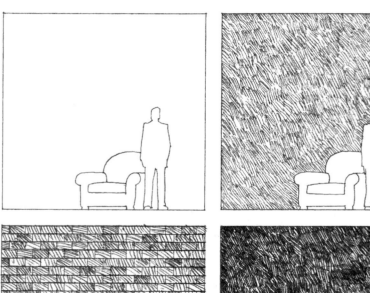

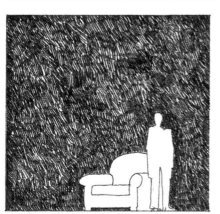

AS WITH COLOR, THE JUXTAPOSITION OF CONTRASTING TEXTURES ENHANCES BOTH THE COARSE AND THE SMOOTH.

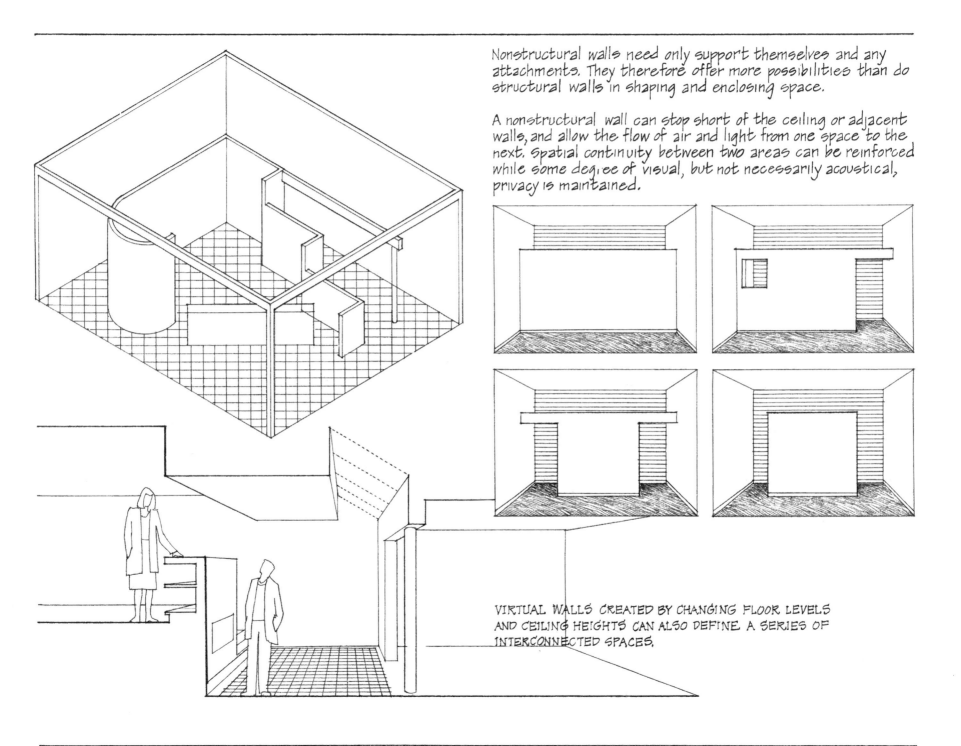

Nonstructural walls need only support themselves and any attachments. They therefore offer more possibilities than do structural walls in shaping and enclosing space.

A nonstructural wall can stop short of the ceiling or adjacent walls, and allow the flow of air and light from one space to the next. Spatial continuity between two areas can be reinforced while some degree of visual, but not necessarily acoustical, privacy is maintained.

VIRTUAL WALLS CREATED BY CHANGING FLOOR LEVELS AND CEILING HEIGHTS CAN ALSO DEFINE A SERIES OF INTERCONNECTED SPACES.

Instead of being strictly a background element in interior space, a wall can also be structured to support furnishing elements, such as seating, shelving, tabletops, and lighting. A wall can also incorporate these elements into its thickness and become itself a piece of furniture.

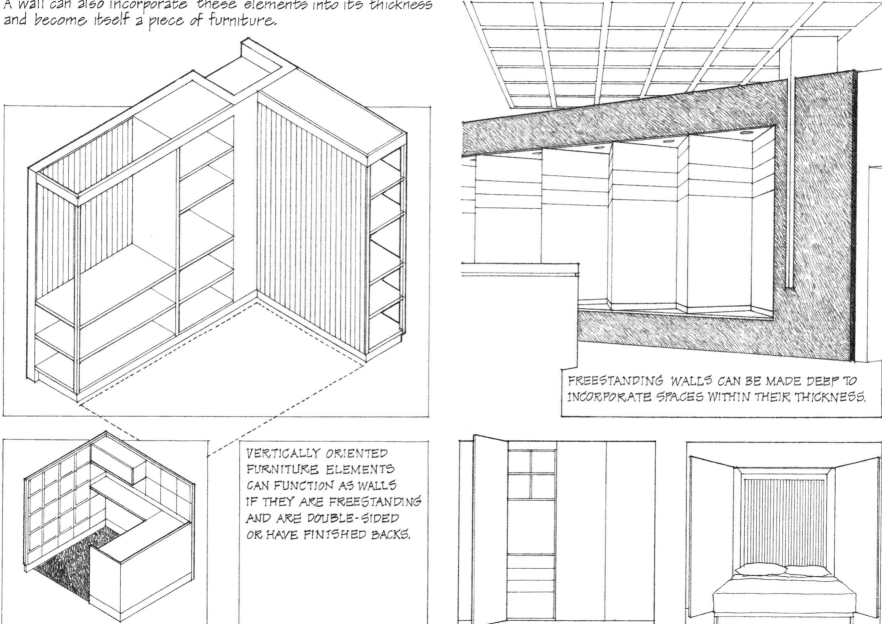

FREESTANDING WALLS CAN BE MADE DEEP TO INCORPORATE SPACES WITHIN THEIR THICKNESS.

VERTICALLY ORIENTED FURNITURE ELEMENTS CAN FUNCTION AS WALLS IF THEY ARE FREESTANDING AND ARE DOUBLE-SIDED OR HAVE FINISHED BACKS.

WALL FINISHES

Some wall finishes are an integral part of a wall's material structure, while others are separate layers attached to a wall frame. Still others are thin coatings or coverings which are applied over a wall surface. In addition to aesthetic factors such as color, texture, and pattern, functional considerations in selecting a wall material and finish include the following.

- If it is an applied material, what type of support or base is required?
- If the wall exists, what type of finish, coating, or covering can it accept?
- How durable must the material or finish be, and how easy is it to maintain?
- What degree of sound absorption, light reflectance, and fire resistance is required?
- How much does it cost to purchase and to install or apply?

The following is an outline of major types of wall materials and finishes, and their general characteristics.

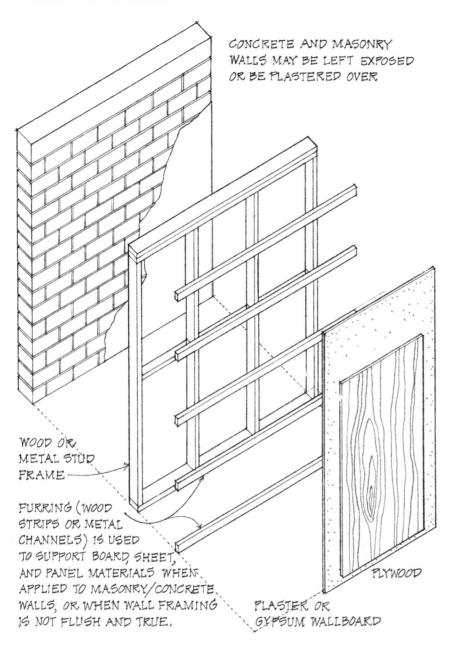

CONCRETE AND MASONRY WALLS MAY BE LEFT EXPOSED OR BE PLASTERED OVER

WOOD OR METAL STUD FRAME

FURRING (WOOD STRIPS OR METAL CHANNELS) IS USED TO SUPPORT BOARD, SHEET, AND PANEL MATERIALS WHEN APPLIED TO MASONRY/CONCRETE WALLS, OR WHEN WALL FRAMING IS NOT FLUSH AND TRUE.

PLASTER OR GYPSUM WALLBOARD

PLYWOOD

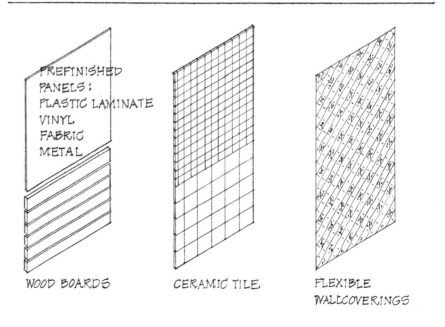

PREFINISHED PANELS:
PLASTIC LAMINATE
VINYL
FABRIC
METAL

WOOD BOARDS

CERAMIC TILE

FLEXIBLE WALLCOVERINGS

BASIC TYPES OF WALL MATERIALS

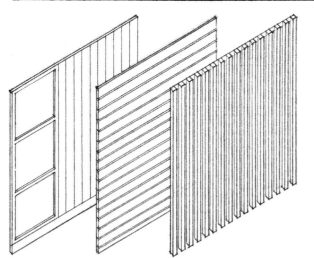

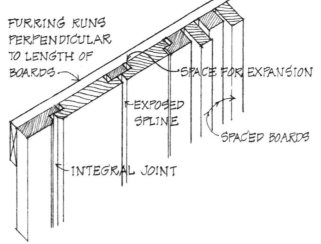

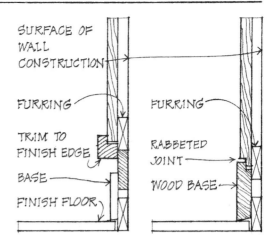

WALL PATTERN AND TEXTURE DEPEND ON BOARD WIDTH, ORIENTATION, SPACING, AND JOINT DETAIL.

FURRING RUNS PERPENDICULAR TO LENGTH OF BOARDS

SPACE FOR EXPANSION

EXPOSED SPLINE

SPACED BOARDS

INTEGRAL JOINT

EXAMPLES OF JOINTS: SPACE SHOULD BE PROVIDED FOR EXPANSION OF WOOD.

SURFACE OF WALL CONSTRUCTION

FURRING

FURRING

TRIM TO FINISH EDGE

RABBETED JOINT

BASE

WOOD BASE

FINISH FLOOR

EXAMPLES OF BASE DETAILS: DETAIL @ CEILING CAN BE TREATED IN A SIMILAR MANNER.

WOOD

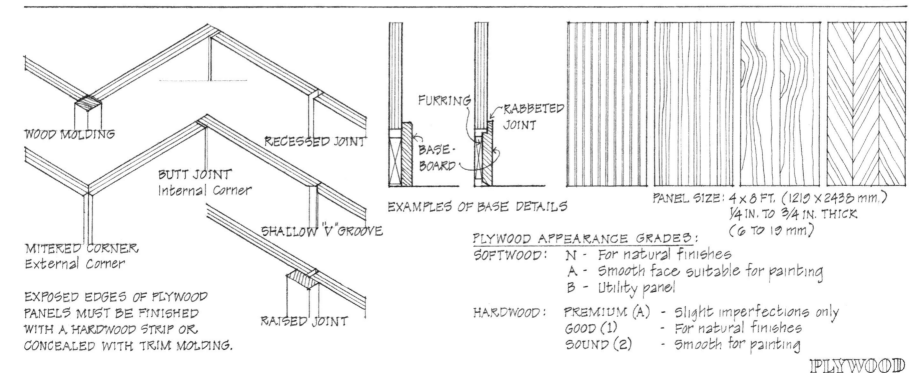

WOOD MOLDING

RECESSED JOINT

BUTT JOINT Internal Corner

MITERED CORNER External Corner

SHALLOW "V" GROOVE

EXPOSED EDGES OF PLYWOOD PANELS MUST BE FINISHED WITH A HARDWOOD STRIP OR CONCEALED WITH TRIM MOLDING.

RAISED JOINT

FURRING

RABBETED JOINT

BASE-BOARD

EXAMPLES OF BASE DETAILS

PANEL SIZE: 4 x 8 FT. (1219 x 2438 mm.) 1/4 IN. TO 3/4 IN. THICK (6 TO 19 mm)

PLYWOOD APPEARANCE GRADES:
SOFTWOOD: N - For natural finishes
A - Smooth face suitable for painting
B - Utility panel

HARDWOOD: PREMIUM (A) - Slight imperfections only
GOOD (1) - For natural finishes
SOUND (2) - Smooth for painting

PLYWOOD

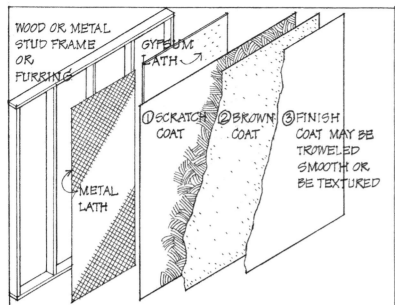

WOOD OR METAL STUD FRAME OR FURRING

GYPSUM LATH

METAL LATH

① SCRATCH COAT ② BROWN COAT ③ FINISH COAT MAY BE TROWELED SMOOTH OR BE TEXTURED

PLASTER IS A MIXTURE OF GYPSUM CEMENT, LIME, SAND, AND WATER WHICH IS APPLIED IN 2 OR 3 COATS OVER METAL OR GYPSUM LATH. TOTAL THICKNESS = ½" TO ¾" (12 TO 19 mm)

PLASTER

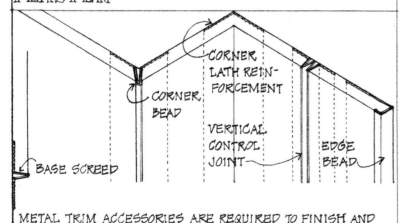

CORNER LATH REIN-FORCEMENT

CORNER BEAD

VERTICAL CONTROL JOINT

EDGE BEAD

BASE SCREED

METAL TRIM ACCESSORIES ARE REQUIRED TO FINISH AND PROTECT THE EDGES AND CORNERS OF PLASTER SURFACES.

¼" TO ⅝" THICK (6 TO 16 mm)

8' TYP. (2438 mm) LONGER LENGTHS AVAILABLE

4' TYP. (1219 mm)

GYPSUM BOARD MAY BE INSTALLED OVER WOOD OR METAL FRAMING OR FURRING

GYPSUM BOARD

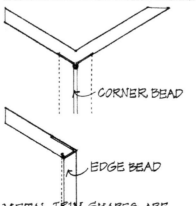

CORNER BEAD

EDGE BEAD

METAL TRIM SHAPES ARE ALSO REQUIRED TO FINISH AND PROTECT THE EDGES AND CORNERS OF GYPSUM BOARD SURFACES.

GYPSUM BOARD CONSISTS OF A GYPSUM CORE SURFACED WITH PAPER OR OTHER COVER MATERIAL. IT MAY BE FINISHED BY PAINTING OR BY THE APPLICATION OF CERAMIC TILE OR A FLEXIBLE WALL COVERING.

MAJOR TYPES OF GYPSUM BOARD:
REGULAR — FOR INTERIOR WALLS AND CEILINGS
MOISTURE-RESISTANT — BACKING FOR CERAMIC TILE IN HIGH-MOISTURE CONDITIONS
FIRE-RESISTANT (TYPE-X) — FOR USE IN FIRE-RESISTANT CONSTRUCTION

PRE-FINISHED PANELS ARE ALSO AVAILABLE IN A VARIETY OF COLORS, TEXTURES, AND PATTERNS.

GYPSUM BOARD MAY BE BENT, DEPENDING ON ITS THICKNESS.

¼" (6) THK. . 5 FT. (1524) RADIUS
⅜" (10) . . . . . 7 FT. (2134)
½" (12) . . . . . 20 FT. (6006)

FOR IMPROVED ACOUSTICAL ISOLATION AND GREATER FIRE RESISTANCE, 2-PLY GYPSUM BOARD CONSTRUCTION CAN BE USED.

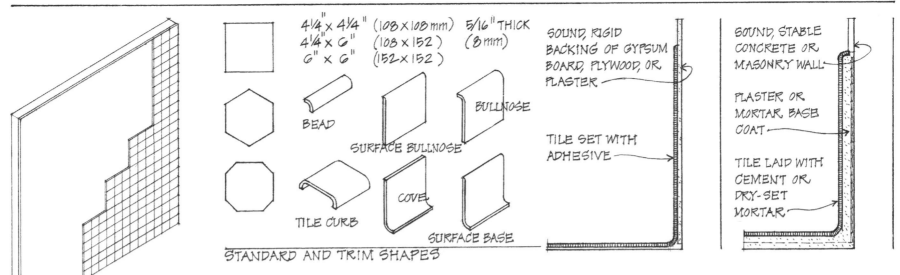

4¼" x 4¼" (108 x 108 mm)   5/16" THICK
4¼" x 6"   (108 x 152)   (8 mm)
6" x 6"   (152 x 152)

BEAD

SURFACE BULLNOSE

BULLNOSE

COVE

TILE CURB

SURFACE BASE

STANDARD AND TRIM SHAPES

SOUND, RIGID BACKING OF GYPSUM BOARD, PLYWOOD, OR PLASTER

TILE SET WITH ADHESIVE

SOUND, STABLE CONCRETE OR MASONRY WALL

PLASTER OR MORTAR BASE COAT

TILE LAID WITH CEMENT OR DRY-SET MORTAR

CERAMIC TILES ARE MODULAR SURFACING UNITS OF FIRED CLAY AND OTHER CERAMIC MATERIALS. THEY PROVIDE A PERMANENT, DURABLE, WATERPROOF SURFACE FOR INTERIOR WALLS. THEY ARE AVAILABLE IN BRIGHT OR MATTE GLAZES IN A WIDE RANGE OF COLORS AND SURFACE DESIGNS. CONSULT MANUFACTURER FOR DETAILS.

CERAMIC TILE MAY BE APPLIED:
① TO MOISTURE-RESISTANT GYPSUM BOARD, PLYWOOD, OR PLASTER, WITH A WATERPROOF ADHESIVE;
② OVER FRAME CONSTRUCTION, SET WITH CEMENT MORTAR OVER METAL OR GYPSUM LATH.

CERAMIC TILE

IN ADDITION TO BEING PAINTED, SMOOTH PLASTER AND GYPSUM BOARD SURFACES CAN BE FINISHED WITH A VARIETY OF FLEXIBLE WALL COVERINGS
• WALLPAPER
• CLOTH OR PAPER BACKED VINYL
• FABRIC (WOOL, LINEN, COTTON)
• GRASS CLOTH
• BURLAP
• CORK

THESE WALL COVERINGS ARE AVAILABLE IN AN ALMOST INFINITE RANGE OF COLORS, PATTERNS, AND DESIGNS. CONSULT MANUFACTURER FOR SAMPLES, ROLL WIDTHS AND LENGTHS, AND TYPE OF ADHESIVE REQUIRED FOR APPLICATION.

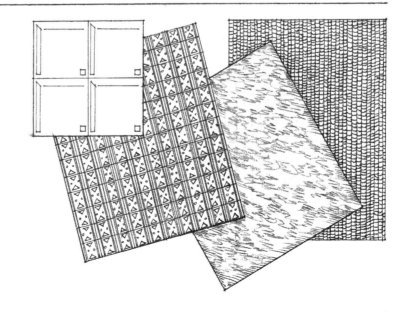

WALL COVERINGS

CEILINGS

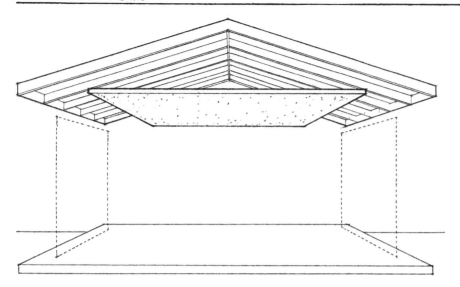

The third major architectural element of interior space is the ceiling. Although out of our reach and not used in the sense that floors and walls are, the ceiling plays an important visual role in shaping interior space and limiting its vertical dimension. It is the sheltering element of interior design, offering both physical and psychological protection for those beneath its canopy.

Ceilings are formed by the undersides of floor and roof structures. The ceiling material can be attached directly to the structural frame or be suspended from it. In some cases, the overhead structure can be left exposed and serve as the ceiling.

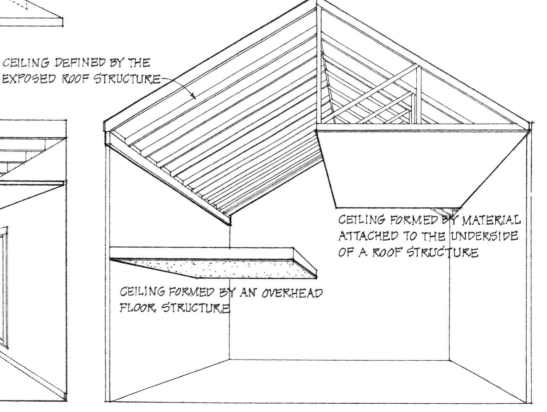

CEILING DEFINED BY THE EXPOSED ROOF STRUCTURE

CEILING FORMED BY MATERIAL ATTACHED TO THE UNDERSIDE OF A ROOF STRUCTURE

CEILING FORMED BY AN OVERHEAD FLOOR STRUCTURE

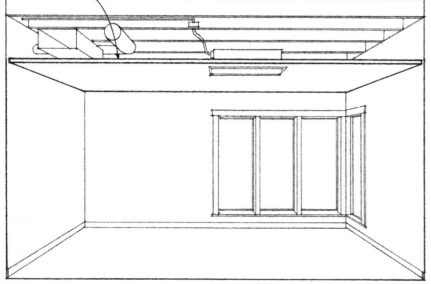

CEILING SUSPENDED FROM A ROOF OR FLOOR STRUCTURE

CEILING FORMATIONS

The height of a ceiling has a major impact on the scale of a space. While a ceiling's height should be considered relative to a room's other dimensions, and to its occupancy and use, some generalizations can still be made about the vertical dimension of space.

High ceilings tend to give space an open, airy, lofty feeling. They can also provide an air of dignity or formality, especially when regular in shape and form. Instead of merely hovering over a space, they can soar.

Low ceilings, on the other hand, emphasize their sheltering quality and tend to create intimate, cozy spaces.

Changing the ceiling height within a space, or from one space to the next, helps to define spatial boundaries and to differentiate between adjacent areas. Each ceiling height emphasizes, by contrast, the lowness or height of the other.

THE "NORMAL" HEIGHT OF A CEILING SHOULD BE IN PROPORTION TO A ROOM'S HORIZONTAL DIMENSIONS AND ITS USE.

HIGH CEILINGS CAN, BY COMPARISON, DIMINISH THE APPARENT WIDTH OF A SPACE.

CEILING HEIGHT AND SCALE

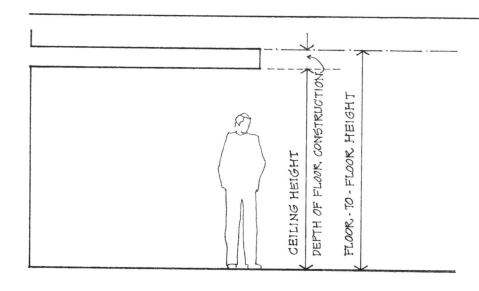

When a flat ceiling is formed by a floor above, its height is fixed by the floor-to-floor height and the depth of the floor construction. Given this dimension, the apparent height of a ceiling can be altered in several ways.

Since light values appear to recede, smooth, light-colored ceilings that reflect light convey a feeling of spaciousness. Carrying the wall material or finish onto the ceiling plane can also make a ceiling appear higher than it is, especially when a cove is used to make the transition between wall and ceiling.

The apparent height of a ceiling can be lowered by using a dark, bright color that contrasts with the wall color, or by carrying the ceiling material or finish down onto the walls.

SMOOTH, LIGHT, COOL-COLORED CEILINGS CONVEY SPACIOUSNESS; CARRYING WALL FINISH ONTO CEILING WITH A COVE ALSO RAISES APPARENT CEILING HEIGHT.

VISUAL WEIGHT OF DARK, BRIGHT COLORS LOWERS APPARENT CEILING HEIGHT; CARRY CEILING FINISH DOWN ONTO WALL PLANE ENLARGES CEILING AND LOWERS WALL HEIGHT.

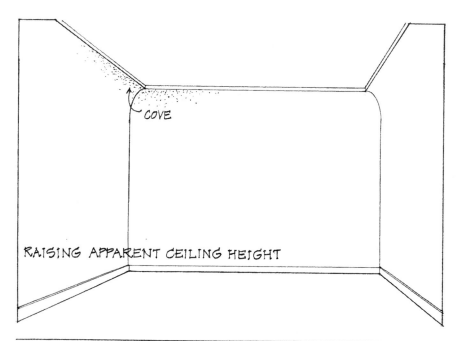

RAISING APPARENT CEILING HEIGHT

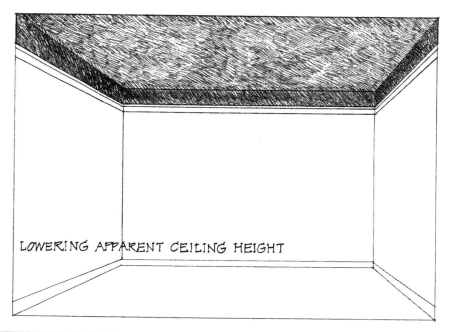

LOWERING APPARENT CEILING HEIGHT

Instead of being surfaced with a smooth, planar material, a ceiling can consist of or express the structural pattern of the floor or roof above. Linear members can create parallel, grid, or radial patterns. Any ceiling pattern will tend to attract our attention and appear to be lower than it is because of its visual weight. Since linear patterns direct the eye, they can also emphasize that dimension of space to which they are parallel.

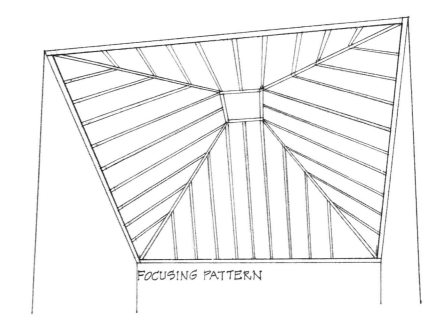

FOCUSING PATTERN

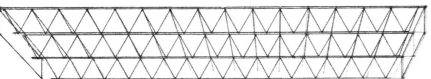

EXPOSED FLOOR AND ROOF STRUCTURES PROVIDE A CEILING WITH TEXTURE, PATTERN, DEPTH, AND DIRECTION. THESE CHARACTERISTICS ATTRACT OUR ATTENTION AND ARE BEST DISPLAYED IN CONTRAST TO SMOOTH WALL PLANES.

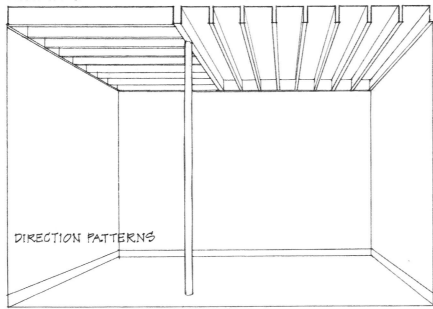

DIRECTION PATTERNS

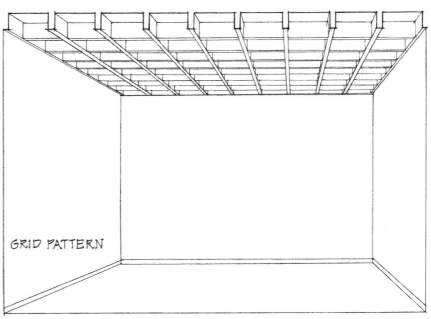

GRID PATTERN

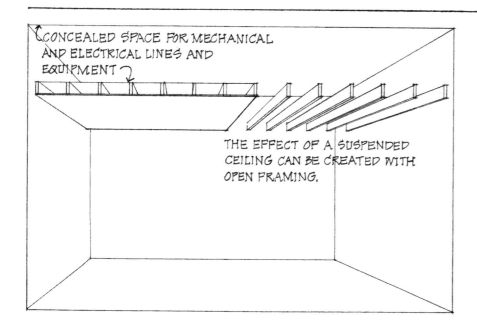

CONCEALED SPACE FOR MECHANICAL AND ELECTRICAL LINES AND EQUIPMENT

THE EFFECT OF A SUSPENDED CEILING CAN BE CREATED WITH OPEN FRAMING.

In a room with a high ceiling, all or a portion of the ceiling can be dropped to lower the scale of the space, or to differentiate an area from the space around it. Because a dropped ceiling is usually suspended from the floor or roof structure above, its form can either echo or contrast with the shape and geometry of the space.

A suspended ceiling creates a concealed space that can be used to house electrical or mechanical lines, recessed lighting fixtures, and insulating materials.

The effect of a suspended ceiling can also be created with nonstructural elements such as fabric or a series of suspended lighting fixtures.

CONTRASTING SPACE CREATED WITHIN A LARGER SPACE ▶

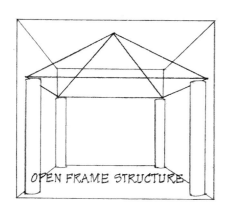

OPEN FRAME STRUCTURE

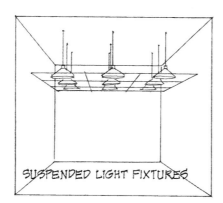

SUSPENDED LIGHT FIXTURES

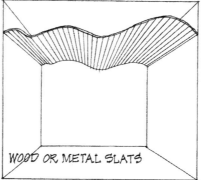

WOOD OR METAL SLATS

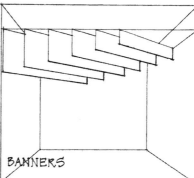

BANNERS

In commercial spaces, a modular suspended ceiling system is often used to integrate and provide flexibility in the layout of lighting fixtures and air distribution outlets. The typical system consists of modular ceiling tiles supported by a metal grid suspended from the overhead structure. The tiles are usually removable for access to the ceiling space.

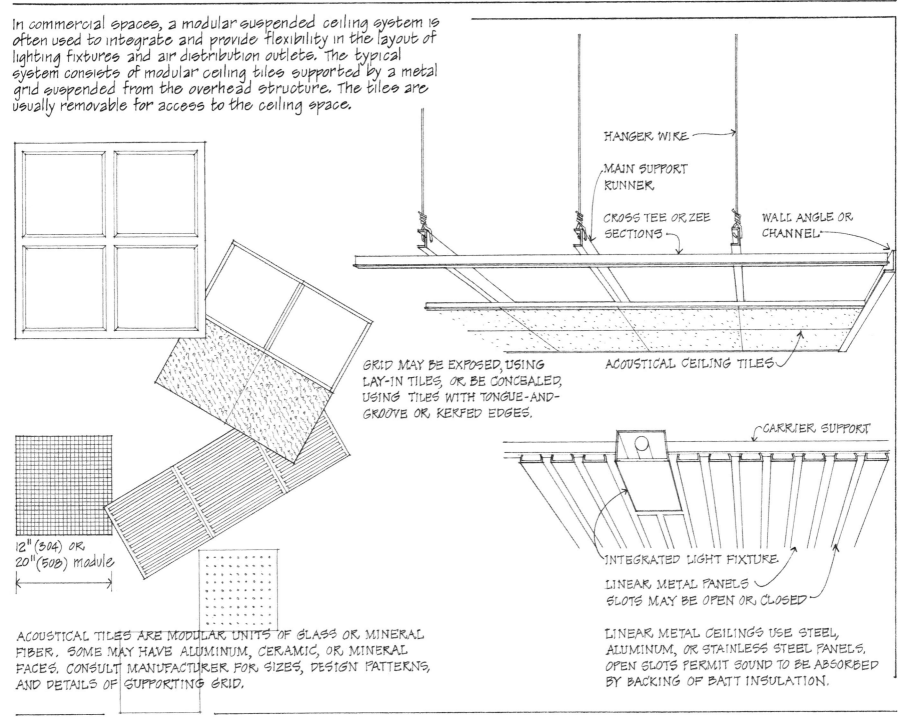

HANGER WIRE

MAIN SUPPORT RUNNER

CROSS TEE OR ZEE SECTIONS

WALL ANGLE OR CHANNEL

ACOUSTICAL CEILING TILES

GRID MAY BE EXPOSED, USING LAY-IN TILES, OR BE CONCEALED, USING TILES WITH TONGUE-AND-GROOVE OR KERFED EDGES.

CARRIER SUPPORT

INTEGRATED LIGHT FIXTURE.

LINEAR METAL PANELS SLOTS MAY BE OPEN OR CLOSED

12" (304) OR 20" (508) module

ACOUSTICAL TILES ARE MODULAR UNITS OF GLASS OR MINERAL FIBER. SOME MAY HAVE ALUMINUM, CERAMIC, OR MINERAL FACES. CONSULT MANUFACTURER FOR SIZES, DESIGN PATTERNS, AND DETAILS OF SUPPORTING GRID.

LINEAR METAL CEILINGS USE STEEL, ALUMINUM, OR STAINLESS STEEL PANELS. OPEN SLOTS PERMIT SOUND TO BE ABSORBED BY BACKING OF BATT INSULATION.

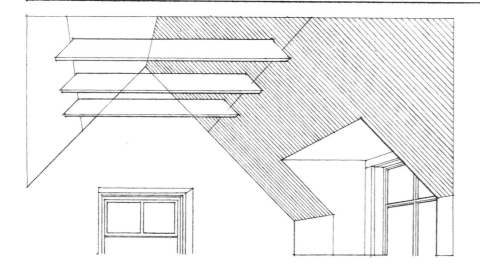

Ceilings supported by a floor structure above are normally flat. When created by a roof structure, however, a ceiling can take on other forms that reflect the shape of the structure, add visual interest, and give direction to the space.

A single slope or shed form may lead the eye upward toward the ridge or down toward the eave line, depending on the location of the daylighting sources within the room.

Gabled ceilings expand space upward toward the ridge line. Depending on the direction of any exposed structural elements, the gabled form may direct our attention to the height of the ridge or to its length.

A pyramid ceiling directs the eye upward to its peak, a focus that can be accentuated further with an illuminating skylight.

SHED OR SINGLE SLOPE   GABLED CEILING

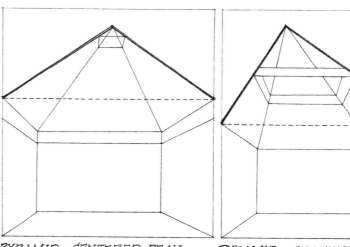

PYRAMID – CENTERED PEAK   PYRAMID – OFF·CENTER PEAK

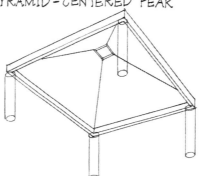

CEILING FORMS

A coved ceiling uses a curved surface to soften its meeting with the surrounding wall planes. The resulting merger of vertical and horizontal surfaces gives the enclosed space a plastic quality.

Increasing the scale of the cove further leads to vaulted and domed ceiling forms. A vaulted ceiling directs our eyes upward and along its length. A dome is a centralized form that expands space upward and focuses our attention on the space beneath its center.

Freeform ceilings contrast with the planar quality of walls and floors, and therefore attract our attention. Whether curvilinear or crystalline in nature, they are decorative and can often dominate the other elements of interior space.

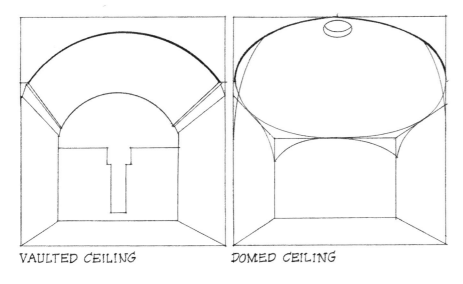

VAULTED CEILING   DOMED CEILING

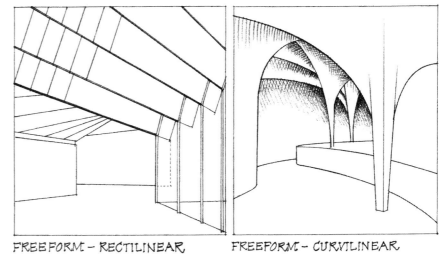

FREEFORM – RECTILINEAR   FREEFORM – CURVILINEAR

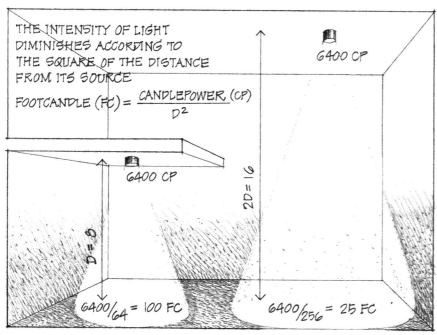

THE INTENSITY OF LIGHT DIMINISHES ACCORDING TO THE SQUARE OF THE DISTANCE FROM ITS SOURCE

$$\text{FOOTCANDLE (FC)} = \frac{\text{CANDLEPOWER (CP)}}{D^2}$$

6400 CP

6400 CP

D = 8

2D = 16

6400/64 = 100 FC

6400/256 = 25 FC

As a functional element, a ceiling affects the illumination of space, its acoustical quality, and the amount of energy required to heat or cool a space.

The height and surface qualities of a ceiling affect the light level within a space. Fixtures mounted on a high ceiling must cast their light a greater distance to achieve the same level of illumination as fewer fixtures suspended from the ceiling.

Because it is not usually encumbered with elements that can block the illumination from light sources, the ceiling plane can be an efficient reflector of light when smooth and light-colored. When directly lit from below or the side, the ceiling surface itself can become a broad surface of soft illumination.

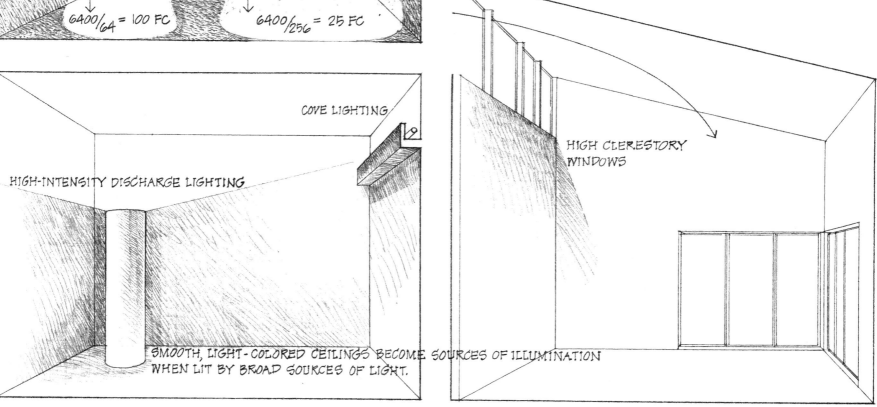

COVE LIGHTING

HIGH-INTENSITY DISCHARGE LIGHTING

HIGH CLERESTORY WINDOWS

SMOOTH, LIGHT-COLORED CEILINGS BECOME SOURCES OF ILLUMINATION WHEN LIT BY BROAD SOURCES OF LIGHT.

Since the ceiling represents the largest unused surface of a room, its form and texture can have a significant impact on the room's acoustics. The smooth, hard surfaces of most ceiling materials reflect airborne sound within a space. In most situations, this is acceptable since other elements and surfaces in a space can employ sound-absorbing materials. In offices, stores, and restaurants, where additional sound-absorbing surfaces may be required to reduce the reflection of noise from numerous sources, acoustical ceilings can be employed.

Undesirable flutter within a space results when repeated echoes traverse back and forth between two non-absorbing parallel planes, such as a hard, flat ceiling opposite a hard-surface floor. Concave domes and vaults focus reflected sound and can intensify echoes and flutter. A remedy for flutter is to add absorbing surfaces. Another is to slope the ceiling plane or use one with a multifaceted surface.

Warm air rises while cooler air falls. Thus a high ceiling allows the warmer air in a room to rise and cooler air to settle at floor level. This pattern of air movement makes a high-ceilinged space more comfortable in warm weather, but also more difficult to heat in cold weather. Conversely, a low-ceilinged space traps warm air and is easier to heat in cold weather, but can be uncomfortably warm in hot weather.

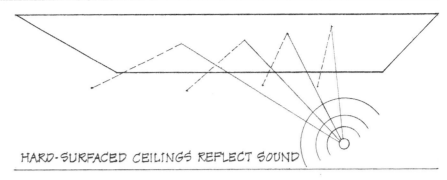

HARD-SURFACED CEILINGS REFLECT SOUND

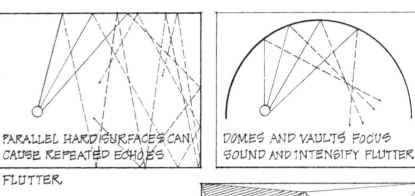

PARALLEL HARD SURFACES CAN CAUSE REPEATED ECHOES

DOMES AND VAULTS FOCUS SOUND AND INTENSIFY FLUTTER

FLUTTER

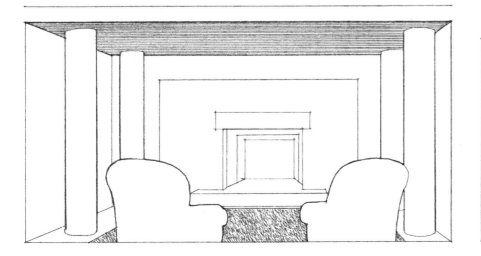

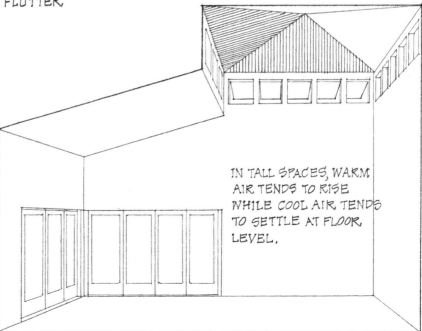

IN TALL SPACES, WARM AIR TENDS TO RISE WHILE COOL AIR TENDS TO SETTLE AT FLOOR LEVEL.

The underside of the floor or roof structure above can be left exposed and serve as the ceiling. More often, however, a separate ceiling material is attached to or hung from a supporting structure. The range of ceiling materials is similar to that for walls except for those which are too heavy to be hung from an overhead structure.

PLASTER & GYPSUM BOARD

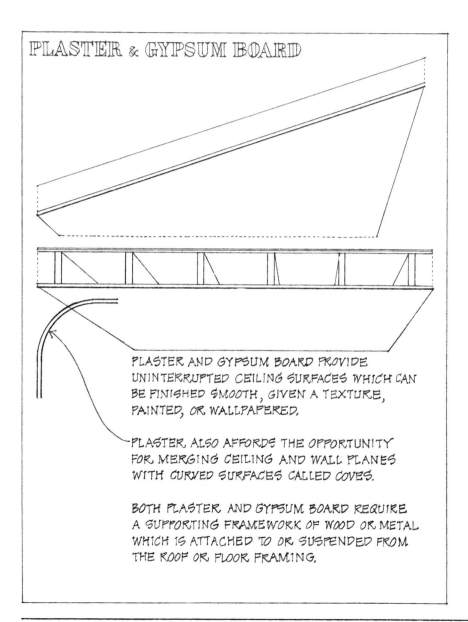

PLASTER AND GYPSUM BOARD PROVIDE UNINTERRUPTED CEILING SURFACES WHICH CAN BE FINISHED SMOOTH, GIVEN A TEXTURE, PAINTED, OR WALLPAPERED.

PLASTER ALSO AFFORDS THE OPPORTUNITY FOR MERGING CEILING AND WALL PLANES WITH CURVED SURFACES CALLED COVES.

BOTH PLASTER AND GYPSUM BOARD REQUIRE A SUPPORTING FRAMEWORK OF WOOD OR METAL WHICH IS ATTACHED TO OR SUSPENDED FROM THE ROOF OR FLOOR FRAMING.

WOOD

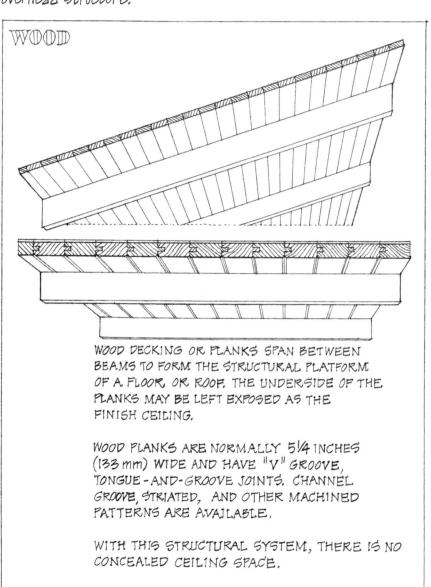

WOOD DECKING OR PLANKS SPAN BETWEEN BEAMS TO FORM THE STRUCTURAL PLATFORM OF A FLOOR OR ROOF. THE UNDERSIDE OF THE PLANKS MAY BE LEFT EXPOSED AS THE FINISH CEILING.

WOOD PLANKS ARE NORMALLY 5¼ INCHES (133 mm) WIDE AND HAVE "V" GROOVE, TONGUE-AND-GROOVE JOINTS. CHANNEL GROOVE, STRIATED, AND OTHER MACHINED PATTERNS ARE AVAILABLE.

WITH THIS STRUCTURAL SYSTEM, THERE IS NO CONCEALED CEILING SPACE.

METAL

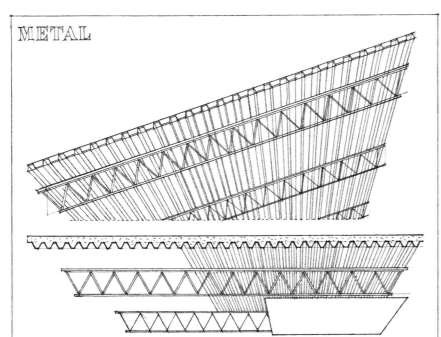

ON ROOFS, CORRUGATED STEEL DECKING FORMS THE STRUCTURAL PLATFORM FOR INSULATION AND THE ROOFING MATERIAL. CELLULAR OR CORRUGATED STEEL DECKING ALSO PROVIDES PERMANENT FORMWORK AND REINFORCEMENT FOR CONCRETE WHEN FORMING COMPOSITE FLOOR SLABS.

THE UNDERSIDE OF STEEL DECKING CAN BE LEFT EXPOSED AS THE CEILING SURFACE. TOGETHER WITH OPEN WEB STEEL JOISTS, STEEL DECKING DEFINES CEILINGS WITH A LINEAR, TEXTURAL QUALITY.

MODULAR

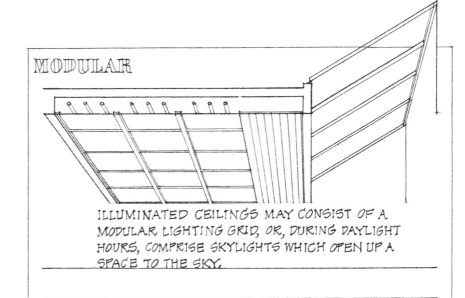

ILLUMINATED CEILINGS MAY CONSIST OF A MODULAR LIGHTING GRID, OR, DURING DAYLIGHT HOURS, COMPRISE SKYLIGHTS WHICH OPEN UP A SPACE TO THE SKY.

MODULAR CEILING MATERIALS ARE NORMALLY SUPPORTED ON A METAL GRID SUSPENDED FROM A ROOF OR FLOOR STRUCTURE. ACOUSTICAL CEILING TILES FORM A SQUARE OR RECTANGULAR GRID PATTERN WHICH MAY BE STRONG OR SUBTLE, DEPENDING ON THE TILE DESIGN. IN CONTRAST TO THIS, LONG, NARROW METAL PANELS FORM A LINEAR PATTERN ON CEILINGS. IN BOTH CASES, LIGHT FIXTURES, AIR DIFFUSERS, AND OTHER EQUIPMENT CAN BE INTEGRATED INTO THE MODULAR SYSTEM.

WINDOWS

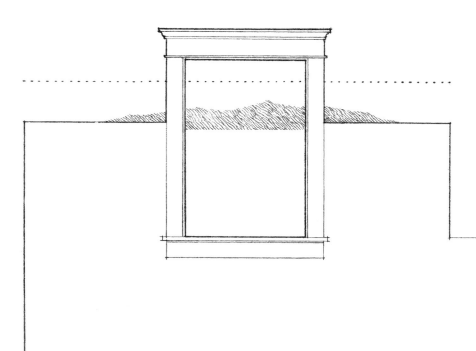

Windows and doorways interrupt the wall planes that give a building its form and interior spaces their definition. They are the transitional elements of architectural and interior design that link, both visually and physically, one space to another, and inside to outside.

The size, shape, and placement of windows affect the visual integrity of a wall surface and the sense of enclosure it provides. A window can be seen as a bright area within a wall, an opening framed by a wall, or a void separating two wall planes. It can also be enlarged to the point where it becomes the physical wall plane - a transparent window wall that visually unites an interior space with the outdoors or an adjacent interior space.

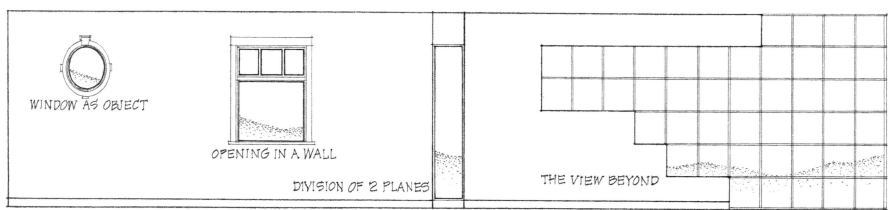

WINDOW AS OBJECT

OPENING IN A WALL

DIVISION OF 2 PLANES

THE VIEW BEYOND

SIZE, SHAPE, AND PLACEMENT OF WINDOW OPENINGS

The scale of a window is related not only to the surrounding wall plane but also to our own dimensions. We are accustomed to a window head height slightly above our height and to a sill height that corresponds to our waistline. When a large window is used to visually expand a space, broaden its outlook, or complement its scale, the window can be subdivided into smaller units to maintain a human scale.

PRIVACY

A "NORMAL" WINDOW

AN OVERSCALED WINDOW

VARYING THE SCALE OF WINDOW OPENINGS

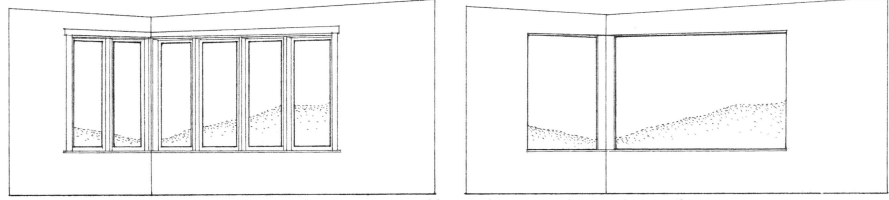

THE FRAMING PATTERN AND TRIM DETAILS OF A WINDOW AFFECTS THE SENSE OF ENCLOSURE WALLS PROVIDE.

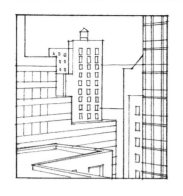

Views from windows become an integral part of the fabric of interior space. They not only provide an outward focus from within a room; they also convey visual information to us about where we are. They form a connection between inside and outside.

In determining the size, shape, and placement of windows in a room, consideration should be given to what can be seen through the window openings, how these views are framed, and how the visual scenes shift as we move about the room.

Windows do more than simply frame views. In daylighting a space and providing for its ventilation, a window may also expose a less than desirable view. In such a case, the treatment of a window can fragment, filter, or divert our view. Exterior landscaping can also aid in shielding an interior space from an undesirable view, or even create a pleasant outlook where none exists.

WAYS TO DEAL WITH AN UNSIGHTLY VIEW:

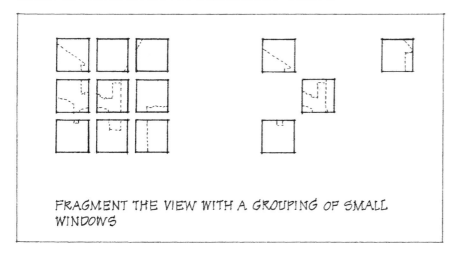 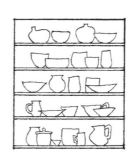

FRAGMENT THE VIEW WITH A GROUPING OF SMALL WINDOWS

FILTER THE VIEW BY SETTING A COLLECTION OF OBJECTS WITHIN THE WINDOW

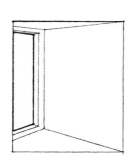 

DIVERT OUR ATTENTION AWAY FROM THE VIEW

WHERE NO VIEW EXISTS, CREATE A GARDEN OR COURTYARD VIEW.

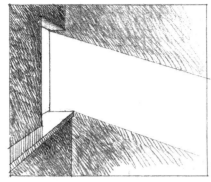

WINDOW

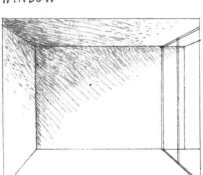

WINDOW WALL

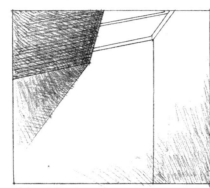

CLERESTORY WINDOW

SKYLIGHT

The size and orientation of windows and skylights control the quantity and quality of natural light that penetrates and illuminates an interior space. Window size is obviously related to quantity of light. The quality of light – its intensity and color – is determined by a window's orientation and placement in a room.

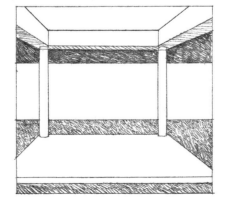

BRIGHT AREAS OF LIGHT
ATTRACT OUR ATTENTION

DAYLIGHT CAN BE USED
EFFECTIVELY AS TASK LIGHTING

CHANGING PATTERNS OF LIGHT
AND SHADOW ANIMATE SPACE

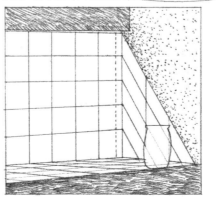

LIGHT CAN BE USED TO
DEFINE SPACE

A problem associated with daylighting is glare, which is caused by excessive contrast between the brightness of a window opening and the darker wall surfaces adjacent to it. When one deals with glare, the placement of windows is as important as their size. The optimum condition is balanced lighting from at least two directions - from two walls or a wall and the ceiling. Skylights, in particular, can help soften the harshness of direct sunlight.

In rooms with windows close to the floor, glare can be caused by the light reflected off of the exterior ground surface. This ground glare can be reduced through the use of shade trees or a vertical screen of horizontal louvers.

Locating a window adjacent to a perpendicular wall or ceiling surface maximizes the light entering the window. The perpendicular surface is illuminated by the entering light and becomes itself a broad source of reflected light.

GLARE RESULTS WHEN OUR EYES CANNOT ADJUST SIMULTANEOUSLY TO WIDELY CONTRASTING AREAS OF BRIGHTNESS.

OUR EYES ADJUST TO THE BRIGHTEST LIGHT, REDUCING OUR ABILITY TO SEE LESS BRIGHTLY LIT AREAS.

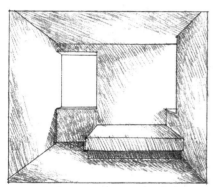

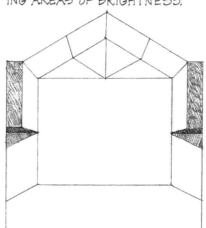
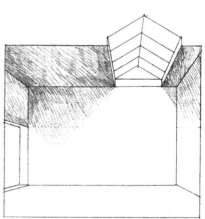

BIDIRECTIONAL DAYLIGHTING RAISES THE LEVEL OF DIFFUSED LIGHT IN A SPACE AND REDUCES THE POSSIBILITY OF GLARE.

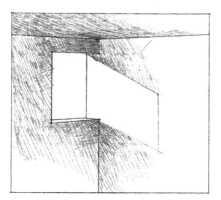
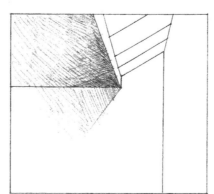
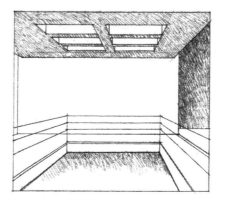
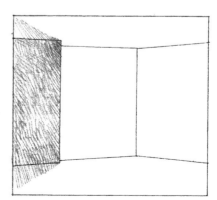

NATURAL VENTILATION REQUIRES THE USE OF OPERABLE WINDOWS.

Wind velocity, temperature, and direction are important site considerations in locating windows in all climatic regions. During hot periods, wind-induced ventilation is desirable for cooling by evaporation or conduction. In cold weather, wind should be avoided or screened from windows to minimize the infiltration of cold air into a building. At all times, some degree of ventilation is desirable for good health and the removal of stale air and odors from interior spaces.

Natural ventilation in the interior spaces of buildings is generated by differences in air pressure as well as temperature. Air flow patterns induced by these forces are affected more by building geometry than air speed.

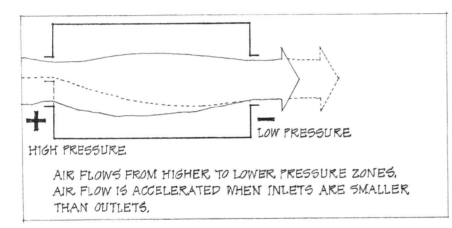

HIGH PRESSURE

LOW PRESSURE

AIR FLOWS FROM HIGHER TO LOWER PRESSURE ZONES. AIR FLOW IS ACCELERATED WHEN INLETS ARE SMALLER THAN OUTLETS.

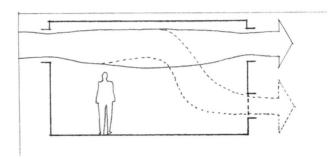

HIGH INLETS AND OUTLETS PRODUCE AIR MOVEMENT ABOVE OUR BODY LEVEL. LOWERING THE OUTLET DOES NOT AMELIORATE THIS CONDITION.

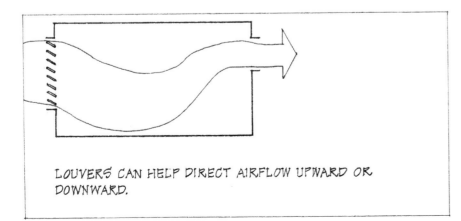

LOUVERS CAN HELP DIRECT AIRFLOW UPWARD OR DOWNWARD.

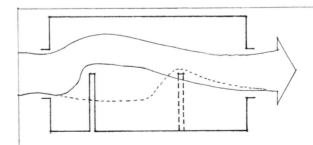

INTERIOR PARTITIONS AND TALL FURNISHINGS CAN ADVERSELY ALTER THE PATTERN OF AIR FLOW.

Ventilation is provided by window openings. Even when closed, windows are sources of heat gain and loss. Heat gain, desirable in cold winter months and undesirable in hot summer months, is due to solar radiation through a window's glazing. Heat loss through a window, undesirable in cold weather, is due to the temperature differential between a heated interior space and the colder outside air.

Glass is a poor thermal insulator. To increase its resistance to heat flow, a window can be double- or triple-glazed, so that the trapped air space between the glass panes can be used as insulation.

A window's orientation is a more cost-effective factor in controlling solar radiation than is its construction.

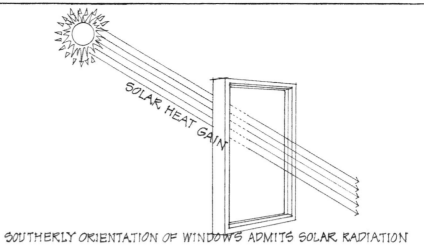

SOUTHERLY ORIENTATION OF WINDOWS ADMITS SOLAR RADIATION

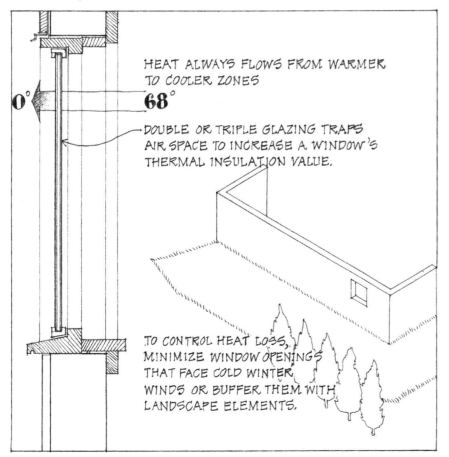

HEAT ALWAYS FLOWS FROM WARMER TO COOLER ZONES

0°   68°

DOUBLE OR TRIPLE GLAZING TRAPS AIR SPACE TO INCREASE A WINDOW'S THERMAL INSULATION VALUE.

TO CONTROL HEAT LOSS, MINIMIZE WINDOW OPENINGS THAT FACE COLD WINTER WINDS OR BUFFER THEM WITH LANDSCAPE ELEMENTS.

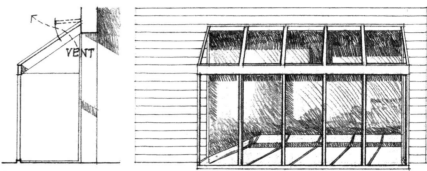

ONE OF THE METHODS FOR PASSIVE SOLAR HEATING UTILIZES A SUN SPACE FOR SOLAR COLLECTION AND THERMAL STORAGE ELEMENTS, SUCH AS MASONRY FLOORS AND WALLS. PROVISION FOR SOME OPERABLE GLAZING IS NECESSARY SO THAT THE SPACE CAN BE VENTILATED IN WARM WEATHER.

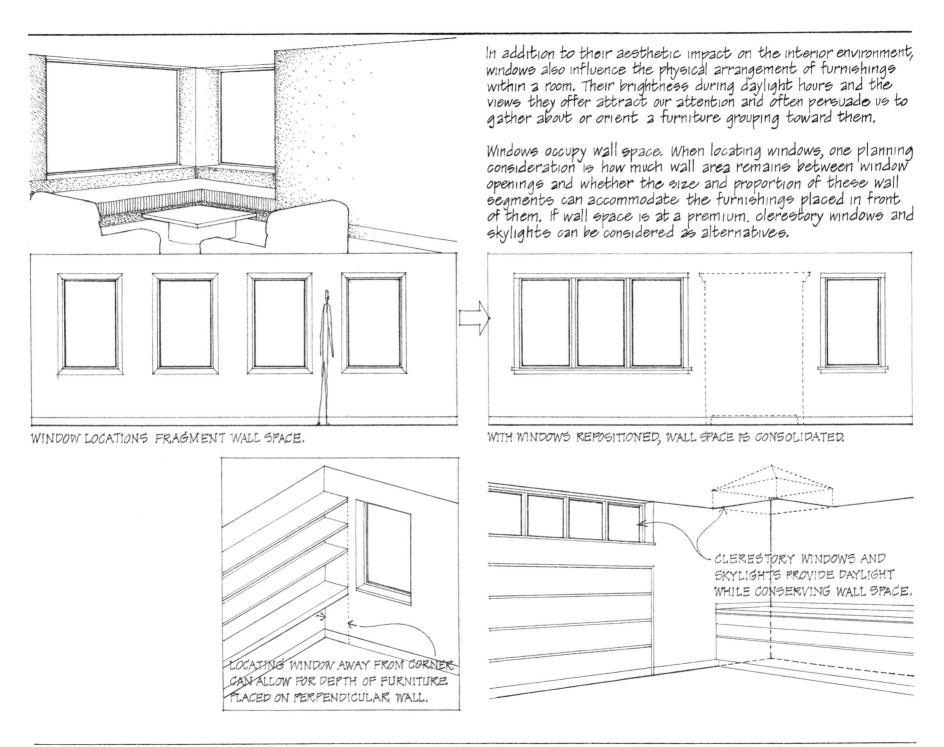

In addition to their aesthetic impact on the interior environment, windows also influence the physical arrangement of furnishings within a room. Their brightness during daylight hours and the views they offer attract our attention and often persuade us to gather about or orient a furniture grouping toward them.

Windows occupy wall space. When locating windows, one planning consideration is how much wall area remains between window openings and whether the size and proportion of these wall segments can accommodate the furnishings placed in front of them. If wall space is at a premium, clerestory windows and skylights can be considered as alternatives.

WINDOW LOCATIONS FRAGMENT WALL SPACE.

WITH WINDOWS REPOSITIONED, WALL SPACE IS CONSOLIDATED.

LOCATING WINDOW AWAY FROM CORNER CAN ALLOW FOR DEPTH OF FURNITURE PLACED ON PERPENDICULAR WALL.

CLERESTORY WINDOWS AND SKYLIGHTS PROVIDE DAYLIGHT WHILE CONSERVING WALL SPACE.

The sill height of a window also affects what can be placed below it. A low sill height may dictate that the floor area in front of the window be left open, thereby reducing the amount of usable floor space in a room. This is especially pertinent when window walls extend down to the floor to promote visual continuity between interior and exterior space.

Another consideration in the placement of windows is the adverse effect direct sunlight can have on a room's occupants (heat and glare) and on the finishes of its carpet and furnishings (fading and deterioration).

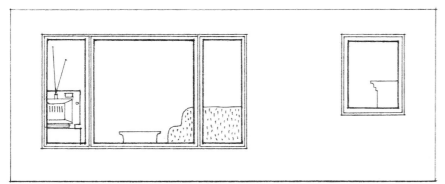

WINDOWS EXPOSE THE BACKS OF FURNITURE PLACED AGAINST THEM.

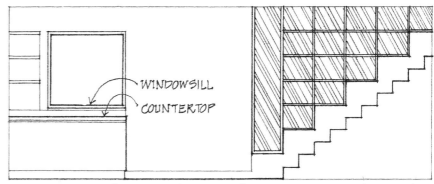

WHEN POSSIBLE, COORDINATE WINDOWS WITH BUILT-IN ELEMENTS.

WINDOW WALLS THAT EXTEND TO THE FLOOR INHIBIT THE PLACEMENT OF FURNITURE AGAINST THEM.

WHEN EXPOSED TO DIRECT SUNLIGHT, SOME MATERIALS ARE SUBJECT TO FADING AND DETERIORATION.

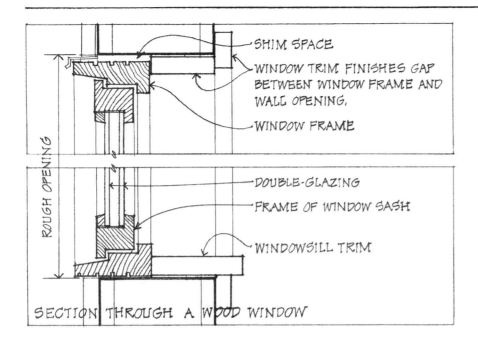

SHIM SPACE

WINDOW TRIM FINISHES GAP BETWEEN WINDOW FRAME AND WALL OPENING.

WINDOW FRAME

ROUGH OPENING

DOUBLE-GLAZING

FRAME OF WINDOW SASH

WINDOWSILL TRIM

SECTION THROUGH A WOOD WINDOW

Most windows used today are prefabricated units with frames of wood or metal. Wood frames are generally constructed of kiln-dried, clear, straight-grain material. They are usually treated in the factory with preservatives or water-repellants. The exterior of the frame may be ordered unfinished, primed for painting, or clad with aluminum or vinyl for reduced maintenance. The interior of the frame is usually left unfinished.

Metal frames are stronger and therefore usually thinner in profile than wood frames. Aluminum and steel are the most common types, although stainless steel and bronze windows are also available. Aluminum frames may have a natural, mill finish, or be anodized for additional protection and color. Steel window frames must be galvanized and/or primed and painted for corrosion-resistance. Since metal is an efficient conductor of heat, moisture can condense on the inner face of metal sashes in cold weather unless a thermal break is built into their construction.

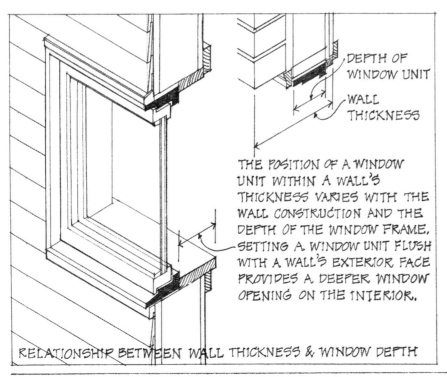

DEPTH OF WINDOW UNIT

WALL THICKNESS

THE POSITION OF A WINDOW UNIT WITHIN A WALL'S THICKNESS VARIES WITH THE WALL CONSTRUCTION AND THE DEPTH OF THE WINDOW FRAME. SETTING A WINDOW UNIT FLUSH WITH A WALL'S EXTERIOR FACE PROVIDES A DEEPER WINDOW OPENING ON THE INTERIOR.

RELATIONSHIP BETWEEN WALL THICKNESS & WINDOW DEPTH

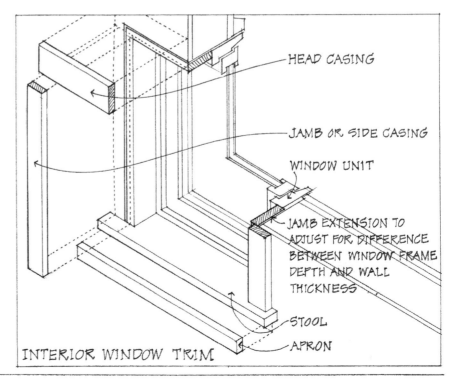

HEAD CASING

JAMB OR SIDE CASING

WINDOW UNIT

JAMB EXTENSION TO ADJUST FOR DIFFERENCE BETWEEN WINDOW FRAME DEPTH AND WALL THICKNESS

STOOL

APRON

INTERIOR WINDOW TRIM

Factory-manufactured windows come in stock sizes, but these vary with each manufacturer. Custom sizes and shapes are available, but often at additional cost.

Rough openings in wall construction usually allow ½ to ¾ inch on each side and along the top for leveling and plumbing up of the window units. Flashing and caulking on the exterior side of the frames help to make the joints weathertight and minimize the infiltration of air.

Casing and trimwork are used to conceal and finish the gaps between a window unit and its rough opening. The type of interior trim used contributes significantly to the character of a space.

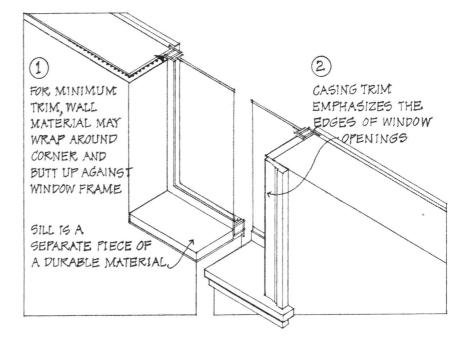

① FOR MINIMUM TRIM, WALL MATERIAL MAY WRAP AROUND CORNER AND BUTT UP AGAINST WINDOW FRAME

SILL IS A SEPARATE PIECE OF A DURABLE MATERIAL.

② CASING TRIM EMPHASIZES THE EDGES OF WINDOW OPENINGS

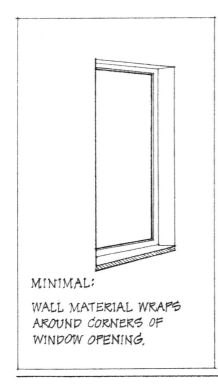

MINIMAL:

WALL MATERIAL WRAPS AROUND CORNERS OF WINDOW OPENING.

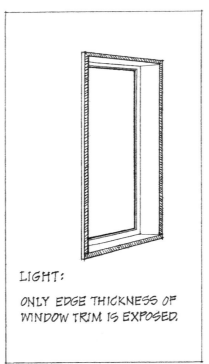

LIGHT:

ONLY EDGE THICKNESS OF WINDOW TRIM IS EXPOSED.

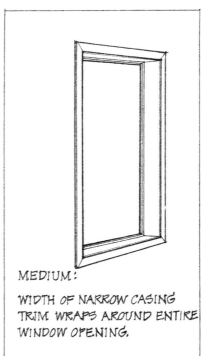

MEDIUM:

WIDTH OF NARROW CASING TRIM WRAPS AROUND ENTIRE WINDOW OPENING.

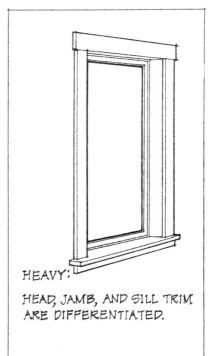

HEAVY:

HEAD, JAMB, AND SILL TRIM ARE DIFFERENTIATED.

Windows can be categorized into two major groups: fixed and ventilating. While both groups provide interior spaces with light and views, fixed windows do not allow for the passage of air as do ventilating windows. Fixed windows can never be opened; ventilating windows can always be closed. It would seem then that the decision to use fixed windows should be a carefully considered one.

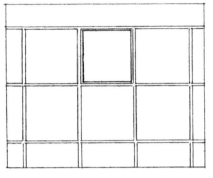
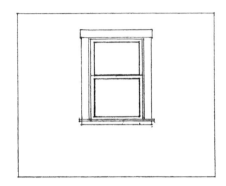
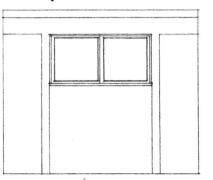
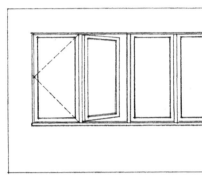

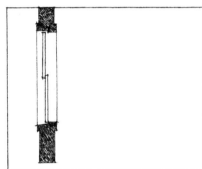
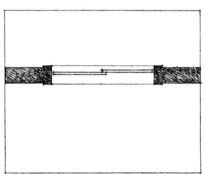
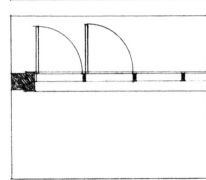

FIXED

- FRAME AND GLAZED SASH ARE STATIONARY
- NO VENTILATION POSSIBLE
- FLEXIBLE SIZE & SHAPE DEPENDING ON GLAZING SIZE AVAILABLE
- CAN TAKE ON A THREE-DIMENSIONAL FORM, I.E., A BAY WINDOW
- NO HARDWARE OR SCREENS REQUIRED

DOUBLE-HUNG

- TWO SASHES TRAVEL VERTICALLY AND ARE HELD IN DESIRED POSITION BY FRICTION OR A BALANCING DEVICE
- NO RAIN PROTECTION
- CAN BE WEATHERPROOFED EFFECTIVELY
- SCREENED ON OUTSIDE
- 50% VENTILATION
- DIFFICULT TO PAINT & CLEAN WITHOUT PIVOTING SASH

SLIDING

- MAY CONSIST OF: Ⓐ TWO SASHES OF WHICH ONE SLIDES HORIZONTALLY (50% VENTILATION), OR Ⓑ THREE SASHES OF WHICH THE MIDDLE IS FIXED WHILE THE OTHER TWO SLIDE (66% VENTILATION)
- NO RAIN PROTECTION
- SCREENED ON OUTSIDE
- SLIDING PATIO DOORS ARE LIKE LARGE SLIDING WINDOWS.

CASEMENT

- OPERATING SASH IS SIDE-HINGED, USUALLY SWINGING OUTWARD; INSIDE SCREEN
- 100% VENTILATION; CAN DIRECT OR DEFLECT BREEZES
- NO RAIN PROTECTION
- PROJECTING SASH CAN BE AN OBSTRUCTION
- ROTO-HARDWARE OR FRICTION HARDWARE USED FOR STABILITY OF SASH WHEN OPEN

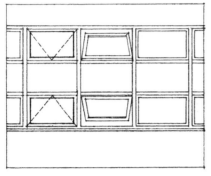

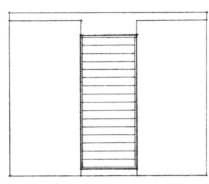

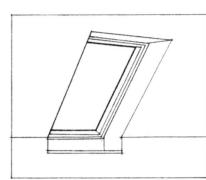

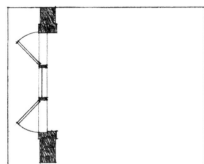

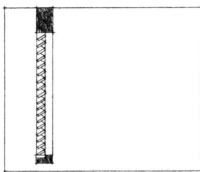

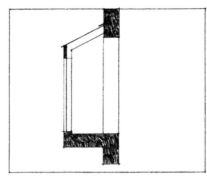

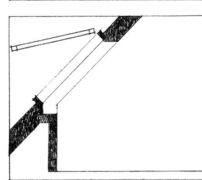

AWNING/ HOPPER

JALOUSIE

BAY WINDOWS & SKYLIGHTS

- SIMILAR TO CASEMENTS BUT HINGED AT TOP (AWNING) OR BOTTOM (HOPPER)
- 100% VENTILATION
- BOTH TYPES PROVIDE DRAFT-FREE VENTILATION; AWNINGS ALSO PROVIDE SOME RAIN PROTECTION
- MAY BE DIFFICULT TO WEATHERPROOF
- REQUIRES SPACE FOR SWING OF SASH

- SIMILAR IN PRINCIPLE TO AWNING WINDOWS EXCEPT THAT A SERIES OF NARROW OPAQUE OR TRANSLUCENT STRIPS ARE USED
- ABLE TO DIRECT FLOW OF INCOMING AIR
- DIFFICULT TO CLEAN & WEATHERPROOF; USED IN WARM CLIMATES WHERE VENTILATION IS REQUIRED ALONG WITH PRIVACY.

- SKYLIGHTS MAY BE FIXED OR VENTILATING UNITS
- SAFETY GLASS (TEMPERED OR WIRE GLASS) OR ACRYLIC REQUIRED
- SKYLIGHTS PROVIDE DAYLIGHTING WITHOUT INTERFERING WITH FURNITURE ARRANGEMENT AND WHILE MAINTAINING PRIVACY FROM UNWANTED VIEW
- VENTILATING SKYLIGHTS CAN BE EFFECTIVE COOLING MECHANISMS, ALLOWING HOT AIR TO ESCAPE IN WARM WEATHER

- BAY WINDOWS MAY USE A COMBINATION OF FIXED AND OPERABLE WINDOWS AND SKYLIGHTS TO PROJECT A PORTION OF INTERIOR SPACE OUTWARD INTO THE SURROUNDING LANDSCAPE

WINDOW TREATMENTS

In the broad category of window treatments are included devices that provide additional control of light, available views, and the passage of air, heat, and cold. Exterior treatments are normally designed as integral elements of a building's architecture. If added to an existing building, such alterations should respect the existing architectural style.

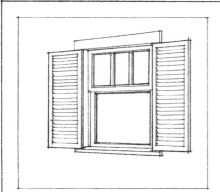

SHUTTERS:
- TRADITIONALLY USED TO MODERATE LIGHT, HEAT, AND COLD
- TRUE SHUTTERS SELDOM USED TODAY

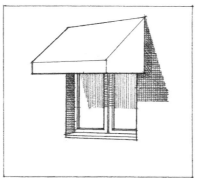

AWNINGS:
- WEATHERPROOF, SOMETIMES TRANSLUCENT, FABRIC STRETCHED OVER A FRAME TO PROVIDE SHADE; SOME ARE RETRACTABLE

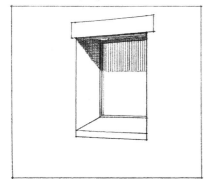

OVERHANGS:
- OVERHANGS AND RECESSED WINDOWS PROVIDE PROTECTION FROM SUN AND RAIN

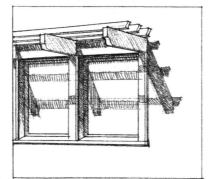

TRELLISES:
- OPEN FRAMEWORK THAT FILTERS LIGHT AND PROVIDES SUPPORT FOR VINES

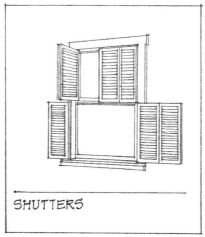

SHUTTERS

- RIGID PANELS, USUALLY OF WOOD, ARE HINGED TO OPEN AND CLOSE LIKE MINIATURE DOORS
- PANELS USUALLY HAVE ADJUSTABLE LOUVERS SO THAT FILTERING OF LIGHT AND VIEW CAN BE CONTROLLED
- SHUTTERS PROVIDE A CLEAN, PRECISE, UNCLUTTERED APPEARANCE
- WHEN CLOSED, SHUTTERS ENHANCE SENSE OF ENCLOSURE

GRILLS

- GRILLS ARE DECORATIVE SCREENS OF WOOD OR METAL THAT CAN BE USED TO MASK VIEWS, FILTER LIGHT, OR DIFFUSE VENTILATION.
- DEGREE OF MASKING, FILTRATION, OR DIFFUSION DEPENDS ON SPACING AND ORIENTATION OF MEMBERS
- MAY BE FIXED OR ADJUSTABLE
- DESIGN OF GRILL PATTERN CAN BE IMPORTANT VISUAL ELEMENT

EXTERIOR   INTERIOR

Interior window treatments vary according to how they temper the light, ventilation, and view a window provides, and how they alter a window's form and appearance. They also differ in how they open and close; a window treatment should not interfere with a window's operation or restrict access to its hardware.

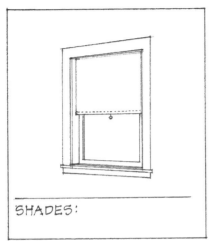

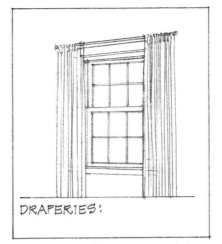

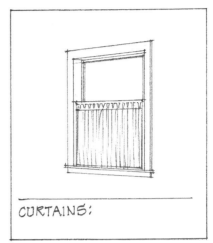

SHADES:

- SHADES ARE ECONOMICAL WINDOW TREATMENTS OF FABRIC, VINYL, OR BAMBOO
- SHADES OPERATE FROM THE TOP DOWN TO COVER PART OR ALL OF A WINDOW OPENING
- SHADE MATERIAL MAY BE TRANSLUCENT OR OPAQUE
- SHADES REDUCE LIGHT WHILE PROVIDING PRIVACY
- BAMBOO PRESENTS A PLEASING TEXTURE WHILE FILTERING LIGHT AND VIEW
- SHADES MAY BE ROLLED OR GATHERED WHEN OPENED

BLINDS:

- HORIZONTAL BLINDS CONSIST OF THIN OR WIDE SLATS
- SLATS MAY BE OF WOOD OR METAL
- SPACING AND ADJUSTABILITY OF SLATS PROVIDE GOOD CONTROL OF LIGHT AND AIR FLOW; THIN SLATS OBSTRUCT VIEW LESS THAN WIDE SLATS
- DIFFICULT TO CLEAN

- VERTICAL BLINDS HAVE SLATS, GENERALLY OF OPAQUE OR TRANSLUCENT FABRIC, THAT PIVOT AT THE TOP AND BOTTOM
- VERTICAL BLINDS ENHANCE THE HEIGHT OF A ROOM, GATHER LESS DUST, AND CAN BE MADE TO FIT ODD-SHAPED OPENINGS

DRAPERIES:

- DRAPERIES REFER TO ANY FABRIC THAT HANGS STRAIGHT IN LOOSE FOLDS
- DRAPERIES ARE USUALLY OF HEAVY FABRIC; THEY MAY BE TIED BACK OR HUNG LIKE A TAPESTRY; THEY OFTEN HAVE A VALENCE OR WIDE CORNICE AT THE TOP

- DRAW CURTAINS OF OPAQUE OR TRANSLUCENT FABRIC ARE MOUNTED ON TRAVERSE RODS
- THEY SHOULD BE FULL AND HANG STRAIGHT, STARTING AT THE CEILING OR SLIGHTLY ABOVE THE TOP OF THE FRAME AND ENDING SLIGHTLY BELOW THE BOTTOM OF THE FRAME OR NEAR THE FLOOR

CURTAINS:

- GLASS CURTAINS ARE OF SHEER, LIGHTWEIGHT MATERIAL HUNG CLOSE TO THE GLASS OF A WINDOW OR FRENCH DOOR
- SHEERNESS SOFTENS AND DIFFUSES LIGHT, FILTERS THE VIEW, AND PROVIDES DAYTIME PRIVACY
- CAN BE HUNG WITHIN WINDOW FRAME, OR OUTSIDE TO UNIFY A GROUP OF WINDOWS

- SASH CURTAINS ARE LIKE GLASS CURTAINS, BUT THEY ARE HUNG OR STRETCHED ACROSS THE SASH OF A WINDOW

DOORS

Doors and doorways allow physical access for ourselves, furnishings, and goods in and out of a building and from room to room within it. Through their design, construction, and location, they can control the use of a room, the views from one space to the next, and the passage of light, sound, warmth, and cool breezes.

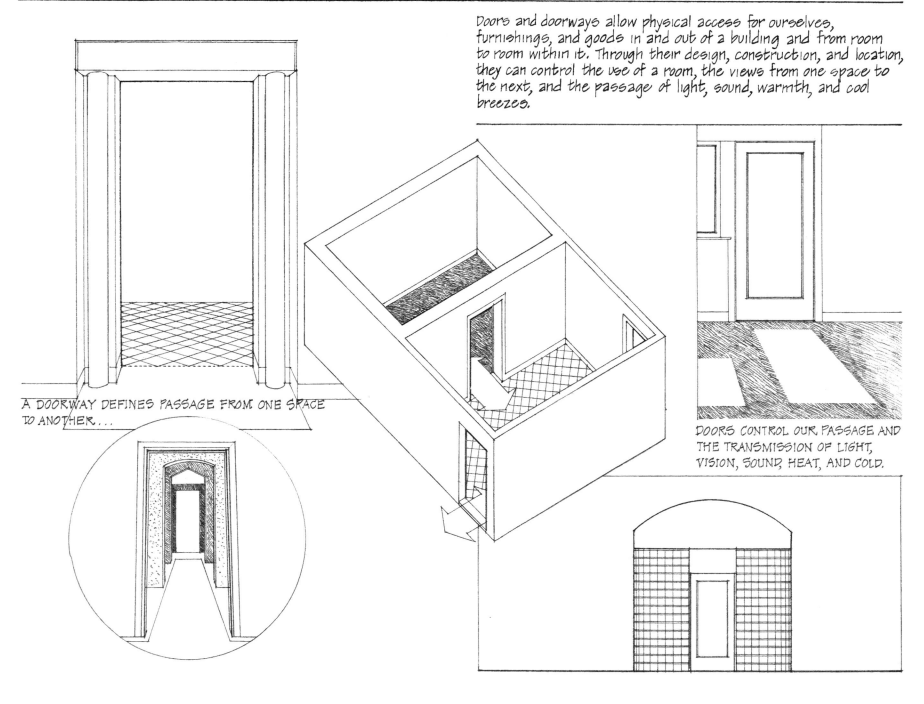

A DOORWAY DEFINES PASSAGE FROM ONE SPACE TO ANOTHER...

DOORS CONTROL OUR PASSAGE AND THE TRANSMISSION OF LIGHT, VISION, SOUND, HEAT, AND COLD.

Doors may have wood or metal frames surfaced with wood, metal, or a specialty material such as plastic laminate. They may be factory-primed for painting, pre-painted, or clad in various materials. They may be glazed for transparency, or contain louvers for ventilation.

Special doors include those constructed to have a fire-resistance rating, an acoustical rating, or entrance doors with a thermal insulation value.

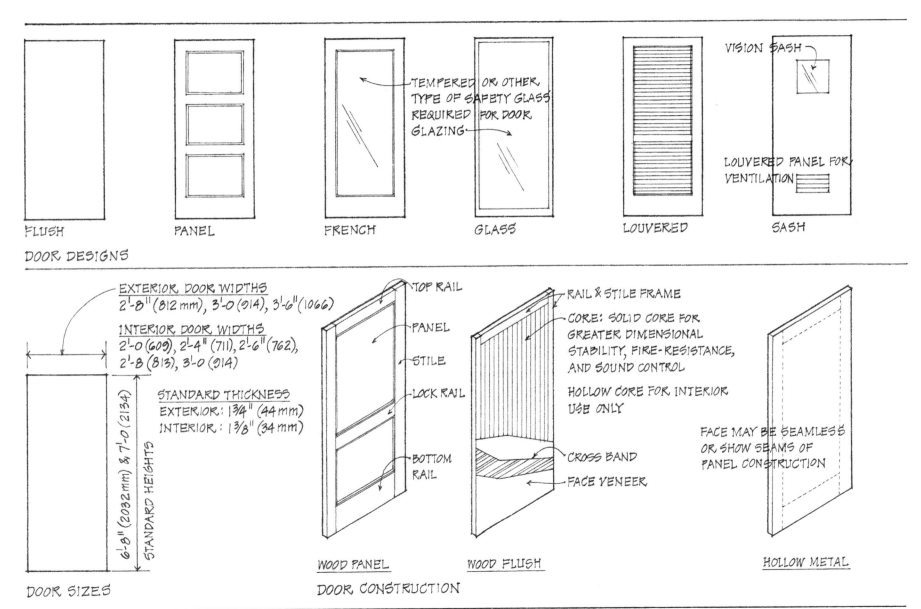

TEMPERED OR OTHER TYPE OF SAFETY GLASS REQUIRED FOR DOOR GLAZING

VISION SASH

LOUVERED PANEL FOR VENTILATION

FLUSH　　　PANEL　　　FRENCH　　　GLASS　　　LOUVERED　　　SASH

DOOR DESIGNS

EXTERIOR DOOR WIDTHS
2'-8" (812 mm), 3'-0 (914), 3'-6" (1066)

INTERIOR DOOR WIDTHS
2'-0 (609), 2'-4" (711), 2'-6" (762), 2'-8 (813), 3'-0 (914)

STANDARD THICKNESS
EXTERIOR: 1¾" (44 mm)
INTERIOR: 1⅜" (34 mm)

6'-8" (2032mm) & 7'-0 (2134) STANDARD HEIGHTS

DOOR SIZES

TOP RAIL
PANEL
STILE
LOCK RAIL
BOTTOM RAIL

WOOD PANEL

RAIL & STILE FRAME
CORE: SOLID CORE FOR GREATER DIMENSIONAL STABILITY, FIRE-RESISTANCE, AND SOUND CONTROL
HOLLOW CORE FOR INTERIOR USE ONLY
CROSS BAND
FACE VENEER

WOOD FLUSH

FACE MAY BE SEAMLESS OR SHOW SEAMS OF PANEL CONSTRUCTION

HOLLOW METAL

DOOR CONSTRUCTION

DOOR TYPES

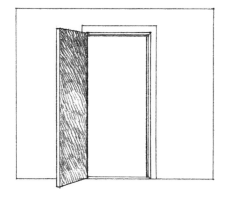

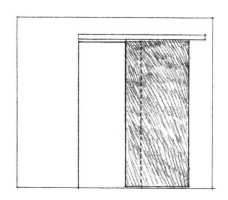

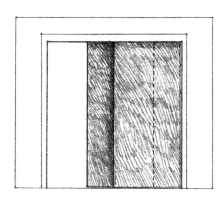

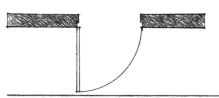

SWINGING:

- HINGED ON SIDE JAMB
- HEAVY OR WIDE DOORS MAY PIVOT AT HEAD AND SILL
- MOST CONVENIENT FOR OUR ENTRY AND PASSAGE
- MOST EFFECTIVE TYPE FOR ISOLATING SOUND AND FOR WEATHERTIGHTNESS
- FOR EXTERIOR AND INTERIOR USE
- REQUIRES SPACE FOR SWING

POCKET SLIDING

- DOOR IS HUNG ON TRACK, AND SLIDES INTO POCKET WITHIN WIDTH OF WALL
- USED WHERE NORMAL DOOR SWING WOULD INTERFERE WITH USE OF SPACE
- PRESENTS A FINISHED APPEARANCE WHEN OPEN
- FOR INTERIOR USE ONLY

SURFACE SLIDING

- SIMILAR TO POCKET DOOR, EXCEPT THAT DOOR IS SURFACE HUNG FROM AN EXPOSED OVERHEAD TRACK
- PRIMARILY FOR INTERIOR USE
- DIFFICULT TO WEATHER-PROOF, BUT CAN BE USED ON EXTERIOR IN WARM CLIMATES

BY-PASS SLIDING

- DOORS SLIDE ALONG AN OVER-HEAD TRACK AND ALONG GUIDES OR A TRACK ON THE FLOOR
- OPENS ONLY TO 50% OF DOORWAY
- USED INDOORS PRIMARILY FOR VISUAL SCREENING
- USED ON EXTERIOR AS SLIDING GLASS DOORS

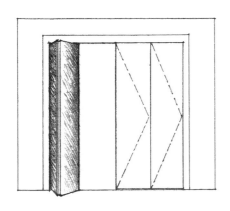
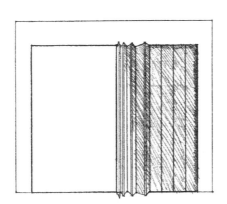
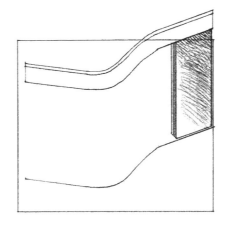
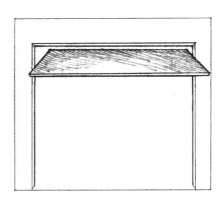

BI - FOLD

- CONSISTS OF HINGED DOOR PANELS THAT SLIDE ON AN OVERHEAD TRACK
- FOR INTERIOR USE ONLY
- COMMONLY USED AS A VISUAL SCREEN TO CLOSE OFF STORAGE AND CLOSET SPACES

ACCORDION FOLDING

- SIMILAR TO BI-FOLD DOORS EXCEPT THAT PANELS ARE SMALLER
- FOR INTERIOR USE ONLY
- USED TO SUBDIVIDE LARGE SPACES INTO SMALLER ROOMS

SPECIAL FOLDING

- DOOR PANELS SLIDE ON OVERHEAD TRACKS
- TRACKS CAN BE CONFIGURED TO FOLLOW A CURVILINEAR PATH
- PANELS CAN BE STORED IN POCKET OR RECESS
- FOR INTERIOR USE

OVERHEAD DOORS

- CONSISTS OF HINGED DOOR SECTIONS THAT ROLL UPWARD ON AN OVERHEAD TRACK
- CAPABLE OF CLOSING OFF UNUSUALLY TALL OR WIDE OPENINGS
- FOR EXTERIOR OR INTERIOR USE
- NOT FOR FREQUENT USE

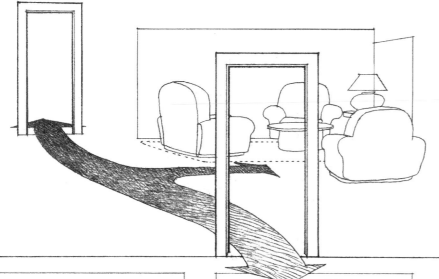

In linking the interior spaces of a building, doorways connect pathways. Their locations influence our patterns of movement from space to space as well as within a space. The nature of these patterns should be appropriate to the uses and activities housed within the interior spaces.

Space must be provided for our comfortable movement and the operation of doors. At the same time, there must also be sufficient and appropriately proportioned space remaining for the arrangement of furnishings.

Generally speaking, a room should have as few doorways as is feasible, and the paths that connect them should be as short and direct as possible without interfering with activity areas within the space.

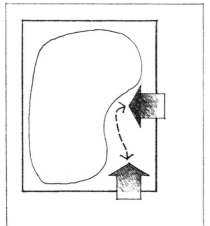

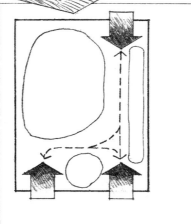

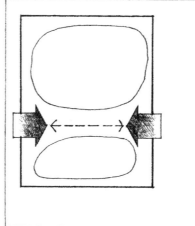

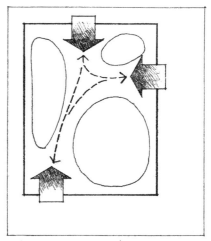

TWO DOORWAYS CLOSE TO EACH OTHER DEFINE A SHORT PATH THAT LEAVES A MAXIMUM AMOUNT OF USABLE FLOOR SPACE.

DOORWAYS SITUATED AT OR CLOSE TO CORNERS CAN DEFINE PATHS THAT RUN ALONG A ROOM'S WALLS. LOCATING THE DOORWAYS A COUPLE OF FEET AWAY FROM THE CORNERS ALLOWS FURNISHINGS SUCH AS STORAGE UNITS TO BE PLACED ALONG THE WALLS.

OPPOSING DOORWAYS DEFINE A STRAIGHT PATH THAT SUBDIVIDES A ROOM INTO TWO ZONES.

THREE DOORWAYS ON THREE WALLS CAN PRESENT A PROBLEM IF THE POSSIBLE PATHWAYS TAKE UP MUCH OF THE FLOOR AREA AND LEAVE A FRAGMENTED SERIES OF USABLE SPACES.

Another consideration in determining the location of a doorway is the view seen through its opening both from the adjacent space and upon entering. When visual privacy for a room is desired, a doorway, even when open, should not permit a direct view into the private zone of the space.

 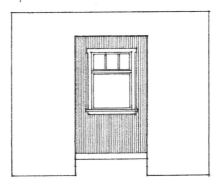 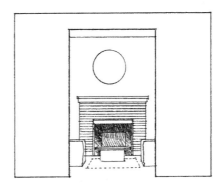 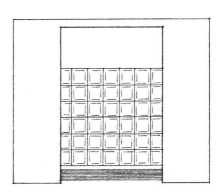

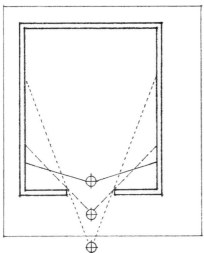

OUR VIEW BROADENS AS WE APPROACH A DOORWAY AND ENTER THROUGH IT INTO A ROOM.

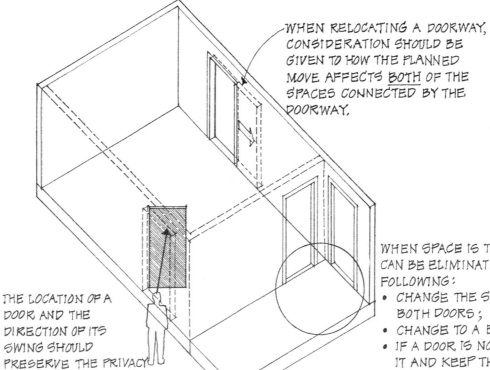

WHEN RELOCATING A DOORWAY, CONSIDERATION SHOULD BE GIVEN TO HOW THE PLANNED MOVE AFFECTS BOTH OF THE SPACES CONNECTED BY THE DOORWAY.

THE LOCATION OF A DOOR AND THE DIRECTION OF ITS SWING SHOULD PRESERVE THE PRIVACY OF A PERSONAL SPACE.

WHEN SPACE IS TIGHT BUT NO DOORWAY CAN BE ELIMINATED, CONSIDER THE FOLLOWING:
- CHANGE THE SWING OF ONE OR BOTH DOORS;
- CHANGE TO A BI-FOLD OR SLIDING DOOR;
- IF A DOOR IS NOT NECESSARY, REMOVE IT AND KEEP THE DOORWAY.

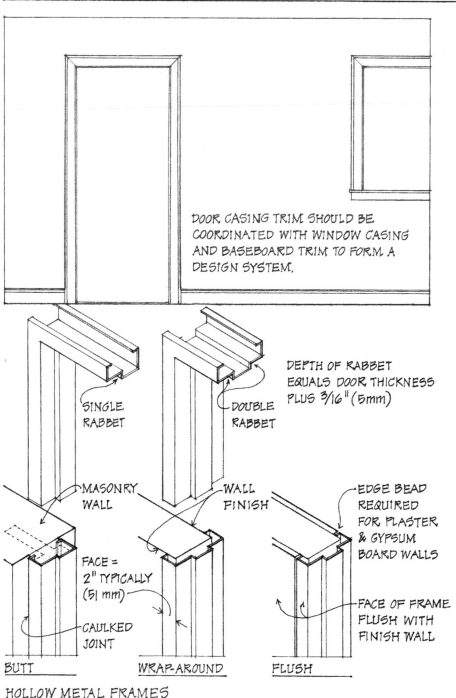

Since most doors are manufactured in a number of standard sizes and styles, the treatment of the opening and the design of the casing trim are the areas where the designer can manipulate the scale and character of a doorway.

Like doors, door frames are standard items. Hollow metal doors are hung in hollow metal frames. These may have single or double rabbets, and may either butt up against or wrap around the wall thickness. In addition to the standard flat face, various trim style moldings are available.

Wood doors use wood frames. Exterior door frames usually have integral stops, while interior frames may have applied stops. Casing trim is used to conceal the gap between the door frame and the wall surface. Casing trim can be omitted if the wall material can be finished neatly and butt up against the door frame.

DOOR CASING TRIM SHOULD BE COORDINATED WITH WINDOW CASING AND BASEBOARD TRIM TO FORM A DESIGN SYSTEM.

DEPTH OF RABBET EQUALS DOOR THICKNESS PLUS 3/16" (5mm)

SINGLE RABBET

DOUBLE RABBET

MASONRY WALL

WALL FINISH

EDGE BEAD REQUIRED FOR PLASTER & GYPSUM BOARD WALLS

FACE = 2" TYPICALLY (51 mm)

CAULKED JOINT

FACE OF FRAME FLUSH WITH FINISH WALL

BUTT   WRAP-AROUND   FLUSH

HOLLOW METAL FRAMES

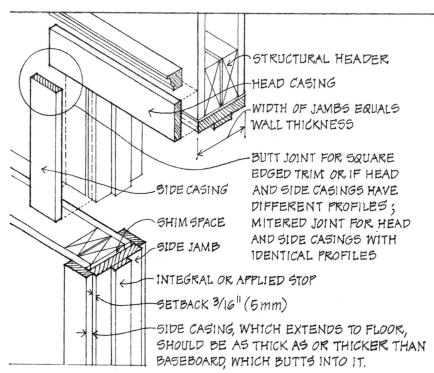

STRUCTURAL HEADER

HEAD CASING

WIDTH OF JAMBS EQUALS WALL THICKNESS

BUTT JOINT FOR SQUARE EDGED TRIM OR IF HEAD AND SIDE CASINGS HAVE DIFFERENT PROFILES; MITERED JOINT FOR HEAD AND SIDE CASINGS WITH IDENTICAL PROFILES

SIDE CASING

SHIM SPACE

SIDE JAMB

INTEGRAL OR APPLIED STOP

SETBACK 3/16" (5mm)

SIDE CASING, WHICH EXTENDS TO FLOOR, SHOULD BE AS THICK AS OR THICKER THAN BASEBOARD, WHICH BUTTS INTO IT.

WOOD FRAMES AND TRIM

Door casing trim, through its form and color, can accentuate a doorway and articulate the door as a distinct visual element in a space. The doorway opening itself can also be enlarged physically with sidelights and transoms, or visually with color and trimwork.

Conversely, a door frame and trim can, if desired, be minimized visually to reduce the scale of a doorway or to have it appear as a simple void in a wall.

If flush with the surrounding wall, a door can be finished to merge with and become part of the wall surface.

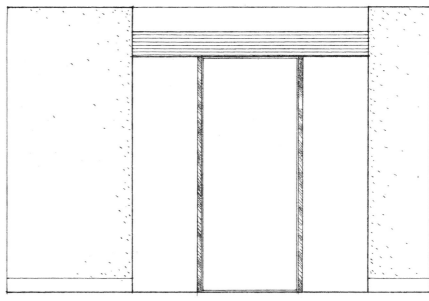

DOORWAY OPENING IS ENLARGED WITH ADDITIONAL GLAZING ABOVE DOOR AND SIDE LIGHTS TO ENHANCE ITS SCALE.

DOORWAY IS ELABORATED WITH TRIM WORK TO VISUALLY PRONOUNCE THE ENTRANCE INTO A ROOM. THE STYLE OF THE ELABORATION CAN GIVE A HINT AS TO WHAT LIES BEYOND.

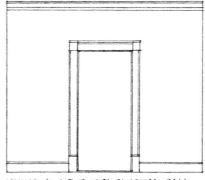

EVEN SIMPLE TRIMWORK CAN EMPHASIZE THE OPENING OF A DOORWAY IN A WALL PLANE.

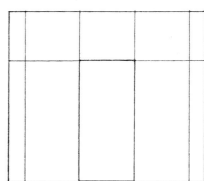

A DOOR CAN MERGE WITH THE SURROUNDING WALL SURFACE AND BECOME AN OBSCURE ELEMENT IN A SPACE.

IN EACH OF THE ABOVE CASES, HOW COLOR AND VALUE IS USED CAN MODIFY OUR PERCEPTION OF THE RELATIONSHIP BETWEEN A DOOR, ITS FRAME AND TRIM, AND THE SURROUNDING WALL SURFACE.

STAIRS

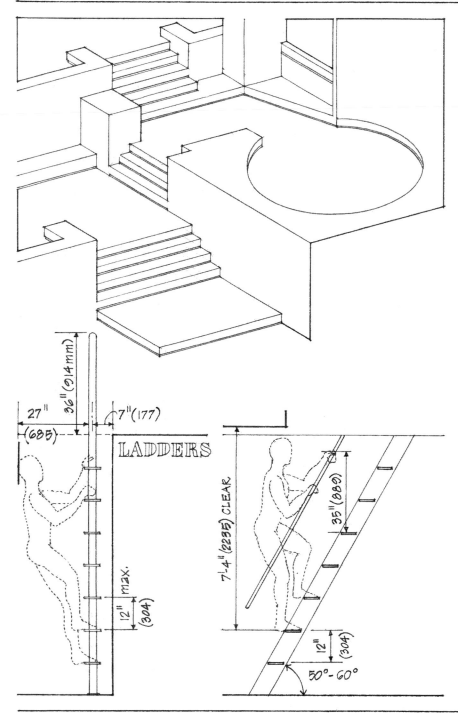

Stairs and stairways provide for our vertical movement between the various floor levels of a building. The two most important functional criteria in the design of stairs are safety and ease of ascent and descent. The dimensions of a stair's risers and treads should be proportioned to fit our body movement. Their pitch, if steep, can make ascent physically tiring as well as psychologically forbidding, and can make descent precarious. If shallow, a stair must have treads deep enough to fit our stride.

Building codes regulate the maximum and minimum dimensions of risers and treads. In addition, there are three rules of thumb that can be used to determine the proper proportion between the riser and tread dimensions of a stairway.

- Riser x Tread   = 70 to 75   (Measurement in inches)
- Riser + Tread   = 17 to 17½
- (2) Riser + Tread = 24 to 25

To determine the actual riser dimension of a stair, divide the total rise (the floor-to-floor height) by a whole number that gives a riser dimension closest to the one desired. The actual tread dimension can then be determined by using one of the rule-of-thumb formulas. Since in any flight of stairs there is one less tread than the number of risers, the total run can be easily determined.

LADDERS

27" (685) 36" (914mm) 7" (177)

7'-4" (2235) CLEAR   35" (889)

12" MAX.   12" (304)

12" (304)   50° - 60°

STAIRS

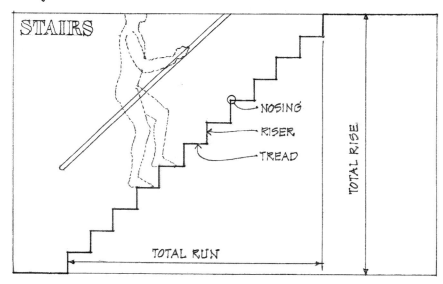

NOSING
RISER
TREAD
TOTAL RISE
TOTAL RUN

A stairway should be wide enough to comfortably accommodate our passage as well as any furnishings and equipment that must be moved up or down the steps. Building codes specify minimum widths based on occupant loads. Beyond these minimums, however, the width of a stairway also provides a visual clue to the public or private quality of the stairway.

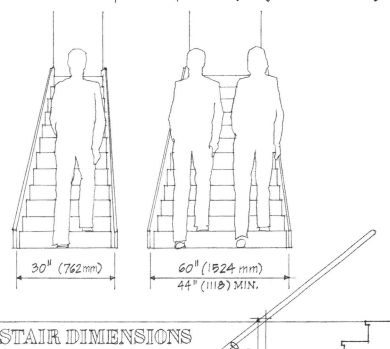

30" (762mm)

60" (1524 mm)
44" (1118) MIN.

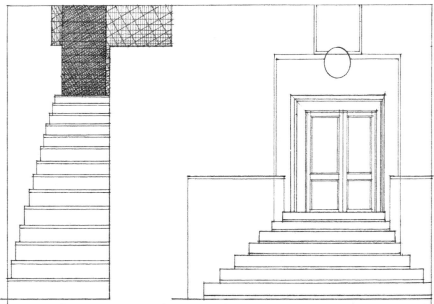

WIDTH AND ANGLE OF ASCENT ARE THE VARIABLES THAT DETERMINE A STAIR'S ACCESSIBILITY.

STAIR DIMENSIONS

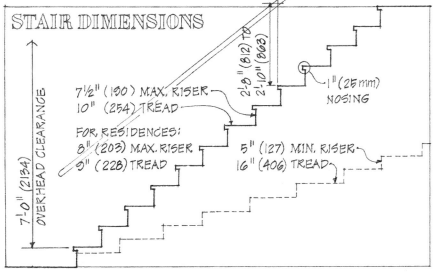

7'-0" (2134) OVERHEAD CLEARANCE

7½" (190) MAX. RISER
10" (254) TREAD

FOR RESIDENCES:
8" (203) MAX. RISER
9" (228) TREAD

2'-8" (812) TO
2'-10" (863)

1" (25 mm) NOSING

5" (127) MIN. RISER
16" (406) TREAD

RAMPS

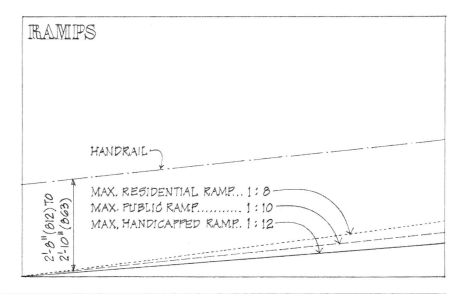

HANDRAIL

2'-8" (812) TO
2'-10" (863)

MAX. RESIDENTIAL RAMP... 1:8
MAX. PUBLIC RAMP............ 1:10
MAX. HANDICAPPED RAMP. 1:12

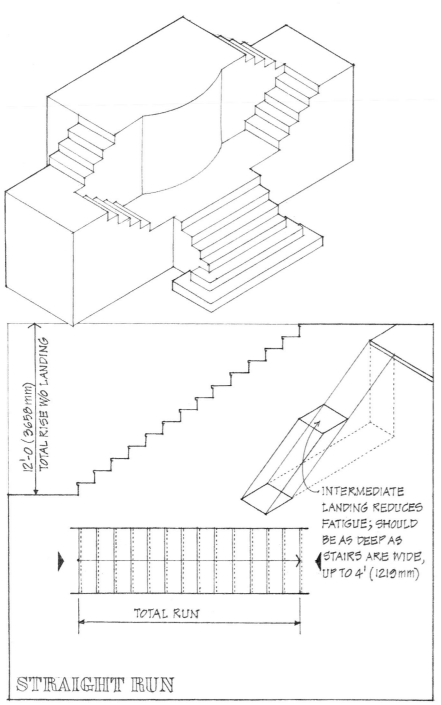

The configuration of a stairway determines the direction of our path as we ascend or descend its steps. There are several basic ways in which to configure the runs of a stairway. These variations result from the use of landings, which interrupt a stair run and enable it to change direction. Landings also provide opportunities for rest and possibilities for access and outlook from the stairway. Together with the pitch of a stair, the locations of landings determine the rhythm of our movement up or down a stair.

An important consideration in the planning of any stairway is how it links the paths of movement at each floor level. Another is the amount of space the stair requires. Each basic stair type has inherent proportions that will affect its possible location relative to other spaces around it. These proportions can be altered to some degree by adjusting the location of landings in the pattern. In each case, space should be provided at both the top and bottom of a stairway for safe and comfortable access and egress.

12'-0 (3658mm) TOTAL RISE W/O LANDING

INTERMEDIATE LANDING REDUCES FATIGUE; SHOULD BE AS DEEP AS STAIRS ARE WIDE, UP TO 4' (1219mm)

TOTAL RUN

STRAIGHT RUN

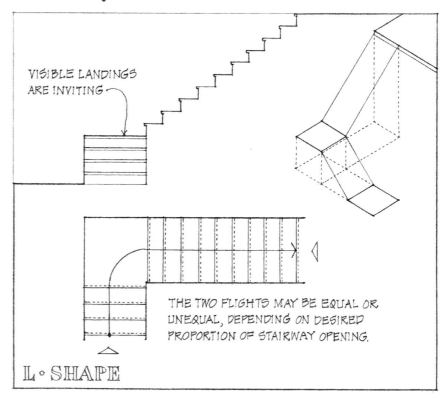

VISIBLE LANDINGS ARE INVITING

THE TWO FLIGHTS MAY BE EQUAL OR UNEQUAL, DEPENDING ON DESIRED PROPORTION OF STAIRWAY OPENING.

L·SHAPE

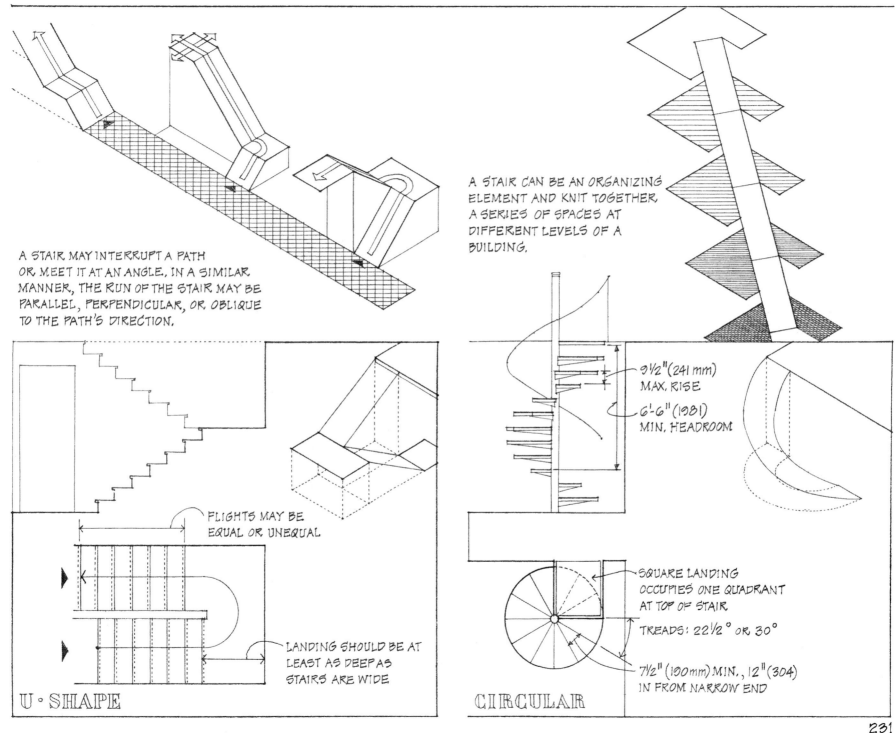

A STAIR MAY INTERRUPT A PATH OR MEET IT AT AN ANGLE. IN A SIMILAR MANNER, THE RUN OF THE STAIR MAY BE PARALLEL, PERPENDICULAR, OR OBLIQUE TO THE PATH'S DIRECTION.

A STAIR CAN BE AN ORGANIZING ELEMENT AND KNIT TOGETHER A SERIES OF SPACES AT DIFFERENT LEVELS OF A BUILDING.

9½" (241 mm) MAX. RISE

6'-6" (1981) MIN. HEADROOM

FLIGHTS MAY BE EQUAL OR UNEQUAL

LANDING SHOULD BE AT LEAST AS DEEP AS STAIRS ARE WIDE

SQUARE LANDING OCCUPIES ONE QUADRANT AT TOP OF STAIR

TREADS: 22½° OR 30°

7½" (190mm) MIN., 12" (304) IN FROM NARROW END

U·SHAPE

CIRCULAR

231

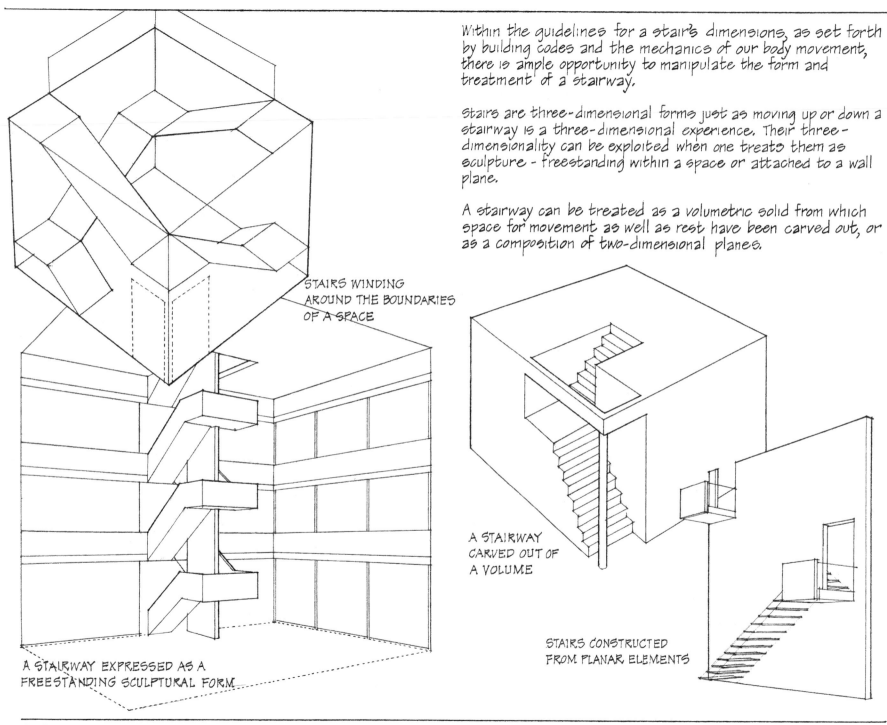

Within the guidelines for a stair's dimensions, as set forth by building codes and the mechanics of our body movement, there is ample opportunity to manipulate the form and treatment of a stairway.

Stairs are three-dimensional forms just as moving up or down a stairway is a three-dimensional experience. Their three-dimensionality can be exploited when one treats them as sculpture - freestanding within a space or attached to a wall plane.

A stairway can be treated as a volumetric solid from which space for movement as well as rest have been carved out, or as a composition of two-dimensional planes.

STAIRS WINDING AROUND THE BOUNDARIES OF A SPACE

A STAIRWAY CARVED OUT OF A VOLUME

STAIRS CONSTRUCTED FROM PLANAR ELEMENTS

A STAIRWAY EXPRESSED AS A FREESTANDING SCULPTURAL FORM

The path of a stair can rise between walls through a narrow shaft of space, or meander through and knit together a series of spaces. A space can itself become a giant, elaborated stairway.

Treads can spill out at the bottom of a stairway as an invitation, or be extended further into platforms for seating or terraces for activity.

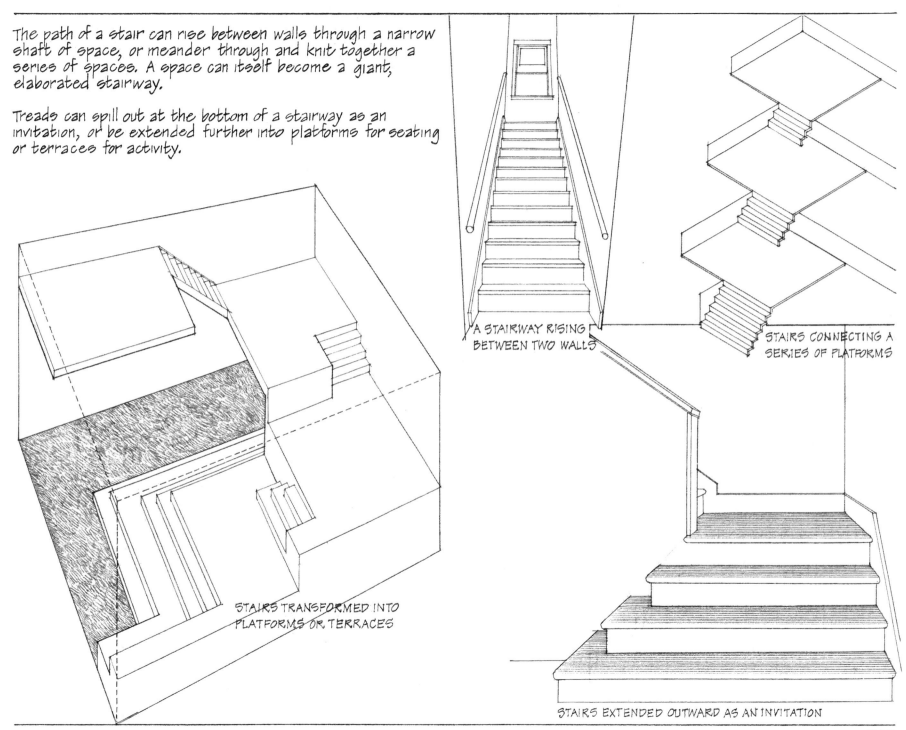

A STAIRWAY RISING BETWEEN TWO WALLS

STAIRS CONNECTING A SERIES OF PLATFORMS

STAIRS TRANSFORMED INTO PLATFORMS OR TERRACES

STAIRS EXTENDED OUTWARD AS AN INVITATION

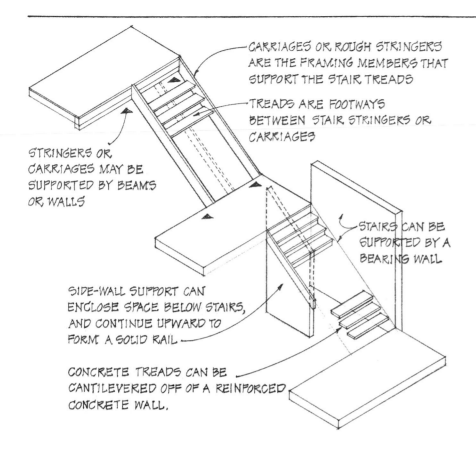

CARRIAGES OR ROUGH STRINGERS ARE THE FRAMING MEMBERS THAT SUPPORT THE STAIR TREADS

TREADS ARE FOOTWAYS BETWEEN STAIR STRINGERS OR CARRIAGES

STRINGERS OR CARRIAGES MAY BE SUPPORTED BY BEAMS OR WALLS

STAIRS CAN BE SUPPORTED BY A BEARING WALL

SIDE-WALL SUPPORT CAN ENCLOSE SPACE BELOW STAIRS, AND CONTINUE UPWARD TO FORM A SOLID RAIL

CONCRETE TREADS CAN BE CANTILEVERED OFF OF A REINFORCED CONCRETE WALL.

Stair construction can be understood by thinking of the stairway first as a sloping floor plane which is supported at its ends or along its sides by beams or walls. Then the individual treads can be thought of as small beams of wood or metal that extend between the stair stringers. Concrete stairs are designed as sloping floor slabs.

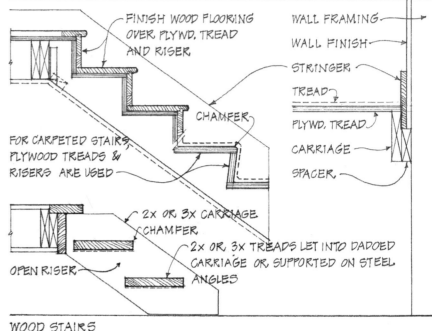

FINISH WOOD FLOORING OVER PLYWD, TREAD AND RISER

WALL FRAMING

WALL FINISH

STRINGER

TREAD

CHAMFER

PLYWD, TREAD

FOR CARPETED STAIRS, PLYWOOD TREADS & RISERS ARE USED

CARRIAGE

SPACER

2x OR 3x CARRIAGE

CHAMFER

2x OR 3x TREADS LET INTO DADOED CARRIAGE OR SUPPORTED ON STEEL ANGLES

OPEN RISER

WOOD STAIRS

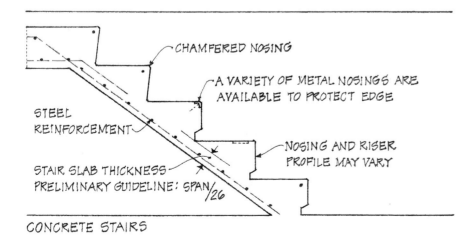

CHAMFERED NOSING

A VARIETY OF METAL NOSINGS ARE AVAILABLE TO PROTECT EDGE

STEEL REINFORCEMENT

NOSING AND RISER PROFILE MAY VARY

STAIR SLAB THICKNESS PRELIMINARY GUIDELINE: SPAN/26

CONCRETE STAIRS

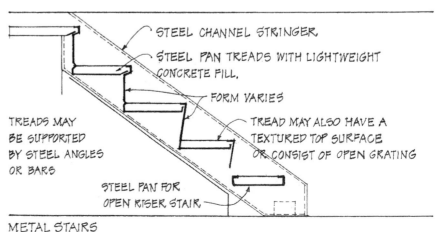

STEEL CHANNEL STRINGER

STEEL PAN TREADS WITH LIGHTWEIGHT CONCRETE FILL.

FORM VARIES

TREADS MAY BE SUPPORTED BY STEEL ANGLES OR BARS

TREAD MAY ALSO HAVE A TEXTURED TOP SURFACE OR CONSIST OF OPEN GRATING

STEEL PAN FOR OPEN RISER STAIR

METAL STAIRS

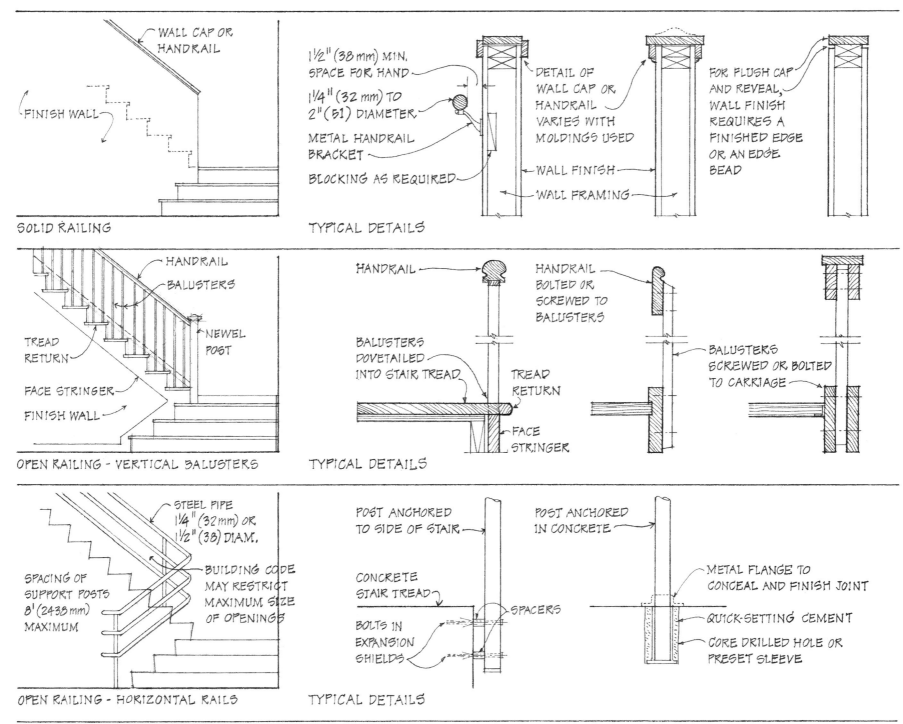

WALL CAP OR HANDRAIL

FINISH WALL

SOLID RAILING

1½" (38 mm) MIN. SPACE FOR HAND

1¼" (32 mm) TO 2" (51) DIAMETER

METAL HANDRAIL BRACKET

BLOCKING AS REQUIRED

DETAIL OF WALL CAP OR HANDRAIL VARIES WITH MOLDINGS USED

WALL FINISH

WALL FRAMING

FOR FLUSH CAP AND REVEAL, WALL FINISH REQUIRES A FINISHED EDGE OR AN EDGE BEAD

TYPICAL DETAILS

HANDRAIL

BALUSTERS

NEWEL POST

TREAD RETURN

FACE STRINGER

FINISH WALL

OPEN RAILING - VERTICAL BALUSTERS

HANDRAIL

BALUSTERS DOVETAILED INTO STAIR TREAD

TREAD RETURN

FACE STRINGER

HANDRAIL BOLTED OR SCREWED TO BALUSTERS

BALUSTERS SCREWED OR BOLTED TO CARRIAGE

TYPICAL DETAILS

STEEL PIPE 1¼" (32 mm) OR 1½" (38) DIAM.

SPACING OF SUPPORT POSTS 8' (2438 mm) MAXIMUM

BUILDING CODE MAY RESTRICT MAXIMUM SIZE OF OPENINGS

OPEN RAILING - HORIZONTAL RAILS

POST ANCHORED TO SIDE OF STAIR

CONCRETE STAIR TREAD

BOLTS IN EXPANSION SHIELDS

SPACERS

POST ANCHORED IN CONCRETE

METAL FLANGE TO CONCEAL AND FINISH JOINT

QUICK-SETTING CEMENT

CORE DRILLED HOLE OR PRESET SLEEVE

TYPICAL DETAILS

FIREPLACES

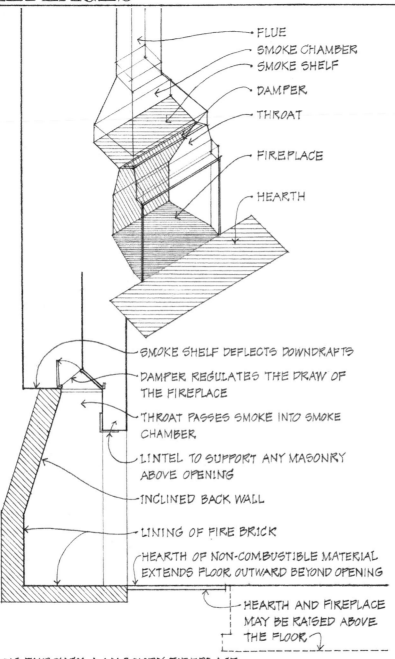

While a traditional fireplace is not as efficient for heating an interior space as a good stove, few would dispute the special attraction it holds for people. The warmth and flames of an open fire are like a magnet, enticing people to gather around a fireplace. Even without a fire, a fireplace can be a unique center of interest, and serve as the focal point about which a room can be arranged.

A fireplace must be designed to draw properly, to sustain combustion safely, and to carry smoke away efficiently. Thus the proportions of a fireplace and the arrangement of its components are subject to both the laws of nature and the local building code. It is important for the interior designer to note the amount of space a fireplace requires, and how the face - the opening, surround, and hearth - can be treated.

- FLUE
- SMOKE CHAMBER
- SMOKE SHELF
- DAMPER
- THROAT
- FIREPLACE
- HEARTH

- SMOKE SHELF DEFLECTS DOWNDRAFTS
- DAMPER REGULATES THE DRAW OF THE FIREPLACE
- THROAT PASSES SMOKE INTO SMOKE CHAMBER
- LINTEL TO SUPPORT ANY MASONRY ABOVE OPENING
- INCLINED BACK WALL
- LINING OF FIRE BRICK
- HEARTH OF NON-COMBUSTIBLE MATERIAL EXTENDS FLOOR OUTWARD BEYOND OPENING
- HEARTH AND FIREPLACE MAY BE RAISED ABOVE THE FLOOR

SECTION THROUGH A MASONRY FIREPLACE

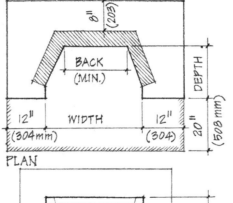

8" (203) · BACK (MIN.) · DEPTH · 20" (508 mm)

12" (304mm) · WIDTH · 12" (304)

PLAN

HEIGHT

8" (203 mm) MIN. CLEARANCE FOR ANY WOOD AROUND OPENING

ELEVATION

GUIDELINES FOR FIREPLACE DIMENSIONS:

WIDTH	HEIGHT	DEPTH	BACK
24"	24"	16"-18"	14"
28"	24"	16"-18"	14"
30"	28"-30"	16"-18"	16"
36"	28"-30"	16"-18"	22"
42"	28"-30"	16"-18"	28"
48"	32"	18"-20"	32"

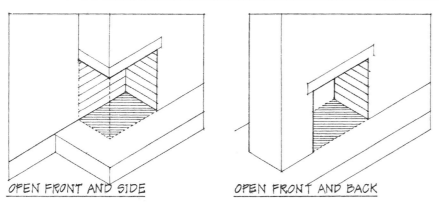

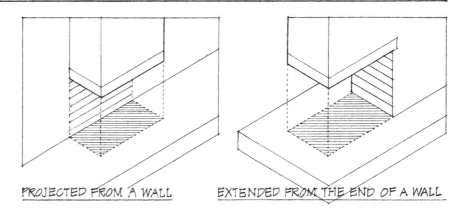

OPEN FRONT AND SIDE   OPEN FRONT AND BACK   PROJECTED FROM A WALL   EXTENDED FROM THE END OF A WALL

In addition to the typical single opening, a fireplace may be open on two, three, or, if freestanding, on all four sides. Even when designed properly, these types must be located and oriented carefully to prevent room drafts from causing smoking problems.

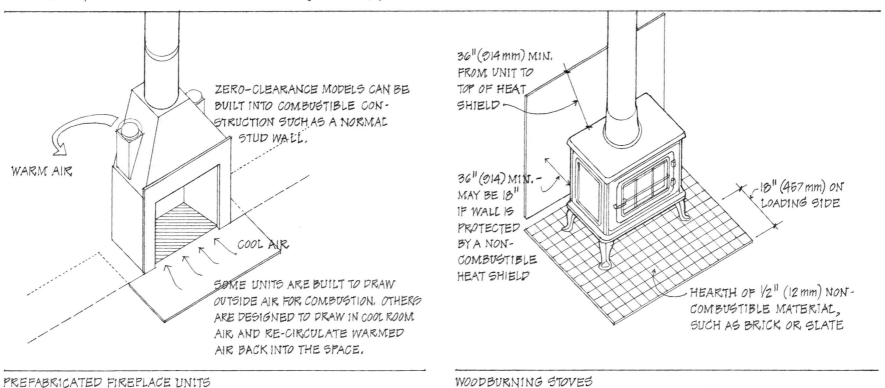

ZERO-CLEARANCE MODELS CAN BE BUILT INTO COMBUSTIBLE CONSTRUCTION SUCH AS A NORMAL STUD WALL.

WARM AIR

COOL AIR

SOME UNITS ARE BUILT TO DRAW OUTSIDE AIR FOR COMBUSTION. OTHERS ARE DESIGNED TO DRAW IN COOL ROOM AIR AND RE-CIRCULATE WARMED AIR BACK INTO THE SPACE.

PREFABRICATED FIREPLACE UNITS

36" (914mm) MIN. FROM UNIT TO TOP OF HEAT SHIELD

36" (914) MIN. MAY BE 18" IF WALL IS PROTECTED BY A NON-COMBUSTIBLE HEAT SHIELD

18" (457mm) ON LOADING SIDE

HEARTH OF 1/2" (12mm) NON-COMBUSTIBLE MATERIAL, SUCH AS BRICK OR SLATE

WOODBURNING STOVES

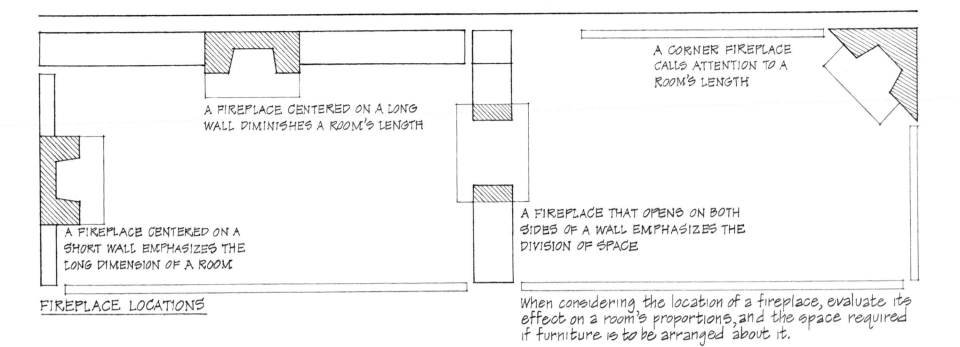

A FIREPLACE CENTERED ON A LONG WALL DIMINISHES A ROOM'S LENGTH

A FIREPLACE CENTERED ON A SHORT WALL EMPHASIZES THE LONG DIMENSION OF A ROOM

A CORNER FIREPLACE CALLS ATTENTION TO A ROOM'S LENGTH

A FIREPLACE THAT OPENS ON BOTH SIDES OF A WALL EMPHASIZES THE DIVISION OF SPACE

FIREPLACE LOCATIONS

When considering the location of a fireplace, evaluate its effect on a room's proportions, and the space required if furniture is to be arranged about it.

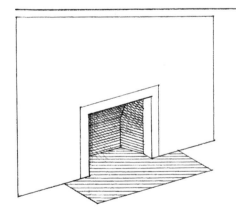 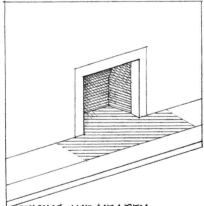 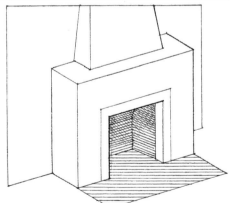

OPENING FLUSH WITH WALL SURFACE

Fireplace can be unobtrusive or be visually active depending on treatment of surround.

OPENING AND HEARTH RAISED OFF FLOOR

Fireplace and hearth together become more of an integral part of a room.

OPENING AND FIREPLACE PROJECTED FROM WALL

Fireplace becomes a three-dimensional form and a forceful element in space.

RELATIONSHIP BETWEEN FIREPLACE AND THE WALL PLANE

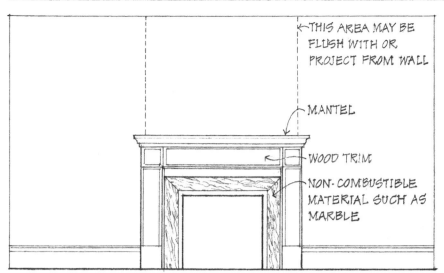

← THIS AREA MAY BE FLUSH WITH OR PROJECT FROM WALL

MANTEL

WOOD TRIM

NON-COMBUSTIBLE MATERIAL SUCH AS MARBLE

THE TREATMENT OF THE SURROUND VISUALLY ENLARGES THE FIREPLACE OPENING, ENHANCES IT AS A FOCAL POINT, AND INTEGRATES IT WITH THE REST OF A ROOM'S TRIMWORK.

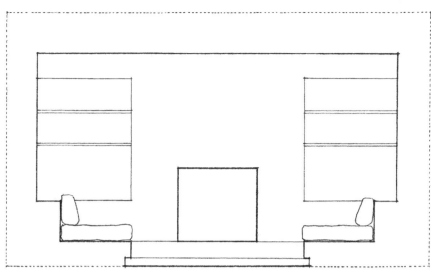

THE RAISED HEARTH OF A FIREPLACE CAN BE EXTENDED TO FORM A PLATFORM FOR SEATING. THIS PLATFORM ALONG WITH THE FIREPLACE CAN BEGIN TO DEFINE AN ALCOVE SPACE.

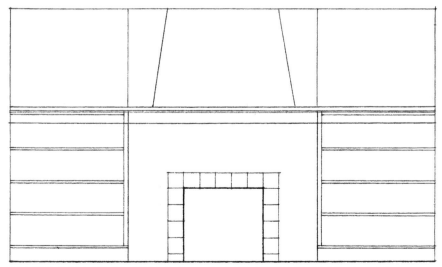

WHEN PROJECTING INTO A ROOM, A FIREPLACE ALSO FORMS RECESSES TO EITHER SIDE THAT CAN BE USED FOR STORAGE.

FIREPLACE TREATMENTS

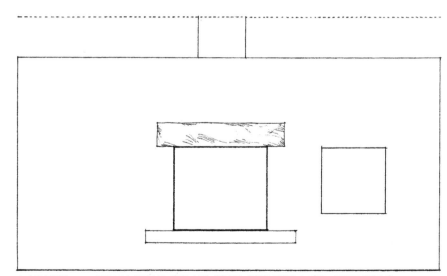

A LINTEL OR BEAM THAT SPANS THE FIREPLACE OPENING IN A MASONRY WALL CAN BE EXPOSED AND EMBELLISHED AS A VISUAL DESIGN ELEMENT.

FURNITURE

Furniture is the one category of design elements that lies almost wholly within the realm of interior design. While walls, floors, ceilings, windows, and doors are established in the architectural design of a building, the selection and arrangement of furniture within the building's spaces are major tasks of interior design.

Furniture mediates between architecture and people. It offers a transition in form and scale between an interior space and the individual. It makes interiors habitable by providing comfort and utility in the tasks and activities we undertake.

In addition to fulfilling specific functions, furniture contributes to the visual character of interior settings. The form, lines, color, texture, and scale of individual pieces, as well as their spatial organization, play a major role in establishing the expressive qualities of a room.

The pieces can be linear, planar, or volumetric in form; their lines may be rectilinear or curvilinear, angular or freeflowing. They can have horizontal or vertical proportions; they can be light and airy, or sturdy and solid. Their texture can be slick and shiny, smooth and satiny, warm and plush, or rough and heavy; their color can be natural or transparent in quality, warm or cool in temperature, light or dark in value.

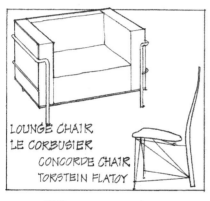

LOUNGE CHAIR
LE CORBUSIER

CONCORDE CHAIR
TORSTEIN FLATOY

WINDSOR CHAIR

EGG CHAIR
ARNE JACOBSEN

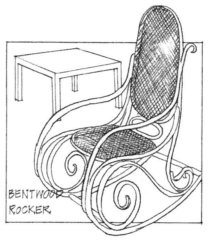

BENTWOOD
ROCKER

MACKINTOSH

HANS WEGNER

LOUIS XVI ARMCHAIR

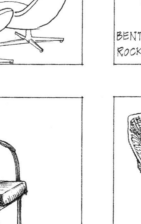

BRNO CHAIR - MIES VAN DER ROHE

BAR HARBOR WICKER

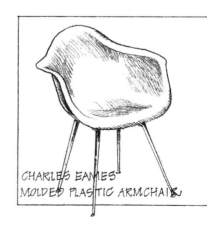

CHARLES EAMES
MOLDED PLASTIC ARMCHAIR

Furniture can, depending on the quality of its design, either offer or limit physical comfort in a real and tangible way. Our bodies will tell us if a chair is uncomfortable, or if a table is too high or too low for our use. There is definite feedback which tells us whether a piece of furniture is appropriate for its intended use.

Human factors, therefore, are a major influence on the form, proportion, and scale of furniture. To provide utility and comfort in the execution of our tasks, furniture should be designed first to respond or correspond to our dimensions, the clearances required by our patterns of movement, and the nature of the activity we are engaged in.

Our perception of comfort is, of course, conditioned by the nature of the task or activity being performed, its duration, and other circumstantial factors such as the quality of lighting and even our state of mind. At times, the effectiveness of a furniture element may depend on its correct use – on our learning how to use it.

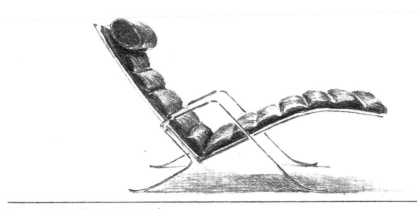

KNOLL INTERNATIONAL INC.

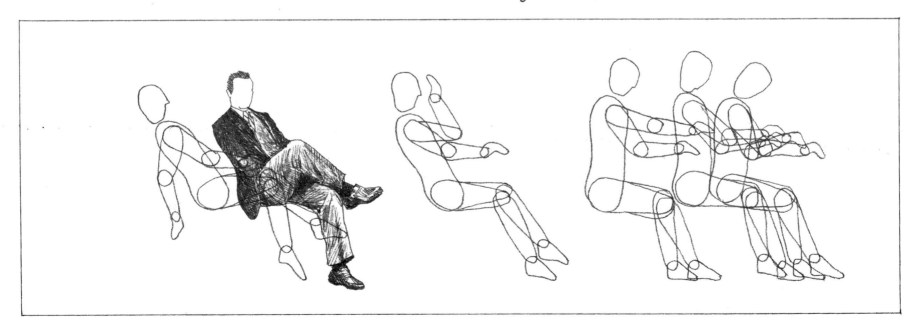

The way furniture is arranged in a room will affect how the space is used and perceived. Furniture can simply be placed as sculptural objects in space. More often, however, furniture is organized into functional groupings. These groupings, in turn, can be arranged to organize and structure space.

Most furniture consists of individual or unit pieces which allow for flexibility in their arrangement. The pieces are movable and may consist of various specialized elements as well as a mix of forms and styles.

Built-in arrangements of furniture, on the other hand, allow for the flexible use of more space. There is generally more continuity of form among the furniture elements with fewer gaps between them.

Modular units combine the unified appearance of built-in furniture with the flexibility and movability of individual unit pieces.

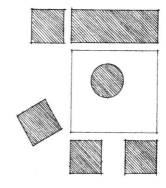

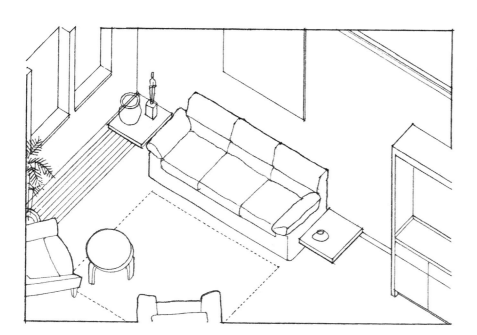

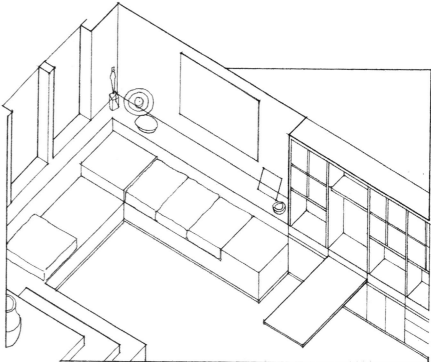

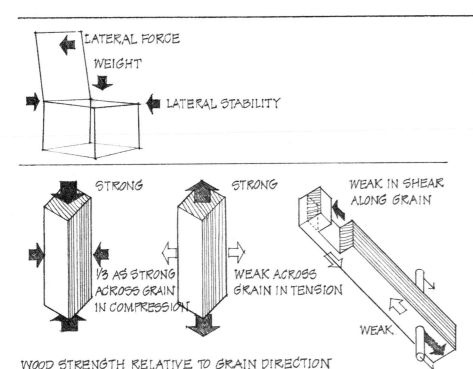

LATERAL FORCE

WEIGHT

LATERAL STABILITY

STRONG   STRONG   WEAK IN SHEAR ALONG GRAIN

⅓ AS STRONG ACROSS GRAIN IN COMPRESSION   WEAK ACROSS GRAIN IN TENSION

WEAK

WOOD STRENGTH RELATIVE TO GRAIN DIRECTION

Furniture may be constructed of wood, metal, or plastic. Each material has strengths and weaknesses which should be recognized in furniture design and construction if a piece is to be strong, stable, and durable in use.

Wood is the standard furniture material. A primary consideration in how it is used and joined is its grain direction. Wood is strong in compression with the grain but can be dented under loading perpendicular to the grain. In tension, wood can be pulled in the direction of its grain, but will split when pulled at a right angle to the grain. Wood is weakest in shear along its grain. Another important consideration is the expansion and contraction of wood across its grain with changes in moisture content. All these factors bear on the way wood members are configured and joined in furniture construction.

Plywood is a sheet material which consists of an odd number of plies layed at right angles in grain direction to each other. Thus, a plywood panel has strength in two directions. In addition, the quality of the face veneer can be controlled in appearance.

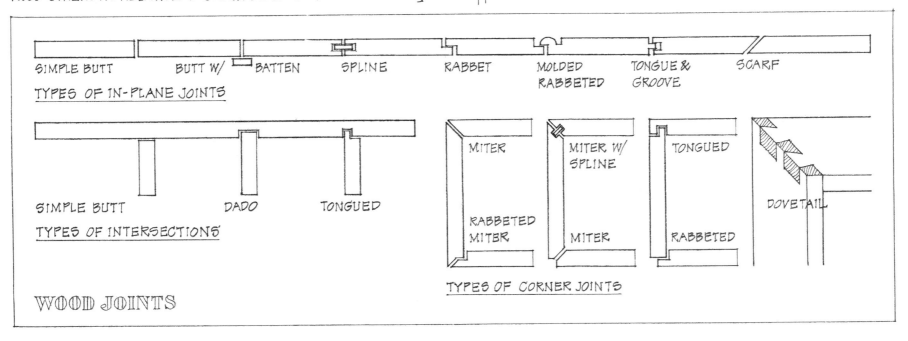

SIMPLE BUTT   BUTT W/ BATTEN   SPLINE   RABBET   MOLDED RABBETED   TONGUE & GROOVE   SCARF

TYPES OF IN-PLANE JOINTS

SIMPLE BUTT   DADO   TONGUED

TYPES OF INTERSECTIONS

MITER

RABBETED MITER

MITER W/ SPLINE

MITER

TONGUED

RABBETED

DOVETAIL

TYPES OF CORNER JOINTS

WOOD JOINTS

Like wood, metal is strong both in compression and tension, but it does not have a strong grain direction and it is ductile. These factors, along with a high strength-to-weight ratio, enable metal to have relatively thin cross sections and to be curved or bent in furniture construction. Methods for joining metal are analogous to those for wood. Instead of being nailed, metal can be screwed, bolted, or riveted; instead of being glued, metal can be welded.

Plastic is a unique material in the way it can be shaped, formed, textured, colored, and used. This is due to the numerous types and variations of plastic materials available and under development today. While not as strong as wood or metal, plastic can be strengthened with glass fiber. More significantly, it can be easily shaped into structurally stable and rigid forms. For this reason, plastic furniture almost always consists of a single piece without joints or connections.

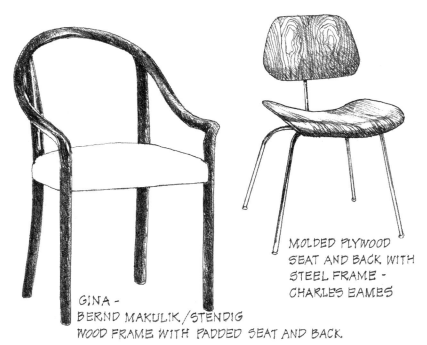

GINA –
BERND MAKULIK/STENDIG
WOOD FRAME WITH PADDED SEAT AND BACK

MOLDED PLYWOOD
SEAT AND BACK WITH
STEEL FRAME –
CHARLES EAMES

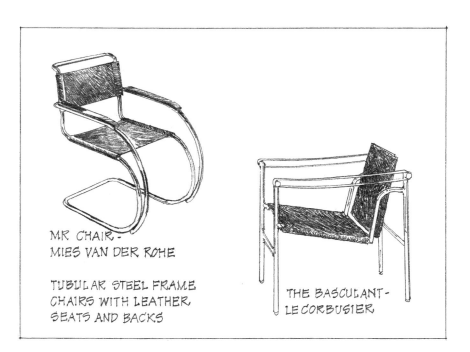

MR CHAIR –
MIES VAN DER ROHE

TUBULAR STEEL FRAME
CHAIRS WITH LEATHER
SEATS AND BACKS

THE BASCULANT –
LE CORBUSIER

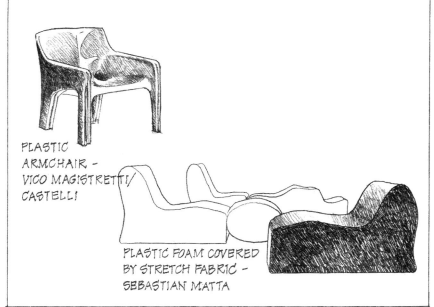

PLASTIC
ARMCHAIR –
VICO MAGISTRETTI/
CASTELLI

PLASTIC FOAM COVERED
BY STRETCH FABRIC –
SEBASTIAN MATTA

SEATING

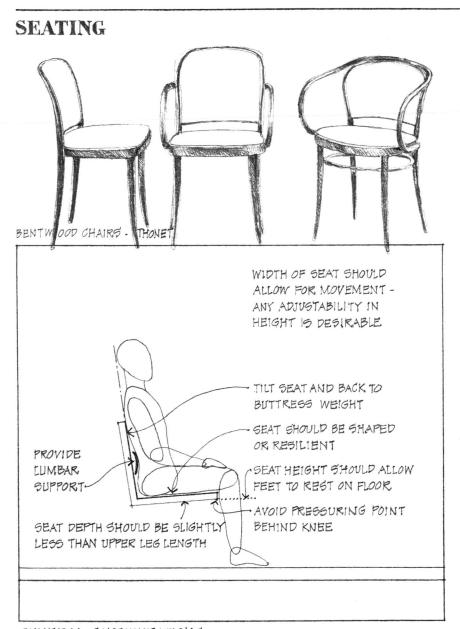

BENTWOOD CHAIRS - THONET

Seating should be designed to comfortably support the weight and shape of the user/occupants. Because of the great variation in body size, however, and the danger of designing too precisely what conditions would result in a comfortable seating device, what is illustrated on these two pages are the factors which affect our personal judgment of comfort and a range of dimensions which should serve only as guidelines.

The comfort factor is also affected by the nature of the activity the user might be engaged in at the time. There are different types of chairs and seating for different uses. On the following pages are illustrations intended to show the range of seating available to the interior designer.

WIDTH OF SEAT SHOULD ALLOW FOR MOVEMENT - ANY ADJUSTABILITY IN HEIGHT IS DESIRABLE

TILT SEAT AND BACK TO BUTTRESS WEIGHT

SEAT SHOULD BE SHAPED OR RESILIENT

SEAT HEIGHT SHOULD ALLOW FEET TO REST ON FLOOR

AVOID PRESSURING POINT BEHIND KNEE

PROVIDE LUMBAR SUPPORT

SEAT DEPTH SHOULD BE SLIGHTLY LESS THAN UPPER LEG LENGTH

GENERAL CONSIDERATIONS

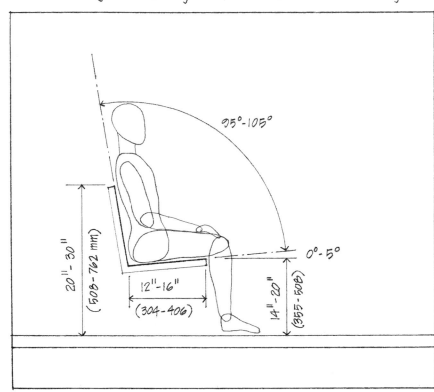

95°-105°

0°-5°

20"-30" (508-762 mm)

12"-16" (304-406)

14"-20" (355-508)

GENERAL PURPOSE CHAIR

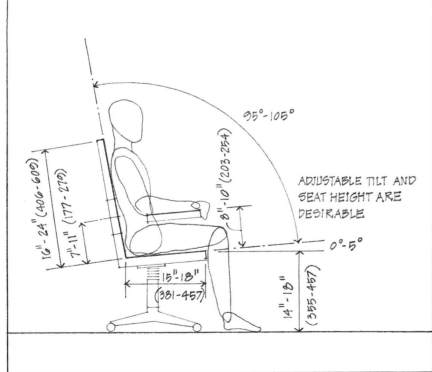

95°-105°

16"-24" (406-609)

7"-11" (177-279)

8"-10" (203-254)

ADJUSTABLE TILT AND
SEAT HEIGHT ARE
DESIRABLE

0°-5°

15"-18"
(381-457)

14"-18"
(355-457)

OFFICE CHAIR

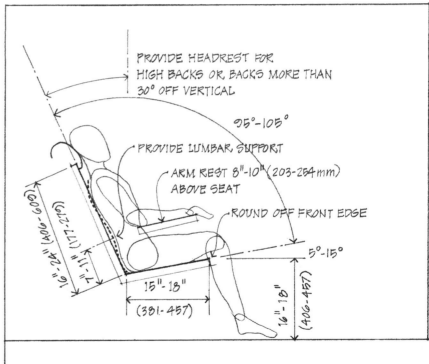

PROVIDE HEADREST FOR
HIGH BACKS OR, BACKS MORE THAN
30° OFF VERTICAL

95°-105°

PROVIDE LUMBAR SUPPORT

ARM REST 8"-10" (203-254mm)
ABOVE SEAT

ROUND OFF FRONT EDGE

16"-24" (406-609)

7"-11" (177-279)

5°-15°

15"-18"
(381-457)

16"-18"
(406-457)

EASY CHAIR

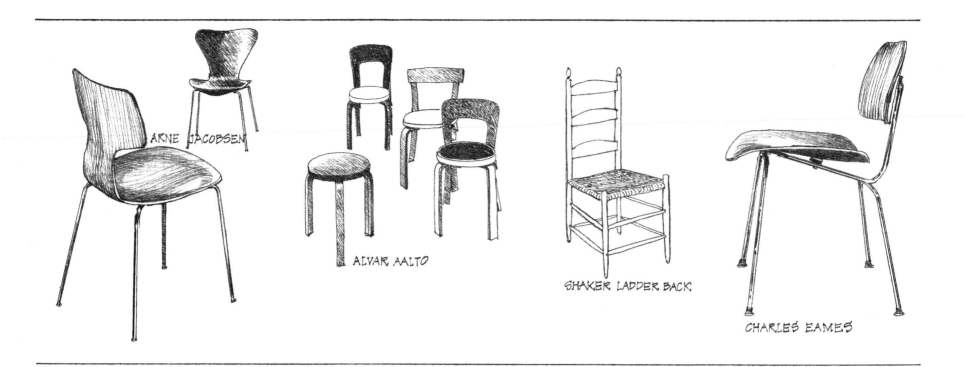

ARNE JACOBSEN

ALVAR AALTO

SHAKER LADDER BACK

CHARLES EAMES

EERO SAARINEN

BILL STEPHENS

THONET
ARMCHAIR

QUEEN ANNE
ARMCHAIR

ANGELO MANGIAROTTI

AFRA & TOBIA SCARPA.

VICO MAGISTRETTI

BJÖRN ALGE

HANS WEGNER

HARRY BERTOIA

HANS WEGNER

ERGON CHAIR- WILLIAM STUMPF
HERMAN MILLER

LINEA - KLÖBER
BRAYTON INTERNATIONAL

WILKHAHN SEATING
VECTA CONTRACT

CHAISE LONGUE - MARTIN SZEKELY

LOUNGE CHAIR - CHARLES EAMES
HERMAN MILLER

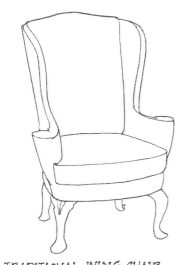

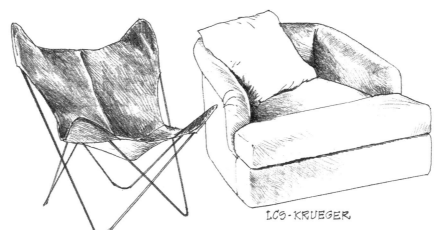

LCS - KRUEGER

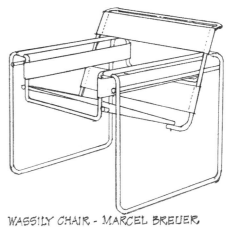

WASSILY CHAIR - MARCEL BREUER

TRADITIONAL WING CHAIR

SLING CHAIR - BONET, HURCHAN, AND
FERRARI - HARDOY

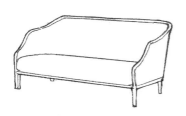

PIERLUIGI MOLINARI

ALESSANDRO MENDINI

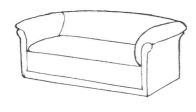

4 SOFAS - WARD BENNETT DESIGNS - BRICKEL ASSOCIATES

MAURO LIPPARINI · ROBERTO TAPINASSI

BURKHARDT VOGTHERR

TABLES

Tables are essentially flat, horizontal surfaces, supported off the floor, and used for dining, working, storage, and display. They should have the following attributes:

- Strength and stability to support items in use
- Correct size, shape, and height off floor for intended use
- Construction of durable materials

Table tops can be of wood, glass, plastic, stone, tile, or concrete. The surface finish should be durable and have good wearing qualities. The surface color and texture should have the proper light reflectance for the visual task.

Table tops can be supported with legs, trestles, solid bases, or cabinets. They can also swing out or down from wall storage units and be supported by folding legs or brackets.

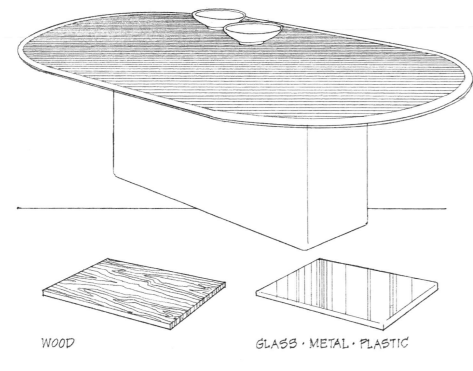

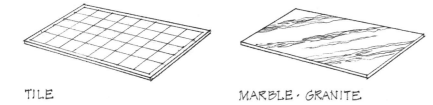

WOOD   GLASS · METAL · PLASTIC

TILE   MARBLE · GRANITE

VARIATIONS: SHAPE, SIZE, MATERIAL, COLOR, TEXTURE

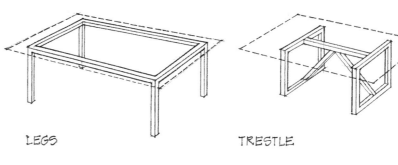

LEGS   TRESTLE

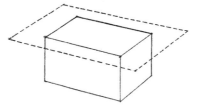

SOLID · PEDESTAL   CABINET · CASEWORK

TABLE TOPS   TABLE SUPPORTS

24" (609 mm)

16" (406)

A MINIMUM OF 24" (609mm) SHOULD BE PROVIDED FOR EACH PERSON AROUND PERIMETER OF TABLE

TABLE SHAPE SHOULD BE COMPATIBLE WITH SHAPE OF ROOM

SURFACE FINISH SHOULD PROVIDE AN ATTRACTIVE BACK- GROUND FOR TABLE SETTINGS

FOR FLEXIBILITY IN ACCOMMODATING BOTH SMALL AND LARGE GROUPS, TABLES THAT EXTEND WITH LEAVES ARE DESIRABLE

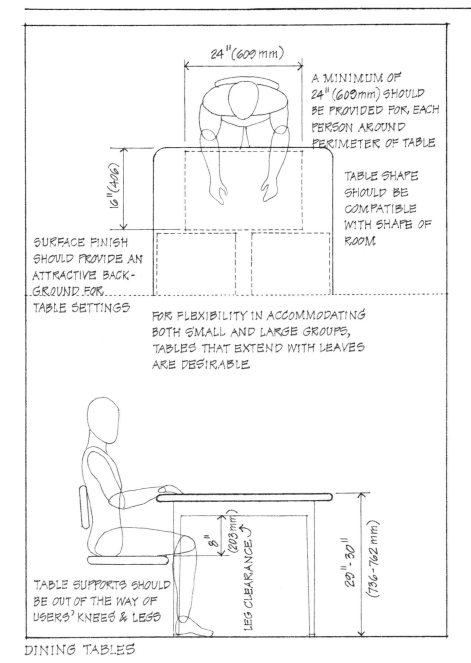

8" (203 mm)

LEG CLEARANCE

29" - 30" (736 - 762 mm)

TABLE SUPPORTS SHOULD BE OUT OF THE WAY OF USERS' KNEES & LEGS

DINING TABLES

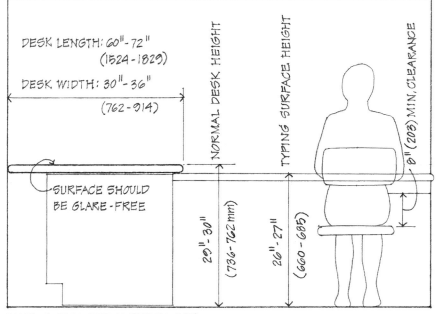

12" - 18" (304 - 457)

17" - 28" (431 - 711)

OCCASIONAL TABLES

DESK LENGTH: 60" - 72" (1524 - 1829)

DESK WIDTH: 30" - 36" (762 - 914)

NORMAL DESK HEIGHT

TYPING SURFACE HEIGHT

8" (203) MIN. CLEARANCE

SURFACE SHOULD BE GLARE - FREE

29" - 30" (736 - 762 mm)

26" - 27" (660 - 685)

DESKS AND WORK SURFACES

TABLE DIMENSIONS

QUEEN ANNE TEA TABLE

DROP-LEAF TABLE

SMALL ACCESSORY TABLE

TILT-TOP TABLE

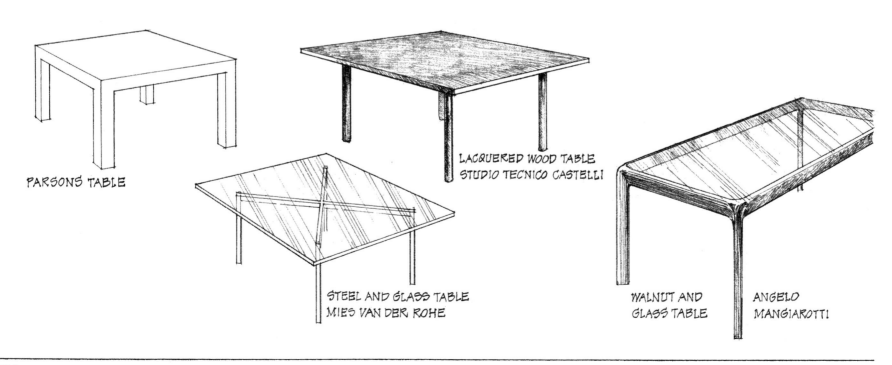

PARSONS TABLE

STEEL AND GLASS TABLE
MIES VAN DER ROHE

LACQUERED WOOD TABLE
STUDIO TECNICO CASTELLI

WALNUT AND
GLASS TABLE

ANGELO
MANGIAROTTI

GLASS TOP AND ENCAUSTIC PAINTED
METAL BASE - LELLA E MASSIMO
VIGNELLI / DAVID LAW

GLASS TOP AND PAINTED METAL BASE
MICHELLE DE LUCHI

MARBLE TOP AND LACQUERED WOOD
BASE - IGNAZIO GARDELLA

MARBLE AND WOOD TOP WITH METAL
LEGS - DANIELA PUPPA

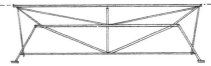

GLASS TOP AND METAL BASE -
KURT ZIEHMER

GLASS TOP - LACQUERED METAL
BASE - CHROME TIE RODS -
R. CARTA MANTIGLIA

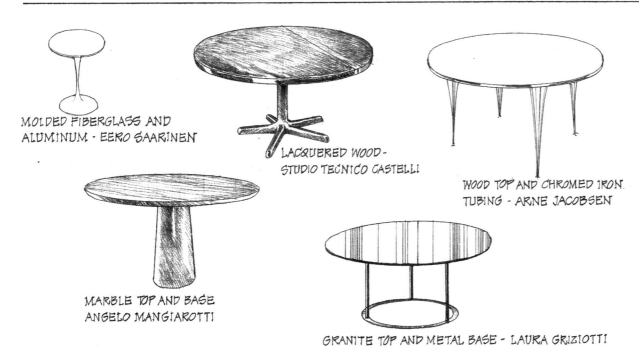

MOLDED FIBERGLASS AND
ALUMINUM - EERO SAARINEN

LACQUERED WOOD -
STUDIO TECNICO CASTELLI

WOOD TOP AND CHROMED IRON.
TUBING - ARNE JACOBSEN

MARBLE TOP AND BASE
ANGELO MANGIAROTTI

GRANITE TOP AND METAL BASE - LAURA GRIZIOTTI

MELAMINE LAMINATE TOP AND WOOD
BASE - GIOVANNI OFFREDI

WORK STATIONS

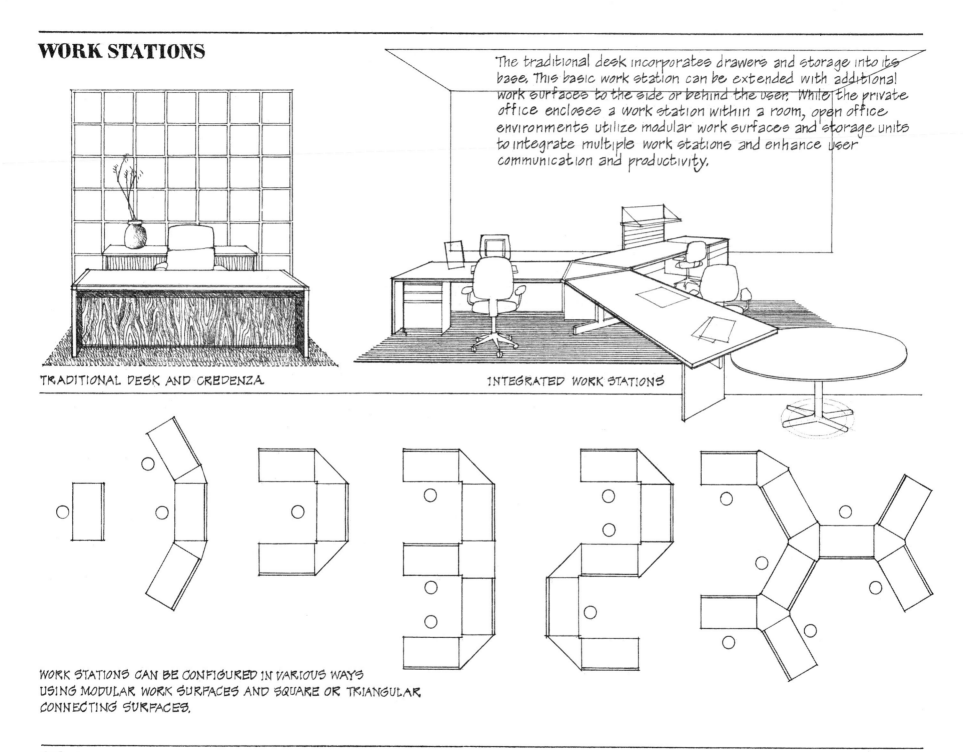

The traditional desk incorporates drawers and storage into its base. This basic work station can be extended with additional work surfaces to the side or behind the user. While the private office encloses a work station within a room, open office environments utilize modular work surfaces and storage units to integrate multiple work stations and enhance user communication and productivity.

TRADITIONAL DESK AND CREDENZA

INTEGRATED WORK STATIONS

WORK STATIONS CAN BE CONFIGURED IN VARIOUS WAYS USING MODULAR WORK SURFACES AND SQUARE OR TRIANGULAR CONNECTING SURFACES.

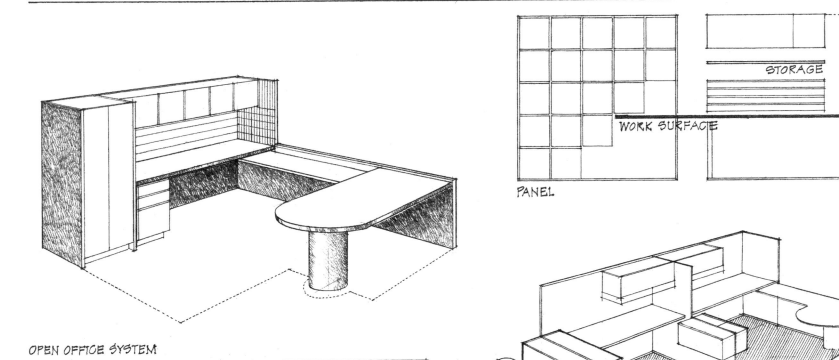

STORAGE

WORK SURFACE

PANEL

OPEN OFFICE SYSTEM

Open office systems offer flexibility in plan arrangements, efficiency in space utilization, and the ability to tailor a work station to suit individual needs and specific tasks. While the details of office systems vary with each manufacturer, the basic components remain the same. Modular panels are configured for stability and support the required work surfaces, storage units, lighting, and accessories. The panels are available in a variety of heights, widths, and finishes; some include glazing. Wiring for power, lighting, and telecommunications is often incorporated into the panel frames.

THE LAYOUT OF OPEN OFFICE SYSTEMS REQUIRES CAREFUL ANALYSIS OF USER NEEDS FOR ACOUSTIC AND VISUAL PRIVACY, COMMUNICATIONS, ACTIVITY REQUIREMENTS, AND EFFICIENT UTILIZATION OF SPACE.

BEDS

Beds consist of two components: the mattress or mattress set, and the base or support frame. There are various types of mattresses, each made in its own way to respond to and support one's body shape and weight. Personal judgment and choice, therefore, are required in the selection of a mattress.

Interior design comes into play particularly in the selection of the base or bed frame, and related furnishings such as headboards, night tables, and the bedding material used to cover and finish the bed set.

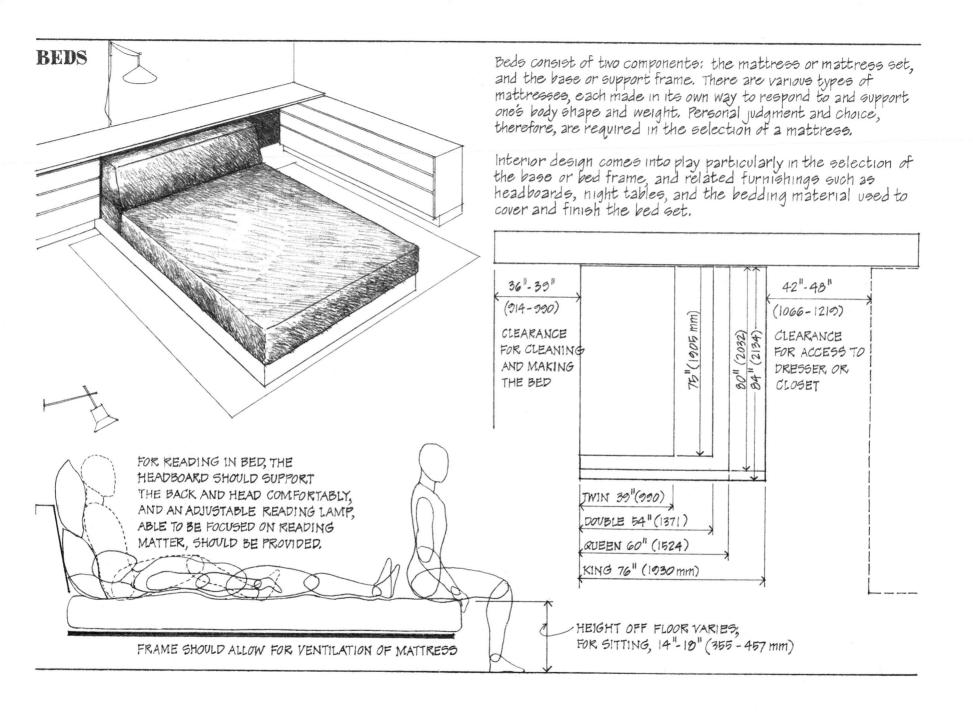

FOR READING IN BED, THE HEADBOARD SHOULD SUPPORT THE BACK AND HEAD COMFORTABLY, AND AN ADJUSTABLE READING LAMP, ABLE TO BE FOCUSED ON READING MATTER, SHOULD BE PROVIDED.

FRAME SHOULD ALLOW FOR VENTILATION OF MATTRESS

36"-39" (914-990)
CLEARANCE FOR CLEANING AND MAKING THE BED

42"-48" (1066-1219)
CLEARANCE FOR ACCESS TO DRESSER OR CLOSET

75" (1905 mm)
80" (2032)
84" (2134)

TWIN 39" (990)
DOUBLE 54" (1371)
QUEEN 60" (1524)
KING 76" (1930 mm)

HEIGHT OFF FLOOR VARIES; FOR SITTING, 14"-18" (355-457 mm)

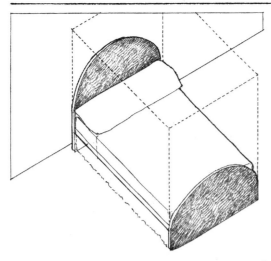

HEADBOARDS, FOOTBOARDS, AND CANOPIES DEFINE THE VOLUME OF SPACE OCCUPIED BY A BED.

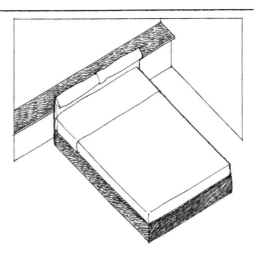

A BED CAN SIMPLY REST ON A PLATFORM BASE, EMPHASIZING THE HORIZONTALITY OF THE SETTING

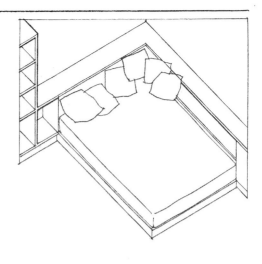

A BED CAN BE NESTLED INTO A CORNER OR ALCOVE. THIS BUILT-IN SETTING TAKES UP LESS FLOOR SPACE BUT BED MAY BE DIFFICULT TO MAKE,

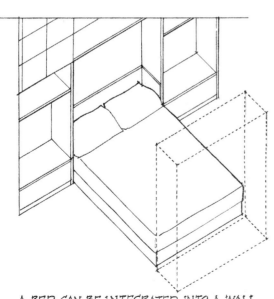

A BED CAN BE INTEGRATED INTO A WALL STORAGE SYSTEM AT THE HEAD AND/OR THE FOOT OF THE BED,

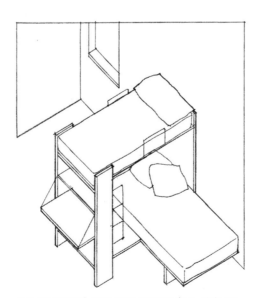

BUNK BEDS UTILIZE VERTICAL SPACE TO STACK SLEEPING LEVELS, STORAGE AND DESK SURFACES CAN ALSO BE INTEGRATED INTO THE SYSTEM,

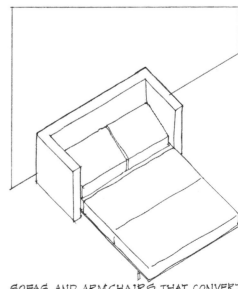

SOFAS AND ARMCHAIRS THAT CONVERT INTO BEDS OFFER CONVENIENT SHORT-TERM SLEEPING ARRANGE-MENTS.

STORAGE

Providing adequate and properly designed storage is an important concern in the planning of interior spaces, particularly where space is tight or where an uncluttered appearance is desired. To determine storage requirements, analyze the following:

- Accessibility: Where is storage needed?
- Convenience: What type of storage should be provided? What sizes and shapes of items are to be stored? What is the frequency of use?
- Visibility: Are items to be on display, or concealed?

Storage should be distributed where needed. How far we can reach while seated, standing, or kneeling should govern the means of access to the storage area. Active storage of often-used items should be readily accessible while dead storage of little-used or seasonal items can be hidden away.

HIGH SHELF

68" - 72" (1727 - 1829 mm)

36" - 48" (914 - 1219 mm)

LOW DRAWER

DIMENSIONAL CRITERIA.

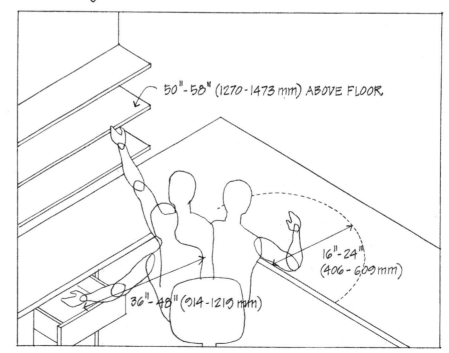

50" - 58" (1270 - 1473 mm) ABOVE FLOOR

16" - 24" (406 - 609 mm)

36" - 48" (914 - 1219 mm)

The size, proportion, and type of storage units used depend on the type and amount of items to be stored, the frequency of use, and the degree of visibility desired. Basic types of storage units are shelves, drawers, and cabinets. These may be suspended from the ceiling, mounted on a wall, or simply be placed on the floor as a piece of furniture. Storage units can also be built into the thickness of a wall, occupy a niche, or utilize otherwise unusable space such as under a stairway.

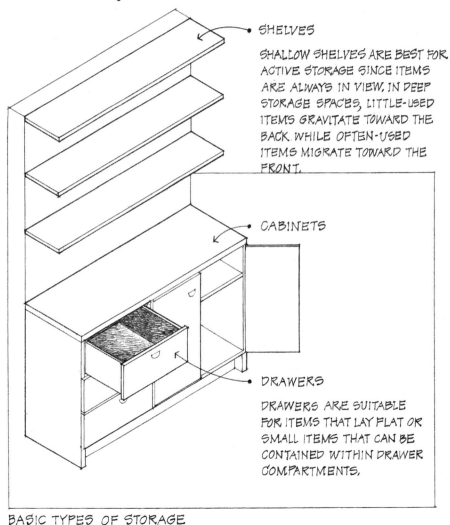

SHELVES

SHALLOW SHELVES ARE BEST FOR ACTIVE STORAGE SINCE ITEMS ARE ALWAYS IN VIEW. IN DEEP STORAGE SPACES, LITTLE-USED ITEMS GRAVITATE TOWARD THE BACK, WHILE OFTEN-USED ITEMS MIGRATE TOWARD THE FRONT.

CABINETS

DRAWERS

DRAWERS ARE SUITABLE FOR ITEMS THAT LAY FLAT OR SMALL ITEMS THAT CAN BE CONTAINED WITHIN DRAWER COMPARTMENTS.

BASIC TYPES OF STORAGE

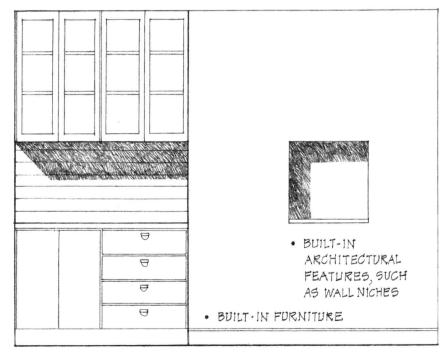

• UNIT FURNITURE

• BUILT-IN ARCHITECTURAL FEATURES, SUCH AS WALL NICHES

• BUILT-IN FURNITURE

FORMS OF STORAGE

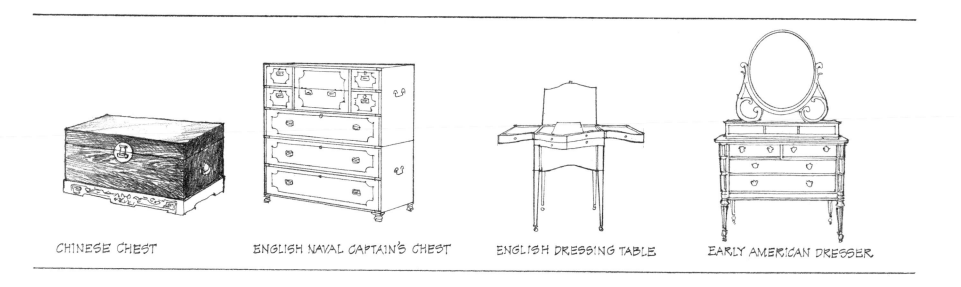

CHINESE CHEST   ENGLISH NAVAL CAPTAIN'S CHEST   ENGLISH DRESSING TABLE   EARLY AMERICAN DRESSER

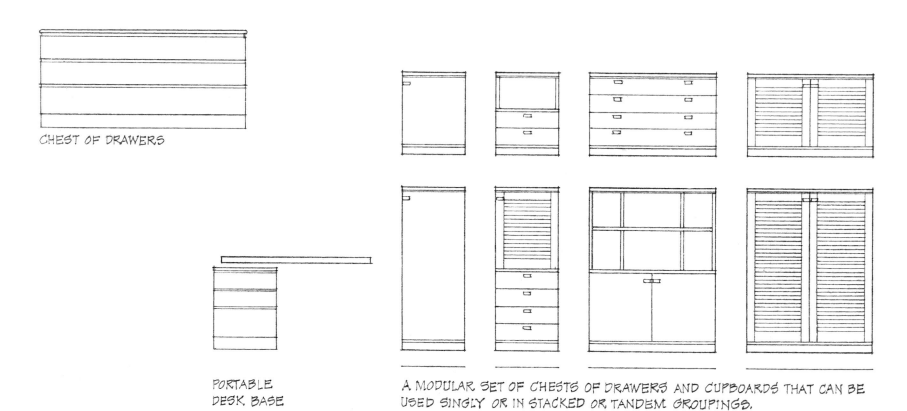

CHEST OF DRAWERS

PORTABLE
DESK BASE

A MODULAR SET OF CHESTS OF DRAWERS AND CUPBOARDS THAT CAN BE
USED SINGLY OR IN STACKED OR TANDEM GROUPINGS.

EARLY AMERICAN CUPBOARD

FRENCH PROVINCIAL ARMOIRE

ITALIAN CREDENZA

AMERICAN BLOCK FRONT SECRETARY

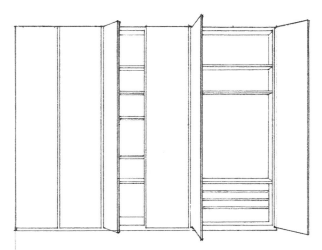

A MODULAR SYSTEM OF CUPBOARDS AVAILABLE WITH PLAIN, GLASS, OR LOUVERED DOORS - UFFICIO TECNICO BRIVIO

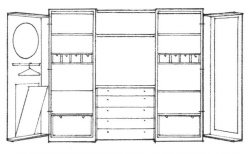

A SYSTEM OF CUPBOARDS, DRAWERS, AND SHELVES - LUIGI MASSONI

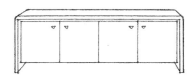

CABINET CREDENZA - HANS WEITZ

CHEST CONVERTIBLE INTO A WRITING TABLE - FRANCO BIZZOZZERO

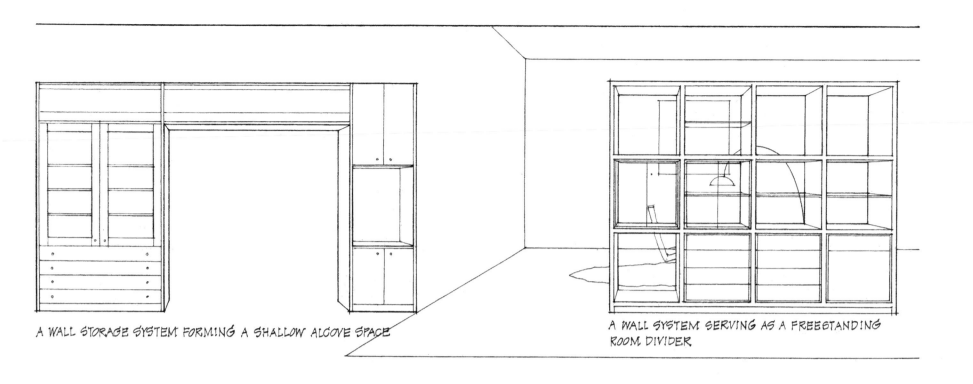

A WALL STORAGE SYSTEM FORMING A SHALLOW ALCOVE SPACE

A WALL SYSTEM SERVING AS A FREESTANDING ROOM DIVIDER

WALL STORAGE SYSTEMS CONSIST OF MODULAR SHELVING, DRAWER, AND CABINET UNITS WHICH CAN BE COMBINED IN VARIOUS WAYS TO FORM SELF-SUPPORTING ASSEMBLIES. THE UNITS MAY HAVE OPEN FRONTS OR BE FITTED WITH SOLID, GLASS, OR LOUVERED DOORS. SOME SYSTEMS INTEGRATE DISPLAY LIGHTING INTO THEIR CONSTRUCTION.

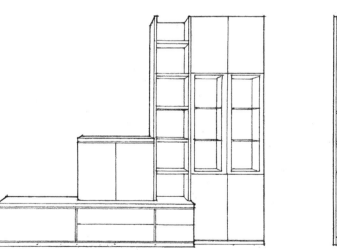
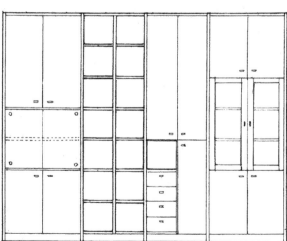

A WALL STORAGE SYSTEM MAY BE A FREESTANDING ASSEMBLY OR BE PLACED INTO A WALL RECESS.

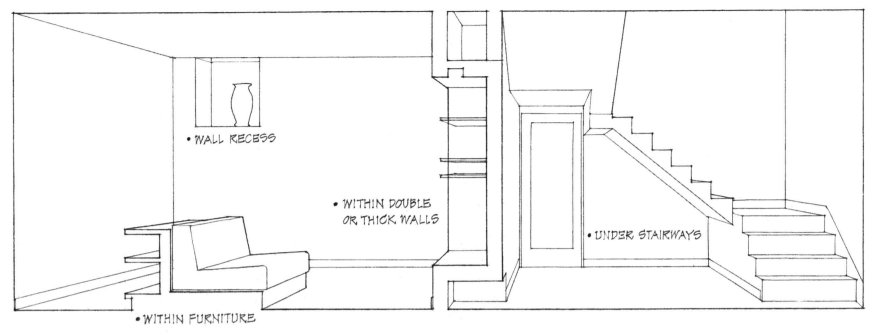

• WALL RECESS

• WITHIN DOUBLE
  OR THICK WALLS

• UNDER STAIRWAYS

• WITHIN FURNITURE

□ FINDING SPACE FOR STORAGE

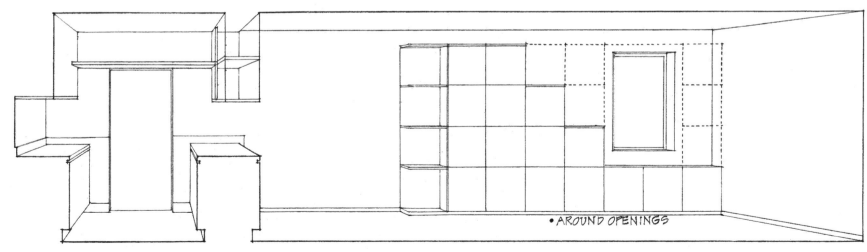

• AROUND OPENINGS

BUILT-IN STORAGE AND CABINETRY ARE MOST COMMON IN KITCHENS,
PANTRIES, AND BATHROOM SPACES, BUT CAN EFFECTIVELY BE
EXTENDED INTO OTHER SPACES AS WELL.

LIGHTING FIXTURES

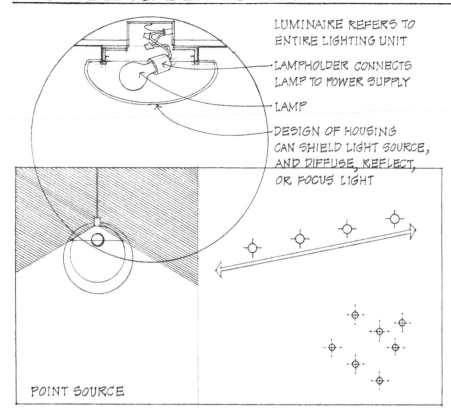

LUMINAIRE REFERS TO ENTIRE LIGHTING UNIT

LAMPHOLDER CONNECTS LAMP TO POWER SUPPLY

LAMP

DESIGN OF HOUSING CAN SHIELD LIGHT SOURCE, AND DIFFUSE, REFLECT, OR FOCUS LIGHT

POINT SOURCE

Light fixtures are integral parts of a building's electrical system, transforming energy into usable illumination. Light fixtures require an electrical connection or power supply, a housing assembly, and a lamp. See Chapter 5 for further discussion of lamps, light distribution, and illumination levels. This section will focus on the light fixtures themselves as design elements.

We are concerned not only with the shape and form of the fixture but also with the form of the illumination it provides. Point sources give focus to a space since the area of greatest brightness in a space tends to attract our attention. They can be used to highlight an area or an object of interest. A number of point sources can be arranged to describe rhythm and sequence. Small point sources, when grouped, can provide glitter and sparkle.

Linear sources can be used to give direction, emphasize the edges of planes, or outline an area. A parallel series of linear sources can form a plane of illumination which is effective for the general, diffused illumination of an area.

Volumetric sources are point sources expanded by the use of translucent materials into spheres, globes, or other three-dimensional forms.

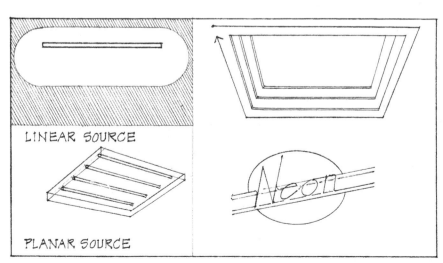

LINEAR SOURCE

PLANAR SOURCE

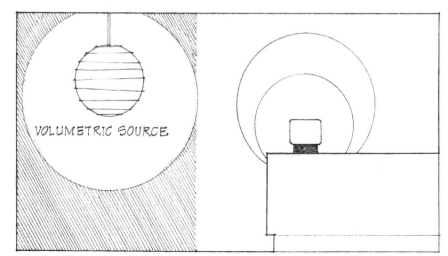

VOLUMETRIC SOURCE

Light fixtures can provide direct and/or indirect illumination. The form of distribution depends on the design of the fixture as well as its placement and orientation in a space.

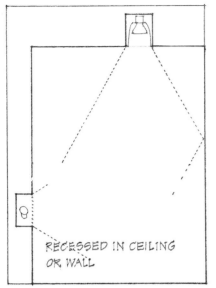

RECESSED IN CEILING OR WALL

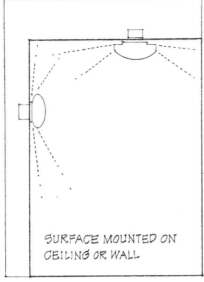

SURFACE MOUNTED ON CEILING OR WALL

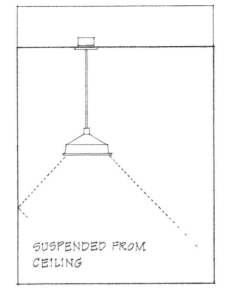

SUSPENDED FROM CEILING

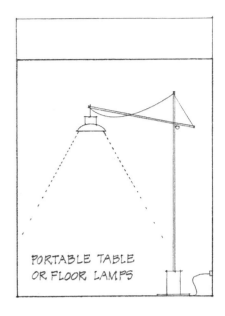

PORTABLE TABLE OR FLOOR LAMPS

DIRECT LIGHTING FIXTURE TYPES

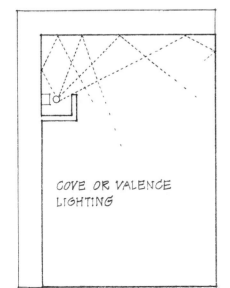

COVE OR VALENCE LIGHTING

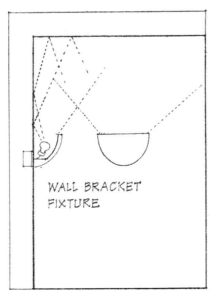

WALL BRACKET FIXTURE

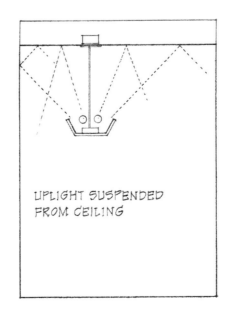

UPLIGHT SUSPENDED FROM CEILING

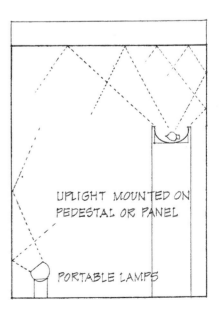

UPLIGHT MOUNTED ON PEDESTAL OR PANEL

PORTABLE LAMPS

INDIRECT LIGHTING FIXTURE TYPES

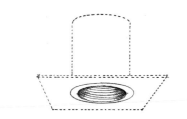

• BAFFLED DOWNLIGHT

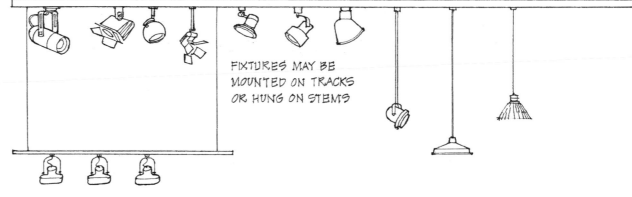

FIXTURES MAY BE
MOUNTED ON TRACKS
OR HUNG ON STEMS

TRACKS MAY ALSO BE SUSPENDED
FROM CEILING

• ADJUSTABLE EYEBALL

EXAMPLES OF TRACK LIGHTING FIXTURES

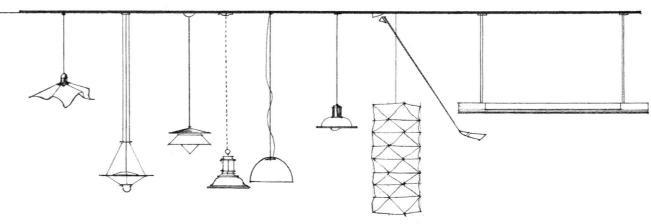

• PINHOLE DOWNLIGHT

• BAFFLED WALL WASHER

TYPES OF RECESSED DOWNLIGHTS

EXAMPLES OF SUSPENDED FIXTURES

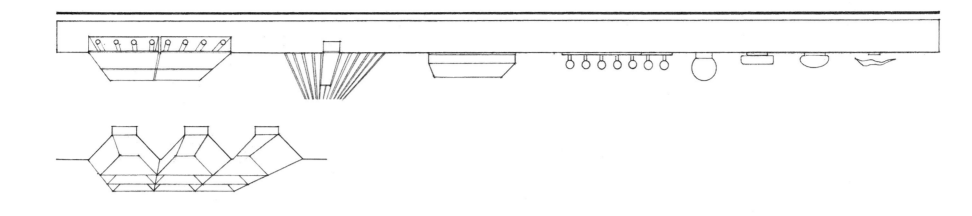

EXAMPLES OF RECESSED AND SURFACE-MOUNTED CEILING FIXTURES

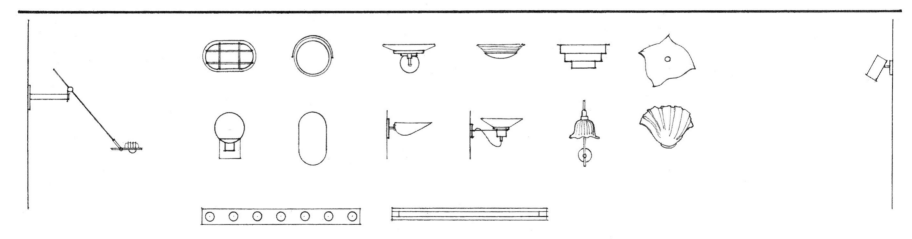

EXAMPLES OF WALL-MOUNTED FIXTURES

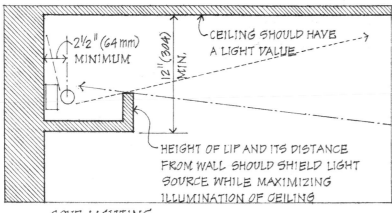

2½" (64 mm) MINIMUM

12" (304) MIN.

CEILING SHOULD HAVE A LIGHT VALUE

HEIGHT OF LIP AND ITS DISTANCE FROM WALL SHOULD SHIELD LIGHT SOURCE WHILE MAXIMIZING ILLUMINATION OF CEILING

COVE LIGHTING

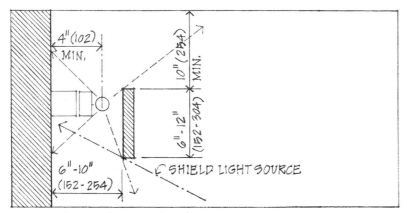

4" (102) MIN.

10" (254) MIN.

6"-12" (152-304)

6"-10" (152-254)

SHIELD LIGHT SOURCE

VALENCE LIGHTING

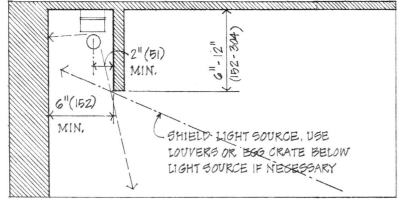

2" (51) MIN.

6"-12" (152-304)

6" (152) MIN.

SHIELD LIGHT SOURCE, USE LOUVERS OR EGG CRATE BELOW LIGHT SOURCE IF NECESSARY

CORNICE LIGHTING

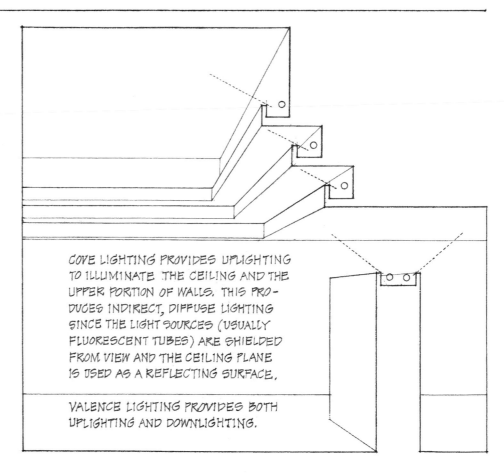

COVE LIGHTING PROVIDES UPLIGHTING TO ILLUMINATE THE CEILING AND THE UPPER PORTION OF WALLS. THIS PRODUCES INDIRECT, DIFFUSE LIGHTING SINCE THE LIGHT SOURCES (USUALLY FLUORESCENT TUBES) ARE SHIELDED FROM VIEW AND THE CEILING PLANE IS USED AS A REFLECTING SURFACE.

VALENCE LIGHTING PROVIDES BOTH UPLIGHTING AND DOWNLIGHTING.

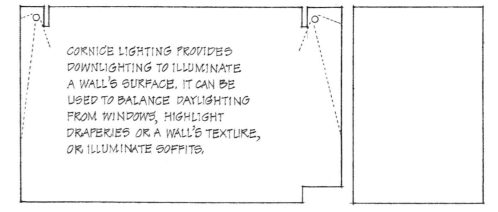

CORNICE LIGHTING PROVIDES DOWNLIGHTING TO ILLUMINATE A WALL'S SURFACE. IT CAN BE USED TO BALANCE DAYLIGHTING FROM WINDOWS, HIGHLIGHT DRAPERIES OR A WALL'S TEXTURE, OR ILLUMINATE SOFFITS.

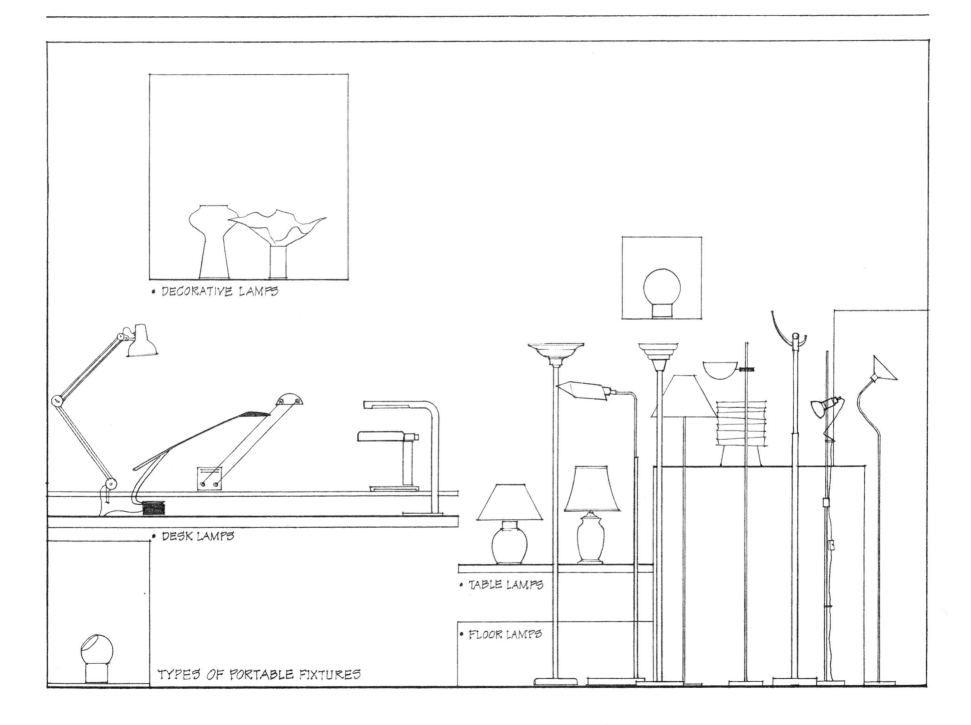

DECORATIVE LAMPS

DESK LAMPS

TABLE LAMPS

FLOOR LAMPS

TYPES OF PORTABLE FIXTURES

ACCESSORIES

Accessories in interior design refer to those items which provide a space with aesthetic enrichment and embellishment. These items may provide visual delight for the eye, textural interest for the hand, or stimulation for the mind. Ultimately, accessories, individually or collectively, are the inevitable evidence of habitation.

Accessories which can add visual and tactile richness to an interior setting may be:

- Utilitarian - useful tools and objects
- Incidental - architectural elements and furnishings
- Decorative - artwork and plants.

Utilitarian accessories come in a range of designs and their selection over time is often a reflection of the personality of those who inhabit a place.

UTILITARIAN

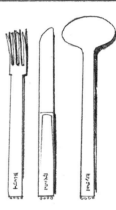

Incidental accessories enrich a space while simultaneously serving other functions. One example is architectural elements and the details which express the way materials are joined. Another would be the forms, colors, and textures of interior furnishings.

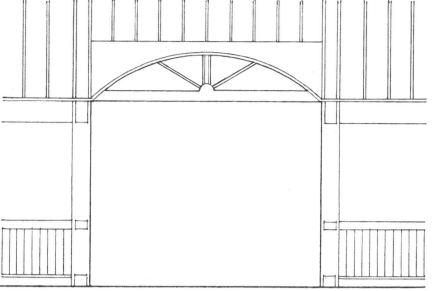

INCIDENTAL

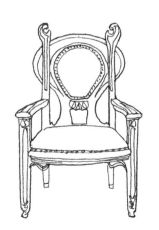

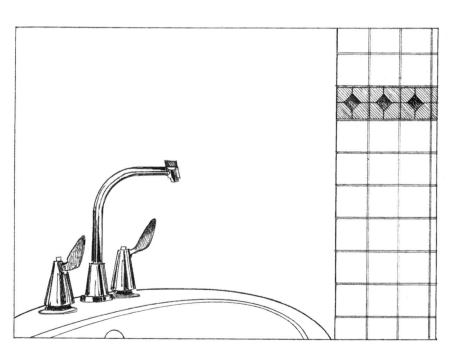

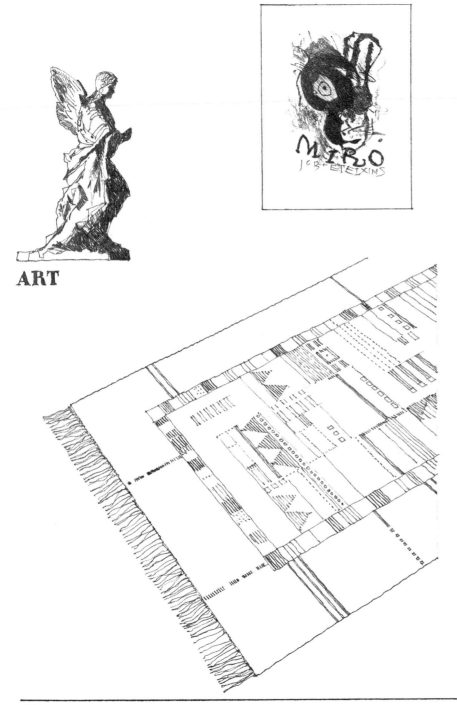

ART

Decorative accessories delight the eye, the hand, or the intellect without necessarily being utilitarian in purpose. These may include:

- Artwork   - Enriching a space with art follows an age-old tradition of decorating objects and surfaces. Many utilitarian and incidental items can be considered as art.

- Collections - Collections of objects may be serious or not so serious but they almost always have personal meaning.

- Plants   - Plants and flowers, as visible signs of nature, bring their expression of life and growth to interior spaces.

COLLECTIONS

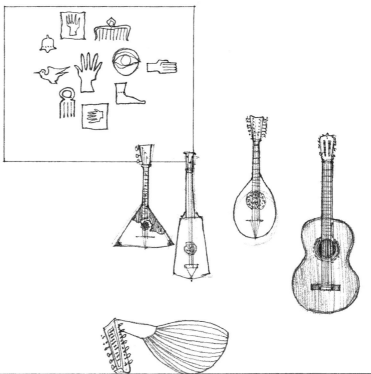

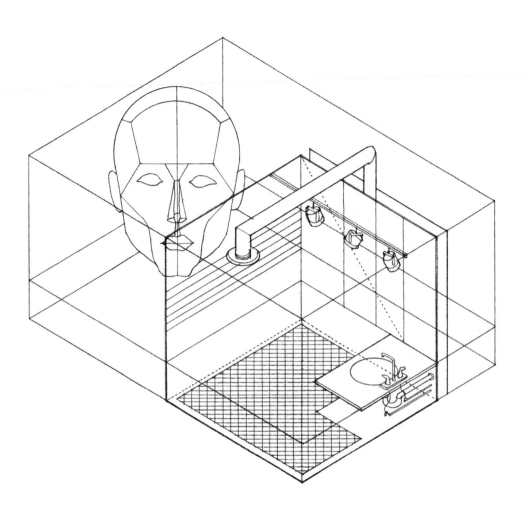

5

INTERIOR ENVIRONMENTAL
SYSTEMS

INTERIOR ENVIRONMENTAL SYSTEMS

HEATING
VENTILATING
AIR CONDITIONING

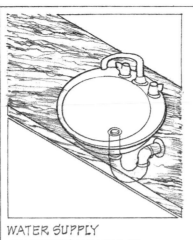

WATER SUPPLY
SANITARY DRAINAGE

Interior environmental systems are essential components of any building since they provide for occupants the thermal, visual, auditory, and sanitary conditions necessary for their comfort and convenience. These systems must be designed and laid out not only to function properly. They must also be coordinated with a building's structural system. This requires the knowledge and expertise of professional engineers and architects. The interior designer, nevertheless, should be aware that these systems exist and know how they affect the quality of the interior environment.

This chapter provides a brief description of the elements of the following systems:

- HEATING AND AIR CONDITIONING SYSTEMS
- WATER SUPPLY AND SANITARY DRAINAGE SYSTEMS
- ELECTRICAL AND LIGHTING SYSTEMS
- ACOUSTICS

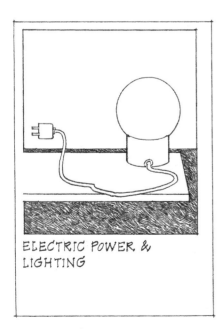

ELECTRIC POWER &
LIGHTING

ROOM ACOUSTICS
NOISE CONTROL

ELECTRIC CIRCUITS

HEATED OR CONDITIONED AIR

RETURN AIR

ELECTRIC SERVICE PANEL

COLD & HOT WATER

OUTSIDE AIR

FURNACE OR AIR-CONDITIONING UNIT

FUEL

WATER HEATER

WATER SERVICE

SYSTEMS

SOURCES

These environmental control systems are similar in the following respects. They all have a source or point of entry, a means of travel, and, ultimately, they deliver a result in an interior space – conditioned air, hot and cold water, electrical power and light.

The means of travel – wiring, pipes, and ducts – run vertically and horizontally through a building. Vertical travel of wiring and small pipes and ducts can be accommodated within the thickness of walls, but large lines require mechanical shaft spaces. Horizontal travel can occur within a floor structure, or if more space is required, between the floor and a hung ceiling.

Where these lines interface with an interior space affect not only their systems' performance but also how the space is used, Just as important for the interior designer is the appearance of those elements that have an impact on the visual quality of a space. Some are low-key, such as an air diffuser or a switch plate; others are more critical, such as a plumbing or light fixture.

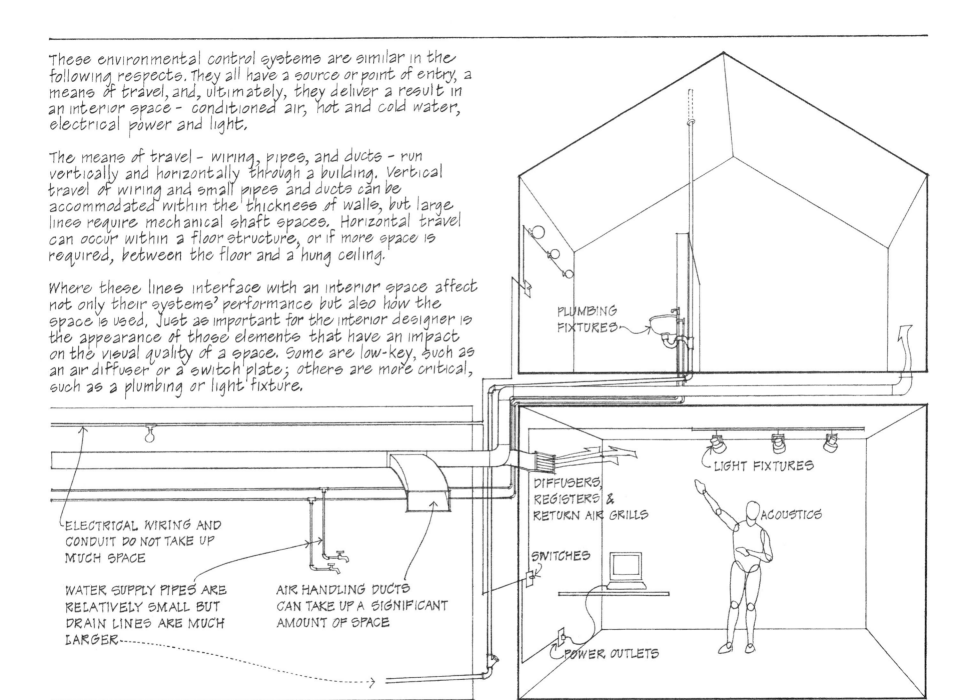

PLUMBING FIXTURES

ELECTRICAL WIRING AND CONDUIT DO NOT TAKE UP MUCH SPACE

WATER SUPPLY PIPES ARE RELATIVELY SMALL BUT DRAIN LINES ARE MUCH LARGER

AIR HANDLING DUCTS CAN TAKE UP A SIGNIFICANT AMOUNT OF SPACE

DIFFUSERS, REGISTERS & RETURN AIR GRILLS

LIGHT FIXTURES

ACOUSTICS

SWITCHES

POWER OUTLETS

TRANSMISSION

CONTROL AND OUTPUT DEVICES

HEATING & AIR CONDITIONING

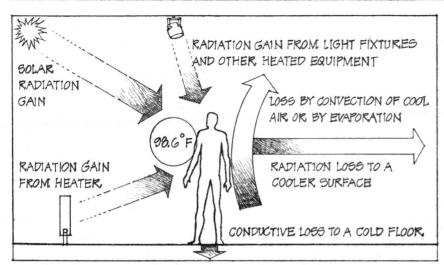

SOLAR RADIATION GAIN

RADIATION GAIN FROM LIGHT FIXTURES AND OTHER HEATED EQUIPMENT

LOSS BY CONVECTION OF COOL AIR OR BY EVAPORATION

98.6°F

RADIATION GAIN FROM HEATER

RADIATION LOSS TO A COOLER SURFACE

CONDUCTIVE LOSS TO A COLD FLOOR.

MODES OF HEAT TRANSFER

The primary objective of a heating system is to replace the heat lost within an interior space. The basic heating system consists of a heat-producing medium, equipment to convert the medium to heat, a means to deliver the heat to a space, and, finally, a method for discharging the heat within the space.

While a heating system supplies heat, an air conditioner is usually considered to be a means for supplying cool air. A true air-conditioning system, however, provides all-year climate control by bringing in outside air, cleaning, heating, or cooling it, adding or removing humidity, and delivering the conditioned air to the interior spaces of a building.

RADIATION: Heat transfer from a warm surface to a cooler surface; not affected by air motion or temp.

CONVECTION: Transfer due to motion of warm or cool air across a body's surface.

CONDUCTION: Direct transfer from a warm surface in contact with a cooler surface.

EVAPORATION: Heat loss due to the process of moisture turning into vapor.

To achieve and maintain thermal comfort, a reasonable balance must be reached among the types of heat transfer that can occur in a room.

• The higher the mean radiant temperature of a room's surfaces, the cooler the air temperature should be.

• The higher the relative humidity of a space, the lower the air temperature should be.

• The cooler the moving air stream, the less velocity it should have.

THERMAL COMFORT CONSIDERATIONS

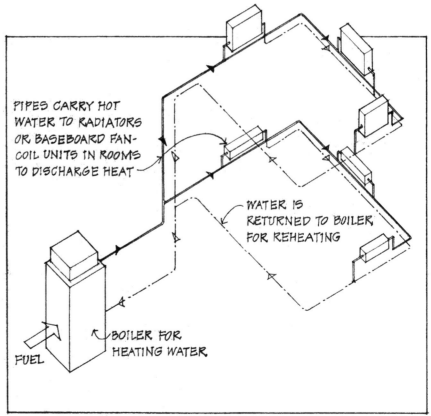

PIPES CARRY HOT WATER TO RADIATORS OR BASEBOARD FAN-COIL UNITS IN ROOMS TO DISCHARGE HEAT

WATER IS RETURNED TO BOILER FOR REHEATING

BOILER FOR HEATING WATER

FUEL

HOT WATER HEATING SYSTEM

An air-conditioning system treats air in several ways since thermal comfort is dependent not only on air temperature, but also on relative air humidity, the radiant temperature of surrounding surfaces, and air motion. Air purity and odor removal are additional comfort factors that can be controlled by an air-conditioning system.

While the architect and engineers plan a heating or air-conditioning system during the design of a building, the interior designer can influence the final result through the selection of wall, window, and floor coverings and by the adjustment of air-flow patterns.

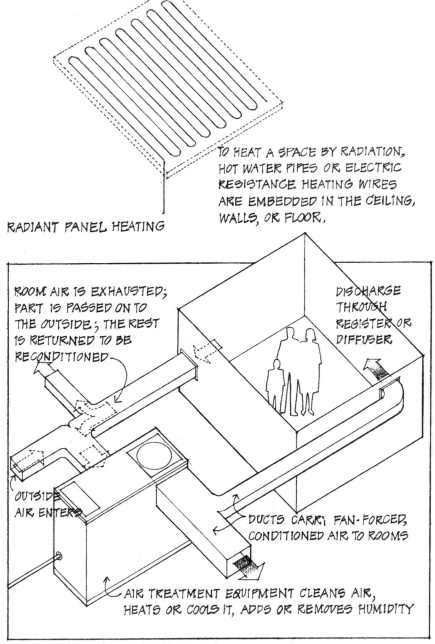

RADIANT PANEL HEATING

TO HEAT A SPACE BY RADIATION, HOT WATER PIPES OR ELECTRIC RESISTANCE HEATING WIRES ARE EMBEDDED IN THE CEILING, WALLS, OR FLOOR.

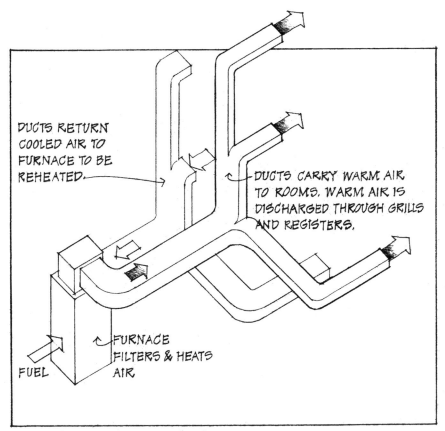

DUCTS RETURN COOLED AIR TO FURNACE TO BE REHEATED.

DUCTS CARRY WARM AIR TO ROOMS. WARM AIR IS DISCHARGED THROUGH GRILLS AND REGISTERS.

FURNACE FILTERS & HEATS AIR

FUEL

WARM AIR HEATING SYSTEM

ROOM AIR IS EXHAUSTED; PART IS PASSED ON TO THE OUTSIDE; THE REST IS RETURNED TO BE RECONDITIONED

DISCHARGE THROUGH REGISTER OR DIFFUSER

OUTSIDE AIR ENTERS

DUCTS CARRY FAN-FORCED, CONDITIONED AIR TO ROOMS

AIR TREATMENT EQUIPMENT CLEANS AIR, HEATS OR COOLS IT, ADDS OR REMOVES HUMIDITY

AIR-CONDITIONING SYSTEM

WATER SYSTEMS

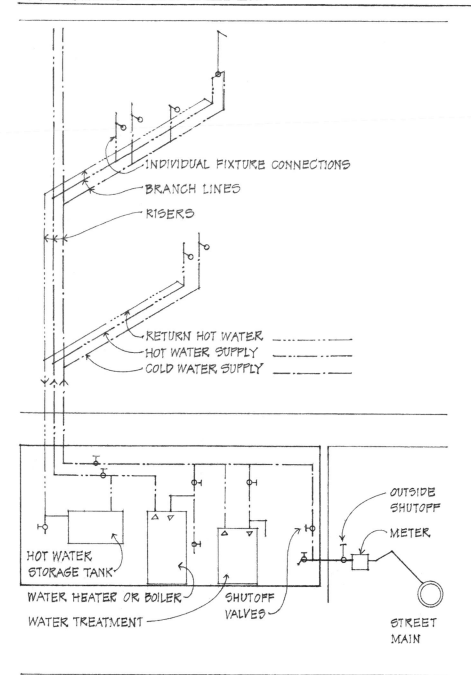

- INDIVIDUAL FIXTURE CONNECTIONS
- BRANCH LINES
- RISERS

- RETURN HOT WATER _____
- HOT WATER SUPPLY _____
- COLD WATER SUPPLY _____

HOT WATER
STORAGE TANK

WATER HEATER OR BOILER

WATER TREATMENT

SHUTOFF
VALVES

OUTSIDE
SHUTOFF

METER

STREET
MAIN

SCHEMATIC OF A WATER SUPPLY SYSTEM

There are two separate but parallel networks in a water system. One supplies water for human use, and use by mechanical and fire protection systems. The other disposes of waterborne waste material once the water has been used. Water is supplied under pressure from a water main; once used, the water along with any waste material is discharged from the building and carried to a sewer line by gravity.

A water supply system must overcome the forces of gravity and friction to deliver water up to its points of use. The pressure required to upfeed water may come from the water main or from pumps within the building. When this pressure is insufficient, water can be pumped to an elevated storage tank for gravity downfeed.

A separate supply subsystem common to all buildings is the hot water supply system, leading from the heater or boiler to each required fixture. To conserve energy, the hot water supply can be a closed and constantly circulating system.

To control the flow of water at each fixture as well as be able to isolate one or more fixtures from the water supply system for repair and maintenance, a series of valves is required.

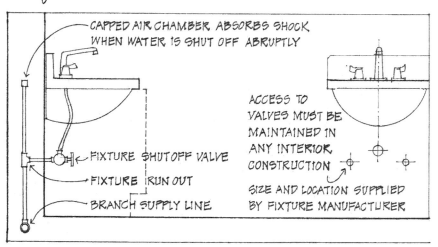

CAPPED AIR CHAMBER ABSORBS SHOCK
WHEN WATER IS SHUT OFF ABRUPTLY

FIXTURE SHUTOFF VALVE

FIXTURE RUN OUT

BRANCH SUPPLY LINE

ACCESS TO
VALVES MUST BE
MAINTAINED IN
ANY INTERIOR
CONSTRUCTION

SIZE AND LOCATION SUPPLIED
BY FIXTURE MANUFACTURER

The water supply system terminates at each plumbing fixture. After the water has been drawn and used, it enters the sanitary drainage system. The primary objective of this drainage system is to dispose of fluid waste and organic matter as quickly as possible.

Since a sanitary drainage system relies on gravity for its discharge, its pipes are much larger than water supply lines, which are under pressure. In addition, there are restrictions on the length and slope of horizontal runs and on the types and number of turns.

Gases are formed in drainage pipes by the decomposition of waste matter. To prevent these gases from entering the interior spaces of a building, traps or water seals are required at each fixture. In addition, the entire sanitary drainage system must be vented to the outside air. Venting prevents water seals in traps from being siphoned out and allows air to circulate within the system.

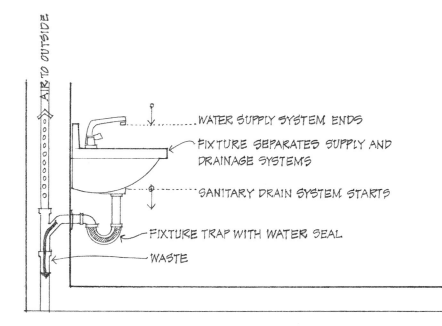

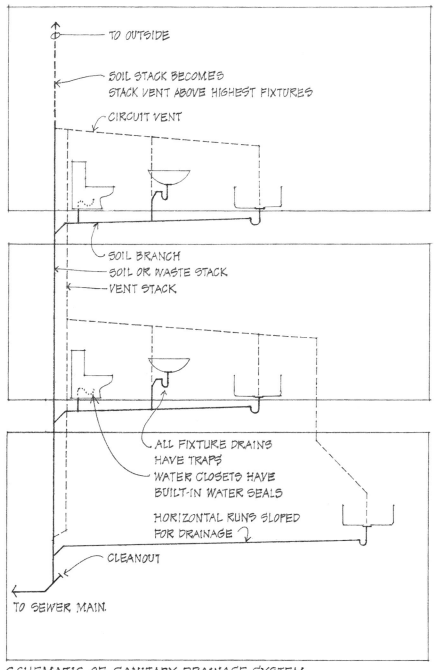

SCHEMATIC OF SANITARY DRAINAGE SYSTEM

ELECTRICAL SYSTEMS

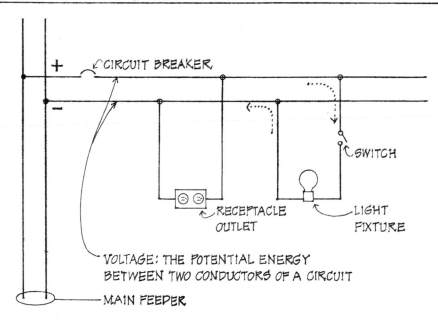

+ ⌐ CIRCUIT BREAKER

–

SWITCH

RECEPTACLE OUTLET

LIGHT FIXTURE

VOLTAGE: THE POTENTIAL ENERGY BETWEEN TWO CONDUCTORS OF A CIRCUIT

MAIN FEEDER

SCHEMATIC OF A BRANCH CIRCUIT

The electrical system of a building supplies power for lighting, heating, and the operation of electrical equipment and appliances. This system should be installed to operate safely, reliably, and efficiently.

Electrical energy flows through a conductor because of a difference in electrical charge between two points in a circuit. This potential energy is measured in volts. The actual amount of energy flow or current is measured in amperes. The power required to keep an electric current flowing is measured in watts. (Power in watts = Current in amperes × Pressure in volts)

For electric current to flow, a circuit must be complete. Switches control current flow by introducing breaks in a circuit until power is required.

Power is supplied to a building by the electric utility company. The service line is first connected to a meter and a main disconnect switch, and then to a panelboard. This panelboard distributes the incoming power supply into smaller, more easily controlled circuits, and protects them from being overloaded with circuit breakers.

Most electric power is used in the form of alternating current (AC). Large pieces of machinery use direct current (DC).

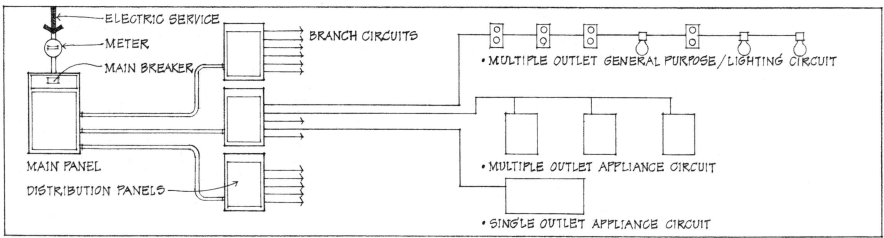

ELECTRIC SERVICE

METER

MAIN BREAKER

BRANCH CIRCUITS

• MULTIPLE OUTLET GENERAL PURPOSE / LIGHTING CIRCUIT

MAIN PANEL

DISTRIBUTION PANELS

• MULTIPLE OUTLET APPLIANCE CIRCUIT

• SINGLE OUTLET APPLIANCE CIRCUIT

SCHEMATIC OF AN ELECTRICAL SYSTEM

Branch circuits distribute electric power to the interior spaces of a building. The wiring in a circuit is sized according to the amount of current it must carry. A fuse or circuit breaker in the distribution panel disconnects a circuit when too much current is drawn for its wiring. The continuous load on a circuit should not exceed 80% of its rated capacity. For example, a 15 Amp. circuit should have a continuous load rating of 12 Amperes. On a 110 Volt line, the circuit could then be assumed to handle (12A x 110V) or 1320 Watts. Since room should be allowed for expansion, the safe capacity of a 15 Amp. circuit on a 110 Volt line is 1200 Watts.

Electrical systems are designed by electrical engineers. The interior designer can influence the location of lighting fixtures, power outlets, and switches to control their operation. The designer should also be aware of the power requirements of an electrical installation so that they can be coordinated with the existing or planned circuits.

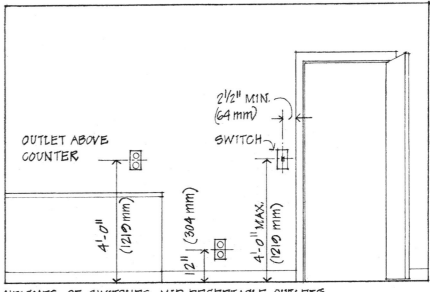

HEIGHTS OF SWITCHES AND RECEPTACLE OUTLETS

Symbol	Name	Symbol	Name
▬	Lighting Panel	▭	Fluorescent Fixture
▨	Power Panel	○	Ceiling Incandescent
S	Single Pole Switch	⊢○	Wall Incandescent
S₃	Three-Way Switch	Ⓡ	Recessed Fixture
⊖	Duplex Receptacle	Ⓧ	Exit Light Outlet
⊟	Floor Duplex Outlet	Ⓕ	Fan Outlet
⊕	Special Purpose Outlet	Ⓔ	Electrical Outlet
◄	Telephone Outlet	Ⓜ	Motor
◄	Floor Telephone Outlet	Ⓙ	Junction Box
TV	Television Outlet	Ⓣ	Thermostat

TYPICAL ELECTRICAL SYMBOLS

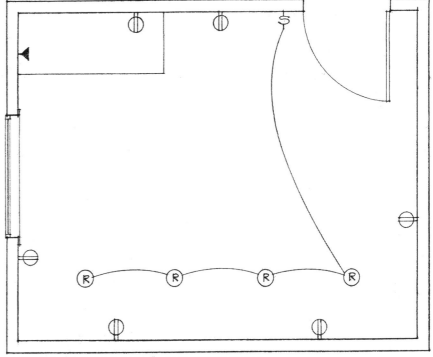

TYPICAL ELECTRICAL & LIGHTING PLAN

LIGHTING

Light is radiant energy. It radiates equally in all directions and spreads over a larger area as it emanates from its source. As it spreads, it also diminishes in intensity according to the square of its distance from the source.

As it moves, light reveals to our eyes the surfaces and forms of objects in space. An object in its path will reflect, absorb, or allow the light striking its surface to pass through.

DIFFUSE OR MULTIPLE REFLECTIONS OCCUR WHEN LIGHT IS REFLECTED FROM MATTE OR UNPOLISHED SURFACES

ANGLE OF INCIDENCE EQUALS ANGLE OF REFLECTION

OPAQUE MATERIALS BLOCK THE TRANSMISSION OF LIGHT, AND CAST SHADOWS.

DIFFUSED TRANSMISSION OCCURS THROUGH TRANSLUCENT MATERIALS SUCH AS FROSTED GLASS. LIGHT SOURCE IS NOT VISIBLE.

NONDIFFUSE TRANSMISSION OCCURS THROUGH CLEAR, TRANSPARENT MATERIALS SUCH AS GLASS AND SOME PLASTICS.

SPECULAR REFLECTION OCCURS WHEN LIGHT IS REFLECTED FROM A SHINY, OPAQUE SURFACE.

The sun, stars, and electric lamps are visible to us because of the light they generate. Most of what we see, however, is visible because of the light that is reflected from the surfaces of objects. Our ability to see well – that is, to discern shape, color, and texture, and to differentiate one object from another – is affected not only by the amount of light available for illumination but also by the following factors:

- Brightness
- Contrast
- Glare
- Diffusion
- Color

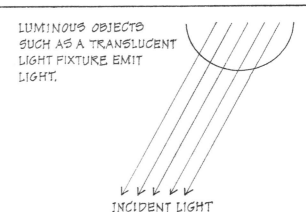

LUMINOUS OBJECTS SUCH AS A TRANSLUCENT LIGHT FIXTURE EMIT LIGHT.

INCIDENT LIGHT

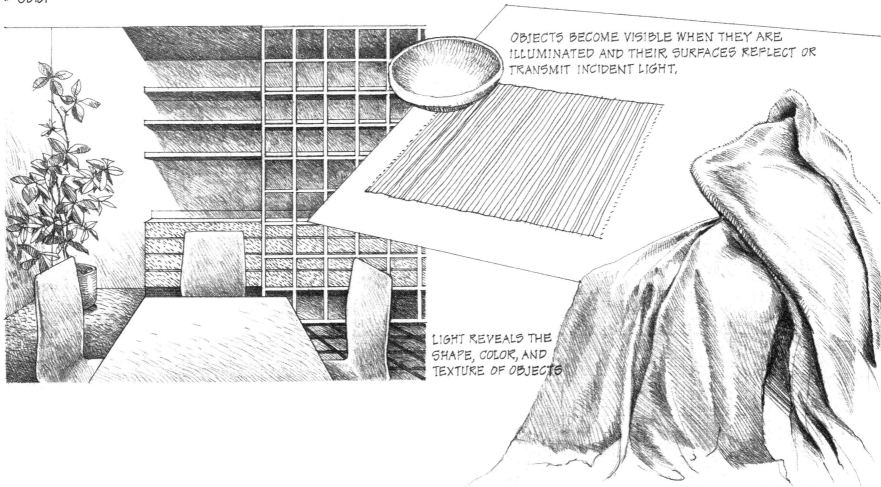

OBJECTS BECOME VISIBLE WHEN THEY ARE ILLUMINATED AND THEIR SURFACES REFLECT OR TRANSMIT INCIDENT LIGHT.

LIGHT REVEALS THE SHAPE, COLOR, AND TEXTURE OF OBJECTS

Brightness refers to how much light energy is reflected by a surface. The degree of brightness of an object, in turn, depends on the color value and texture of its surface. A shiny, light-colored surface will reflect more light than a dark, matte, or rough-textured surface, even though both surfaces are lit with the same amount of illumination.

Generally speaking, visual acuity increases with object brightness. Of equal importance is the relative brightness between the object being viewed and its surroundings. To discern its shape, form, and texture, some degree of contrast or brightness ratio is required. For example, a white object on an equally bright white background would be difficult to see, as would a dark object seen against a dark background.

EVEN THOUGH THESE OBJECTS MAY BE UNIFORMLY ILLUMINATED, THEIR SURFACES DIFFER IN BRIGHTNESS ACCORDING TO THEIR COLOR VALUE AND TEXTURE AND CONSEQUENTLY, THEIR ABILITY TO REFLECT LIGHT.

BRIGHTNESS = ILLUMINATION × REFLECTANCE

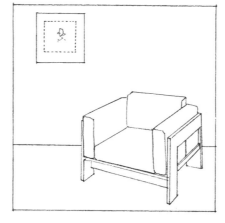
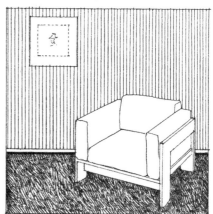

CONTRAST IN BRIGHTNESS AIDS IN OUR PERCEPTION OF SHAPE AND FORM ▷

BRIGHTNESS

Contrast between an object and its background is especially critical for visual tasks that require the discrimination of shape and contour. An obvious example of this need for contrast is the printed page where dark letters can best be read when printed on light paper.

For seeing tasks requiring discrimination of surface texture and detail, less contrast between the surface and its background is desirable because our eyes adjust automatically to the average brightness of a scene. Someone seen against a brightly illuminated background would be silhouetted well but it would be difficult to discern that person's facial features.

The surface brightness of a task area should be the same as its background or be just a bit brighter. A maximum brightness ratio of 3:1 between the task surface and its background is generally recommended. Between the task area and the darkest part of the surrounding room, the brightness ratio should not exceed 5:1. Higher brightness ratios can lead to glare and associated problems of eye fatigue and loss in visual performance.

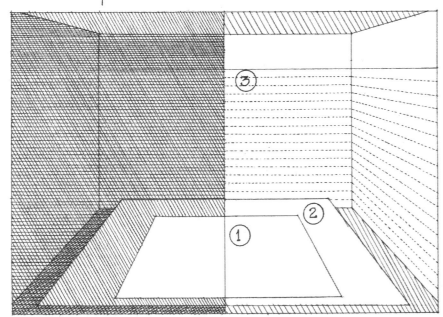

CONTRAST

HIGH BACKGROUND BRIGHTNESS IS HELPFUL IN DELINEATING SHAPE AND OUTLINE.

TO AID IN DISCRIMINATING SURFACE DETAIL, SURFACE BRIGHTNESS MUST BE INCREASED.

SURROUNDING AREA ③ SHOULD RANGE FROM 1/5 TO 5X THE BRIGHTNESS OF THE VISUAL TASK AREA ①

3:1
MAXIMUM RECOMMENDED BRIGHTNESS RATIO BETWEEN VISUAL TASK AREA ① AND ITS IMMEDIATE BACKGROUND ②

BRIGHTNESS AND CONTRAST CAN BE DESIRABLE IN CERTAIN SITUATIONS.

GLARE

DIRECT GLARE IS CAUSED BY THE BRIGHTNESS OF LIGHT SOURCES IN A PERSON'S NORMAL FIELD OF VISION.

Even though our eyes prefer even lighting, particularly between a task surface and its background, our eyes are able to adapt to a wide range of brightness levels. We can respond to a minimum brightness ratio of 2:1 as well as to a maximum of 100:1 or more, but only over a period of time. Our eyes cannot respond immediately to extreme changes in lighting levels. Once our eyes have adjusted to a certain lighting level, any significant increase in brightness can lead to glare, eyestrain, and impairment of visual performance.

There are two types of glare, direct and indirect. Direct glare is caused by the brightness of light sources within our normal field of vision. The brighter the light source, the greater the glare. Possible solutions to problems of direct glare include the following:

- Locate the sources of brightness out of the direct line of vision.
- If this is not possible, use properly shielded or baffled luminaires.
- In addition, raise the background brightness of the light sources and reduce their brightness ratio.

POSSIBLE SOLUTIONS TO DIRECT GLARE:

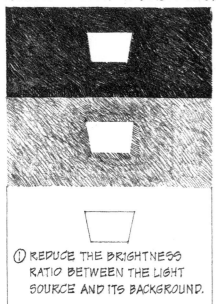

① REDUCE THE BRIGHTNESS RATIO BETWEEN THE LIGHT SOURCE AND ITS BACKGROUND.

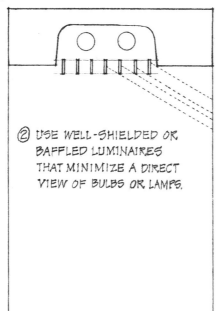

② USE WELL-SHIELDED OR BAFFLED LUMINAIRES THAT MINIMIZE A DIRECT VIEW OF BULBS OR LAMPS.

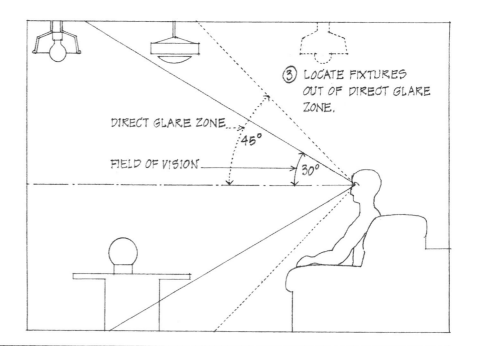

③ LOCATE FIXTURES OUT OF DIRECT GLARE ZONE.

DIRECT GLARE ZONE

45°

FIELD OF VISION

30°

Indirect glare is caused by a task or viewing surface reflecting light from a light source into the viewer's eyes. The term _veiling reflection_ is sometimes used to describe this type of glare because the reflection of the light source creates a veiling of the image on the task surface and a resultant loss of contrast necessary for seeing the image.

Reflected glare is most severe when the task or viewing surface is shiny and has a high specular reflectance value. Using a dull, matte task surface can help alleviate, but will not eliminate, veiling reflections.

Possible solutions to problems of reflected glare include the following:

- Locate the light source so that the incident light rays will be reflected away from the viewer.
- Use luminaires with diffusers or lenses that lower their brightness levels.
- Lower the level of general overhead lighting and supplement it with localized task light closer to the work surface.

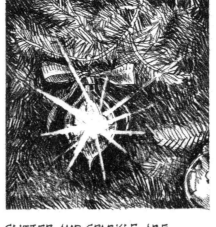

GLITTER AND SPARKLE ARE DESIRABLE TYPES OF GLARE.

INDIRECT OR REFLECTED GLARE AFFECTS OUR ABILITY TO PERFORM CRITICAL SEEING TASKS SUCH AS READING OR DRAFTING.

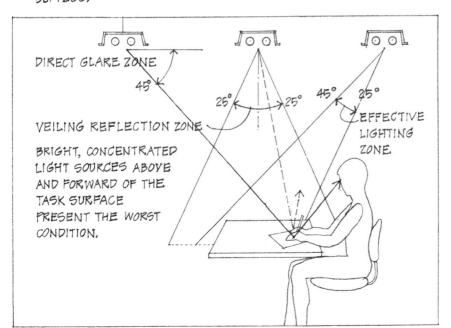

DIRECT GLARE ZONE

45° 25° 25° 45° 25°

VEILING REFLECTION ZONE

EFFECTIVE LIGHTING ZONE.

BRIGHT, CONCENTRATED LIGHT SOURCES ABOVE AND FORWARD OF THE TASK SURFACE PRESENT THE WORST CONDITION.

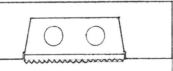

TO MINIMIZE VEILING REFLECTIONS WHEN THE TASK LOCATIONS ARE UNKNOWN, USE LOW-BRIGHTNESS LUMI-NAIRES, OR RELY ON A LOW LEVEL OF AMBIENT LIGHTING.

LOW-LEVEL AMBIENT LIGHTING SUPPLEMENTED BY INDIVIDUAL TASK LIGHTING - WHICH IS ADJUSTABLE BY THE USER - IS A GOOD GENERAL PURPOSE SOLUTION.

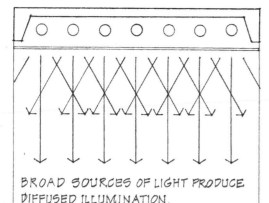

BROAD SOURCES OF LIGHT PRODUCE DIFFUSED ILLUMINATION.

DIFFUSE

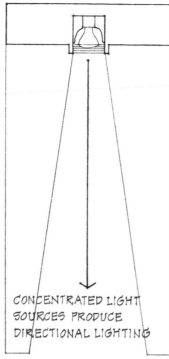

CONCENTRATED LIGHT SOURCES PRODUCE DIRECTIONAL LIGHTING

Diffuseness is a measure of a light's direction and dispersion as it emanates from its source. This quality of light affects both the visual atmosphere of a room and the appearance of objects within it. A broad source of light such as a luminous ceiling produces diffused illumination that is flat, fairly uniform, and generally glare-free. The soft light provided minimizes contrast and shadows, and can make the reading of surface textures difficult.

On the other hand, a point source of light such as an incandescent bulb produces a directional light with little diffusion. Directional lighting enhances our perception of shape, form, and surface texture by producing shadows and brightness variations on the objects it illuminates.

While diffused lighting is useful for general vision, it can be monotonous. Some directional lighting can help relieve this dullness by providing visual accents, introducing brightness variations, and brightening task surfaces. A mix of both diffused and directional lighting is often desirable and beneficial, especially when a variety of tasks are to be performed in a room.

DIFFUSED ILLUMINATION MINIMIZES CONTRAST AND SHADOWS.

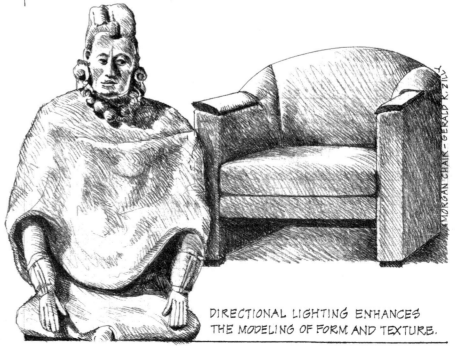

DIRECTIONAL LIGHTING ENHANCES THE MODELING OF FORM AND TEXTURE.

Another important quality of light is its color and how it affects the coloration of objects and surfaces in a room. While we assume most light to be white, the spectral distribution of light varies according to the nature of its source. The most evenly balanced white light is noon daylight. But in the early morning hours, daylight can range from purple to red. As the day progresses, it will cycle through a range of oranges and yellows to blue-white at noon, and then back again through the oranges and reds of sunset.

The spectral distribution of artificial light sources varies with the type of lamp. For example, an incandescent bulb produces a yellow-white light while a cool-white fluorescent produces a blue-white light.

The apparent color of a surface is a result of its reflection of its predominant hue and its absorption of the other colors of the light illuminating it. The spectral distribution of a light source is important because if certain wavelengths of color are missing, then those colors cannot be reflected and will appear to be missing or greyed in any surface illuminated by that light.

THE COLOR OF LIGHT

COLOR TEMPERATURE SCALE

°KELVIN	LIGHT SOURCE
10,000°	Clear blue sky (up to 25,000°K)
9000°	
8000°	North light
7000°	
	Daylight fluorescent
6000°	Overcast sky
5000°	Noon sunlight
	Cool white fluorescent
4000°	Daylight incandescent
	Warm white fluorescent
3000°	
	Incandescent lamp
2000°	Sunrise

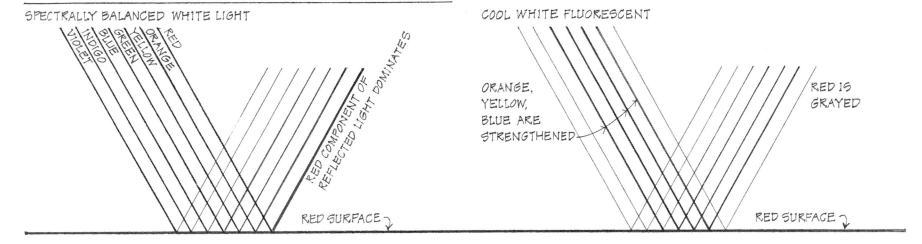

SPECTRALLY BALANCED WHITE LIGHT

VIOLET INDIGO BLUE GREEN YELLOW ORANGE RED

RED COMPONENT OF REFLECTED LIGHT DOMINATES

RED SURFACE

COOL WHITE FLUORESCENT

ORANGE, YELLOW, BLUE ARE STRENGTHENED

RED IS GRAYED

RED SURFACE

LIGHT SOURCES

The source of all natural daylight is the sun. Its light is intense but will vary with the time of day, from season to season, and from place to place. It can also be diffused by cloud cover, haze, precipitation, or any pollution that may be present in the air.

In addition to direct sunlight, two other conditions must be considered when designing the daylighting of a space, reflected light from a clear sky and light from an overcast sky. While direct sunlight emphasizes hot, bright colors, skylight is more diffuse and enhances cool colors.

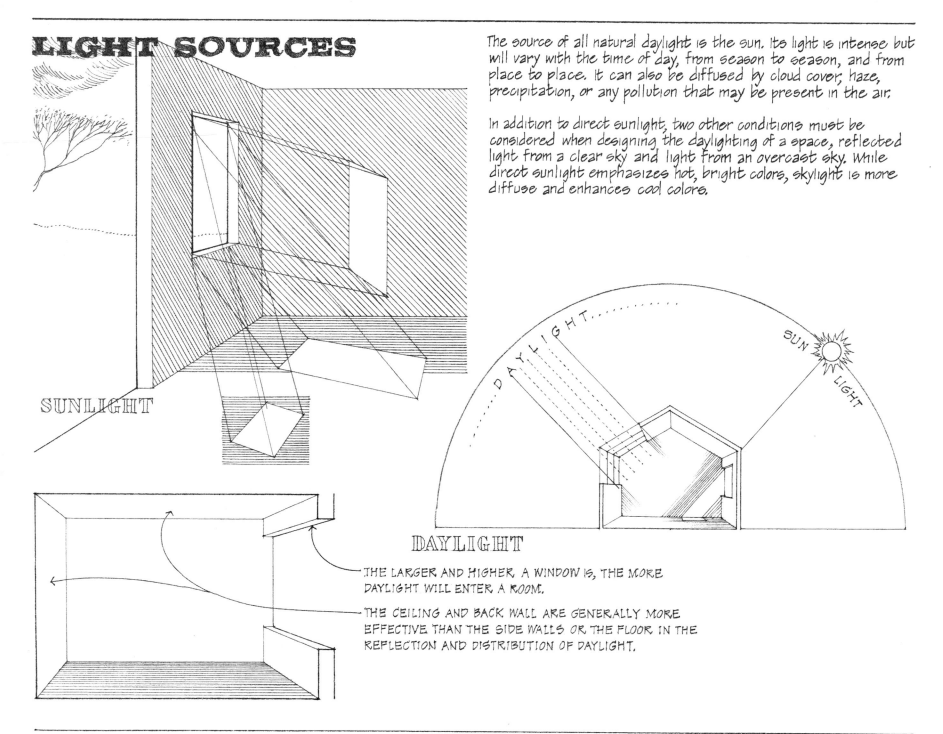

SUNLIGHT

DAYLIGHT

THE LARGER AND HIGHER, A WINDOW IS, THE MORE DAYLIGHT WILL ENTER A ROOM.

THE CEILING AND BACK WALL ARE GENERALLY MORE EFFECTIVE THAN THE SIDE WALLS OR THE FLOOR IN THE REFLECTION AND DISTRIBUTION OF DAYLIGHT.

Artificial light is natural light that is produced by manufactured elements. The quantity and quality of light produced differ according to the type of lamp used. The light is further modified by the housing which holds and energizes the lamp.

There are two major types of artificial light sources in common use, incandescent and fluorescent lamps. Incandescent lamps consist of material filaments which are heated within a glass enclosure until they glow. They are generally less expensive, easier to dim with rheostats, and warmer in color than fluorescent lamps. Their relatively small size and compact shape allow them to be used as point sources of light which emphasize the form and texture of objects.

Incandescent lamps have a low efficacy rating. Only about 12% of the wattage used goes toward the production of light; the remainder is heat. They also have a comparatively short life.

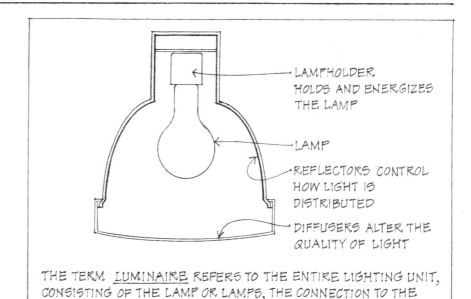

- LAMPHOLDER HOLDS AND ENERGIZES THE LAMP
- LAMP
- REFLECTORS CONTROL HOW LIGHT IS DISTRIBUTED
- DIFFUSERS ALTER THE QUALITY OF LIGHT

THE TERM LUMINAIRE REFERS TO THE ENTIRE LIGHTING UNIT, CONSISTING OF THE LAMP OR LAMPS, THE CONNECTION TO THE POWER SUPPLY, AND ELEMENTS THAT SHIELD, REFLECT, OR DIFFUSE THE LIGHT.

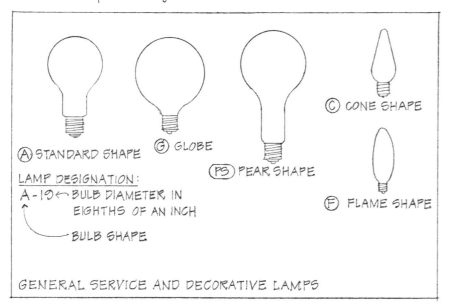

(A) STANDARD SHAPE (G) GLOBE

(PS) PEAR SHAPE

(C) CONE SHAPE

(F) FLAME SHAPE

LAMP DESIGNATION:
A-19 ← BULB DIAMETER IN EIGHTHS OF AN INCH
↑
BULB SHAPE

GENERAL SERVICE AND DECORATIVE LAMPS

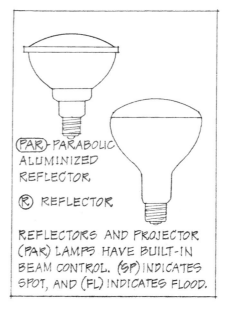

(PAR) PARABOLIC ALUMINIZED REFLECTOR

(R) REFLECTOR

REFLECTORS AND PROJECTOR (PAR) LAMPS HAVE BUILT-IN BEAM CONTROL. (SP) INDICATES SPOT, AND (FL) INDICATES FLOOD.

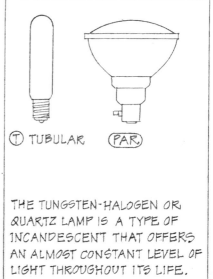

(T) TUBULAR   (PAR)

THE TUNGSTEN-HALOGEN OR QUARTZ LAMP IS A TYPE OF INCANDESCENT THAT OFFERS AN ALMOST CONSTANT LEVEL OF LIGHT THROUGHOUT ITS LIFE.

INCANDESCENT LAMPS

LAMP LENGTH: .... 18" (457mm) - 15 WATTS

FLUORESCENT LAMPS

24" (609) - 20 W
36" (914) - 30 W
48" (1219) - 40 W
96" (2438) - 75 W

A BRIEF COMPARISON:

ONE F48 T12 FLUORESCENT: 40 W - 3150 LUMENS
TWO 100 W INCANDESCENT : 200 W - 3420 LUMENS
FOUR 60 W INCANDESCENT : 240 W - 3480 LUMENS

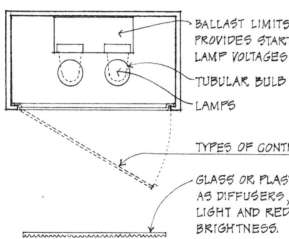

BALLAST LIMITS CURRENT AND
PROVIDES STARTING AND OPERATING
LAMP VOLTAGES

TUBULAR BULB

LAMPS

TYPES OF CONTROLLING ELEMENTS:

GLASS OR PLASTIC LENSES SERVE
AS DIFFUSERS, REDIRECTING THE
LIGHT AND REDUCING THE FIXTURE
BRIGHTNESS.

ONE-WAY BAFFLING CAN BE PROVIDED
BY SLATS WHICH SHOULD SHIELD
THE LENGTH OF THE TUBES.

SHIELDING ANGLE

EGG CRATE LOUVERS PROVIDE
TWO-WAY BAFFLING AND ALSO
DIFFUSE THE LIGHT.

Fluorescent lamps are tubular, low-intensity, electric discharge lamps. They produce light by generating an electric arc which passes through the mercury vapor sealed within their tubes. This produces ultraviolet light which energizes the phosphors that coat the tubes' inner walls, thus emitting visible light.

Fluorescent lamps are more efficient (efficacy of 50-80 lumens per watt) and have a longer life (9,000 - 20,000 hours) than incandescent lamps. They produce little heat.

The long, tubular form of fluorescent lamps results in a linear light source which produces diffused light. This light can be difficult to control optically, and the resulting flat light can be monotonous. Circular and U-shaped lamps are also available for use in more compact fixture housings.

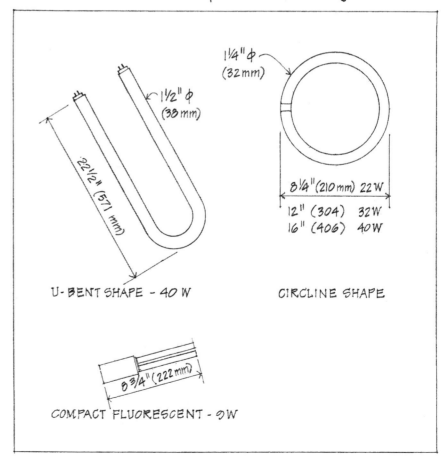

1¼" ϕ (32mm)

1½" ϕ (38 mm)

22½" (571 mm)

8¼" (210 mm) 22 W
12" (304) 32 W
16" (406) 40 W

U-BENT SHAPE - 40 W

CIRCLINE SHAPE

8¾" (222 mm)

COMPACT FLUORESCENT - 9 W

One can control the lamp's output and color by changing the fluorescent phosphors that coat the inner wall of the tube. There are, therefore, many types of "white" light produced by the various types of fluorescent lamps.

FLUORESCENT ········ → **F48 T12 CW · HO**

TUBE LENGTH ········

LAMP SHAPE (TUBULAR) ········
LAMP DIAMETER IN EIGHTHS OF AN INCH ········

········INDICATES HIGHER OUTPUT LAMP –
········REQUIRES SPECIAL CIRCUIT AND BALLAST

········TYPE OF COLOR TINT

COLOR PROPERTIES OF FLUORESCENT AND INCANDESCENT LAMPS				SOURCE: GENERAL ELECTRIC CO. LAMP DEPARTMENT	
TYPE OF LAMP	EFFECT ON A NEUTRAL SURFACE	EFFECT ON ATMOSPHERE	COLORS STRENGTHENED	COLORS GRAYED	REMARKS
COOL WHITE CW	WHITE	NEUTRAL TO MODERATELY COOL	ORANGE YELLOW BLUE	RED	BLENDS WITH NATURAL DAYLIGHT
DELUXE CWX COOL WHITE	WHITE	NEUTRAL TO MODERATELY COOL	ALL NEARLY EQUALLY	NONE	BEST OVERALL COLOR RENDITION
WARM WHITE WW	YELLOWISH WHITE	WARM	ORANGE YELLOW	RED GREEN BLUE	BLENDS WITH INCANDESCENT LIGHT
DELUXE WWX WARM WHITE	YELLOWISH WHITE	WARM	RED, ORANGE YELLOW GREEN	BLUE	SIMULATES INCANDESCENT LIGHT
DAYLIGHT	BLUISH WHITE	VERY COOL	GREEN BLUE	RED ORANGE	
INCANDESCENT	YELLOWISH WHITE	WARM	RED ORANGE YELLOW	BLUE	GOOD COLOR RENDERING

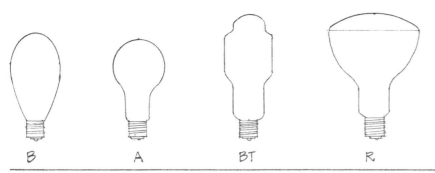

MERCURY VAPOR LAMP SHAPES

B   A   BT   R

> FOR ACCURATE, CURRENT DATA ON LAMP SIZES, WATTAGES,
> LUMEN OUTPUT, AND AVERAGE LIFE, CONSULT MANUFAC-
> TURER'S CATALOGS.

A third major group of artificial light sources consists of high intensity discharge (HID) lamps - mercury vapor, high pressure sodium, and metal halide lamps. These lamps have a long life expectancy and consume little energy to produce a great amount of light from a relatively small source. They combine the form of an incandescent lamp with the efficiency of a fluorescent.

HID lamps were originally used primarily for street and sidewalk lighting and in large industrial spaces. Despite their efficiency, they had uneven spectral distributions and acutely distorted the color of objects they illuminated. Because of improvements in their rendition of color, however, HID lamps are increasingly being used in large commercial and public interior spaces.

Mercury lamps produce light when an arc is struck in a quartz tube containing vaporized mercury. Available in 40W to 1000W sizes, they produce twice as much light as a comparable incandescent lamp and have about the same efficacy (40-60 lumens/watt) as fluorescent lamps. Since they have a life of 16,000 - 24,000 hours, they are often used when burning hours are long and service is difficult. Clear mercury lamps cast a definite blue-green light. Phosphor-coated lamps have improved efficiency and color quality, making them usable for interior lighting.

HIGH INTENSITY DISCHARGE LAMPS

COLOR PROPERTIES OF MERCURY LAMPS

SOURCE: GENERAL ELECTRIC CO. LAMP DEPARTMENT

TYPE OF LAMP	EFFECT ON NEUTRAL SURFACE	EFFECT ON ATMOSPHERE	COLORS STRENGTHENED	COLORS GREYED	REMARKS
CLEAR MERCURY	GREENISH BLUE-WHITE	VERY COOL, GREENISH	YELLOW BLUE GREEN	RED ORANGE	POOR COLOR RENDERING
WHITE MERCURY	GREENISH WHITE	MODERATELY COOL, GREENISH	YELLOW GREEN BLUE	RED ORANGE	MODERATE COLOR RENDERING
DELUXE WHITE MERCURY	PURPLISH WHITE	WARM, PURPLISH	RED BLUE YELLOW	GREEN	COLOR ACCEPTABILITY SIMILAR TO CW FLUORESCENT

Metal halide lamps are similar to mercury lamps except that metal halide is added to provide more light (efficacy of 80-100 lumens/watt) and better color. They are available in 400W-1500W sizes, and have a life of 1,500-15,000 hours. Because of their compact shape, their light can be optically controlled. And because they render color fairly well, they can be used both for outdoor and interior applications.

High-pressure sodium lamps are the most efficient sources of white light. Available in 75W-1000W sizes, they have an efficacy of 100-130 lumens/watt and a life of 10,000-20,000 hours. Their light has a slightly yellowish cast similar to that of a warm-white fluorescent.

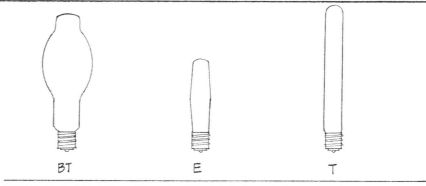

BT   E   T

METAL HALIDE AND HIGH PRESSURE SODIUM LAMP SHAPES

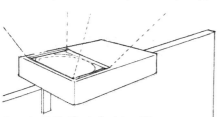

PORTABLE UNITS MAY BE PLACED ON SHELVES OR ATOP PANELS ABOVE EYE LEVEL.

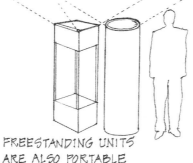

FREESTANDING UNITS ARE ALSO PORTABLE

HID LIGHTS ARE AN ALTERNATIVE TO CONVENTIONAL OVERHEAD LIGHTING IN COMMERCIAL INTERIOR SPACES. THEY PROVIDE INDIRECT, AMBIENT LIGHTING BY USING THE CEILING SURFACE TO REFLECT AND DIFFUSE THEIR LIGHT.

COLOR PROPERTIES OF METAL HALIDE AND HIGH PRESSURE SODIUM LAMPS

SOURCE: GENERAL ELECTRIC CO. LAMP DEPARTMENT

TYPE OF LAMP	EFFECT ON NEUTRAL SURFACE	EFFECT ON ATMOSPHERE	COLORS STRENGTHENED	COLORS GRAYED	REMARKS
METAL HALIDE	GREENISH WHITE	MODERATELY COOL, GREENISH	YELLOW GREEN BLUE	RED	COLOR ACCEPTABILITY SIMILAR TO CW FLUORESCENT
HIGH PRESSURE SODIUM	YELLOWISH	WARM, YELLOWISH	YELLOW GREEN ORANGE	RED BLUE	COLOR ACCEPTABILITY APPROACHES THAT OF WW FLUORESCENT

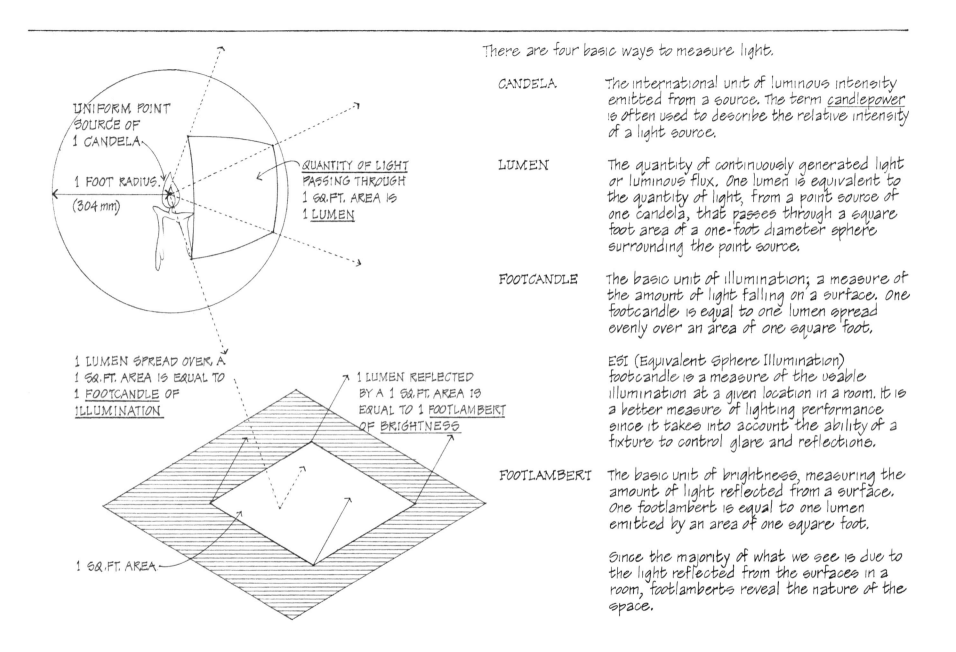

There are four basic ways to measure light.

CANDELA   The international unit of luminous intensity emitted from a source. The term <u>candlepower</u> is often used to describe the relative intensity of a light source.

LUMEN   The quantity of continuously generated light or luminous flux. One lumen is equivalent to the quantity of light, from a point source of one candela, that passes through a square foot area of a one-foot diameter sphere surrounding the point source.

FOOTCANDLE   The basic unit of illumination; a measure of the amount of light falling on a surface. One footcandle is equal to one lumen spread evenly over an area of one square foot.

ESI (Equivalent Sphere Illumination) footcandle is a measure of the usable illumination at a given location in a room. It is a better measure of lighting performance since it takes into account the ability of a fixture to control glare and reflections.

FOOTLAMBERT   The basic unit of brightness, measuring the amount of light reflected from a surface. One footlambert is equal to one lumen emitted by an area of one square foot.

Since the majority of what we see is due to the light reflected from the surfaces in a room, footlamberts reveal the nature of the space.

UNIFORM POINT SOURCE OF 1 CANDELA

1 FOOT RADIUS. (304 mm)

QUANTITY OF LIGHT PASSING THROUGH 1 SQ.FT. AREA IS 1 <u>LUMEN</u>

1 LUMEN SPREAD OVER A 1 SQ.FT. AREA IS EQUAL TO 1 <u>FOOTCANDLE</u> OF <u>ILLUMINATION</u>

1 LUMEN REFLECTED BY A 1 SQ.FT. AREA IS EQUAL TO 1 <u>FOOTLAMBERT</u> OF <u>BRIGHTNESS</u>

1 SQ.FT. AREA

LIGHTING CALCULATIONS

The basic unit of illumination, the footcandle, can be defined by the formula:

1 Footcandle = $\dfrac{\text{1 Lumen (evenly distributed over)}}{\text{1 Square Foot of Area}}$

This formula also provides the basis for calculating the average level of illumination in a space generated by a number of known light sources.

Illumination (Footcandles) = $\dfrac{\text{Lumens (from sources)}}{\text{Square Footage (of space)}}$

or

$\boxed{FC = L/A}$ This formula assumes all of the light generated by a room's light sources becomes usable illumination. In reality, however, there are several factors that diminish the actual lumen output of luminaires and how well this amount is utilized for task illumination in a given room.

- Fixture Efficiency:
  As soon as light is generated by a luminaire, a portion of it is lost within the fixture itself.

- Room Characteristics:
  The proportion of a room (the ratio of its vertical-to-horizontal areas) as well as the reflectances of its surfaces affect the amount of light that is lost as it strikes, and is absorbed by, the room's surfaces.

The one factor that takes these considerations into account is the Coefficient of Utilization (CU). It represents the percentage of generated light that ultimately arrives at the work plane. It is usually supplied by the fixture manufacturer for the specific luminaire being considered for use. Its use modifies the basic formula for illumination as follows:

$$FC = \frac{L \times CU}{A}$$

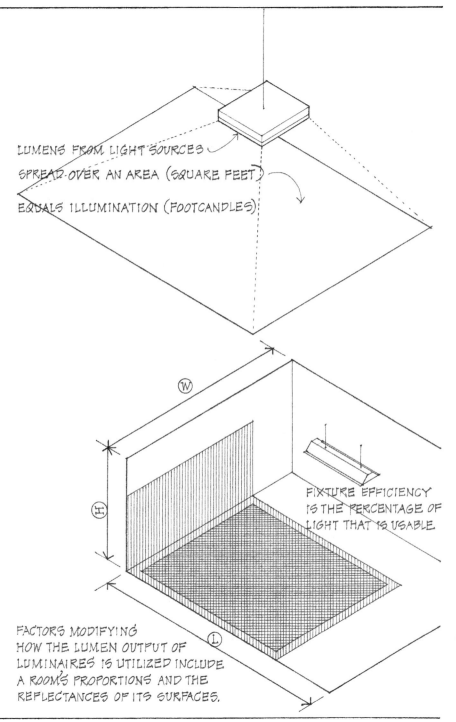

LUMENS FROM LIGHT SOURCES SPREAD OVER AN AREA (SQUARE FEET) EQUALS ILLUMINATION (FOOTCANDLES)

FIXTURE EFFICIENCY IS THE PERCENTAGE OF LIGHT THAT IS USABLE

FACTORS MODIFYING HOW THE LUMEN OUTPUT OF LUMINAIRES IS UTILIZED INCLUDE A ROOM'S PROPORTIONS AND THE REFLECTANCES OF ITS SURFACES.

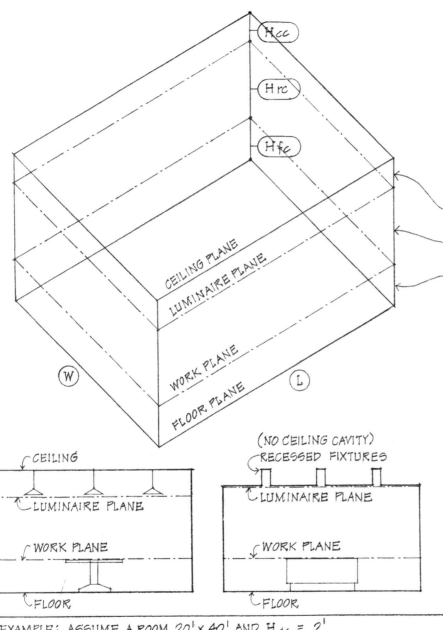

Before the CU tables for a specific luminaire can be used, some preliminary calculations regarding a room's proportions and surface reflectances must be made. These calculations are based on the Zonal Cavity Method, developed by the Illuminating Engineering Society (IES) to determine the number of luminaires required to deliver a specified amount of illumination at a predetermined horizontal work plane.

The Zonal Cavity Method assumes a room to be divided into a number of horizontal cavities, each bounded vertically by the room's walls and horizontally to form a:

- Ceiling Cavity (cc) between the ceiling and a horizontal luminaire plane;
- Room Cavity (rc) between the luminaire plane and a horizontal work plane across the task surfaces;
- Floor Cavity (fc) between the work plane and the floor.

Note that there always is a room cavity. The existence of a ceiling or floor cavity depends on the suspension of the luminaires and the location of the work plane.

Dividing a room into cavities permits the study of how light behaves differently in each cavity — according to the light distribution of the luminaires, the surface reflectances, and the vertical-to-horizontal areas — before the light reaches the assumed work plane.

The Cavity Ratio (CR) for each cavity is the relationship of the cavity's vertical area to its horizontal area as defined by the following formula:

$$CR = \frac{5 \times H \times (W+L)}{W \times L} ,$$

where H = cavity height
W = cavity width
L = cavity length

EXAMPLE: ASSUME A ROOM 20' × 40' AND H$_{cc}$ = 2'
H$_{RC}$ = 8'
H$_{FC}$ = 3'

① RCR = $\frac{5 \times 8 \,(20+40)}{20 \times 40}$ = 3.0

CCR = 2/8 OF RCR = 0.75

FCR = 3/8 OF RCR = 1.13

The "percent effective cavity reflectance," represented by the Greek letter rho (P), is a measure of how much light escapes the ceiling or wall cavities after a portion is absorbed within the cavity by surface reflectances. The effective reflectances for the ceiling and floor cavities, based on the cavity Ratio and the actual ceiling, wall, and floor reflectances, can be found in tables in the <u>IES Lighting Handbook</u> (Illuminating Engineering Society, New York).

Given the Room Cavity Ratio (RCR), the percent effective ceiling and floor cavity reflectances, and the percent wall reflectance, the overall Coefficient of Utilization (CU) for a specific luminaire can be extracted from tables supplied by the fixture manufacturer.

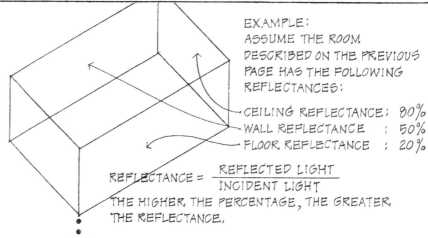

EXAMPLE:
ASSUME THE ROOM DESCRIBED ON THE PREVIOUS PAGE HAS THE FOLLOWING REFLECTANCES:

- CEILING REFLECTANCE : 80%
- WALL REFLECTANCE : 50%
- FLOOR REFLECTANCE : 20%

$$\text{REFLECTANCE} = \frac{\text{REFLECTED LIGHT}}{\text{INCIDENT LIGHT}}$$

THE HIGHER THE PERCENTAGE, THE GREATER THE REFLECTANCE.

---

③ DETERMINE THE COEFFICIENT OF UTILIZATION ASSUMING A SPECIFIC TYPE OF LUMINAIRE

TYPE OF LUMINAIRE	DISTRIBUTION AND PER CENT LAMP LUMENS	P_{CC} 80		(70)			50		
		P_W	30 . 10	(50)	30 . 10		50 . 30 . 10		
	MAINT. CAT. / MAX. S/MH GUIDE	(RCR)	CU TABLE FOR $P_{FC} = \underline{20}$						
IV 1.3	0% ↑ 83½% ↓	0	.90	.97	.97	.97	.92	.	.
		1	.82	.86	.83	.81	.83	.	.
		2	.68	.76	.72	.67	.73	.	.
		(3) →.57	(.67)	.61	.57	.65		.	.
		4	.49	.60	.53	.48	.58	.	.
		5	.41	.53	.46	.41	.51	.	.
		6	.35	.47	.40	.35	.96	.	.
		7	.30	.42	.35	.30	.41	.	.
		8	.26	.38	.31	.26	.37	.	.
		9	.23	.34	.27	.23	.33	.	.
		10	.20	.31	.24	.20	.30	.	.

$\boxed{CU = .67}$

If the effective floor cavity reflectance is not equal to 20, then the value for CU must be adjusted. The CU value is higher if P_{FC} is greater than 20, and lower if P_{FC} is less than 20.

---

② DETERMINE EFFECTIVE CEILING AND FLOOR CAVITY REFLECTANCES

PERCENT BASE (CEILING OR FLOOR) REFLECTANCE	(80) ceiling						(20) floor					
PERCENT WALL REFLECTANCE	90	80	70	60	(50)	40	90	80	70	60	(50)	40
CAVITY RATIO												
0.2	79	78	78	77	77	76						
0.4	79	77	76	75	74	73						
0.6	78	76	75	73	71	70						
0.8	78	75	73	71	(69)	67						
1.0	77	74	72	69	67	65	25	23	22	20	19	18
1.2							25	23	22	20	19	17
1.4							26	24	22	20	18	17
1.6							27	24	22	20	18	17
1.8							27	25	23	20	18	17

CCR = 0.75 (at cavity ratio 0.6–0.8 region)

FCR = 1.13 (at cavity ratio 1.0–1.2 region)

<u>INTERPOLATING</u>, $P_{CC} = 70$ and $P_{FC} = 19$

Note that, in principle, the <u>effective</u> reflectances for ceiling and floor cavities decrease as their cavity ratios increase and and wall reflectances decrease.

LAMP LUMEN DEPRECIATION (LLD) FACTORS FOR SOME TYPICAL LAMPS			
LAMP TYPE	WATTS	MEAN	MINIMUM
INCANDESCENT	75	.90	.86
	100	.93	.90
	300	.91	.87
FLUORESCENT	40	.87	.83
	60	.93	.89
	75	.93	.89
HID - MERCURY	250	.81	.75
HID - METAL HALIDE	250	.83	.76

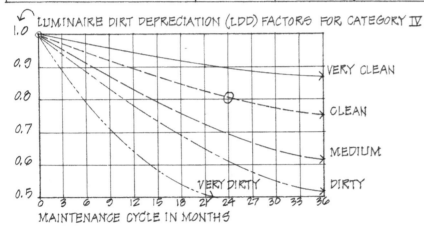

LUMINAIRE DIRT DEPRECIATION (LDD) FACTORS FOR CATEGORY IV

MAINTENANCE CYCLE IN MONTHS

EXAMPLE CONTINUED FROM PREVIOUS PAGE:
ASSUME: LUMINAIRE USES A SINGLE 300 W INCANDESCENT WITH A LUMEN OUTPUT OF 6360; A CLEANING CYCLE OF 24 MONTHS UNDER CLEAN CONDITIONS.

▶ MF = LLD × LDD = .91 × 0.8 = 0.73

FROM PREVIOUS PAGES:
▶ ROOM = 20' × 40'
▶ CU = .67

DESIRED FOOTCANDLE LEVEL = 100 FC ◀

THEREFORE, REQUIRED NUMBER OF LUMINAIRES =

$$\frac{(100) \times (20 \times 40)}{0.67 \times 0.73 \times 6360 \times 1} = 25.7,\ldots.\underline{26 \text{ LUMINAIRES REQUIRED}}$$

There are two additional factors that contribute to the loss of light available for illumination. The Lamp Lumen Depreciation (LLD) factor takes into account the inherent loss of lumen output of lamps over time. This LLD factor varies with the type of lamp used.

The Luminaire Dirt Depreciation (LDD) factor compensates for light loss due to the accumulation of dirt on the lamp and fixture housing. The LDD factor used will depend on the type of luminaire used, the type of atmosphere in the room, and the expected maintenance practice.

Consult the IES Lighting Handbook or the manufacturer's photometric tables for LLD and LDD values. An overall Maintenance Factor (MF) combines these two values into a single quantity that modifies the working equation for illumination.

$$FC = \frac{L \times CU \times LLD \times LDD}{A}; \quad \text{IF } MF = LLD \times LDD, \text{ then}$$

$$\boxed{FC = \frac{L \times CU \times MF}{A}}$$

The working formula for illumination has assumed solving for Footcandles (FC). Since the desired footcandles is normally determined by the function of a space, the formula can be transposed to solve for required Lumens (L).

$$\boxed{L \text{ (total lumens required)} = \frac{FC \text{ (desired)} \times Area}{CU \times MF}}$$

Since each luminaire has a known number of lamps and each lamp generates a known quantity of lumens, the required number of luminaires can be found by the following:

$$\boxed{N^{\underline{o}} \text{ of luminaires} = \frac{FC \text{ (desired)} \times Area}{CU \times MF \times lumens/lamp \times lamps/luminaire}}$$

COEFFICIENT OF UTILIZATION TABLES FOR THREE TYPES OF LUMINAIRES:
Consult the IES Lighting Handbook, or for the most current data, refer to manufacturer's catalogs.

TYPE OF LUMINAIRE	TYPICAL DISTRIBUTION AND PERCENT LAMP LUMENS		MAINT. CAT. / MAXIMUM SM/H GUIDE	RCR	ρcc → 80			70			50			30			10			0
				ρw →	50	30	10	50	30	10	50	30	10	50	30	10	50	30	10	0
					COEFFICIENTS OF UTILIZATION FOR ρFC = 20															
DIFFUSING SPHERE WITH INCANDESCENT LAMP	V 1.5 35%↑ 45%↓			1	.71	.67	.63	.66	.62	.59	.56	.53	.50	.47	.45	.43	.39	.37	.35	.31
				2	.61	.54	.49	.56	.50	.46	.47	.43	.39	.39	.36	.33	.32	.29	.27	.23
				3	.52	.45	.39	.48	.42	.37	.41	.36	.31	.34	.30	.26	.27	.24	.22	.18
				4	.46	.38	.33	.42	.36	.30	.36	.30	.26	.30	.26	.22	.24	.21	.18	.15
				5	.40	.33	.27	.37	.30	.25	.32	.26	.22	.26	.22	.19	.21	.18	.15	.12
				6	.36	.28	.23	.33	.26	.21	.28	.23	.19	.23	.19	.16	.19	.15	.13	.10
				7	.32	.25	.20	.29	.23	.18	.25	.20	.16	.21	.16	.13	.17	.13	.11	.09
				8	.29	.22	.17	.27	.20	.16	.23	.17	.14	.19	.15	.12	.15	.12	.09	.07
				9	.26	.19	.15	.24	.18	.14	.20	.15	.12	.17	.13	.10	.14	.11	.08	.06
				10	.23	.17	.13	.22	.16	.12	.19	.14	.10	.16	.12	.09	.13	.09	.07	.05
RECESSED R-40 FLOOD WITH REFLECTOR SKIRT	IV 0.7 0% 85%			1	.96	.94	.92	.94	.92	.91	.90	.89	.88	.87	.86	.85	.84	.84	.83	.82
				2	.91	.88	.86	.90	.87	.85	.87	.85	.83	.84	.83	.82	.82	.81	.80	.79
				3	.87	.84	.81	.86	.83	.81	.84	.81	.79	.82	.80	.78	.80	.78	.77	.76
				4	.83	.80	.77	.82	.79	.77	.81	.78	.76	.79	.77	.75	.78	.76	.74	.73
				5	.79	.76	.73	.79	.75	.73	.77	.74	.72	.76	.73	.71	.75	.73	.71	.70
				6	.76	.73	.70	.76	.72	.70	.75	.72	.69	.74	.71	.69	.73	.70	.68	.67
				7	.73	.69	.66	.73	.69	.66	.72	.68	.66	.71	.68	.66	.70	.67	.65	.64
				8	.70	.66	.63	.70	.66	.63	.69	.65	.63	.68	.65	.63	.67	.65	.63	.62
				9	.67	.63	.60	.67	.63	.60	.66	.62	.60	.65	.62	.60	.65	.62	.60	.59
				10	.64	.60	.58	.64	.60	.58	.63	.60	.58	.63	.60	.57	.62	.59	.57	.56
2 LAMP FLUORESCENT WITH WRAPAROUND PRISMATIC LENS	V 1.2 24%↑ 50%↓			1	.71	.68	.65	.67	.65	.62	.60	.58	.56	.53	.51	.50	.47	.45	.44	.41
				2	.63	.58	.54	.59	.55	.52	.53	.50	.47	.47	.45	.42	.42	.40	.38	.35
				3	.56	.50	.46	.53	.48	.44	.47	.44	.40	.42	.39	.37	.38	.35	.33	.31
				4	.50	.44	.40	.48	.42	.38	.43	.39	.35	.38	.35	.32	.34	.32	.29	.27
				5	.45	.39	.34	.43	.37	.33	.38	.34	.31	.35	.31	.28	.31	.28	.26	.24
				6	.41	.35	.30	.39	.33	.29	.35	.30	.27	.32	.28	.25	.28	.25	.23	.21
				7	.37	.31	.27	.35	.30	.26	.32	.27	.24	.29	.25	.22	.26	.23	.20	.19
				8	.33	.27	.23	.32	.26	.23	.29	.24	.21	.26	.22	.20	.23	.20	.18	.16
				9	.30	.24	.20	.29	.23	.20	.26	.22	.18	.24	.20	.17	.21	.18	.16	.14
				10	.27	.22	.18	.26	.21	.18	.24	.19	.16	.22	.18	.15	.19	.16	.14	.13

TYPES OF LUMINAIRE DISTRIBUTION

Luminaires may be classified according to how they distribute the light emitted by their lamps, and the characteristic spread of their beams. This information, along with the S/MH ratio, is normally supplied by the fixture manufacturer for each luminaire.

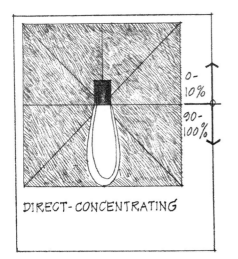

DIRECT-CONCENTRATING

0-10%

90-100%

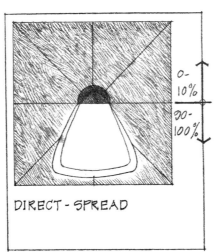

DIRECT - SPREAD

0-10%

90-100%

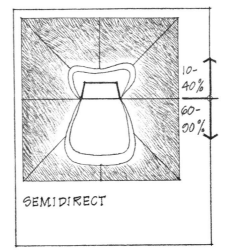

SEMIDIRECT

10-40%

60-90%

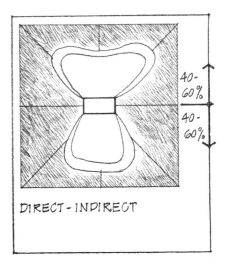

DIRECT - INDIRECT

40-60%

40-60%

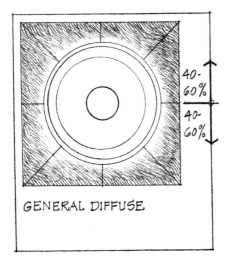

GENERAL DIFFUSE

40-60%

40-60%

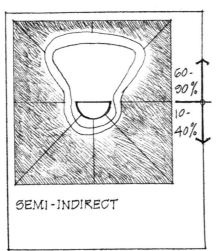

SEMI - INDIRECT

60-90%

10-40%

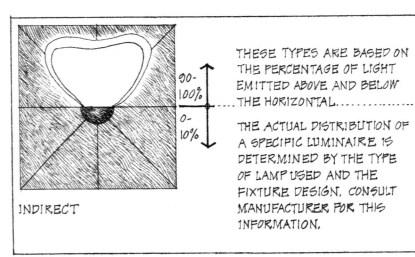

INDIRECT

90-100%

0-10%

THESE TYPES ARE BASED ON THE PERCENTAGE OF LIGHT EMITTED ABOVE AND BELOW THE HORIZONTAL.

THE ACTUAL DISTRIBUTION OF A SPECIFIC LUMINAIRE IS DETERMINED BY THE TYPE OF LAMP USED AND THE FIXTURE DESIGN. CONSULT MANUFACTURER FOR THIS INFORMATION.

The S/MH guideline specifies the ratio of maximum luminaire spacing to mounting height in order to achieve an acceptable uniformity of illumination. For most luminaires, the mounting height is measured from the luminaire to an assumed work plane. For semi-indirect and indirect lighting systems that utilize the ceiling plane as a reflector, the mounting height is measured from the ceiling to the work plane.

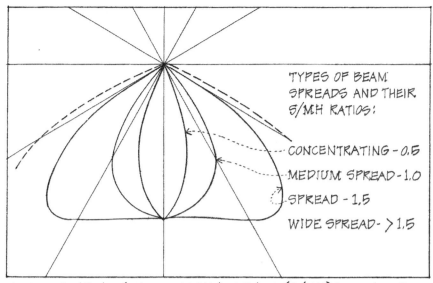

TYPES OF BEAM SPREADS AND THEIR S/MH RATIOS:

CONCENTRATING - 0.5

MEDIUM SPREAD - 1.0

SPREAD - 1.5

WIDE SPREAD - >1.5

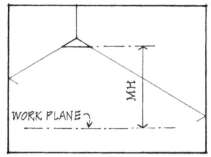

DIRECT LIGHTING OF THE WORK OR VISUAL TASK PLANE

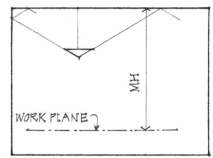

INDIRECT LIGHTING, USING THE CEILING PLANE AS A REFLECTOR.

MAXIMUM-SPACING-TO-MOUNTING-HEIGHT (S/MH) RATIOS ARE CALCULATED AND SUPPLIED BY THE FIXTURE MANUFACTURER.

PLACING LUMINAIRES TOO FAR FROM WALL REDUCES WALL BRIGHTNESS AND MAY RESULT IN LOWER LEVEL OF ILLUMINATION.

FOR INCREASED WALL BRIGHTNESS AND GENERALLY HIGHER LEVEL OF ILLUMINATION, SPACE LUMINAIRES AWAY FROM WALL 1/3 TO 1/2 OF (S)

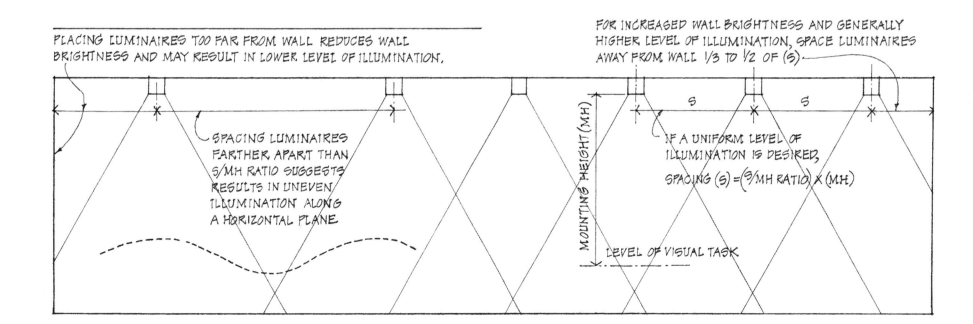

SPACING LUMINAIRES FARTHER APART THAN S/MH RATIO SUGGESTS RESULTS IN UNEVEN ILLUMINATION ALONG A HORIZONTAL PLANE

MOUNTING HEIGHT (MH)

LEVEL OF VISUAL TASK

IF A UNIFORM LEVEL OF ILLUMINATION IS DESIRED,

SPACING (S) = (S/MH RATIO) × (MH)

ACOUSTICS

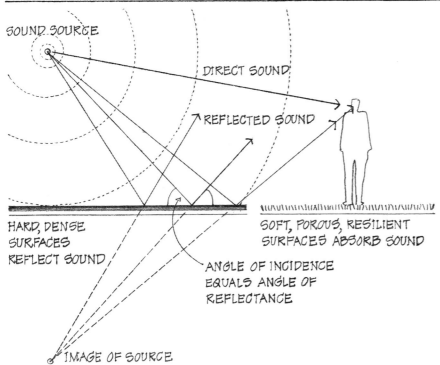

SOUND SOURCE

DIRECT SOUND

REFLECTED SOUND

HARD, DENSE
SURFACES
REFLECT SOUND

ANGLE OF INCIDENCE
EQUALS ANGLE OF
REFLECTANCE

SOFT, POROUS, RESILIENT
SURFACES ABSORB SOUND

IMAGE OF SOURCE

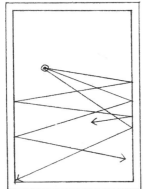

PARALLEL REFLEC-
TIVE SURFACES CAN
CAUSE ECHOES OR
FLUTTER

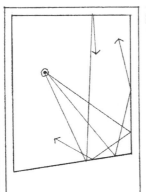

SPLAYED SURFACES
CAN FRAGMENT
SOUND

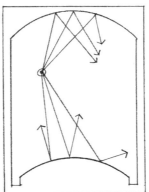

CONCAVE SURFACES
FOCUS SOUND; CONVEX
SURFACES DIFFUSE
SOUND

In interior design, we are concerned with the control of sound in interior spaces. More specifically, we want to preserve and enhance desired sounds and reduce or eliminate sounds which would interfere with our activities.

Sound is a form of kinetic energy caused by vibration. The resulting wave motion travels outward spherically from its source until it encounters an obstacle or surface in its path. Hard, dense, rigid materials reflect sound while soft, porous, resilient materials absorb and dissipate sound energy.

When a sound wave reaches our ears, it vibrates our ear drums, resulting in the sensation of hearing. In a room, we first hear a sound directly from its source and then a series of reflections of that sound. Reflective surfaces are useful when they reinforce desirable sounds by directing and distributing their paths in a room. The continued presence of reflected sounds, however, can also cause problems of echo, flutter, or reverberation.

Echoes can occur in large spaces when parallel reflective surfaces spaced more than 60 feet (18 m) apart cause the interval between direct and reflected sounds to be more than 1/15 th of a second. In smaller rooms, parallel reflective surfaces can cause mini-echoes or flutter. Reverberation refers to the continued presence of a sound in a space. While some music is enhanced with long reverberation times, speech can become muddled in such an acoustic environment. To correct these situations, it may be necessary to alter the shape and orientation of a room's surfaces or install more sound-absorbing materials.

The requirements for sound level, reverberation time, and resonance vary with the nature of the activity and the types of sounds generated. An acoustical engineer, given stated criteria, can determine the acoustical require-ments for a space. The interior designer should be aware of how the selection and disposition of reflective and absorbent materials affect the acoustical qualities of a room.

Unwanted noise generated outside a room can be controlled in three ways. The first is to control and isolate the noise at its source. The second is to organize the building plan such that noisy areas are located as far away as possible from quiet areas. The third is to eliminate possible paths - through the air or through a building's structure - that the noise can take from its source to the space.

Sound can be transmitted through the solid materials of a building's structure. Since structure-borne sounds are difficult to control, they should be isolated at their source. Using quiet equipment, resilient mountings, and flexible connections can help reduce structure-borne sound.

Sound can be transmitted through any clear air path, even the tiniest cracks around doors, windows, and electrical outlets. Careful weatherstripping to block these openings can help prevent airborne noise from entering a room.

Sound can also penetrate a room's wall, floor, or ceiling construction. This transmission can be reduced by introducing discontinuity in the construction assembly and using heavy, rigid materials that resist sound vibration. As a guide to designers, various construction assemblies have been tested for their theoretical insulation value and assigned an STC (Sound Transmission Class) rating.

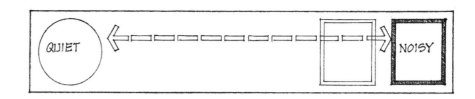

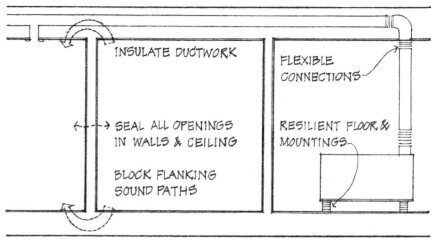

CONTROLLING AIR-BORNE AND STRUCTURE-BORNE SOUND

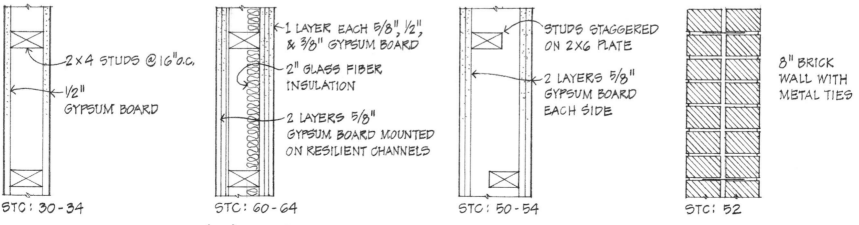

2 x 4 STUDS @ 16" o.c.

1/2" GYPSUM BOARD

STC: 30-34

1 LAYER EACH 5/8", 1/2", & 3/8" GYPSUM BOARD

2" GLASS FIBER INSULATION

2 LAYERS 5/8" GYPSUM BOARD MOUNTED ON RESILIENT CHANNELS

STC: 60-64

STUDS STAGGERED ON 2x6 PLATE

2 LAYERS 5/8" GYPSUM BOARD EACH SIDE

STC: 50-54

8" BRICK WALL WITH METAL TIES

STC: 52

SOUND TRANSMISSION CLASS (STC) RATINGS OF SEVERAL WALL ASSEMBLIES

STANDARDS & CODES

This final section outlines some considerations of a system which, while not immediately visible, affects the design of a building and its interior spaces. This system consists of a variety of laws and regulations enacted by federal, state, and local governments in an effort to protect the public health, safety, and general welfare.

Zoning regulations control the size, location, and use of buildings. Building codes regulate how a building is constructed and occupied. Many of these regulations incorporate standards established by governmental or independent testing agencies. (See page 312 for a listing of model codes and standards.)

While architects and engineers bear the primary responsibility for complying with code requirements, the interior designer should be aware of these regulatory devices and be sensitive to how they might affect the design of interior spaces. It should also be remembered that codes often set minimum standards, and mere compliance will not ensure that a building will be efficient, comfortable, or well designed.

The following are some specific areas of concern which affect the work of the interior designer. For further detailed requirements, always check the applicable codes.

The applicable building code usually specifies minimum standards for the structural stability of a building and the quality and design of its materials and construction. When planning the interior of a new building or the remodeling of an existing one, an architect or engineer should be consulted if any alterations to a building's structural elements are anticipated.

Fire safety is a prime area of concern of building codes. Requirements for the noncombustibility or fire-resistance of a building's structural elements and exterior walls are specified according to the building's occupancy, floor area, height, and location. In addition, fire-resistant walls and doors may be required to subdivide a building into separate areas and prevent a fire in one area from spreading to others.

Even when a building's structure would not support combustion, a fire can occur because of its finish materials and contents. This is of particular significance for interior designers when specifying such materials as carpet, draperies, upholstery, and furniture finishes. Regulations may prohibit the use of materials with a low flash point or set standards for the degree of flame spread and smoke emission allowed.

Sprinkler systems are increasingly being relied on to control a fire that does start. In addition, a type of fire/smoke detector and alarm system is usually required to warn of fire.

The means-of-egress requirements of fire codes provide for the safe and efficient evacuation of a building in case of fire. These requirements are usually based on a building's size, construction, and type of occupancy. In principle, there should be at least two alternative ways of exiting a building from any space within in case one route is cut off by fire or smoke. Exit passages, stairs, ramps, and doorways should be clearly marked, well lit, and wide enough to accommodate the number of occupants. Exit doors should swing outward in the direction of travel and, in places of public assembly, be equipped with panic hardware that will unlatch under pressure.

In addition to structural and fire safety, general areas of health and safety are dealt with in building codes. These include the design of stairways in terms of allowable riser-to-tread ratios, minimum widths based on occupancy, the use of landings, and requirements for handrails.

For habitable spaces, natural light must be provided by exterior glazed openings, and natural ventilation by means of exterior openings. These requirements are usually based on a percentage of a room's floor area. For some types of occupancy, artificial light and a mechanically operated ventilating system can be substituted.

Increased attention is being paid to making buildings, particularly government and other public facilities, accessible to the physically handicapped - to the blind, the deaf, or those confined to a wheelchair. Specific concerns include the use of ramps and elevators for access to the various levels of a building, adequate space and uncluttered layouts for ease of movement, provision of usable restrooms and other facilities, accessibility of hardware such as door handles, light switches, and elevator controls, and non-visual means of orientation for the sight-impaired.

MODEL CODES AND SPONSORING ORGANIZATIONS

Basic Building Code
Basic Fire Protection Code
Basic Plumbing Code

- Building Officials and Code Administrators
  International, Inc.

National Building Code
Fire Prevention Code

- American Insurance Association
  (formerly National Board of Fire Underwriters)

Uniform Building Code

- International Conference of Building Officials

National Electrical Code
Life Safety Code

- National Fire Protection Association

National Plumbing Code

- American Society of Mechanical Engineers

Uniform Plumbing Code

- International Association of Plumbing and
  Mechanical Officials

ORGANIZATIONS THAT ISSUE STANDARDS

ANSI	American National Standards Institute
ASTM	American Society for Testing and Materials
FHA	Federal Housing Administration
GSA	General Services Administration
HUD	Department of Housing and Urban Development
NBS	National Bureau of Standards
NFPA	National Fire Protection Association
UL	Underwriters' Laboratories Inc.

BIBLIOGRAPHY

Albers, Anni. On Weaving. Wesleyan University Press, 1965.

Allen, Edward. How Buildings Work. Oxford University Press, 1980

Arnheim, Rudolph. Art and Visual Perception. University of California Press, 1971.

Ball, Victoria. The Art of Interior Design. 2nd Ed. John Wiley and Sons, 1982.

Bevlin, Marjorie Elliott. Design Through Discovery. Holt, Rinehart & Winston, 1980

Birren, Faber. Light, Color, and Environment. Van Nostrand Reinhold Company, 1969.

Birren, Faber. Principles of Color. Van Nostrand Reinhold Company, 1969.

Ching, Francis D.K. Building Construction Illustrated. Van Nostrand Reinhold Company, 1975.

Dreyfuss, Henry. Measure of Man: Human Factors in Design. Watson-Guptill, 1967.

Faulkner, Ray, and Sarah Faulkner. Inside Today's Home. 4th Ed. Holt, Rinehart & Winston, 1975.

Friedmann, Arnold, John Pile, and Forrest Wilson. Interior Design: An Introduction to Architectural Interiors. 3rd Ed. Elsevier Science Publishing, 1982.

Garner, Philippe. Twentieth Century Furniture. Van Nostrand Reinhold Company, 1980.

General Electric. Light and Color. General Electric, Nela Park, Cleveland, Ohio, 1968.

Hall, Edward T. The Hidden Dimension. Doubleday, 1966.

Illuminating Engineering Society. IES Lighting Handbook. John E. Kauffman, Ed. Illuminating Engineering Society, 1972.

Itten, Johannes. The Elements of Color. Van Nostrand Reinhold Company, 1970.

Munsell, Albert H. A Color Notation System. The Munsell Color Company, 1954.

Nelson, George. How To See. Little, Brown and Company, 1977.

Nelson, George. Living Spaces. Whitney Library of Design, 1952.

Panero, Julius, and Martin Zelnick. Human Dimension and Interior Space. Whitney Library of Design, 1979.

Pile, John. Design: Purpose, Form and Meaning. University of Massachusetts Press, 1979.

Pile, John. Open Office Planning. Whitney Library of Design, 1978.

Pye, David. The Nature and Aesthetics of Design. Van Nostrand Reinhold Company, 1978.

Ramsey, C., and H. Sleeper. Architectural Graphic Standards. 7th Ed. Wiley-Interscience, 1981.

Rasmussen, Steen Eiler. Experiencing Architecture. MIT Press, 1962.

Salvadori, M., and R. Heller. Structure in Architecture. Prentice-Hall, 1975.

Siegel, Harry. A Guide to Business Principles and Practices for Interior Designers. Whitney Library of Design, 1968.

Sommer, Robert. Personal Space: The Behavioral Basis for Design. Prentice-Hall, 1969.

Whiton, Sherrill. Interior Design and Decoration. Lippincott Company, 1974.

Wilson, Forrest. Structure: The Essence of Architecture. Van Nostrand Reinhold Company, 1971.

. . . .

Other important sources of information for the interior designer include current periodicals such as Abitare, Architecture, Architectural Record, Contract, Domus, Interior Design, Interiors, and Progressive Architecture.

For information on current materials and product offerings, always consult manufacturers' catalogs or sales representatives.

INDEX

Accessories, 272-275
Acoustical tile, 197, 203
Acoustics, 308-309
    Effect of ceilings on, 201
Activity
    Relationships, 72
    Requirements, 54
Air conditioning, 281
Ambient lighting, 127
Ampere, 284
Asymmetrical balance, 144, 148
Awnings, 218

Balance, 140-145
Beams, 11, 18-19, 177
Bearing wall systems, 20, 176
Beds, 258-259
Bilateral symmetry, 142
Brightness, 288
Building
    Elements, 16-17
    Loads, 16
    Systems, 16-17, 278-279
Built-in furniture, 76-77

Candlepower, 300
Carpets, 172-174
Ceiling finishes, 202-203
Ceiling heights, 34-35, 193-194
Ceilings, 190-203
    Forms, 198-199
    Patterns, 195
    Suspended, 196-197
Ceramic tile, 170, 191
Chairs, 248-251
Circle, 10
Circuit breakers, 284

Color, 106-110, 147, 182, 203, 207
    Dimensions, 108
    Effect on form, 114-115
    Schemes, 116-117
    Tonal distribution, 118-119
Columns, 11, 18-19, 177
Concrete slabs, 21, 163
Contrast, 289
Cornice lighting, 270
Cove lighting, 270
Curvilinear spaces, 32-33

Dado, 183, 244
Daylighting, 208, 294
Design criteria, 52
Design principles, 130
Design process, 48-51
Design vocabulary, 91
Diffusion, 292
Dimensional guidelines, 62-69
Doors, 220-227
    Construction, 226
    Defining paths, 224
    Designs, 221
    Frames, 226-227
    Types, 222-223
Doorways, 37
Dovetail, 244
Draperies, 219
Drawing grids, 80-85

Electrical systems, 284-285
Emphasis, 154-157
Environmental control systems, 278-300
ESI Footcandle, 300

Fibonacci Series, 132
Figure-ground relationships, 26-27, 88-89
Fireplaces, 236-239
Floor coverings, 172-175
Flooring, 164-167
    Resilient, 171
    Tile and stone, 170
    Wood, 168-169
Floors, 162-166
Fluorescent lighting, 296-297
Focal points, 156
Footcandle, 300
Footlambert, 300
Forces on buildings, 16
Form, 92-101
Furnishing requirements, 54
Furniture, 240-265
    Arrangements, 74-77
    Construction, 244-245
    Form, 241, 243

Glare, 209, 290-291
Golden section, 132
Graphic representation, 80-85
Gypsum wallboard, 190

Handrails, 235
Harmony, 146-147
Heating and air conditioning, 280-281
HID Lighting, 298-299
Hierarchy, 154
Human dimensions, 60-69, 228-229, 242, 246-247,
    253, 258, 260
Human factors, 58
Human scale, 138

Incandescent lighting, 295
Indirect lighting, 127, 270, 306
Interior design, 46-47
    Elements, 160-161
    Structuring space, 24-25
Isometric grid, 82

Jambs, 214, 226
Joints, wood, 244

Lamps, 271, 295-299
Light, 126-129, 208-209
    And color, 107, 111, 293
    And texture, 122
    Effect of ceilings on, 200
Lighting, 286-307
    Accent, 129
    Calculations, 300-307
    General, 127
    Sources, 294-299
    Task, 128
    Zonal cavity method, 302-305
Lighting fixtures, 266-272
Line, 94-97
Luminaire distribution, 306

Mechanical systems, 278-283
Metal ceilings, 197, 203
Miter joints, 244
Modular furniture, 76-77, 243, 257, 262, 264-265
Munsell color system, 109

Oblique grid, 83
Open plans, 76, 243
Outlets, electrical, 284

Panelboard, 284
Patterns, 43, 125, 130, 195
Perspective grids, 84-85
Pigments, 107, 110
Plan arrangements, 74-77
Plan grid, 80
Plane, 98-99
Plaster walls, 190
Plumbing, 282-283
Plywood paneling, 189
Point, 92-93
Post-and-beam systems, 18-19, 177
Prang color wheel, 108
Programming requirements, 53-57
Proportion, 131-135
Proportional relationships, 134-135

Rabbeted joints, 244
Radial balance, 143
Rafters, 16
Rectangular proportions, 30-31
Resilient flooring, 171
Reverberation, 308
Rhythm, 150-153
Rugs, 175

Sanitary drainage systems, 283
Scale, 136-139
Seating, 246-251
Section grid, 81
Shape, 96, 98, 102-105, 146-147
Simultaneous contrast, 112-113
Site, building, 12
Slab construction, 21, 163

Space, 10-15
    Architectural, 11
    Analysis, 55, 71
    Exterior, 12
    Interior, 14-15
    Modifying, 40-42
    Planning, 70-73
    Structuring, 16-25
Spatial dimensions, 28-35
Spatial form, 26-27
Spatial transitions, 13, 36-39
Spline joints, 244
Square proportions, 29, 105
Stairways, 39, 228-235
    Construction, 235
    Dimensions, 228-229
    Form and treatment of, 232-233
    Types, 230-231
Storage, 260-265
Structural systems, 18-23
Surface characteristics, 98
Symmetry, 142

Tables, 252-255
Task lighting, 128
Texture, 120-125, 146-147, 185
    And light, 122
    And pattern, 125
    And scale, 121, 124
Thermal comfort, 280
Tonal contrast, 88
Triangle, 104
Trimwork, 182-183, 214-215, 226

Unity, 148-149
User requirements, 53, 70

Variety, 147-149
Veiling reflectance, 291
Ventilation, 210
Vision, 90
Visual characteristics, 91
Visual perception, 88-89
Volt, 284
Volume, 100-101

Waffle slab, 21
Wall finishes, 188-191
Wall storage systems, 264-265
Walls, 176-187
    Bearing, 176-177
    Construction, 178-179
    Form, 180
    Nonstructural, 186-187
    Openings in, 181
Water supply systems, 282
Watt, 284
Window treatments, 218-219
Windows, 38, 204-219
    And furnishings, 212-213
    And light, 208-209
    And ventilation, 210-211
    Construction, 214-215
    Framing views, 206-207
    Scale of, 205
    Thermal insulation of, 211
    Trim, 214-215
    Types of, 216-217
Wood joints, 244
Wood paneling, 180
Work stations, 256-257